Langenscheidt Publishers, Inc.

Lisa Checchi Ross

Stephen Brewer, Mark Greenberg, Lenore
Malen, Donald S. Olson, Jane Opper
Mitchell Nauffts, Pamela Nelson, Dana
Schwartz

Gert Oberländer; Adaptations by Polyglott-
Redaktion

Vera Solymosi-Thurzó

Diane Wagner

Jules Zalon, Image Bank, New York

Irving Perkins Associates

Ripinsky & Company

Erdmann Gormsen, No. 2, No. 7, No. 17; Jutta
Gormsen, No. 1, No. 6, No. 12, No. 22;
Andreas Gross, No. 3, No. 4, No. 5, No. 8,
No. 10, No. 11, No. 13, No. 14, No. 15, No.
16, No. 19, No. 20, No. 21; Sr. Martinez, No.
18; Gertraud Trox, No. 9

Translation Company of America

Dr. Jutta Schutz-Gormsen (author); Polyglott-
Redaktion (editorial)

We welcome your comments and suggestions.
Our address:
Langenscheidt Publishers, Inc.,
46–35 54th Rd.
Maspeth, N.Y. 11378.

SELF-GUIDED

Mexico

Publishe
Managing Edito
U.S. Editorial Adaptatio

U.S. Editorial Sta

Cartograph

Illustratio
Cover Desig
Cover Photograp
Text Desig
Productio
Photograph

Translati
Original German Te

Lette

I

With 122
32 map

Manuf

LANGEN

Contents

Foreword

To explore Mexico on your own is to discover infinite possibilities. Outside the great sophisticated metropolis, away from the fabulous coastal resorts, awaits a nation as bursting with tourism opportunities as it is with the vigor of its people. Evocative Colonial capitals, world-class scuba diving and deep-sea fishing, great ruins and museums of ancient civilizations, remote villages, and industrial megacomplexes—today's traveller may be startled to discover not one, but many Mexicos.

Langenscheidt's *Self-Guided Mexico* puts any or all of these Mexicos within reach of every independent traveller. Written especially for seasoned travellers by writers who specialize in the areas they cover, this unique guide covers extensive detailed tours of Mexico City, Mexico's other great cities, and the countryside. Travellers will find all the information they need to explore Mexico at their own pace and follow their own interests.

Self-Guided Tours

The heart of this book is its self-guided tours. Walking tours of each major city describe all important sites and put them in historical perspective. Travel routes connect major cities and other areas of interest, covering many fascinating and beautiful areas of the countryside. Detailed maps outline every route.

Because many travellers begin in Mexico City, we begin our tours with a selective guide to Mexico City and a series of seven drives from the capital that can be done in a day, or extended into two or three day trips. The remaining 24 Travel Routes cover the most scenic and interesting areas in each major region: the Central Highlands, Northern Mexico, including the Baja peninsula, the Pacific coast, the Gulf coast, the Southern Highlands, and the Yucatán peninsula.

Using This Guide

This travel guide helps you plan, organize, and enjoy your holiday in Mexico. In "Getting Your Bearings," a brief rundown of Mexico's different regions will help you choose the areas in which you'd like to spend the most time. It also offers insights into Mexican culture. An historical chronology and essays on art, literature, and architecture provide helpful background and perspective on the sights you'll be seeing. A special essay on Mexico's great ancient Indian civilizations helps to round out your introduction to this historic land.

Langenscheidt's writers also offer a subjective guide to the most appealing sights. Our unique three-star system appears throughout the guide:

> *** Worth a special trip—don't miss it!
> ** The most important sights on the tour
> * Highlights

Other sights along the way are also worth seeing, but are not necessarily as important as the starred sights.

Total mileage is provided in kilometers and miles from the departure point of each tour. Major towns and sights appear in boldface for easy reference, while other notable places appear in italics. Numbers in parentheses correspond to locations on the maps.

The guide concludes with a Practical Information chapter divided into two parts. The first is General Trip Planning, to help you gather information you'll need before you depart for Mexico. The second part is specific information—such as local tourist information offices and hotels—listed town by town.

Notes and Observations

Travel information, like fruit, is perishable. We've made every effort to double-check information in this guide. But hotels do close and museums do shut down for renovation, so check ahead wherever possible.

We welcome your comments and updates of our information. Please write us at:

> Langenscheidt Publishers, Inc.
> 46–35 54th Road
> Maspeth, N. Y. 11378

Getting Your Bearings

The vacation possibilities Mexico provides are as varied as exploring the ancient remains of sophisticated Mesoamerican cultures; sun-bathing at chic, modern coastal resorts; basking on cool Colonial patios; or hiking on remote mountain trails.

Mexico City offers the glories of pre-Columbian Aztec civilization, Spanish Colonial charm, and the bustle of the largest metropolitan area in the world. Using this vibrant, crowded, diverse city as a base, there are a variety of fascinating nearby attractions you can visit in one- and two-day trips: Teotihuacán, one of the oldest and largest Aztec cities in the region; the Colonial city of Cuernavaca, where Hernán Cortés retired after conquering much of Mexico; and picturesque Taxco, with its cobblestone streets, flower-filled balconies, and world-renowned silversmiths.

Mexico's central highlands lie between two impressive mountain ranges: the Sierra Madre Oriental and Sierra Madre Occidental. The generally mountainous terrain is dotted by the architectural remains of old Indian cultures and beautiful Colonial towns, and is also the birthplace of the country's independence movement.

Northern Mexico shares a long border with the United States that divides "Anglo" and "Latin" America. The eastern and central part of this region is characterized by low mountains, arid deserts, and dry plateaus that are sparsely settled. The western slope of the Sierra Madre Occidental offers a more lush, hospitable landscape. The peninsula of Baja California dangles from the northwest corner of the country, and attracts vacationers with its wild, desolate beauty, unspoiled beaches, and spectacular sport fishing.

The Pacific coast offers a year-round tropical paradise with famed resorts such as Acapulco, secluded seaside retreats, and tiny fishing villages. The Gulf coast, in contrast, has a more changeable climate, endless beaches, and comparatively few resorts (it's also where Mexico's petroleum industry is based).

Jutting into the Caribbean Sea and acting as the southern flank of the Gulf coast is the starkly contrasting Yucatán peninsula. Characterized by low hills, isolated *cenotes,* and tropical scrub forests, this is the land of the Mayas and their magnificent legacy; archaeological sites such as Chichén-Itzá and Uxmal are among the most visited destinations in the country. The Yucatán also boasts two of Mexico's most popular modern resorts: Cancún and the offshore island of Cozumel, one of the premier diving spots in the world.

The Yucatán gives way in the west to the southern highlands, an area rich in Indian and Colonial history, as evidenced by the cities of Oaxaca and San Cristóbal. It was also a key region in the development of high

Mesoamerican cultures, and boasts such ruined jungle cities as Palenque and Bonampak, as well as the excavated remains of Monte Albán near Oaxaca.

Location and Size

Bordered on the north by the United States, the west by the Pacific, the east by the Gulf of Mexico and Caribbean Sea, and the south by Guatemala and Belize (formerly British Honduras), Mexico is a vast ice cream cone–shaped country covering much of the southern third of the North American continent. With an area of almost 1.5 million square km. (761,000 square miles), Mexico is the fifth-largest country in the Western Hemisphere and three times the size of Texas. From its 2,597-km.- (1,800-mile-) long border with the U.S., Mexico narrows to a width of 210 km. (126 miles) at the Isthmus of Tehuantepec before it widens again into the Yucatán peninsula. (The isthmus is generally considered the geographical threshold of the Central American subcontinent, an area that includes the highlands of Chiapas and the tropical Yucatán.) Dangling like a slender earring from the northwestern corner of the country is Baja California, a narrow peninsula longer than Italy and separated from the mainland by the Gulf of California (also called the Sea of Cortés). Mexico's Pacific coast, at over 7,427 km. (4,600 miles), is almost three times as long as its combined Gulf and Caribbean coasts. The Tropic of Cancer more or less bisects the country latitudinally on a line running from Mazatlán on the Pacific to Ciudad Victoria in the east-central state of Tamaulipas.

Topography

Legend has it that the Spanish conqueror of Mexico, Hernán Cortés, tried to describe the terrain of Spain's latest acquisition to his king, Charles V, by crumpling a piece of paper in his hand. True or not, it is an apt comparison, for Mexico is an overwhelmingly mountainous country. The dominant geological feature of the north and central regions is a massive highland block, or *altiplano,* whose basins and valleys are separated from each other by a series of transverse mountain chains ranging in elevation from 1,300 meters (4,200 feet) in the north to 2,500 meters (8,200 feet) in the vicinity of Mexico City. This central plateau, which comprises nearly three-quarters of the country's area, is hemmed in on either side by an impressive mountain range following a roughly northwest-southeast axis. To the west, the Sierra Madre Occidental, a rugged upheaval of mostly volcanic rock, reaches heights of over 3,050 meters (10,000 feet) and is made virtually impassable by numerous steep-

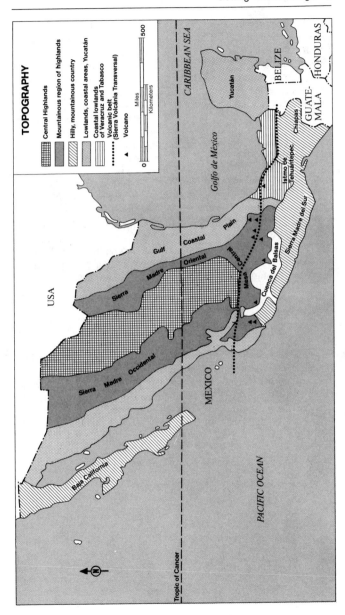

walled gorges. To the east, the Sierra Madre Oriental, a 1,200-km.-
(750-mile-) long jumble of Jurassic and Cretaceous limestone, runs the
length of the Gulf coastal plain. As you travel farther south, the highland
block gradually lifts, so that, in effect, the mountains around it do not
appear quite so formidable. In fact, you will sometimes have the impression, in places like Pachuca or Puebla, that you're riding *down* into the
mountains as they tumble toward the Gulf of Mexico.

The southern boundary of the central plateau is formed by a neo-
volcanic belt known as the Sierra Volcánica Transversal. Rising at a point
north of Puerto Vallarta on the Pacific, this chain of geologically younger
and sometimes still-active volcanoes traverses the country to the Gulf
near Veracruz and includes Mexico's most famous peaks, all perpetually
snow-capped: Orizaba (or Citlaltépetl) at 5,700 meters (18,700 feet),
Popocatépetl (the "Smoking Mountain") at 5,450 meters (17,877 feet),
and Iztaccíhuatl, (also spelled Ixtaccíhuatl, the "Sleeping Woman") at
5,287 meters (17,343 feet). You'll also find the country's youngest volcano in this chain, now-dormant Parícutan, which emerged suddenly
and violently in 1943 and over the next nine years built itself to a height of
610 meters (2,000 feet), causing the abandonment of the village of San
Juan Parangaricutiro in the process.

The great Balsas basin (*Cuenca de Balsas*) separates the southern
terminus of the Sierra Madre Oriental from yet another range, the Sierra
Madre del Sur, which consists of a hodgepodge of smaller mountains
rising precipitously from an almost nonexistent Pacific coastal plain at
that point and extending into the rugged highlands of Oaxaca. This
region, in turn, is linked to the mountains of Chiapas by a band of hills
running across the Isthmus of Tehuantepec.

Unlike much of the rest of the country, the humid Gulf coastal plain
gets more than its share of rain and is drained by a number of rivers. The
adjacent Yucatán peninsula—geologically speaking, a massive limestone slab—juts into the Gulf of Mexico to form a barrier between it and
the Caribbean. Its tropical coastline is strewn with matchless lagoons
and coral reefs; the dry karst landscape of the interior, in contrast, is
dotted with sinkholes, or cenotes, that have acted as loci for human activity for thousands of years.

In the far northwest, at the opposite corner of the country, is a region
that at times seems as far removed from the Yucatán as the moon is from
earth. Sonora is chiefly a land of mountains (some over 3,050 meters,
10,000 feet, in elevation) and desert, with a long coastline and sparkling
beaches on the Gulf of California. Across the gulf from Sonora lies Baja,
a narrow (only 50–250 km., 30–150 miles, wide) desert peninsula with a
rugged, mountainous spine and coastal strips punctuated by numerous
coves and bays—jumping-off points for some of the finest deep-sea fishing in the world.

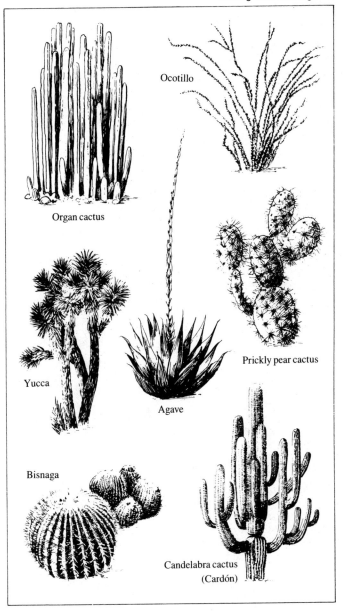

Organ cactus

Ocotillo

Yucca

Agave

Prickly pear cactus

Bisnaga

Candelabra cactus
(Cardón)

Rivers and Lakes

The longest river in Mexico, the Río Grande (or Río Bravo as it's called south of the border), rises in the San Juan mountains of southwestern Colorado and flows south-southeast to form Mexico's border with the United States for some 1,500 km. (930 miles), from El Paso/Ciudad Juarez to the Gulf of Mexico east of Brownsville/Matamoras. The central plateau is drained by three major rivers: The Río Balsas has its source in the mountains of Puebla, meanders through its large basin in the state of Guerrero, and finally spills into the Pacific through a deep mountain gorge; the Río Lerma rises in the highlands of Toluca, flows into the Río Grande de Santiago near Lake Chapala, and also empties into the Pacific through a spectacular gorge; the Río Moctezuma, rising in the mountains of Hidalgo, flows northeastward into the Panuco, which then winds its way through the Gulf coastal plain in well-defined loops. The water-rich Grijalva and Usumacinta, with their sources in Guatemala, meander through Chiapas and meet in the swamps of Tabasco before flowing into the Bay of Campeche.

Mexico's most important natural lakes (*lagos*) are found in the central highlands, which, not coincidentally, is the country's most populous region. Lago de Chapala south of Guadalajara is the largest at 80 km. (50 miles) long and 20 km. (12.5 miles) wide (it's also the site of the largest U.S. retirement community in Mexico). Lago de Cuitzeo, north of Morelia, is also quite large but shrinks considerably during the dry season (December to May). To the south of Morelia lies fabled Lago de Pátzcuaro, with its story-book mountain setting and picturesque volcanic islands. Equally scenic, though far less visited, is Laguna Catemaco, some 175 km. (100 miles) southeast of Veracruz, with its very own green-blanketed islands and the volcanic peaks of the Tuxtla massif serving as a picture-postcard backdrop.

In a country where only 20 percent of the land is arable, Mexicans are dependent on artificial lakes, or *presas,* for much of their agricultural irrigation, power generation, and public water supplies.

Constitution and Government

The *Estados Unidos Mexicanos* (United Mexican States) is a federal republic with 31 states and a Federal District (*Distrito Federal*) comprised of Mexico City and its environs. (When you mention "Mexico," remember that the natives will assume you're talking about the city, not the country.) The Constitution of 1917, with a few amendments, is still the law of the land, and, in theory at least, provides for far-reaching social guarantees and an extensive agrarian reform program.

All Mexican citizens above the age of 18 have the right to vote. The Constitution provides for a tripartite system, with a theoretical separa-

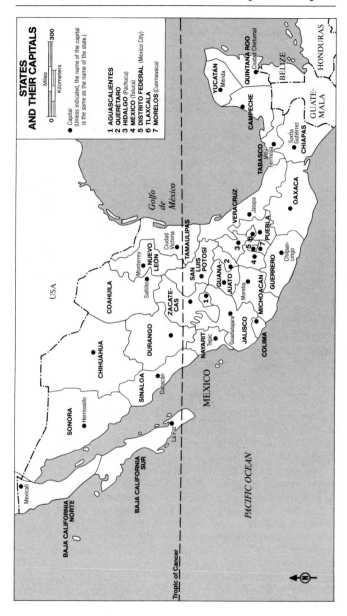

STATES AND THEIR CAPITALS

● Capital
(Unless indicated, the name of the capital is the same as the name of the state.)

1 AGUASCALIENTES
2 QUERÉTARO
3 HIDALGO (Pachuca)
4 MÉXICO (Toluca)
5 DISTRITO FEDERAL (Mexico City)
6 TLAXCALA
7 MORELOS (Cuernavaca)

Miles
Kilometers
0   300

tion of powers enforced among the executive, legislative, and judicial branches of government. However, the bulk of the political power rests with the executive branch. The president, elected for a single six-year term, is the highest official in the country, the commander-in-chief of the armed forces, and the head of the "revolutionary family," an elite circle of several hundred individuals who play key roles in politics, business, and the administration of the arts. Among the president's constitutional powers are the rights to initiate legislation, to veto all or only parts of legislative bills, to refuse to enforce laws of which he disapproves, to intervene in the affairs of the various states, and to appoint a Cabinet without consulting Congress.

The Mexican Congress is a bicameral legislature, with a Chamber of Deputies and a Senate, both elected by popular vote. Members are prevented only from serving consecutive terms, and Congress has the right to override the president's veto. The Mexican Supreme Court is more of an interpreting than a controlling branch of government. Under the Constitution, it sits at the behest of the president, and Congress is excluded from any participatory role in its decisions. Likewise, every state elects a governor and chamber of deputies for six-year terms, but here, too, the Constitution grants the president extraordinary powers, even allowing him to dismiss governors and deputies for "insubordination."

Traditions: Clothing, Festivals, Music, and Dance

In addition to its natural attractions and scenic countryside, Mexico offers visitors a distinctive culture rich in history, folklore, traditional handcrafts, music, and dance. The variety, vitality, and ubiquity of folk customs in everyday Mexican life can be a welcome change from the mass-produced conformity of our own culture.

Indian Dress. Among the most remarkable of Mexico's folk arts is its astonishing variety of native dress, and while the wearing of these distinctive costumes is declining in many Indian villages, it's still common enough so that you shouldn't have to look hard to find it. Your best bet to see the more traditional styles will be on weekly market days in the southern part of the country, Oaxaca City or San Cristóbal in Chiapas, for example, or in one of the more remote highland villages in the state of Puebla, but on occasion they'll still turn up on the outskirts of Mexico City on the backs of new immigrants to the big city.

The costumes of Indian women are usually more elaborate than those of their male counterparts, and consist of a gathered wraparound skirt with a woven belt (which can easily be let out during pregnancy), and topped by either a *huipil* or *quechquemetl*. The latter is a triangular-shaped garment made of two rectangular pieces of cloth sewn together and worn over a blouse, and is generally found throughout the north and central highlands. The *huipil,* a rectangular-shaped dress with openings for the head and arms, can be worn without a skirt as a sort of chemise (as the Chinantecas of Oaxaca do) or open at the sides (as it is in Chiapas), and is quite common throughout southern Mexico. Color, stitching, and the very particular way in which a garment is worn varies from region to region and village to village.

The article of clothing most common to both Indian communities and *mestizo* (the term for people of mixed Indian/European descent) villages is the *rebozo,* essentially a broad shawl or stole. It's believed to have made its first appearance during the early days of the Colonial period due to the Spanish custom that required a woman to keep her head covered in church. Today, though elegant versions of it are made out of silk, it's more of an all-purpose garment, serving at any given moment as head covering, baby carrier, coat, or blanket, and is worn or wrapped in a variety of styles.

The Indian men's clothing can be quite striking, too. The typical outfit consists of white cotton pants worn with a woven belt, a loose homespun shirt, and a wool pancho, or *serape.* There are, of course, variations on this theme as you travel from one part of the country to another. The men of the Tzeltal and Tzotzil tribes of Chiapas, for example, are noted for their finely embroidered shirts, their woven shawls, and their knee-length pants. The Huichol men from the remote, mountainous areas in Jalisco and Nayarit wear traditional cotton clothing distinguished by the intricacy of its embroidered geometric designs.

Fiestas. Nowhere is the festival calendar more crowded than in Mexico. Religious holidays, patriotic holidays, civil holidays—at times it seems as if every day is a holiday in the self-styled "Land of the Fiesta." The overwhelming majority of Mexicans (96 percent) are Roman Catholics; thus a mass and the procession of a saint through the streets are usually at the center of any celebration, with music, dancing, fireworks, and the consumption of alcohol important components on the periphery.

The most important annual festival in Mexico is the one held in honor of the Virgin of Guadalupe, Mexico's patron saint, on December 12. While the whole country celebrates it, the most lavish processions and festivities center around the Basílica de Guadalupe on the northern edge of Mexico City, a pilgrimage site for Catholics from around the country. (It is interesting to note that the four major pilgrimage sites in Mexico—Guadalupe and Los Remedios in Mexico City, Chalma, and Amecameca—roughly coincide with the cardinal points of the compass, and were all sites of ancient Indian worship in pre-Conquest times before "miracles" sanctified them as holy Christian shrines.) Despite its religious overtones and lines of penitents crawling on their knees to the basilica, Guadalupe Day is, generally speaking, a festive day, with much dancing, eating, and socializing.

Right after this holiday, the country moves into the Christmas season and another round of festivities. The nine days of the *posada,* which means "inn" in Spanish, begin December 16 and commemorate Mary and Joseph's search for accommodations in the days before Jesus' birth. The traditional *posada* calls for house guests bearing images of the Holy Family on a tray to march around the outside of their hosts' home, finally stopping at the front door and asking for a place to stay. These days, however, it has become more of an excuse to have a cocktail party. Still, it is the occasion for the wonderful Mexican tradition of the *piñata.* Probably familiar to most *norteamericanos* from their grade-school days, the *piñata* is a large, decorated papier-mâché receptacle filled with toys, sweets, and other delights. Children are gathered in a circle and blindfolded in turn, with each one getting a whack at breaking open the *piñata* with a stick as it's pulled up and down by a rope.

Perhaps the most unique Mexican holiday is the one set aside to honor the dead, which, like our own Halloween, has its roots in ancient pagan beliefs. A visit at this time of year will be something you always remember, for nowhere else in the world do people treat the subject of death with more candor and cheerful casualness than do Mexicans. It all starts in the middle of October when bakers begin to display their *pan de muerto* ("dead man's bread") and confectioners offer little skulls and coffins of decorated sugar. On October 31st, villagers greet the *muertos chicos,* or "souls of dead children," as they return to earth on the night of November 1. The following evening, a grand repast is prepared for the souls of long-dead adults, and is often followed by an all-night vigil at the local cemetery to keep the departing souls company as they head back to the other world.

Carnival, the Latin American equivalent of Mardi Gras, celebrated almost everywhere in Mexico, can last up to two weeks and is especially colorful in Veracruz, Mazatlán, and Mérida. The Easter Holy Week is also observed almost everywhere and is noted for its passion play presentations. The *Feria de San Marcos* ("Fair of St. Mark") at the end of April in Aguascalientes; Corpus Christi Day in Mexico City or Papantla (where you can witness the spectacular *El Volador,* or "flying pole dance") at the end of May; the Festival of St. Ignatius on July 31st in Chetumal; the Festival of Our Lady of the Remedies in Cholula during the first week of September—the list is seemingly endless, as are the opportunities to soak up an eye and earful.

Folk Music, Dances and Other Entertainment. The rich musical traditions of pre-Hispanic culture are readily apparent in the pictorial representations of ancient dances found by archaeologists, as well as the legacy of musical instruments that have been handed down over the millenia. Flutes, pipes, rattles made of gourds and wood, and drums (the most common being the *teponaztli,* a slotted drum made from the trunk of a tree) were all used by ancient Indian peoples, especially in their war and religious ceremonies. String instruments were introduced by the Spanish in the Colonial period and were quickly adopted by native populations. By the 18th century, the guitar in all its variations was the most popular instrument in Mexico, with each region busy developing its own distinctive melodies and rhythms. Subsequent European inventions such as the accordion and mouth organ also found an eager audience, and the German and Polish polkas they inspired, the so-called *rancheras,* were quickly adapted by Mexican musicians, especially in the northern cattle-raising areas.

Still, the music most closely identified with Mexico is the noisy, exuberant, happy-to-sappy music of the mariachi bands (the name is said to derive from the French *mariage,* or "marriage," and refers to the original vocation of such groups, which was to play at weddings). Mariachi music and the bands that play it are said to have originated in the state of Jalisco and its capital of Guadalajara. The bands can range in size from four to fourteen, and feature an idiosyncratic combination of violinists, guitarists, and trumpeters, with an occasional harp thrown in to keep things interesting. The musicians always perform in the elegantly ostentatious clothing of the *charros* (the expert horsemen who made their living on the old *haciendas*)—tightly fitted jacket and trousers of suede or deerskin studded with silver buttons along seams and sleeves, a frilled white shirt, and a wide-brimmed sombrero embroidered in silver—and can be rented for an evening, a serenade at dawn, or just a song. (The price is agreed to in advance.)

In southern Mexico, folk music has developed more in line with Caribbean influences, and melodies are characterized by the warm sounds of the marimba. Although long believed to have been introduced into Africa by Malay settlers and then brought to Central and South America by black slaves, recent evidence seems to indicate that pre-Hispanic Indian cultures were already familiar with a variation of the instrument.

Unlike *mestizos* and *criollos,* tradition-bound Indians do not usually perform music for mere entertainment. Instead, music and dance are used as ritual elements to help them communicate with the supernatural forces that abound in the world, and are confined to the male population who act as the guardians of sacred ceremonies. Of course, there are exceptions to the rule and one of the most spectacular is the "flying pole dance," or *El Volador,* which, these days, is performed almost exclusively for visitors by the Totonacs of Veracruz. Thought to have originally been an expression of pre-Hispanic sun worship, today's *El Volador* is part acrobatics and part performance art. In it, four "flying men" mount a tall pole (representing the sun) topped by a small platform and hook their feet into ropes that have been wound around the top of the pole. After a musical prelude by the fifth member of the troupe, the capitán, the flyers hurl themselves headfirst backwards off the platform and descend to the ground in ever-widening circles as the ropes unwind. Just before they hit ground, the flyers perform somersaults and land on their feet. Apparently, the dance is related to the Mesoamerican religious calendar: if you multiply *13* (the number of circles around the pole the flyers make as they descend to the ground) by *4* (the number of flyers), you end up with *52,* the number of months in an Aztec "year" and years in an Aztec "century."

Fantastic masks are a staple in many Mexican dances, their religious-mystical significance originating in pre-Hispanic traditions and passed down over the centuries. Animal masks were used in hunting and harvesting ceremonies, and still figure prominently in the Deer Dance performed by the Yaquis and Mayos of the northwest. During the colonial period, missionaries who were unable to completely eradicate Indian cultural habits began to use their ceremonial masks to explain Christian motifs. Not to be outdone, Indian priests soon started creating their own masks with European features and long beards to mock their would-be conquerors.

Other, purely Spanish imports have also been integrated into Mexico's rich cultural heritage. The dance of the *Moros y Cristianos,* or "Moors and Christians" more or less reenacts the Crusaders' victories over the Moors. *Jarabes* and *huapangos* betray their Andalusian origins by the coquettish behavior of the performing couples as well as their rapid, stamping steps (the Guadalajaran version of the *jarabe,* the Jarabe Tapatío, is performed in *charro* costume and is Mexico's national dance). You can sample a potpourri of these wonderful dances and traditional musical styles courtesy of the world-famous Ballet Folklórico (performances several times a week, depending on the season, in the Palace of the Fine Arts) in Mexico City.

Although considered cruel by most *norteamericanos* (and certainly not recommended for the squeamish), cockfighting is popular in Mexico. In this "sport," roosters with sharp spurs attached to their feet are set against each other, with spectators placing heavy bets on the outcome. *Charreadas* are much-loved exhibits of horsemanship (similar to rodeos) that are put on by clubs of *charros* throughout the year. Bullfighting was introduced to the country by the Spanish, and remains wildly popular with most Mexicans (in fact, the largest *plaza de toros* in the world, with 60,000 seats, is in Mexico City). Held on Sunday afternoon and holidays in arenas throughout the country, each contest is an elaborately ritualized spectacle in which human guile is pitted against brute animal strength. In bullfighting, however, it's not so much the fact of winning as the manner in which the victory is achieved that counts. The main season runs from November to March; in the rainy months from April to October, novices, or *novilleros,* fight against younger and smaller bulls in most of the bigger cities.

Food and Drink

With over 80 varieties of chile pepper—small and large, *muy pico* (very spicy) or mild and aromatic, red, yellow, and green—used in traditional dishes in Mexico it's no wonder that the subtleties of Mexican cooking have eluded duplication outside the country and many of us have not had the opportunity to experience this truly wonderful cuisine at its best.

Mexican cooking has enriched and been enriched in turn by Spanish, French, Italian, and Austrian cuisines over the centuries, and the end result is truly exciting and delicious—that is, *if* you manage to find the genuine article during your visit. If you're fortunate enough to count yourself among the knowledgeable *and* adventurous, your best bet is to head out to the provinces to try the many regional specialties. With a good measure of common sense (eat seafood near the coast; pork, poultry, and beef dishes in the highlands) and a little luck, your efforts should be richly—and deliciously—rewarded.

Indians introduced the Old World to corn, or *maize* (also pineapple, avocado, squash, peanuts, vanilla, and cocoa), and it remains the most important ingredient of the average Mexican's diet. The tortilla—a thin pancake made out of *masa* (cornmeal paste), and then baked on a griddle—is the basic component of many Mexican dishes, and serves as bread, plate, and spoon. Tacos and tostadas are fried tortillas, the former stuffed with meat, cheese, and onions, the latter topped with the same. Enchiladas are rolled and stuffed tortillas cooked in a seasoned tomato sauce. (Burritos are rolled and stuffed tortillas made from wheat flour.) Quesadillas are tortillas baked with cheese (often as a component of the paste). The many variations of these basic items frequently will be garnished with a dollop of sour cream or *guacamole,* a Mexican favorite made from mashed avocados pureed with tomatoes, onions, chile, coriander, and lemon juice. *Frijoles,* black or navy-style beans, usually mashed and refried, are almost always served as a side dish.

Of course, one of the beauties of Mexican cooking is its variety; while it can be as simple as a tortilla wrapped around a few pieces of beef or poultry, it can also be as elaborate as any concocted by an Old World chef. A typical meal, for example, might begin with a *coctel de mariscos* (seafood cocktail), *guacamole,* or a salad. This is usually followed by a soup—the robust *chili con queso* of Sonora, maybe, or *menudo,* a tripe soup that's a national favorite, or a thick, pureed *crema,* or even a *caldo de res* or *caldo de pollo* (clear beef or chicken consommés). Rice or noodles may be served as an additional course before the main entrée, which will either be meat (*carne*), poultry (*pollo*), or fish (*pescado*), with the type of preparation usually determined by the sauce. Most likely, the dessert, or *postre*, will be sweet and flavored with cinnamon and vanilla, like *arroz con leche,* a favorite rice pudding. Other favorites include *flan*, a caramel custard pudding introduced by the Spanish, fried bananas, preserved and candied fruit, and *ate de membrillo*, or "quince bread" (not really a bread, but a sheet of sticky quince paste with white cheese).

Regional Specialties. As mentioned earlier, the real action in Mexican cooking is out in the provinces. The cities on both coasts, for example, abound in fabulous seafood dishes. Mazatlán is famed for its *ostiones*, or oysters, that are so fresh, they're usually opened right under your nose! Farther south, the normally undistinguished international-style cooking of Acapulco is brightened by the refreshing *ceviche*, a cocktail of raw fish marinated in lemon or lime juice and seasoned with oil, oregano, fresh onion, chile, and tomato. Across the country on the Gulf, Veracruz has an established reputation as a seafood-lover's paradise, and is especially noted for its red sauces *a la cruzana*—made with sherry, olives, capers, sweet peppers, almonds, raisins, and *no* spicy chiles. Be sure to try the *huachinango* (red snapper) *a la verucruzana*.

The cooking of Puebla is famous throughout the country but is probably best known for an indescribably complex concoction from pre-Hispanic times, *mole poblano*, a dark brown chocolate sauce seasoned with chiles and dozens of other spices that give it a unique sweet-piquant flavor. Late summer is the time for another Puebla specialty, *chile en nogada*, green peppers stuffed with meat, nuts, and raisins, lightly battered and fried, then covered with a white sauce garnished by ground walnuts and red pomegranate seeds. (The dish was created especially for Mexico's Independence Day on September 16, and its colors—green, white, and red—are those of the Mexican flag.)

Separated from the rest of the country for most of its history by impenetrable jungles, the Yucatán has developed its own unique cuisine, with a somewhat milder, more aromatic flavor. The *sopa de limas* (the "lime" is actually a type of sweet lemon) is a local favorite, as is *cochinita pibil*, suckling pig seasoned with *achiote*, garlic, and black pepper, then wrapped in banana leaves and baked slowly in a *pibil*, or underground oven. And, of course, given the fact that the peninsula is surrounded by water on three sides, the *mariscos* is out of this world.

Beverages. Cocoa was the king of beverages among the Aztecs, and is still loved in Mexico, where it's usually prepared with cinnamon. Today, however, Mexico's most famous beverage is tequila, which, along with its rawer sister mescal, is distilled from the cooked hearts, or *tlachi-*

quero, of the maguey cactus, a species of the agave plant. The end product has a strong taste all its own (the difference between tequila and mescal is the difference between regular unleaded and premium) and is rumored to be mildly hallucinogenic when consumed in sufficient quantities (but so is cough syrup). The best way to drink either is mixed with lime juice and triple sec (a "margarita") but it's also drunk straight, usually with a pinch of salt and a section of lime as a chaser (you lick the salt off your hand, drink the tequila or mescal, and then suck on the lime).

Pulque, long popular with indigenous peoples, though rarely offered to visitors, is slowly fading out of fashion. It, too, is made from the maguey, but instead of distilling the juice of the plant, it is simply allowed to ferment, resulting in a milky-sticky liquid with approximately the same alcoholic content as beer.

Speaking of beer, the Mexican variety, with a tip of the hat to the immigrant German brewmeisters who shared their secrets, is excellent, and brands such as Corona, Dos Equis, and Carta Blanca have already made inroads into the huge U.S. market. The domestic wines from the vineyards of the northwest are surprisingly good, though expensive; imported wines are exorbitantly priced.

If you prefer non-alcoholic beverages, Mexico has a variety to offer. *Refrescos* are refreshing carbonated drinks available just about everywhere. Better yet are the *jugos,* natural fruit juices available from street vendors who extract juice from fruits right in front of your eyes (in fact, if they're *not* freshly squeezed while you wait, it's better to stay away from them). Plain water or water served with fruit juice or a fruit flavoring (the so-called *agua frescas*) should be avoided unless served in a private home or restaurant where the water is bottled or purified.

The Arts of Mexico

The Grid Pattern of the Colonial City

It was King Ferdinand (1479–1516) who first recommended that Colonial governors introduce a grid pattern of parallel intersecting streets, and his recommendation soon became a binding plan for New Spain towns under the name *Codigo de las Indias.* (While a few such towns had been built on the Iberian peninsula, the major inspiration for the layout was derived from ancient Rome and reinforced by Renaissance planners.) As a result, most of the cities of Colonial Mexico, including Mexico City, follow this plan.

Of course, the center of any new town in Colonial Mexico was the plaza (Plaza des Armas), on which would be found the local church or cathedral, the town hall, the market, and the homes of the *criollo* aristocracy.

Domestic Architecture

Like the town plan, the houses of the well-to-do betrayed Roman as well as Iberian influences. Colonial houses were each built around a "patio," or inner courtyard, surrounded on four sides by colonnaded galleries and decorated with mosaic floors and fountains.

Churches, Convents, and Cathedrals

16th-Century Architecture. Missionary zeal in the New World led to the construction of hundreds of religious buildings, many of which were erected on the sites of destroyed Indian pyramids or temples. Compared to their European counterparts, however, churches in Mexico were usually modest, having single naves and lacking towers. In most cases, they were built to serve an additional purpose as thick-walled battlements, offering protection against Indian attacks. Walled atriums and outer courtyards were common features of monasteries during this period as were central stone crosses and side chapels (*capillas posas*), an architectural feature of church construction that is unique to Mexico. Because of the dry, frequently broiling climate, mass was often celebrated in open chapels called *capillas abiertas* that, like *posas,* were constructed specifically for the worship of converted Indians. Splendid examples of atriums and *posas* can be found in Huejotzingo, San Andrés de Cálpan, Izamal, Actopan, and Tlaxcala. You'll find fascinating *abiertas* in Teposcolula, Coixtlahuaca, and Cuernavaca.

The style of the early fortress-like Mexican churches usually derived from the European Romanesque or Gothic. In some instances, however, the architectural decoration of these Colonial buildings reflected the influence of the *mudéjar* style, so-named for the Mudejares, or Moors, who remained in Spain after their defeat in 1492. Among the most common *mudéjar* motifs are the *alfiz,* a carved embellishment above an arched entranceway, and (in churches of a later date) *azulejos* (glazed tiles) and timber paneling known as *alfarje* and *artesonado.*

The *Plateresque* decorative style (from the Spanish *platero,* meaning silversmith) dominated the stone reliefs and sculpture around the portals of most churches. While it was a style predominately influenced by late Gothic and Renaissance motifs, it, too, incorporated some *mudéjar* decorative forms and was subject to local interpretation as well.

Frescoes of this period, which were almost always executed in two colors by Indian apprentices, sometimes concerned themselves with native themes. At Ozumba, Huejotzingo, and Ixmiquilpan one can see the depiction of embattled Aztec warriors.

17th-Century Architecture. The influence of independent religious orders gradually declined in the face of more centralized authority exercised by the Roman Catholic Church and the Spanish crown. Small parish churches and isolated missions gave way to large cathedrals constructed in a relatively restrained Baroque style. The great age of elaborately decorated church interiors with gilded altarpieces and polychrome stucco was about to begin. Examples of this type of cathedral can be seen at Mérida, Puebla, La Soledad in Oaxaca, Mexico City, Morelia, Guadalajara, and San Luís Potosí.

18th–20th Century Architecture. The 18th century was the age of the Mexican High Baroque, a period when gilded decorative motifs were incorporated into all interior surfaces. The combination of the native Indian and Spanish temperaments made Mexico the center of the Baroque at its most extravagant. This trend toward elaborate and increasingly bizarre ornamentation which often included depictions of plants and animals, came to a climax with the *Churrigueresque* style, named for a Spanish architect, José de Churriguera (though it was his younger disciples in New Spain who took the master's theories to extremes). One interesting feature of the style was the pilaster, or *estípite,* designed as an inverted and truncated pyramid that embellished church façades and interiors. Prominent examples of the *Churrigueresque* style can be found in the church of Santa María, Tonantzintla, and La Casa de Alfeñique (the Almond-Cake House), both in the Puebla region, as well as the church of San Francisco in nearby Acatepec. In Mexico City this style can be found in the Sagrario Metropolitano, the church of La Santisima, and the Casa de los Mascarones. The *Poblano* style, a regional variation appearing in the towns of Puebla and Tlaxcala, features ornate stucco ornamentation combining colored tiles and red brick. It can be found at the churches of Santa María Tonantzintla and San Bernardino de Tlax-calancingo, the church of La Merced, and the Rosary Chapel in Atlixco.

By the end of the 18th century the Neoclassical style had superceded the Baroque. In fact, Baroque extravagances were often removed from existing cathedrals and replaced by severe Neoclassical motifs. Some of the best Neoclassical architecture and sculpture was produced by the Spanish-born Manuel Tolsá (1759–1816), who created the equestrian statue of Emperor Charles IV in Mexico City among other masterpieces. Tolsá's work can also be seen on the dome of the Cathedral in Mexico City. A list of other important Neoclassical architects would have to include Francisco Eduardo Tresguerras (1759–1833) and Pedro Patino Ixilinque (1774–1835).

The 19th century saw very little in the way of architectural innovation. Two interesting exceptions are the Mexican variations on the Art Nouveau style and the updated Neo-Gothic architectural style of Zeferino Gutierrez. Twentieth-century architecture has been strongly influenced by the International Style. Prominent 20th-century architects include Felix Candela, Enrique de la Mora Y Palomar, Luis Barragán, José García Villagrán, Mario Pani, Enrique del Moral, Mathias Goeritz, Pedro Ramírez Vázquez, and Rafael Mijares.

Four Centuries of Mexican Painting

Mexican painting throughout the 17th century stood in the service of the Church, and was only occasionally influenced by Old World masters and the importation of artwork, particularly prints. Mexican painters drew heavily from the Baroque styles of Murillo and Rubens, but imbued their art with its own unique quality of pious sentimentality. Among the more significant painters of this period were the Dominican Alonso López de Herrera (b. 1579), and nicknamed "the Divine," Baltazar de Echave Orío (1548–1620), Baltazar de Echave Ibía (1585–1645), Luis Juárez (1600–1635), José Juárez (1615–1667), Baltazar de Echave Ríoja (1632–1682), and Pedro Ramírez (1650–1678).

Painting during the Mexican Baroque reached its climax from the late-17th to mid-18th centuries. The works of Cristóbal de Villalpando (1652–1714), Juan Rodríguez Juárez (1675–1728), Juan Correa (1674–1739), and his pupils José María de Ibarra (1688–1768) and Miguel Cabrera (1695–1768) are characteristic of Mexican art in the later stages of the Colonial era. The religious subject matter and themes, and the style of sweet affectation are telling evidence of the artists' distance from the realities of Mexican civic and political life. Their work can be seen in churches, convents, and the museums of Mexico City, Puebla, Morelia, Tepotztlán, San Miguel de Allende, Guadalajara, and Taxco.

The Mexican Baroque eventually yielded to the international taste for Neoclassical style. By decree of Charles III of Spain, the Royal Academy of San Carlos de la Nueva España was established in Mexico City in 1785, its faculty devoted to Neoclassicism. Closely allied to the spirit of the French and American Revolutions, the Neoclassical style prevailed during the Mexican War for Independence. Yet despite its exalted political aims, the idealized subject matter imposed by the prestigious Academy was often stultifying and academic, reflecting little of authentic Mexican culture. The handful of Mexican painters who rejected the stereotypical themes dictated by the Academy were called *costumbristas,* (from the Spanish *costumbre,* meaning "custom" or "usage") and received little recognition in their lifetimes.

During this period a number of European artists were hard at work in Mexico, many drawn by the vivid descriptions of the Mexican landscape and Mexican folklore penned by the German explorer Alexander von Humboldt (1769–1859). Humboldt particularly influenced the German artist Johann Moritz Rugendas (1802–1858), who painted exotic images of the Mexican landscape as well as genre scenes, and eventually became an artistic chronicler of Mexican life. At approximately the same time the Italian printmaker Claudio Linati and the English artist Daniel Thomas Egerton were visitors to Mexico and subsequently produced works with a variety of Mexican themes. One of the most authoritative descriptions of the cultural life of this period is *Life in Mexico,* a collection of letters written by Madame Calderón de la Barca that was first published in 1843.

By the close of the 19th century the Academy had lost much of its prestige, though it still claimed some prominent painters as its own, most notably the landscapist José María Velasco (1840–1912), who was considered the official painter of the "Porfiriate." One of Velasco's most common images was a Mexican landscape dotted with signs of industrialization—his contribution to President Díaz's efforts to modernize Mexico. Velasco's works can be seen in the Museo Nacional de Arte in Mexico City.

In the last decades of the 19th century Mexican artists began to create prints and political cartoons that dramatized the social injustices of the Díaz regime. One of the most distinguished political satirists of the time was the printmaker José Guadalupe Posada (1852–1913), who is best known for his 1913 woodcut titled *Calavera Huertista,* which depicted a tarantula-like General Victoriano Huerta devouring the skeletons of his victims. Another interesting figure of the period was Julio Ruelas (1870–1907), an engraver who specialized in macabre scenes of eroticism and death. Along with the home-grown intellectuals of the day, the Mexican artists who came of age in the post-revolutionary period shared a disdain for the academic, the European, and the artificially sentimental.

Mexican Muralismo

Mexican muralism was inspired by calls for a new social agenda at the turn of the century. Soon an entire generation of artists, many of them strongly influenced by the satire of José Guadalupe Posada, had enlisted in the service of *muralismo*. Notable among this group was Saturnino Herrán (1887–1918), whose depictions of regional themes reflected the primitivism of indigenous Mexican art. Still better known was the legendary Gerardo Murillo (1895–1964), whose pseudonym "Dr. Atl" incorporated the Náhuatl word for *water*, and who founded the first Mexican artists organization, *Centro Artistico*.

The three artists most closely associated with *muralismo*, however, are José Clemente Orozco (1883–1949), David Alfaro Siqueiros (1896–1974), and Diego Rivera (1886–1957). Orozco's fiery expressionist frescoes, which are somewhat reminiscent of the work of the painter El Greco, range in subject matter from historical to biblical themes. His finest works were frescoes made in Guadalajara during the late 1930s, particularly those painted on the walls and domes of the Hospicio Cabañas. David Alfaro Siqueiros painted bold, energetic murals of modern Mexican life that featured machine parts and human forms, sometimes outlined with black contours. Many of Siqueiros' best-known murals are located in Mexico City and can be found at the Palacio de Bellas Artes (the former Royal Academy), the Palacio Nacional, and the Hospital de la Raza.

Diego Rivera and his wife Frida Kahlo (1910–1954) may be the best-known artists of their generation. As a young man Rivera travelled to Europe, and his early work was heavily influenced by Cézanne, Renoir, and the Cubists. Later, the themes of his mature frescoes would derive from Indian life, reinterpreting Indian culture on a heroic scale, his calm narrative style and figural representation recalling Mayan frescoes. In Mexico City his works can be found at the Palacio de Bellas Artes and the Ministry of Health.

Unlike her husband, Frida Kahlo created art, mostly oils and nearly all of them self-portraits, on a small scale. Partially lame as a result of a car accident suffered in her youth, Kahlo's almost surrealistic paintings are devastatingly expressive of the physical pain she endured for most of her life.

Juan O'Gorman was trained as an architect and built one of the first modern residences in Mexico, the Rivera house in Coyoacán. Among his contributions to Mexican muralism were the frescoes that once colored the walls of the waiting room of the Mexico Airport (sadly destroyed in 1939). O'Gorman nevertheless continued to paint, producing landscapes and portraits in a meticulous but highly inventive style. One of his most interesting surviving works can be seen in the library of the National University (UNAM) in Mexico City.

Born in 1899 in Oaxaca of Zapotec parents, Rufino Tamayo had his first important show in Mexico City in 1926. His work typifies the mood of a younger generation that was less politically inclined and gravitated toward an aesthetic based on abstract values of form and color. One of the foremost Mexican painters of the century, Tamayo was soon considered a member in good standing of the international avant-garde, but lack of receptivity toward his work prompted him to move to New York for a time in the late 1930s. He eventually returned to his native country, where the Conservatoire in Mexico City has a nice collection of his work. Other 20th-century artists of note include Carlos Mérida (1891–1984), who emerged in the 1950s as a lyrically abstract painter, and Pedro Coronel, who attempted a synthesis of mural painting with Mexican themes and geometric abstraction. Coronel's work can be seen in the Museo Goitia in his home town of Zacatecas.

Contemporary Mexican painters such as Lilia Carrillo, Fernando García Ponce, and Ricardo Rocha have adopted Mérida's style of lyrical abstraction. The work of Alberto Gironella, José Luis Cuevas, Francisco Corzas, and Rafael Coronel, on the other hand, seems to owe a debt to German Expressionism. Perhaps the contemporary artist most influenced by Indian concerns is the Zapotec Francisco Toledo, who conveys the nightmare world of Mexican poverty in a lurid, almost visionary manner.

The Mirror of Literature

Mexico's literary traditions, which date back to the Aztec and Mayan empires, are the oldest and among the richest in the New World. Tragically, much of this written record was destroyed in the 16th century by overzealous missionaries who thought they recognized in it the unmistakable hand of Satan. The little that did survive, spared the torch of fanaticism by a few courageous priests and soldiers, portrays vibrant communities with complex socio-economic arrangements and deeply intellectual concerns. These so-called "codices"—folding sheets of animal-skin or tree-bark parchment bound between wooden "covers"— recorded, in hieroglyphic or pictographic form, everything from plant and animal descriptions to tax returns and mortality rates to ritual ceremonies and historical events. The tragedy of their destruction is further compounded by the fact that Mesoamerican poetry and ritual lyrics were transmitted from generation to generation orally, and thus never set down in a permanent form. Again, we have a handful of enlightened men to thank for the preservation of the few examples that have survived. Foremost among these scholars was Fra Bernardino de Sahagún (c. 1500– 1590), who recorded accounts of religious rituals, descriptions of daily life, and verse related to him by his Indian pupils (mostly the sons of Aztec chiefs) and eventually published them as *A History of Ancient Mexico* (*Historia General de las cosas de Nueva España*), which remains the most important compendium of ancient Aztec ways and wisdom. Of the approximately 2,000 Nahuatl-based poems (Nahuatl is the root tongue of all Aztec languages) recorded by Father Bernardino, almost 30 are ascribed to the poet-king Neazhuacóyotl (1402–1472), a remarkable individual and the ruler of Texcoco (near present-day Mexico City) who, in addition to his literary abilities, designed temples, built grand palaces containing special music and poetry rooms, and initiated extensive public works such as the aqueduct to the island city of Tenochtitlán (now Mexico City).

The Maya, too, managed to preserve some of their ancient wisdom predating the arrival of the Spanish, most notably in the prose of the *Popul Vuh* (or *Book of the Counsel*), which was written in the Quiché language using Latin characters between 1554 and 1558, and the *Books of the Chiam Bilam*, accounts of religious beliefs, medical practices, and creation stories compiled in the 18th century.

Mexico's Colonial literature dates back to the first *conquistador* himself, Hernán Cortés (1485–1547), whose five letters to the Emperor Charles V, written between 1519 and 1526, attempted to defend his rebellious actions and expressed, at the same time, his astonishment and admiration for the culture of the "barbarian" peoples he and his soldiers so ruthlessly surpressed. While it's apparent from these letters that Cortés suffered from Caesar-like delusions of grandeur (*"Veni, vidi, vinci"*), a little-known foot soldier in his expedition, Bernal Díaz del Castillo, expressed the viewpoint of the simple man caught up in events greater than himself in his *True History of the Conquest of New Spain* (*Historia Verdadera de la Conquista de la Nueva España*). Written when he was 70 years old, some 50 years after his own experiences in Cortés' army, Castillo's memoir of the clash of two cultures worlds apart is still moving.

The same period witnessed a flowering of works in other literary genres as well, though they were usually overshadowed by the output of the mother country. Among the most notable authors of the time were Bernardo de Balbuena (1562–1627), whose verse epic *Mexican Grandeur* (*Grandeza Mexicana*) transfigured the country poetically, and the wholly admirable Sister Juana Inés de la Cruz (1648–1695), a native-born *criollo* who wrote her first poems at the age of eight. She developed into an exceptionally beautiful and intelligent young woman at the court of the viceroy and then entered a convent—the only place in her day where a woman could devote herself to intellectual pursuits. Besides a steady stream of plays and poems discussing the religious and secular disputes of the age, she most tellingly explained her predicament in the autobiographical *Reply to Sor Filotea*. Then, at the height of her fame, Sister Juana turned her back on her intellectual activities, sold her 4,000-volume library, and spent the rest of her short-lived days nursing the sisters in her convent who had contracted the plague. The most famous Mexican dramatist of the period was Juan Ruiz de Alarcón y Mendoza (1580–1639), who soon realized his talents were being wasted in a country where there was no public theater and eventually emigrated to Spain, where he became one of the leading figures of that country's Golden Age. Likewise the novel, due to Church decrees forbidding their import, made a rather late and tentative appearance on the Colonial literary scene. The first native example of the genre, *The Misfortunes of Alonso Ramirez* (*Infortunios de Alonso Ramírez*), a *Robinson Crusoe* imitation, was written by Carlos de Sigüenza y Góngora (1645–1700), who also produced a large body of scientific writing. Still, practitioners of the art of the novel remained few and far between until the early years of the 19th century, when José Joaquín Fernandez de Lizardi (1176–1827) figured out a way to get around church censors with his picaresque allegory *The Itching Parrot* (*El Periquillo Sarniento*), published in 1816.

For much of the 19th century, Mexican novels and short stories were heavily influenced by French Romanticism and, later, a Spanish variant of the same school, with few authors establishing a lasting reputation. Three important exceptions were José López Portillo y Rojas (the grandfather of the future president), Ignacio Altamirano, and Manuel Payno (1810–1894). Altimarano, an Indian who didn't learn Spanish until he was 14, made a splash with his novel about banditry—a common Mexican preoccupation in the 19th century—called *The Zarco*. Payno's three long novels, the best known of which was *The Outlaws at the Cold River* (*Los Bandidos de Río Frío*), also mined much the same ground while painting a realistic portrait of the society of his day.

Contemporary Literature. While it goes without saying that the Revolution changed every aspect of Mexico's social and economic relationships, the impact on her intellectual life cannot be underestimated; even today, as Mexico's politicians and technocrats continue to struggle to deliver on the Revolution's promises, its ideals and rhetoric have already been fully integrated into her art and literature. Perhaps not surprisingly, given the country's long and tortured past, the preoccupation with the Revolution and attempts to place it into an "acceptable" historical context are, more often than not, used by her artists, poets, and writers to further their own explorations of the unique "Mexican" psychology.

Verse, especially, seems to have appealed to the 20th-century Mexican sensibility, and the list of the country's noteworthy poets is a long one: Salvador Díaz Míron, Ramon López Velarde, Armando Nervo, Luis Urbina, Enrique Gonzalez Martínez, Carlos Pellicer, Ortiz de Montellano, Gonzalez Rojo, José Gorostiza, Jaime Torres Bodet, Salvador Novo, and Xavier Villaurrutia—all have addressed themselves to the legacy of the Revolution while, at the same time, capturing the hearts of their countrymen with the lyrical quality of their poetry.

Similarly, after centuries of benign neglect, if not outright inter-
ference, our own century has been witness to an explosion of Mexican
prose works, many of them of the highest order. Two of the cornerstones
of this relatively recent tradition are Octavio Paz (b. 1914) and Juan
Rulfo (1918–1986). The multi-talented Paz, a noted poet in his own
right (as well as a respected diplomat with a long record of service), is
best known for his perceptive criticism and wide-ranging essays, the
most famous of which appeared in his seminal *The Labyrinth of Solitude*
(*El laberinto de la soledad*), which remains, some 40 years after its publication, perhaps the most important introduction to the collective
psyche of "this Castilian people with Aztec traits." Rulfo's fame is based
on a collection of short stories, *The Burning Plain* (*El llano en Llamas*),
and a thin novel, *Pedro Páramo,* that he published two years apart while
in his mid-30s. Nevertheless, his compressed, masterful tales penetrate
to the true essence of the Mexican landscape as well as the characters
whose souls are shaped by it.

The best-known contemporary Mexican novelist is Carlos Fuentes (b.
1928), who first came to international prominence with the publication
of his novels *The Death of Artemio Cruz* and *Where the Air Is Clear,* both
of which portray the upper middle class—and often seamier side—of
Mexican society. Fuentes, who has divided his time between Mexico and
the States for years now, imbues his narratives with a uniquely objective
perspective, along with a fondness for point-of-view experiments. Other
members of Fuentes' generation include Rosario Castellanos (1925–
1974), who conjured up life in the remote province of Chiapas during her
youth and then described the dawn of the new age brought about by the
Revolution in her novel *The Nine Guards* (*Balún Canán*), and whose
lyrical poetry puts her among the first rank of modern Latin American
poets, and Elena Poniatowska (b. 1933), the daughter of a Polish father
and Mexican woman who settled permanently in Mexico after the Second World War. Poniatowska served her "apprenticeship" as a journal-
ist, a period during which she mastered the Mexican language and found
herself gravitating toward the country's socially and politically commit-
ted writers. The result was a nonfiction account titled *The Night of
Tlatelolco* (*La noche de Tlatelolco*), which she has since followed with
other works in a similar vein—among them, *Silence Is Strong, Five
Reports From Mexico,* and *Defying Everybody: The Life of Jerusa.*

More recent developments on the literary scene include the founding
in 1960 of the *La espiga Amotinada* group (roughly translated as "The
Corn in Mutiny") by the likes of Jaime Labastidas and Oscar Olivas,
writers concerned with renewing Mexico's rich tradition of lyrical poetry
as it relates to more contemporary themes. Finally, you might also want
to check out the novels of the mysterious B. Traven, a pseudonym for the
German Ret Marut, who lived in Mexico from the middle of the 1920s

(after his ill-fated participation in the Munich Räte republic) until his death in 1969. Best-known for his *Treasure of Sierra Madre* (which is also the least "Mexican" of his works), Traven became a passionate spokesman for the downtrodden and oppressed, particularly Mexico's Indians, and captured to a remarkable degree the feeling of the southern part of the country in such novels as *The Cotton Pickers, The Bridge in the Jungle, The General From the Jungle,* and *The Rebellion of the Hanged.*

Great Civilizations of Mesoamerica

The term "Mesoamerica" refers to that part of what is now Mexico and Central America that was inhabited prior to the Spanish Conquest. Smaller than present-day Mexico, the northern border of Mesoamerica extended from just above modern Tampico on the Gulf coast to a region parallel to the tip of Baja California on the Pacific. Its southern border was located in what is now Honduras. It was divided climatically into two regions, the coastal lowlands and the central highlands and valleys, and while the first signs of civilization appeared in the lowlands, actual cities only developed in the highlands at a later date.

An extraordinarily gifted people, the Mesoamericans are known for the giant earth pyramids they built, their monumental sculpture and jade figurines, and their wall paintings. Their religious rites and ceremonial rituals were recorded in ideograms and, later, glyphs, which were then bound into books, or "codices" made of deerskin or bark paper. They were brilliant mathematicians and astronomers, and invented a calendar based on two cycles, a solar year of 365 days and another cycle of 260 days that repeated every 52 "years." Religious life closely followed this calendar. But despite their intellectual sophistication, Mesoamericans were also warlike and violent, and regularly practiced human sacrifice to appease a pantheon of rapacious gods.

The cloudy history of Mesoamerica is one of civilizations suddenly emerging and just as suddenly vanishing into the humid jungles. Over the last hundred years, archaeologists have been hard at work excavating the remains of these ancient cultures, and their discoveries continue to change our ideas and theories of the development of entire regions. Firm chronologies of this epoch of mankind's past are extremely hard to establish since so few written records survived the depredations of the Spanish conquistadors, and many of the glyphic carvings that do exist have yet to be translated. Fortunately, calendars left behind by different Mesoamerican cultures have helped to place many major events in a relative historical framework. Other more technical means of establishing a chronology include radiocarbon dating, thermoluminescence, stratigraphy, pollen analysis, tree-ring dating, and linguistic analyses.

The Olmecs (c. 1200 B.C.–175 B.C.)

The earliest Mesoamerican culture developed along the Gulf coast in what are now the modern states of Veracruz and Tabasco. In these humid lowlands the Olmecs (meaning "inhabitants of the rubber country") created three great ceremonial centers in succession: San Lorenzo (1150 B.C.–900 B.C.), La Venta (800 B.C.–400 B.C.), and Tres Zapotes, which was completely destroyed about 175 B.C.

Not surprisingly, given their achievements, the Olmecs influenced virtually all later Mesoamerican civilizations, from the Mayan in the Yucatán to the Aztec of the highlands. Central to their culture was the worship of gods of fire, rain, maize (corn), and the feathered serpent Quetzalcóatl. One of the most distinctive Olmec images, appearing on numerous stone statues and reliefs, was a frightening hybrid of a jaguar and human infant, often grimacing or crying with open mouth. Just as impressive are the Olmec's colossal basalt heads with their flat faces and fixed, staring eyes. Some of these heads are as tall as 3 meters (9 feet) and weigh as much as 44 tons. The Olmecs typically wore beautiful iron ore mirrors around their necks, and fashioned elaborately carved stelae depicting contemporary events of significance.

At their chief ceremonial city of La Venta, archaeologists have discovered a huge beaten-earth pyramid flanked by buildings aligned on a north-south axis. The pyramid itself may have had funerary origins, developing out of the Indian custom of burying the dead beneath the floor of the home and then abandoning that home. Excavations at La Venta have also uncovered a ball court similar to those that appeared in virtually every civilization in Mesoamerica. The court was designed for a game played with a hard rubber ball (representing the sun) in which the players could not use their hands or feet. Oddly enough, it was the winners who were ritually sacrificed to the gods. Artifacts of the Olmec civilization are displayed in museums at Villahermosa and Santiago Tuxtla, the Jalapa and Tres Zapotes open-air museums, and the National Museum of Anthropology in Mexico City.

Teotihuacán (c. 300 B.C.–A.D. 700)

Teotihuacán, the "City of the Gods," is located about 50 km. (30 miles) north of Mexico City at an altitude of 2,135 meters (7,000 feet). The largest pre-Colonial city of central Mesoamerica, in its heyday it spread over 13 square km. (8 square miles) and probably housed a population of 150,000 people. By the time the Spanish discovered the site in the early 16th century, it had been in ruins for almost 800 years. To the Aztecs who found it in the 14th-century, however, Teotihuacán was venerated as a sacred place. They named its longest avenue (aligned on a north-south axis for astronomical reasons) the Street of the Dead, and marveled at the pyramids, courtyards, and palaces that lined either side of it. Today, the 60-meter- (200-foot-) high Pyramid of the Sun on one side of the avenue and the smaller Pyramid of the Moon at the northern end are especially impressive. You might also want to note the inclined bearing walls and horizontal cornices of the existing structures, both of which were designed to ensure the stability of the building in this earthquake-prone region. Among the more common craft and artworks found at the site are

Jaguar frescoes, Teotihuacán

three-legged cylindrical vessels that were stuccoed and then painted, carved snake heads, stone reliefs and maquettes, inlaid masks, and wall paintings.

One of the largest pre-Columbian structures in Mesoamerica is the gigantic pyramid of Cholula in the state of Puebla, which was probably constructed in the first century by a culture strongly influenced by the one centered around Teotihuacán.

El Tajín (A.D. 300–1100)

The ceremonial center of El Tajín is situated near the Gulf of Mexico between Tampico and Veracruz. Emerging in the fifth century, El Tajín reached its cultural zenith between A.D. 600-1100, when invading Toltecs from the highlands put an end to its Golden Age. Though the surrounding area is inhabited by Totonac Indians, the original builders remain shrouded in obscurity. (Most anthropologists consider the Totonacs latecomers to the coast). What we do know is that they were very much a ball court culture, with 11 courts having been discovered at the site, along with carved stone objects that appear to be reproductions of wooden protective gear worn during the games. The extreme brutality of such games is illustrated by the narrative relief carvings that decorate the walls of the courts. Also located at El Tajín is the extraordinary Pyramid of the Niches, so-named for the 365 recesses (17 of which decorated the temple that once topped the summit) in its four sides, one for each day of the year.

Monte Albán (c. 700 B.C.–A.D. 1521)

Monte Albán, or "White Mountain," stands in serene and splendid isolation on a hilltop 1,615 meters (5,300 feet) above sea level, 366 km. (220 miles) southeast of Mexico City in the valley of Oaxaca. Archaeologists have been able to identify five distinct historical periods (labeled Monte Albán I–V), suggesting that the region had been populated as early as 800 B.C.: first by the Olmecs (Monte Albán I), then a different group of Indians (Monte Albán II) around 300 B.C., and still later by the Zapotecs (Monte Albán III), who occupied it between A.D. 300–900. The Mixtecs (Monte Albán IV–V), occupied Monte Albán after A.D. 900 using it only as a funerary center.

One of the earliest sites at Monte Albán is called the Courtyard of the Dancers, which features *Los Danzantes,* reliefs depicting dwarflike figures in bizarre, contorted poses. The early tombs at Monte Albán are simple walled-in burial chambers. Much later, the Mixtecs created tombs that were cruciform in shape. In 1932, archaeologists discovered the remains of a Mixtec prince buried with 500 precious objects at one of these tombs—a find that today can be seen at the church of Santo Domingo in Oaxaca.

Mayas (A.D. 150–900)

The Mayas built a vast jungle civilization that extended from Mexico into present-day Guatemala, Belize, Honduras, and El Salvador. Eschewing "urbanization," Mayan civilization reached its height between A.D. 650–900, when it mysteriously came to an abrupt end. An industrious

Two characteristic representations of a woman carrying a child: Mayan (left), culture of West Coast (right).

and brilliant people, the Mayas created an elaborate network of trade routes, built an extensive canal system, and developed highly efficient farming techniques. Their astronomy and mathematics were advanced enough to employ the zero notation and Mayan astronomers measured the solar year at precisely 365.242 days (modern astronomy has improved that to 365.2422 days). Mayan architecture used corbel vaulting to span open spaces, Mayan stone carvers produced statues in abundance, and Mayan "chemists" developed a form of bark paper coated in white plaster.

Mayan stone carving may have had its most brilliant flowering in northern Petán at the ceremonial centers of Tikal and Uaxactún (Guatemala). Here the Mayas evolved a highly narrative, almost painterly style of relief. The highest pyramid in Mesoamerica, measuring 65 meters (213 feet) high, was also constructed at Tikal.

Mayan archaeological sites have been grouped into three geographic zones: north, central, and south. The northern region includes the provinces of Yucatán, Quintana Roo, and the eastern part of Campeche, and includes the sites at Dzibilchaltún (near Mérida), Chichén Itzá, Mayapán, Uxmal, Labná, Sayil, Kabah, and Río Bec. The central region encompasses the provinces of Tabasco, southwestern Campeche, northern Chiapas, and Petán in Guatemala, and includes sites at Tikal, Uaxactún, and Bonampak, Yaxchilán, and Palenque. (Nearly half the inhabitants of Guatemala are directly descended from the Mayas.) The southern region encompasses southern Chiapas, areas of Guatemala, western Honduras, and El Salvador, with sites of Zaculeu, Kaminaljuyú, Chincultic, Chamá, Alta Verapaz, Quirigua, and Copán.

Toltecs (A.D. 900–1300)

The Aztecs considered the militaristic Toltecs to have been the founders of civilization, and the Aztecs' own self-image as warrior-priests was lifted directly from Toltec culture. The Toltec capital was located at Tula (meaning "City of God"), about 92 km. (55 miles) northwest of Mexico City near present-day Hidalgo, and wasn't positively "rediscovered" until 1938. The Toltecs' legacy to the New World includes their large pillared halls, their colossal statues of warlike figures, their numerous reliefs incorporating human skulls, and their worship of the feathered serpent-god Quetzalcóatl.

Shortly after the collapse of Mayan civilization, a branch of the Toltecs invaded the Yucatán peninsula and established a capital at Chichén Itzá as well as a ceremonial center at Izamal. The Mayan-Toltec culture that evolved thereafter produced numerous reliefs of the rain-god Chac, half man and half beast, with a sweeping trunklike snout.

Aztecs (c. 1300–1521)

The Spanish conquistadors who discovered the great Aztec city of Tenochtitlán ("the place where cactus grows from rock") on the site of what is now Mexico City considered it as impressive as any of the major cities of Europe. The city, which had spread over two small islands in Lake Texcoco since its founding around 1325, was a huge metropolis 3 km. (5 miles) square, with a population of 300,000, making it the largest and most densely populated urban site in Mesoamerica. The emperor Moctezuma's palace alone had 300 rooms grouped around three courts, with a royal zoo and aviary.

The Aztecs, who had once been a poor nomadic tribe, believed they had risen to greatness as the chosen people of the sun-god Huitzilopochlti. Much of their culture, however, including their pyramids, ball courts, pantheon of deities, and calendar, had been adapted from earlier Mesoamerican civilizations. One of their most notable achievements was their calendar stone, the "Stone of the Fifth Sun." The Aztecs believed they were living in the epoch of the Fifth Universe, the first four having already been destroyed by cosmic events. Their divine mission, as they saw it, was to prevent the destruction of the current (and last) world by appeasing the gods with sacrifices of human hearts and blood, called chalchiuatl ("precious water").

As a result, war was waged on an almost continual basis to obtain victims for these sacrifices. This practice undoubtedly bolstered the conquistadors' perception of the Aztecs as bloodthirsty savages, which in turn encouraged Hernán Cortés to burn the magnificent city of Tenochtitlán to the ground in April, 1521. Phoenix-like, Mexico City soon emerged from its ashes.

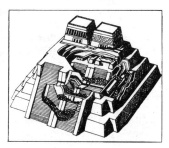

Aztec feather shield

Pyramid model, Tenochtitlán

Chronology

Paleo-Indian Period

to 6500 B.C. The earliest inhabitants are nomadic hunter-gatherers who enter the Western Hemisphere across a land bridge linking present-day Siberia and Alaska, then migrate south as far as the Andes region of South America during the last Ice Age (about 50,000–9,000 B.C.). Tools and other relics from Mexican archaeological excavations have been dated to at least 21,000 B.C. At this time, Mexico is cool and wet, with glaciers in the mountains and considerable volcanic activity. About 7,000 B.C. the temperature begins to rise and the ice sheets retreat.

Early Agriculture

6500–1500 B.C. By 3500 B.C. beans, squash, and hybrid maize are being planted. By 3000 B.C. fired clay vessels are being produced in Ecuador and Colombia.

Early Formative Period

1500–900 B.C. Permanent villages are established in moist lowlands on the Pacific coast near present-day Chiapas. The Olmec civilization emerges in the lowlands of southern Veracruz and Tabasco. San Lorenzo, the oldest Olmec site, is founded by 1150 B.C. and destroyed by 900 B.C. All other Mesoamerican cultures ultimately derive from the Olmecs.

Middle Formative Period

900–300 B.C. The transition to a fully settled life has taken place everywhere and growing populations are centered around villages and small towns. Regional cultures prevail, but the Olmec influence is predominant. La Venta, the most important Olmec site, is founded and flourishes from 800–400 B.C. Other important Olmec sites are established in Puebla, the Valley of Mexico, and Morelos. Monte Albán is founded near Oaxaca around 800 B.C.

Late Formative Period

300 B.C.–A.D. 100 Pyramids are developed at this time and the first fully urban Mesoamerican culture is founded at Teotihuacán in the Valley of

Mexico. An advanced calendar system is developed by the "Epi-Olmec" peoples at Tres Zapotes. The Izapan civilization, a transitional stage of development between Olmec and classic Mayan culture, appears. The first flowering of Mayan civilization occurs in the Petán–Yucatán peninsula.

Early Classical Period

A.D. 100–600 Urban Teotihuacán culture reaches its heights and the less centralized Mayan civilization begins to evolve. Cholula develops on broad fertile plains near the present-day city of Puebla, its 50-meter- (180-foot-) high pyramid an outstanding achievement of Teotihuacán culture.

Classical Period

300–900 The lowland Mayas reach intellectual and artistic zeniths. Mixtec peoples occupy the northern part of Oaxaca. The great ceremonial center of El Tajín near the Gulf of Mexico is inhabited by Totonacs.

Post-Classical Period

900–1519 Mayan civilization ends and the Toltecs found their capital city of Tula near modern Hidalgo. The Aztecs develop the great city of Tenochtitlán. Mesoamerican history ends with the arrival of the Spanish led by Hernán Cortés in 1519, and the destruction of Tenochtitlán three years later.

Colonial Period (1519–1821)

Three centuries of Spanish rule see the suppression and exploitation of the Indians by their conquerors. The native economy is replaced in part by a transplanted Spanish economy, with the importation of Spanish domestic animals and products supplanting indigenous products. Spanish-owned *haciendas* and *estancias* (large agricultural or cattle concerns) take up huge tracts of land. Plantations in the tropical lowlands that use African slave labor profit by the exportation of cocoa and sugar cane. The Spanish educational system is introduced into Mexico, with most schools run by monastic orders. By 1568 disease has decimated Mexico's Indian population to a third of its former size. The Spanish crown, fearing that the *conquistadors* will create an independent power in the new territories, eventually replaces the leaders with a Colonial administration directly responsible to the king.

1519–1521 Hernán Cortés and a small army of men arrive from Cuba and enter Aztec territory. Aztec ruler Moctezuma II, believing Cortés to be the "returning" god Quetzalcóatl, welcomes him with lavish gifts. On August 13, 1521, Cortés defeats Moctezuma's successor Cuauhtémoc and destroys the Aztec capital of Tenochtitlán. Cortés is appointed governor of the territory of New Spain, and rebuilds Tenochtitlán, calling it "Mexico."

1527–1535 The responsibility for governing New Spain is transferred to a five-member committee, the *Audiencia*. Then, in 1535, Charles V appoints Antonio de Mendoza the first viceroy of the territory.

1551 The first Mexican university is founded, the third in the New World after those of Santo Domingo and Lima.

1600 Eighty years after the arrival of the Spanish over 250 convents and monasteries have been established.

1700–1800 The territory of New Spain is more than doubled through the establishment of missions and military expeditions into what are now the Mexican states of Nayarit, Sinaloa, Sonora, Durango, Chihuahua, Coahuila, and Baja, as well as Texas, New Mexico, Arizona, and California. Immigration from Spain creates a sharp rise in population. Silver ore becomes a major trade commodity. This new economic growth benefits only a small minority of the Spanish- and native-born aristocracy, however. Toward the end of the period, the small but growing middle class begins to espouse the principles of the French and American Revolutions, along with a growing desire for independence.

1808–1821 The turmoil in Spain caused by Napoleon's dreams of empire opens the way for a *criollo* conspiracy in the Mexican state of Querétaro led by Mayor Miguel Domínguez and his wife Doña Josefa Ortiz. The rebellion is sustained by a parish priest from Dolores named Miguel Hidalgo Y Costilla, but is ultimately put down.

1813 The struggle for independence continues in Chilpancingo (state of Guerrero) under the leadership of José María Morelos, another priest. A constitution for a republic is drafted but never instituted.

1815 Rebellious armies are defeated by troops loyal to the Spanish crown.

1820 The Liberal movement in Spain implements the Cadiz constitution proclaiming the legal equality of Mexicans and Spaniards, and furthering the cause for independence in Mexico.

Republic of Mexico (1821–1911)

1821 Agustín de Iturbide signs the Cordoba Agreement, which grants Mexico national sovereignty (not recognized by Spain until 1836).

1822 Agustín de Iturbide is proclaimed Emperor of Mexico but is deposed after eleven months.

1824 The monarchy is dissolved and a new constitution modeled after that of the United States establishes Mexico as a federal republic. Guadalupe Victoria is proclaimed president. Political turmoil continues.

1845 Texas is annexed by the United States, an act that leads to the outbreak of the Mexican-American War a year later.

1848 The Treaty of Guadalupe, in which Mexico cedes Texas, California, New Mexico, and Arizona to the United States for compensation of $18,250,000, is signed.

1855 Liberals led by General Ignacio Comonfort and Benito Juárez, a full-blooded Zapotec Indian, draft radical reform laws.

1857 A new constitution calling for a federal republic and representative democratic government is adopted.

1858–1861 Reform wars rage between Liberals and Conservatives.

1862–1867 French troops allied with Mexican Conservatives offer the imperial crown to Hapsburg Archduke Maximilian. In 1867 the Liberals regain power, Maximilian is executed, and the Republic is restored.

1867 Benito Juárez is confirmed as president in 1867 and continues to implement Liberal policies until his death in 1872.

1876–1911 Porfirio Díaz is elected president. His stay in office (almost 30 years) is the longest uninterrupted period of peace in Colonial Mexico's history and is dubbed the "Porfiriate." Mexico becomes modernized: foreign investment contributes to the construction of industrial plants, telegraph lines, and railroads. At the same time, Díaz's administration evolves into a dictatorship, with exploitation of Mexico's middle and lower classes its trademark. Díaz resigns under pressure in 1911.

Mexican Revolution (1910–1920)

1911 Moderate Francisco I. Madero, supported by a rebel army in the north led by Francisco "Pancho" Villa and another in the south led by Emiliano Zapata, assumes the presidency. Zapata, a radical, seeks land reform under the slogan *Tierra y Libertad*, ("Land and Freedom").

1913 The Conservative opposition under the leadership of Victoriano Huerta stages a coup with the tacit approval of the United States. Madero is assassinated. Venustiano Carranza, the governor of Coahuila, spurs a civil war that forces Huerta to flee. Villa and Zapata refuse to recognize Carranza as the new leader.

1915 Carranza, with his ally General Alvaro Obregón, occupies the capital and then defeats Villa and Zapata at Celaya in one of the bloodiest battles in Mexico's history.

1917 Carranza institutes a new constitution based on the Constitution of 1857 (but with more extreme anticlerical and socialist provisions) on February 5, 1917.

1921–1933 A more peaceful era in Mexico's political life is presided over by Presidents Obregón (1921–1924) and Plutarco Elías Calles (1924–1928). Reforms brought about include the redistribution of landed estates and the development of an educational system. There is a rise in anticlericalism, cultural nationalism, and trade unionism, and the *Partido Revolucionario Institucional,* or Institutional Revolutionary Party (better known as the *PRI*), the dominant political party of the next fifty years, is founded.

Nationalism (1934–1940)

The presidency of Lázaro Cárdenas coincides with numerous social and nationalistic reforms, including the further redistribution of land; the promotion of *ejidos,* or collective farms; the nationalization of the petroleum industry; and an emphasis on moving away from foreign sources of capital.

Mexico since 1940

1942 Mexico declares war on the Axis powers; economic development increases as a result of the war-induced shutdown in imports.

1950s Mexico continues to move toward socialism, as land is redistributed and industry is nationalized. The Treaty of Tlatelolco establishes atomic neutrality in Latin America.

1960s An exploding population outstrips Mexico's ability to feed itself or create enough jobs to keep pace with the growing labor pool. Imports rise and Mexico is forced to fall back on foreign capital.

1970s The devaluation of the peso by almost 50 percent leads to political unrest and triple-digit inflation. Extensive oil reserves are discovered in the Gulf of Mexico, creating hope for a solution to the country's economic crisis.

1982 Miguel de la Madrid Hurtado is elected president. Mexico continues to stagger under the twin burdens of its rapidly growing population and escalating foreign debt.

1985 A major earthquake devastates parts of Mexico City, the world's most populous metropolitan area, underscoring the need to decentralize Mexico's economy.

**Mexico City

See color map.

Over 2 km. (1 mile) high and ringed by mighty mountains, Mexico City—or as residents usually call it, simply "Mexico"—is breathtaking. It is also the world's largest city, with an estimated population of 18 million. The capital of the Republic, it is technically known as the Distrito Federal, or "D. F.," a political entity governed indirectly by the president of Mexico, who appoints the city's mayor.

The setting is stunning. Mexico City lies at the foot of two magnificent snow-covered volcanoes rising to over 5,200 meters (17,000 feet): Popocatépetl and Iztaccíhuatl. Its once crystal-clear air is now unfortunately fouled by the exhaust of the city's millions of autos and many factories, but on clear days the vistas are splendid.

The population has nearly doubled since 1979, in part thanks to the tremendous influx of immigrants drawn from rural areas by the dream of a job. The newcomers generally settle on the outskirts of the city, and as a result, the city is sprawling into the plateau of Anáhuac. A century ago, with fewer than 350,000 inhabitants, Mexico City was a quieter capital, surrounded by Indian villages. But during the Revolution of 1910, large numbers of people began to stream into the city from embattled areas in the countryside, and by 1930 the city had over a million inhabitants. Industrialization during and after World War II drew people to the city, and densely packed slums grew up in and around it. The rich moved to new quarters just outside the city limits—Lomas de Chapultepec and El Pedregal, for example—and the city spread out, eventually outgrowing the old boundaries of the Federal District and spilling into the adjacent state of México. Planned satellite cities were built but—more frequently—wild, unplanned suburbs also grew to accommodate the constant flow of immigrants.

To look closely at Mexico City's overcrowding and pollution is to look into the abyss of 20th-century urban sociology. But beyond these problems lies the soul of Mexico itself, awe-inspiring, beautiful, and seductive.

You will enjoy Mexico City nonetheless—despite the infernal traffic and polluted air. Oases abound: quiet Colonial patios and squares in the old center, picturesque corners and streets in the Coyoacán and San Ángel districts, and the spacious and modern university campus. The city's excellent museums are among the finest and most diverse in the world. The boulevards, dense with traffic and hurrying crowds during the week, are peaceful on Sundays, when many of the city's inhabitants retreat to country homes and resorts, enjoy the quiet green of Chapultepec Park, or visit the "floating gardens" (*chinampas*) of Xochimilco.

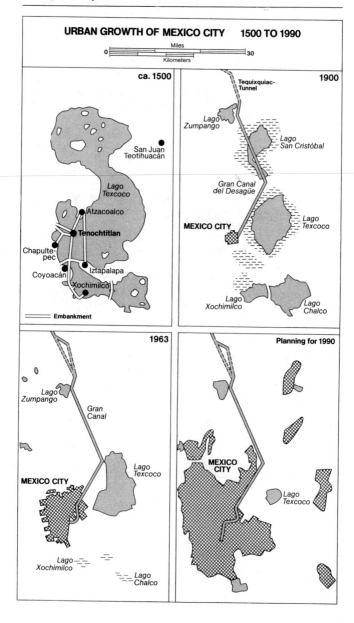

URBAN GROWTH OF MEXICO CITY 1500 TO 1990

History

Modern Mexico City stands on the site of the ancient Aztec capital of Tenochtitlán. Settled in the 14th century on the salt lake of Texcoco, a lake with no natural outlet, Tenochtitlán was built on islands in the lake connected by landfill. More land area was created by floating other islands, which became the famous *chinampas*; a part of these is preserved today at Xochimilco ("place of the flower fields"). The *chinampas* did not in truth float; they were anchored to the lake floor by willows planted at the edges of these man-made islands.

To reduce the danger of flooding during the rainy season, the Spanish tried, after the Conquest of 1521, to drain the salt lake: They dug canals and tunnels to create an outlet into the rivers that flowed north, such as the Río Panuco. Complete success eluded them (as, later, it eluded the Mexicans), but in about 1900 a central canal did finally reach the headwaters of the Panuco.

While this centuries-long reclamation project at last eliminated the problems of flooding, it spawned two new and seemingly insurmountable problems: a scarcity of drinking water that becomes more acute each year, and a gradual sinking of the city's foundations. (You will see this effect clearly in buildings such as the Palacio de Belles Artes or the Basílica de Guadalupe, both of which had to be closed and restabilized.) In 1971 the city established a program to restore some ecological balance to the region, but it has been implemented only fitfully and without much success.

When the Spanish first saw the Aztec city, with its bridges, waterways, palaces, and temples, they were "astonished beyond measure at this magic realm," according to Captain Bernal Díaz del Castillo. By the time the Spanish actually won the city from the Aztecs, in 1521, they had virtually destroyed it; and modern Mexico City rose on the ruins of Tenochtitlán.

To be sure, the Spanish had destroyed what must have been a truly remarkable Aztec city; but in its place they built one of the finest European-style cities of the world, which rivals in plan and architecture the great capitals of the Old World. Although most of the city is modern, you can still see the magnificent Colonial architecture that so impressed 19th-century visitors around the Zócalo, the city's main square.

Transportation

Public transportation in Mexico City is quite inexpensive but usually over-crowded. The subway system (see map on page 40) is new and efficient and still expanding. But during rush hours (lasting until 11:00 in the morning and from 5:00 to 10:00 P.M.), the center of the city is jammed, both above and below ground.

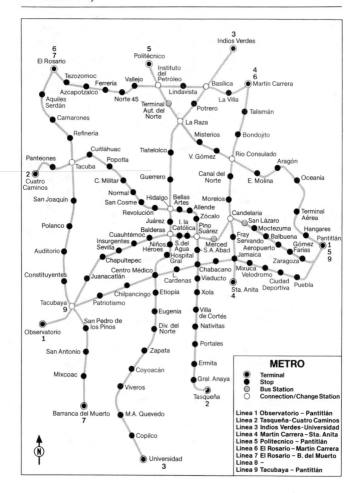

There are about 60 city bus lines, but most of them follow routes so inscrutable that, unless you know the city well, they may deposit you at an unanticipated destination. The easiest routes to follow, and the ones visitors chiefly use, are those along the Paseo de la Reforma and the Avenida de los Insurgentes, the two main arteries of the city. Maps and route information are available from the city bus company.

The green *pesero* cabs are faster than buses because they generally travel along one street from end to end, picking up and letting off passengers every few blocks. There is little chance of getting lost and prices are reasonable—though more than the *peso* from which these cabs got their name many years ago!

There are two types of officially sanctioned taxis in Mexico City. The small Volkswagen taxis that cruise throughout the city are small and poorly maintained but offer the cheapest fares. The *sitio* taxis, which are white with red stripes, pick up passengers only at specified taxi stations. They are larger and more expensive than the Volkswagen taxis. Since the taxi meters do not reflect the rapid pace of Mexico's inflation, drivers post signs on the windows to let you know by how much to multiply the fare shown on the meter. (If there is no meter or the driver tells you it's "broken," be sure to negotiate the price before you begin the trip.) It's a good idea to give the driver as complete a set of directions as possible since he may not know the city perfectly. At a minimum, you should know the address, the street and cross street and the *colonia* (district) of your destination.

One Day in the Capital . . .

Mexico City is a rich capital, a place that rewards endless exploration; but if you have only one or two days here, you can easily take in a few of the city's high points. (Fuller information on these sights is found in the descriptions of Walks 1–6).

Start with the **Zócalo—the largest public square in the Western Hemisphere—and the two great buildings that face it, the **Palacio Nacional (National Palace) and the **cathedral. In the Palacio Nacional, along the gallery and staircase, are Diego Rivera's great murals depicting the history of Mexico. Even if your time in the capital is brief, you should not miss this moving portrayal of Mexico's ancient roots and modern struggles. After visiting the murals, go to the cathedral and stop to peruse the **Sagrario Metropolitano*, or Metropolitan Tabernacle. From the cathedral and Palacio Nacional, it is only a few steps to the excavated ruins of the Aztec **Templo Mayor, the former center of the Aztec city of Tenochtitlán.

When you leave the Zócalo, take the Calle Madero to the **Casa de los Azulejos* (House of Glazed Tiles), once the palace of the counts of Orizaba, now a Sanborns store with an elegant patio restaurant. Visit the nearby *Torre Latinoamericana* (Latin-American Tower) for the best view of the city.

In the afternoon try to see either the ***Basílica de Guadalupe* or the *pyramids of Teotihucán*.

In the evening, sample Mexican food and music at any of a number of restaurants featuring the national cuisine and the national music, mariachis. Try to catch the *Ballet Folklórico* if the world-famous troupe is performing at the *Palacio de Bellas Artes.* (The ballet also gives morning performances.)

If You're Staying a Second Day . . .

If you have a little more time in the capital, then be sure to spend some time at the ***Museo Nacional de Antropología** (National Anthropological Museum) which also has a restaurant, **Chapultepec Park,* and the **Museo Nacional de Historia* (National Historical Museum), which is located in Chapultepec Castle. Enjoy a boat ride in **Xochimilco,* site of the famous floating gardens, or catch the sound-and-light show in the Polyforum Siqueiros at the Insurgentes Sur, where you'll also find several moderately priced restaurants.

If you have more time, consider taking the tours laid out in Walks 1–6 that follow.

WALK 1: Around the Zócalo

Subway stop: Zócalo

See map on page 50.

At the Zócalo, the heart of Mexico City, you can experience centuries of Mexican history for here was the center of the Aztec metropolis, Tenochtitlán, and its principal temple has now been excavated. It was on this spot that Hernán Cortés, the leader of the conquering Spanish, chose to build his own capital, and in the palace built by Spanish viceroys the president of Mexico now officially resides.

The name of this square is properly Plaza de la Constitución, but it has been known popularly for decades as the Zócalo. (The word means "base of a monument"; on this spot for many years, a monument to independence was planned. Although the monument was never built, the base stood on the square until about 1920. Now almost all main squares in Mexican towns are called "Zócalo.")

A walk around the Zócalo takes you to the excavations of the awesome Templo Mayor, the impressive cathedral, the Palacio Nacional where the president of Mexico resides, and other nearby attractions.

The capital's **Zócalo** was once a market square and later a park, but today it forms an impressive stage for the Mexican flag, which flies in the center. Facing the flag are the two seats of power in modern Mexico: the civil authority, housed in the **Palacio Nacional,* and the religious authority, based in the great **Cathedral.* On the Zócalo, national festivals are celebrated, parades are held and demonstrations take place for and against the government. When there is neither celebrating, parading, nor protesting to be done, the Zócalo is crowded with the ordinary players in the great national drama.

You can view the whole square from the roof of the *Hotel Majestic,* at the corner of Calle Madero, and if you arrive by subway, you can see an exposition documenting its history in the Zócalo station. In the pedestrian area to the right of the cathedral, there is a fountain with a copper model of the island city of Tenochtitlán. A little farther on you can see the excavations and reconstruction of the ****Templo Mayor** (1), the main temple of the Aztecs.

The Spanish Conquistadors had reported that in Tenochtitlán there was a pyramid over 50 meters (150 feet) high, with places of worship for the war god Huitzilopochtli and the rain god Tláloc. Human sacrifices to these deities were made to them on the platform. Portions of the Aztec temple district have been discovered since 1913. In 1978, during a construction

Coyolxauhqui

project, workers stumbled upon an 8-ton round altar stone with a relief of the moon goddess Coyolxauhqui; it was then that the Mexican Institute for Anthropology intervened and started the huge project of excavating the Templo Mayor, a project for which two city blocks were demolished.

Archaeologists found that several buildings had been superimposed on each other, leading to the gradual rise of the temple pyramid. Now you can tour this site on foot bridges, seeing the various layers and finds. Take note especially of the eight nearly life-size *figures* on the third level—they were probably standard bearers—and of the heads and bodies of serpents. There is also a figure of a so-called *Chac-mool,* a sitting messenger of the gods, which the Mexica Indians adopted from the Toltec pantheon. The figure's polychrome paint is still completely preserved. A copy of the *monolith of Coyolxauhqui* is now on view;

Templo Mayor, Tenochtitlán
(Florence codex)

the fine carving illustrates a legend, which holds that the goddess was decapitated and cut into pieces by her brother, Huitzilopochtli.

For archaeologists, an equally exciting discovery was an altar (*tzompantili*) whose walls are decorated with more than 200 stone skulls. Many hidden storage sites contained offerings from all over old Mexico, paid in tribute to the Aztec overlords. These trophies are to be exhibited in a museum at the site.

In 1525 the Spanish built their first church in the ruined ceremonial center of the Aztecs, using its stones for the work. The church soon became too small for the capital of New Spain, and so in 1563 construction on the ****Cathedral** (2) was begun. This great structure was not finished until 1813, and consequently it is an interesting blend of the architectural styles of three centuries. Its *façade* shows characteristics of the Renaissance spirit with which it was begun, and the gradual transition to mannered Baroque, then finally the Neoclassical taste of the builders who completed it. Indeed, it is Neoclassicism that finally wins out in this war of styles: the *clock tower* by Manuel Tolsá and the imposing *bell towers* by José Ortiz de Castro dominate every other aspect of the façade.

Because the interior of this three-nave church is rather dark, you only gradually become aware of the impressive proportions within. The works of art were damaged during a fire in 1967, but they have largely been restored. Located right at the entrance is the *Altar del Perdón* (Altar of Forgiveness); it was fashioned by Jerónimo de Balbás in the

Cathedral and Sagrario Metropolitano

Churrigueresque style—the flamboyant and characteristically Spanish combination of all the decorative elements of Baroque and Mannerism. In Mexico, de Balbás gave the Churrigueresque a more specific connotation: the use of the *estípite*, a column with a shaft shaped like an inverted obelisk or cone and made up of elaborately carved components incorporating abstract, floral, and sometimes human decorative elements. Balbás also made the onyx *Altar de los Reyes* (Altar of the Magi), located in the apse behind the main altar. The Altar de los Reyes overflows with gilded carvings and far outshines the rather dark paintings by José Rodríguez y Juárez representing the Assumption of the Virgin and the Adoration of the Magi.

In the central aisle are statues that were ordered from Macao in the 18th century, as was the wonderful *choir screen*. The *choir stalls*, carved by Juan de Rojas in 1696, are another treasure of the Cathedral.

There are 14 side chapels. The first one, west of the Altar de los Reyes, has an urn containing the remains of Emperor Iturbide (see page 34). The others are dedicated to miracle-working saints or paintings of Christ or the Virgin. In the third chapel to the left of the main entrance is *Nuestro Señor del Cacao,* a Christ figure set up before the doors of the original church to accept the offerings for the building of the cathedral; the Indians made these offerings in their own currency, the cocoa bean. The chapter room and the sacristy were painted in 1665 by Juan Correa and Cristóbal de Villalpando; the bishops of the city are buried in the crypt. The treasury is exhibited at the *Museo de Arte Religioso* at Calle Republica de Guatemala 17, behind the Cathedral. The ***Sagrario Metropolitano,** a church serving as a tabernacle, was erected next to the Cathedral in the middle of the 18th century. The rich sculptures and reliefs of its façade, which was executed by the Spaniard Lorenzo Martinez in the Churrigueresque style, is framed by dark red volcanic stone—the same stone that the Aztecs used for construction.

The ****Palacio Nacional** (3) is the official residence of the president of Mexico; its long front occupies the eastern edge of the Zócalo. This is the site of Moctezuma's (or Montezuma's) palace, which Cortés had rebuilt and expanded, using forced Indian labor. After 1562 it became the viceroy's residence and it was burned down during an Indian uprising in 1692. Eventually rebuilt, the building was enlarged in 1927, when the third floor was added. Above the central portal hangs the "freedom bell," which Father Hidalgo rang in Dolores on September 16, 1810, signaling the beginning of the War of Independence. The president reenacts the "call from Dolores" (*grito de Dolores*) annually on September 15, the eve of Independence Day.

Parts of the Palacio Nacional are

open to the public. In the first inner court are Diego Rivera's murals—probably his most important—depicting the history of Mexico. He worked on these paintings for over 25 years, beginning in 1929. In the second-floor gallery are his series of paintings representing old Mexican tribes, and along the stairway is Rivera's personal political statement, presented in the monumental fresco entitled *Class Struggle.*

The former living quarters of Benito Juárez, liberal statesman and two-time president of the Republic, are open to the public, as is the chamber of deputies in which the 1857 reform constitution was decided.

The *Palacio de Ayuntamiento* (Town Hall) on the Zócalo (now the Departamento del Distrito Federal), was built around 1700 and later altered. The *Suprema Corte de Justicia* (Supreme Court) building dates from the 20th century, but it was designed in the Colonial style in order to preserve the architectural character of the square.

When you make the Zócalo your starting point, you can find interesting sights in any direction. If you walk along Avenida Pino Suárez to number 30, you reach the ****Museo de la Ciudad de Mexico** (6). Located in the townhouse of the count of Santiago de Calimaya, it contains items illustrating the history of the city, including a remarkable serpent's head from a corner of a building in the religious center of Tenochtitlán.

Diagonally opposite the museum is the **Hospital de Jesús Nazareno** (7), founded in the year of Cortés's conquest and at the spot where he is said to have met Moctezuma for the first time. From its founding, the hospital has treated Spaniards and Indians equally, and it was the first institution of its kind in America. Cortés is buried in its church. Because of anti-Spanish sentiment in Mexico, his remains were hidden in the hospital from the time of his death in 1547 for over a hundred years. On a ceiling fresco in the church choir, José Clemente Orozco painted his version of the Apocalypse.

If you return to the Zócalo via Avenida 20 de Noviembre, you will see at the corner of Calle Carranza, on the left, the *Palacio de Hierro,* the young people's department store. The palacelike structure is lighted inside through a wonderful roof of colored glass. If you continue along Calle Carranza a little toward the west, you will reach Calle Isabel la Católica, where stands the stately *palace of the count of Valparaiso* (8). Dating from the 18th century, it has been the head office of the Mexican National Bank since 1882.

You can make a somewhat longer tour from the Hospital de Jesús by travelling eastward. If you take the Calle Republica de Uruguay, you reach an old quarter of houses dating from the Colonial period. They are poorly maintained, but hidden among them is an architectural jewel, which you'll find just past the corner of

Convento de la Merced

Calle Jesús Maria: the **Convento de la Merced** (Mercy Convent) (9). The cloister, which contains many early 17th-century sculptures, has been quite carefully preserved. From here it is not far to the large city market, **La Merced** (10), located in a modern hall and spilling into the surrounding streets. The market can also be visited as part of a subway tour of the southern edge of the old city (see page 55).

Following Calle Jesús Maria north, you reach the area of Corregidora and Alhondiga streets. The neighborhood was once crisscrossed with canals, along which canoes transported the produce of nearby Indian villages into Mexico City. The canals are now dry.

At the eastern end of Calle Corregidora is the *Palacio Legislativo,* the ultramodern legislative headquarters of Mexico's senate and lower chamber, which was dedicated in 1981. If you continue through Calle Alhondiga to Calle de Moneda, you will reach the ***Iglesia de la Santisima Trinidad** (Church of the Holy Trinity) (11), whose façade offers a particularly beautiful example of the Churrigueresque style. As its name implies, Calle de Moneda— "Money Street"—was once the

Patio at Calle Moneda No. 13

site of the mint of New Spain. Located at *Casa de la Moneda* 13, it was built in 1734. The mint now houses the *Museo Nacional de las Culturas* (12), which is dedicated to non-Mexican cultures. On this street you can also see the *Archbishop's Palace* and the first Mexican university, which was founded in 1553, at the corner of the Zócalo.

Going north from the Zócalo will lead you past the **Templo Mayor* excavation (1). At the corner of Calle Argentina and Calle Donceles, the architect Manuel Tolsá built a *stone house* (13) for the Marquis del Apartado in the Neoclassical style, using stones from an Aztec pyramid. Be sure to look into the *Iglesia de la Enseñanza* (14) diagonally across the street. Its *high altar,* built in 1778, is in a style called "Ultrabaroque" in Mexico: Columns dissolve into ornament, and instead of the excessive flourishes of the Churrigueresque, a more geometric design is used in which only the figures of the saints preserve their recognizable and traditional attributes.

If you go back toward the Zócalo along Calle Argentina, you will come on the **Anfiteatro Bolívar** at Calle Justo Sierra 16. This amphitheater is where Diego Rivera first experimented with fresco painting, signaling the beginning of this important 20th-century art form in Mexico. The amphitheater is not open to the public; it is part of the **Escuela Nacional de Preparatoria** (15), formerly the Jesuit college of San Ildefonso and now a preparatory school for the university. You can enter the school from Calle San Ildefonso or through the pretty *Plaza de Loreto* (16), with its fountain and two Colonial-style churches. The school itself is a Baroque building of dark volcanic stone, which has sunk deep into the subsoil. It now houses offices of the *National University* (UNAM). Orozco painted murals in the three arcade courts of the school.

Diego Rivera's first important commission was to design the interior courts of the *Secretaría de Educación Pública* (Ministry of Education) (17), an otherwise unattractive building at Calle Argentina, between Calle Obregon and Calle Venezuela. In 124 panels, totaling 1,600 square meters (5,712 square feet), the artist painted an encyclopedic panorama of his country as it appeared to him in the years 1923 through 1928: agriculture and industry, art and architecture, science, and scenes from everyday life, as well as folk and religious festivals and celebrations of the Revolution. Rivera's vision of a socialist future is clearly evident in this exuberant fresco series.

One block farther west is the **Plaza Santo Domingo** (18), with the Baroque *church* of the Dominican monastery. At the northeast corner is the building that once housed the Court of the Inquisition and that now is home to the *museum* attached to the former medical university. On the square is a monument to Josefa

Ortiz de Dominguez (see page 141), erected to commemorate her decisive role in instigating the War of Independence.

On the west side of the square, under the arcades, scribes sit before ancient typewriters; for a small fee they hammer out letters and other documents—providing a valuable service to illiterate members of the population. Small print shops around the square also provide business cards and other stationery on the spot. At the corner of Calle Chile and Calle Donceles is another charming town house from the second half of the 18th century, the *home of Count Heras y Soto*. West of Calle Donceles is the elegant *Teatro de la Ciudad* (city theater), built in 1918, and the buildings that formerly housed the Antigua Camara de Deputados (lower chamber) (19) and the Antigua Camara de Senadores (Senate) (20).

WALK 2: Avenida Madero–*Alameda Park–Avenida Juárez–Plaza de la República–La Ciudadella–Salto del Agua–La Merced

Subway stops: Zócalo, Bellas Artes, Hidalgo, Revolución; Balderas, Salto del Agua, Isabél la Católica, Pino Suárez, Merced

See map on page 50.

This long walk offers you a sample of the diverse sights the city has to offer: from the elegant areas around Avenida Madero, to the lively Plaza Garibaldi, to the shaded serenity of the Alameda, and to the interesting crafts markets.

Between the Zócalo and Alameda Park there is a carefully restored Colonial quarter with pedestrian malls; older, well-kept hotels; elegant stores and small restaurants with moderate prices; and some remarkable buildings erected during the Spanish period, many of which can be found along the Avenida Madero.

The ***Iglesia La Profesa** (Church of the Solemn Vow) (21), built in 1720, was part of a Jesuit convent demolished during uprisings in 1861. The church has a beautiful Baroque façade; its high altar was made by Manuel Tolsá.

The ***Palacio Iturbide** (22) was the residence of Augustín de Iturbide (1783–1824), first ruler of independent Mexico and self-styled emperor. Because of a disputed claim to the property, the palace and its grounds went to the Italian Count Moncada, who allowed Iturbide to reside there during his short reign as emperor; Iturbide was forced into exile in 1823 and upon his illegal return to the country, he was executed before a firing squad. The palace building was designed by the most famous architect of New Spain, Francisco Guerrero y Torres, in

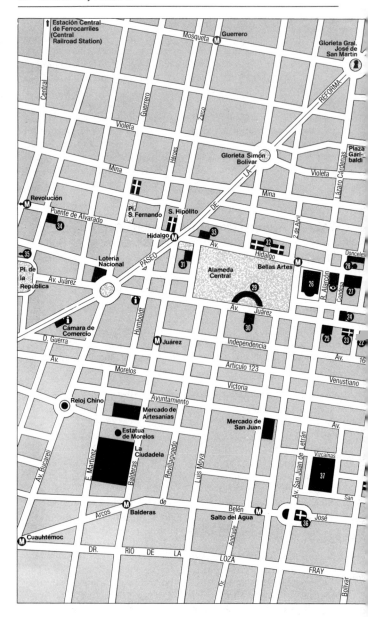

Estación Central
de Ferrocarriles
(Central
Railroad Station)

Mosqueta Guerrero

Glorieta Gral.
José de
San Martín

Central

Violeta

Guerrero

Zarco

Héroes

REFORMA

Glorieta Simón
Bolívar

LA

Plaza
Gari-
baldi

Lázaro Cárdenas

Violeta

Mina

Mina

Revolución

Puente de Alvarado

34

Pl.
S. Fernando

S. Hipólito

Hidalgo

Av.

2 de Abril

Hidalgo

32

Donceles

35

Pl. de
la
República

Av. Juárez

Lotería
Nacional

PASEO

31

33

Alameda
Central

Bellas Artes

26

28

R. Alarcón

Conesa

27

29

24

Cámara de
Comercio

D. Guerra

Humboldt

Juárez

30

Av. Juárez

Independencia

25

23

Av.

16

Av.

Morelos

Artículo 123

Venustiano

Ayuntamiento

Victoria

Reloj Chino

Mercado de
Artesanías

Estatua
de Morelos

Mercado de
San Juan

Av.

La
Ciudadela

Av. San Juan de Letrán

Vizcaínas

Av. Bucareli

E. Martínez

Balderas

Revillagigedo

Luis Moya

37

Arcos

Balderas

de

Belén

José

Cuauhtémoc

Salto del Agua

36

DR.   RÍO   DE   LA

LOZA

FRAY

Bolívar

Pl. de las Tres Culturas
Monumento Anahuac
Basílica de Guadalupe

MEXICO CITY WALKS 1 AND 2
(Zócalo - Plaza Santo Domingo;
Avenida Madero - La Merced)

Yards
0 ▭▭▭▭▭ 250
Meters

La Lagunilla

Rayon

Brasil

Aztecas

Héroes

de

Granaditas

Rep. de Ecuador

Argentina

República

de

Costa

Rica

Chile

Rep.   de   Honduras

Perú

Apartado

Peña y Peña

epública   de

Allende

de

de

Carmen

Colombia

B.   Dominguez

Museo

República   de   Cuba

Rep. de Venezuela

República

19   Teatro

18

17

Hemeroteca
Nacional

20   Allende

14   Gonzáles Obregon

San

Mayor

Ildefonso

M Tacuba

Doncelles

15

16

Bolivar

Molina

Nac. Monte
de Piedad

13   Justo

Sierra

Santísima

1

11

21

2

Moneda

Francisco

Madero

12

Correo

Academia
de S. Carlos

de Septiembre

Zócalo M

3

Soledad

8

Pal. de
Hierro

Corregidora

Alhondiga

Carranza

4

5

República

Febrero

de

Uruguay

9

Palacio Legislativo

República

6

Maria

Roldan

Salvador

Mesones

7

Mesones

San

Talavera

Anillo Circunvalación

erónimo

5

PINO

10

aría M
atólica

38

Izazaga

20 DE

NOVEMBRE

SUÁREZ

del

Pablo

M
La Merced

Isabel

M
Pino Suárez

Jesús

SERVANDO   TERESA   DE   MIER

1780, under commission from the Moncadas, who had the patio made according to a model from Palermo, their hometown. It has now been roofed over and is used for exhibitions by its present owner, the National Bank of Mexico.

On the same side of the street as the Palacio Iturbide is the **Iglesia San Francisco** (23), which has sunk deep into the subsoil. Its *portal* is a masterpiece of the Churrigueresque style. The church was part of the main convent of the Franciscans in Mexico, also destroyed during the unrest in 1860. Across the street is the ***Casa de los Azulejos** (24), with a magnificently tiled façade in the Puebla style. The building was once the palace of the count of Orizaba. The Sanborn chain now operates a restaurant in the roofed patio and sells artifacts in the gallery. The staircase has a mural by Orozco, and the ceiling is decorated in wood and tile.

At the corner of Madero and Avenida Letrán Ruiz de Alarcon—the north–south central axis now called Lázaro Cardenas—is the **Torre Latinoamericana** (Latin American Tower) (25). At 181 meters (593 feet) high, it is the tallest building in the city and a good point of orientation. Its foundation lies on hollow boxes, conceived as "floating reservoirs," which have successfully prevented the building from sinking into the soft subsoil. They also allowed the tower to sway and remain standing during

the strong earthquake in 1985, despite the fact that some of the worst damage in the city was sustained along the Avenida Juárez in this area. This proven sturdiness should reassure you as you gaze down on the city from the 41st-floor restaurant or the 42nd-floor observatory.

At the foot of the tower is the ***Palacio de Bellas Artes** (Palace of Fine Arts) (26), a magnificent Art Nouveau building made of white Carrara marble. It was built between 1901–1934, according to designs by the Italian architect Adamo Boari. During construction in 1907, the building began to sink, but cement and lime injections under the foundation have arrested the process. The interior is fitted out in precious Mexican marble and wood, but the chief attraction in the theater is the curtain, a glass mosaic representing a landscape in the valley of Mexico with the two high volcanoes. The design is by Dr. Atl

Palacio de Bellas Artes

(Gerardo Murillo) (see p. 20), and it was executed by the New York firm of Tiffany and Company. The covered walkways in the galleries bear the works of Mexico's best-known muralists and include a reproduction of Diego Rivera's *Man at the Crossroads.* The original, commissioned for New York City's Rockefeller Center, was rejected because it disparaged capitalism. Art exhibitions are held in the museum of the Palacio.

Casa de Corréos, the main *post office,* looking for all the world like a palace, is located across the street on the Cardenas axis. Adamo Boari was also responsible for this building, which he designed in the Spanish Colonial style in 1907. The postal history of Mexico is traced through exhibits in the *museum* located in the upper floors, and there is also a special section for philatelists.

If you follow the Cardenas axis northward, you'll reach the junction of Calle Honduras and ***Plaza Garibaldi,** a square that livens up considerably in the evening when mariachis begin to serenade their customers. These musical groups will play on the spot in the square or anywhere the customer desires—Mexicans are especially fond of the *gallo,* or rooster, a serenade at dawn. At midnight on November 21, hundreds of mariachis gather here after a public festival and serenade their patron, Saint Cecilia.

Plaza Garibaldi has long been considered unsafe at night because

of petty crime. Despite efforts by the government to renovate the area and make it safer, you must be extremely cautious about jewelry and money, and remain sober no matter how strongly tempted you may be by the tequila and pulque served in the many cantinas that surround the square. One popular cantina is *Tenampa,* where many famous singers and mariachi groups play. The *Mercado de San Camilito* (St. Camilito Market) serves typical Mexican *antojitos* (appetizers) in the clean, new building erected during renovation of the square.

Before going on to Alameda Park, make a detour into Calle Tacuba to see the ***Palacio de Minería** (27), the former mining college built between 1797–1813 by Manuel Tolsá in the Neoclassical style. Its generous dimensions radiate the majesty of the Spanish empire at its zenith.

The former *Palacio de Comunicaciones* (28) across the street at Calle Tacuba 8, was built about a century after the Palacio de Mineria. Since 1982 it has been the **Museo Nacional de Arte* featuring Mexican art from the pre-Columbian period to the present. Its front courtyard appears to be the final resting place for *El Caballito* (The Little Horse)—the popular nickname for the equestrian **statue of Charles IV* (1716–1788). The statue, by Manuel Tolsá, was moved from the Zócalo after independence; some consider it to be one of the finest equestrian statues ever made.

Now it's time for a stroll in the
*Alameda—this popular term
may mean either a grove of poplars
or a public mall, but in Mexico
City, the Alameda is a park laid
out at the end of the 16th century
by Viceroy Luis de Velasco II.
While the capital chokes on its
smog, the Alameda offers cool
shade and some breatheable air.
Until fairly recently, the courtly
custom of the *paseo* was observed
here; the word denotes a rather for-
mal "stroll," where boys met girls
with their chaperones and, if very
lucky, were allowed to accompany
them for part of the walk. In the
mezzanine lounge of the *Hotel del
Prado* (29), Diego Rivera's mural
*Dream of a Sunday Afternoon in
the Alameda* reflects his own
youthful exuberance and captures
what the Alameda must have been
like half a century ago, in a very
different Mexico. The Alameda is
still a haven where Mexicans and
visitors can escape the city's bustle
and noise, and enjoy informal per-

Alameda and Torre Latinoamericano

formances by clowns, mimes,
fire-eaters, and other entertainers
who use the *tribuna pública* in the
park to practice their art.

Back on the Avenida Juárez,
you may want to take some time to
shop for souvenirs at number 44.
In the rebuilt *Iglesia de Corpus
Christi*, originally constructed in
1724, the Instituto Nacional de
Indigenista (INI; Mexican Indian
Institute) has installed the
***Museo de Artes e Industrias
Populares** (Museum for Ethnic
Art) (30) on the second floor.
There is a shop on the first floor. At
numbers 70, 89, and 92 on the
Avenida Juárez are the *FONART*
stores, government-run handi-
crafts stores that sell good prod-
ucts at fixed prices.

To the west of the Alameda is
the ***Pinacoteca Virreinal** (31),
a museum containing the picture
collections of the Spanish viceroys. It is housed in the former
church and convent of San Diego,
built in the early 17th century. The
works are largely religious, and
many of them are quite good.

On the north side of the park,
facing each other across a small
square are two Baroque churches
dating from the 18th century, *San
Juan de Dios* and *Santa Veracruz*
(32).

At Avenida Hidalgo 85, is a particularly attractive oasis, the patio
of the **Hotel de Cortés,* the small-
est and oldest hotel in the city. It
dates from 1780 and was initially
the Augustinian hospice San
Nicolas Tolentino.

Beyond the Paseo de la Reforma, which runs diagonally across the Juárez, stands the *Iglesia San Hipolito,* dating from the 17th century. A right turn at Calle Puente de Alvarado, just a short distance away, will lead you to the enticing **Plaza San Fernando,* with benches and many shade trees. Following the Calle Puente de Alvarado westward, you will reach the ***Palacio de Buenavista** (34), a townhouse by Manuel Tolsá. The **Museo de San Carlos* is located here and houses a collection of works by Mexican and foreign artists.

Turn left and you'll come to the **Monumento a la Revolución** (35). This massive domed structure (67 meters; 220 feet, high) was intended to cap a legislative assembly hall. Work on the hall began in 1910, but in that year Porfirio Díaz, the president who had ruled for 30 years, was overthrown and the project was halted. Two of the columns of the monument contain the graves of the great revolutionary presidents of Mexico: Francisco Madero, Venustieno Carranza, Plutarco Elres Calles, Lázaro Cárdenas and Francisco Villa.

This is a good place to begin your exploration of the *Paseo de la Reforma* (see page 57); or you may wish to take the subway (Revolución station on Linea 2) to the southern area of the old city.

If you opt for the subway, take the train in the direction of Tasqueña only one stop to Hidalgo, then transfer to Linea 3 and take the train two stops in the direction

of Universidad to the Balderas. Get out here to explore *La Ciudadela,* the former citadel built in the early 19th century. Next to La Ciudadela is a large handicrafts market, the *Mercado Ciudadela,* which—because it is not very well known—offers goods at fairly reasonable prices.

From Balderas station, take the train on Linea 1 one stop in the direction of Zaragoza to Salto del Agua. The Baroque fountain *Salto del Agua* (35) marks the end of the old Aztec aqueduct, which ran from Chapultepec Park to the inner city. Remains of its stone arches are preserved at Avenida Chapultepec, between the Insurgentes and Sevilla stations (see map on page 40). Opposite the fountain is the little *Iglesia de la Purísima Concepción* (Church of the Immaculate Conception) which boasts a fine Baroque masonry façade.

Between Calle Jerónimo and Calle Vizcaína is the large complex of the *Colegio de Vizcaínas* (37), built in the 18th century as a boarding school for the daughters of the Basque community. With its four patios, the layout is a good example of Spanish Baroque recreated with Mexican materials, in this case red volcanic stone.

At the corner of Ayuntamiento Dolores, on the old market place of San Juan, you will see a modern building with a winding staircase in which more than 150 stores sell handicrafts and other souvenirs. At the *Museo de la Charrería* (38) on Avenida J. M. Izazga, you can see the wide-brimmed sombreros and richly adorned outfits of the *charros* (horsemen); the museum also contains paintings of their traditional, elegant sport played on horseback. At the Piño Suárez subway station you can see portions of an Aztec pyramid discovered during the station's construction.

WALK 3: Paseo de la Reforma–**Bosque de Chapultepec

Subway stops: Hidalgo, Chapultepec, Auditoria

See map on page 58.

In 1864, in an attempt to establish a New World empire for France, the Austrian Archduke Maximilian was installed as emperor of Mexico. During his brief three years on the throne, Maximilian tried to make his capital resemble the great capitals of Europe. Part of this ambitious plan involved constructing a grand boulevard much like the Champs-Elysées in Paris or the Ringstrasse in his own city of Vienna. The boulevard, moreover, would connect his residence, the castle in Bosque de Chapultepec (Chapultepec Park), with the governor's palace on the Zócalo. Maximilian's reign was too short to allow him to see this project to completion; in 1867 he was captured and executed by troops loyal to President Benito Juárez. Ten years later, however, his boulevard was finished, and in a nose-thumbing gesture to the Austrian's imperial ambitions, the street was named Paseo de la Reforma—in commemoration of Juárez's reform laws of 1861.

Elegant, patrician houses were built along the broad boulevard, which became the principal pedestrian and vehicular route through the capital. People strolled along the Paseo, and carriages crowded the thoroughfare. Later, mule-driven streetcars carried riders from the park to the center of town. Statues honoring the heroes of Mexican history lined the center of the boulevard, making it a true promenade through Mexico's past. Today the statues are surrounded by *glorietas,* circular enclosures around which eight-lane traffic circles have been constructed.

Although the occasional mansion has survived, the Paseo is today largely given over to modern office buildings, and the genial promenade has yielded to the hurried pace of 20th-century urban life. Despite the urgency of modern life, however, the Paseo de la Reforma remains one of the great urban thoroughfares.

Walk 3 explores the magnificent Paseo de la Reforma, and includes visits to the elegant Zona Rosa district and the activity-filled Bosque de Chapultepec.

Beginning at the corner of Avenida Juárez and going south-west along the **Paseo de la Reforma,** you come to the *Monumento a Colón* (39) in the first glorieta. This monument to Christopher Columbus was built by the French sculptor Charles Cordier and placed here in 1877. On the corner of the Avenida Insurgentes—one of the world's longest (41.5 km.; 26 miles) streets, and forming the north-south axis of Mexico City—stands the monument to the last Aztec ruler, the *Monumento a Cuauhtémoc* (40), portrayed in his warrior's costume. The second glorieta from there encloses the **Monumento a la Independencia** (41), popularly called "El Angel" for the gilded angel of liberty that tops the high Corinthian column.

Just at El Angel, Calle Florencia branches off to the left, leading into the **Zona Rosa,** the area famous for expensive shops, restaurants, galleries and nightclubs. Some of the best hotels are located in this quarter of the city and tourists naturally gravitate here. The Zona Rosa is quite elegant, and its fashionable streets are named after European cities such as London, Nice, and Hamburg.

At the *Fuente de Diana Cazadora* (Diana Fountain) the Paseo turns into Chapultepec Park, just north of the hill on which the palace is built. The roads form a cloverleaf here, and the traffic thunders off in all directions. Here also are statues of President Venustiano Carranza (1915–

Monumento a la Independencia

1920) and Simón Bolívar, the glorious hero who led much of Latin America in its fight for independence from Spain. A bit farther on is the **Monumento a los Niños Héroes** (42); its six columns are topped by bronze torches. It is dedicated to the military cadets who in 1847 defended to the last man the castle (then a military academy) against the American army.

**Bosque de Chapultepec (Chapultepec Park) begins here, where the Aztec rulers, after founding the city of Tenochtitlán, built a summer residence for

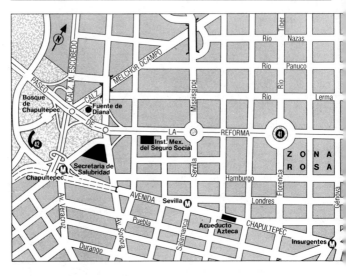

themselves. The name means "cricket hill" in the Náhuatl language. Like great urban parks everywhere nowadays, Chapultepec is filled with morning joggers, afternoon strollers, and Sunday picnickers. There are boats for rowing, carriages, a zoo, and museums. As the city's residents know, Chapultepec is the perfect place to seek refuge from the crowded streets.

A walk through the park can begin at the Monumento a los Niños Héroes. The hike up to the ****Castillo de Chapultepec** (43), is fairly steep; less vigorous visitors may want to take the elevator (which can be reached through the gate to the left and then through the rock tunnel). There is also a minitrain.

The viceroys began construction of the palace in 1785, and Maximilian expanded it for his own residence. Later, the presidents of Mexico (all except Juárez) occupied it until Lázaro Cárdenas, (president from 1934–1940), decided to convert the palace to a museum. (He then moved into a townhouse called Los Piños in the southwestern part of Chapultepec, which has been the presidential residence ever since.)

The palace is now the **Museo Nacional de Historia.** Within its 20 rooms Mexican history is documented; interpretations of that history are offered in murals by such famous painters as Juan O'Gorman and Clemente Orozco. The upper floor is devoted to Mexican painting and artifacts from the 17th–19th centuries. To the left of the exit are rooms containing flags and historic carriages— including the one Maximilian had

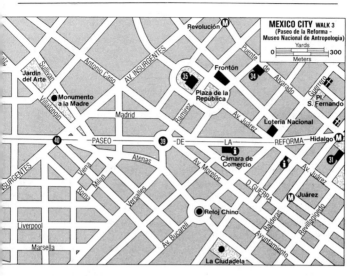

imported from Milan. In the former residential section of the palace you can see the emperor's rooms and the parlor where the presidents signed treaties. The terrace provides one of the best views of the city.

Farther down the hill, Mexican history is presented somewhat more didactically in the *Galería de Historia* (44), which is also called the *Museo del Caracol* (Snail Museum) because of its shape. At the foot of the hill is the ****Museo Nacional de Arte Moderno** (45), designed by

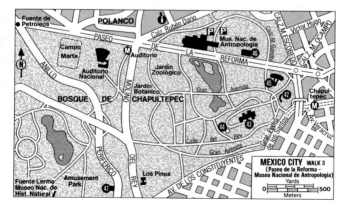

Rafael Mijares and Pedro Ramirez Vazquez, which opened in 1964. It is primarily devoted to Mexican art of the 19th and 20th centuries. If you cross the Paseo de la Reforma here, you will be at the ****Museo de Arte Contemporáneo Internacional Rufino Tamayo** (46), where the works of the dean of contemporary Mexican art, Rufino Tamayo, are displayed, along with his collection of 20th-century painting and sculpture. The museum and the collections were the artist's gift to the nation.

Near the Tamayo Museum is the ****Museo Nacional de Antropología* (see Walk 4).

Cross the Paseo again, to an artificial lake, and the *Casa del Lago* (Lake House)—the setting for plays and other cultural events. In the newer, southern section of the park is another artificial lake with the elegant *Del Lago* restau-

rant on its shore. In this part of the park you will find the *Museo Nacional de Tecnológico* (47) and the *Museo Nacional de Historia Natural.* Here, too, is the large *Parque de Diversiones,* an amusement park whose gigantic roller coaster (Montaña Rusa—or Russian Mountain) can be seen from the Periférico highway.

The Paseo de la Reforma continues past the city's largest audience hall, the *Auditorio Nacional* (near the Auditorio subway station), and reaches the western end of Chapultepec Park at the Fuente de Petróleos (Oil Fountain), which commemorates the nationalization of the nation's oil wells in 1938. From here the Paseo winds up the chain of hills called Las Lomas and through an elegant residential neighborhood, Lomas de Chapultepec, where lordly mansions are tucked away behind lush gardens and greenery.

WALK 4: ***Museo Nacional de Antropología

Subway stop: Chapultepec

Some have called it the most beautiful museum in the world; it is surely one of the most successful examples of modern architecture. The Museo Nacional de Antropología is located in Bosque de Chapultepec (Chapultepec Park) off Paseo de la Reforma. Designed by Pedro Ramírez Vázquez, the museum, which opened in 1964, harmoniously blends modern, large-scale architecture with the many diverse styles and types of objects it houses. A hushed grandeur pervades the building, almost as if modern Mexico were paying homage to the glories and mysteries of its past.

During the Colonial period, Mexico's Indian past was little valued. Indeed, the official reason for Spain's presence in the New World was the conversion of these peoples, and the result of her presence was their enslavement. Only after independence did the Indian cultures and the archaeological traces of their long past assume some importance. In 1825 the foundation for a collection was laid, and some 40 years later it was moved to a palace in the Calle de Moneda that Maximilian had converted into a national museum. As interest in the pre-Columbian past expanded, especially after the Revolution, so grew the amount of archaeological material and the need for a place to house and display it.

The entrance to the museum is guarded by the basalt monolith of the rain god Tláloc (7 meters, 21 feet, high and weighing 165 tons). This is an unfinished Teotihuacán statue brought here in an incredible technical *tour de force* from Coatlinchán, near Texcoco.

The spacious inner courtyard is devoted to water, the life-giving element. The front half is roofed over by a huge rectangular umbrella that sinks down toward the middle. Its supporting column, covered with reliefs, is surrounded by a veil of water. The museum galleries are arranged around the inner courtyard.

On the ground floor are the archaeological treasures of the vanished cultures, while the upper floor is devoted to Indian cultures that still thrive in modern Mexico.

The galleries are arranged so that the visitor will learn not only about the specific cultures represented by the museum's collections but also about the science of anthropology. The museum permits photography without flash or tripod for a fee. There is a bookshop in the basement and a restaurant. Guided tours are available.

If you have only a limited time to spend here, you should see at least the Mexica room (XI), the Tula (X) and Teotihuacán (IX) rooms, and the Maya (XIV) room. And, of course, you should try to see the rooms devoted to the cultures of the particular areas in Mexico that you will be seeing during your travels through Mexico.

The ground floor is organized as follows, starting from the right side of the entrance and working your way counterclockwise:

Room I offers orientation films and slides about the museum and its collection while *Room II* is given over to special exhibits. The auditorium is in *Room III. Room IV* is devoted to findings from recent excavations. The permanent displays begin with an instructive introduction to anthropology and its related disciplines in *Room V.*

Mesoamerica (Room VI): This room shows the locations of the many Mesoamerican cultures as well as their common foundation.

Prehistory (Room VII): The theme of this room deals with the origin of human life on the American continent. The emigration from Asia, hunting, and the beginning of agriculture by the first inhabitants are documented with diagrams and primitive artifacts.

Preclassic Period (Room VIII): Displays in this room show how the formative cultures slowly developed in the central highlands. Most of the pottery figures represent female fertility idols and scenes of daily life. The so-called "*acrobat vase*" from Tlatilco is remarkable—it is a container formed in the shape of a man twisted like a circus performer.

*Teotihuacán (Room IX): This room offers a glimpse of the colorful city of Teotihuacán where a culturally rich and influential civilization flourished from A.D. 300–900. A corner of the temple to Quetzalcóatl, with its serpent heads and rain-god masks, is reproduced in its original color. A copy of a fresco showing the "*Paradise of Tlaloc,*" where it was believed the souls of departed warriors and drowned people frolicked in the afterlife, is an example of temple wall painting. Stone sculptures of deities, polychrome pottery from the various epochs of this culture, as well as masks and figurines of semiprecious stones, testify to the extraordinary artistry of this "primitive" people.

*Tula (Room X): This section shows the fortified enclosure of Xochicalco, influenced by the

Early Teotihuacán figures

Teotihuacán culture. The Toltecs, whose center became Tollan (Tula), mastered sculpture in relief and in the round. Typical *Chacmool* figures are exhibited; they were no doubt messengers of the gods carrying offerings to the sun. There is also a column from Tula 4.6 meters (15 feet) high. A warrior's head, inlaid with a mother-of-pearl mosaic and hidden behind a coyote mask, is a particularly striking piece.

*Mexica (Room XI): The largest room at the end of the patio is set aside for the Mexica, or Aztecs. The effect of the illuminated stone sculptures in the darkened room is particularly dramatic. The famous ****Calendar** *(or Sun) Stone* of the Aztecs hangs here. In the center of this 24-ton round basalt disk is the sun god Tonatiuh, depicted with his forked tongue hanging out of his mouth. Around his face are the Aztec hieroglyphs for the cosmic periods, as well as the symbols for the months and days. These motifs, reproduced many times, have become almost a symbol of Mexico. The **Tizoc Stone* is also exhibited here. Around the stone's circumference are reliefs that describe the conquests of the ruler Tizoc who dedicated his efforts to the sun.

The life of the Mexica is depicted in three objects: a mural by Miguel Covarrubias showing the island of Tenochtitlán; a model of its ceremonial center; and a three-dimensional model of the large market of Tlatelolco. There is also a reproduction of Moc-

Aztec calendar stone

tezuma's headdress of brilliant green quetzal feathers (the original is in Vienna). Contrasting with the sacrificial altars and martial sculptures is the stone figure of **Xochipillis* (Lord of the Flowers)—the god of love, dance, and poetry is shown sitting cross-legged on his throne. His flower-bedecked body is a symbol of joy, a commodity apparently plentiful in this warrior culture.

Oaxaca (Room XII): This room pays tribute to the Zapotecs who were excellent potters and architects—they built the famous city of Monte Albán. Urns in the shape of gods are characteristic Oaxaca motifs. The ornate Mixtec façades were decorated with stone mosaics, as the reproduction of the frieze of Mitla in this room demonstrates. The Mixtecs were also gifted codex painters and goldsmiths, as can be seen from the grave pieces here.

On the night of December 25, 1985, some 173 priceless artifacts were stolen from the museum; none has ever been recovered. Among the items taken were some important pieces from the Oaxaca room, including a Zapotec jade mask of the bat god, and the famous gold-and-turquoise breastplate of Yanhuitlán.

Gulf Coast (Room XIII): This room is devoted to the early Olmecs who were very influential in the development of early Mesoamerican culture in the Gulf Coast region. Their stone works are of human forms with Negroid traits; some of them have exaggerated heads, like the colossal head from Tres Zapotes (Veracruz) and a dynamic wrestling figure. A model of the ceremonial center of El Tajín shows the architectural aptitude of the Totonac culture, who also gave us the famous smiling pottery figures on display here. The Huastecs are represented by painted pottery and by their characteristic stelae (marble slabs) covered with reliefs.

*Maya (Room XIV): This section is particularly compelling—unfortunately, it attracted the thieves, too, during the spectacular Christmas 1985 break-in. They took 64 objects from this room, plundering the cases containing the precious grave offerings of the priest-king of Palenque, whose pyramid crypt has been reconstructed in the basement. The relief work on the heavy sarcophagus plates is easier to see here in the museum than in the narrow tomb chamber in Palenque itself. Stelae and figures from the tomb island of Jaina testify to the physical appearance of the Maya, with their pronounced "hook" noses and their celebrated woven garments. The temple of Bonampac, with its unique wall paintings has been reconstructed in the open air. The museum setting offers a less arduous approach to the temple than does the steamy jungle of Chiapas.

Northern Mexico (Room XV): On the other side of the stairway that leads to the restaurant is the room containing items from the hunting and nomadic cultures of arid northern Mexico. Influences on them from the native peoples of the southwestern United States are unmistakable. The cultural links are particularly apparent in the adobe houses of La Quemada or Casas Grandes and the pottery painted with geometric motifs.

Western Mexico (Room XVI): The adjacent room contains items from the western cultures, whose realistic and expressive ceramic grave offerings give an attractive insight into the daily life of Mexican Indian tribes.

The **ethnological collection** on the upper floor was assembled with the aid of Indian tribes still living in Mexico. Shapes of houses and corn silos, clothing, tools, and artifacts testify to the amazing diversity that persists among the surviving groups of indigenous inhabitants.

Starting from the right and moving counterclockwise, the upper floor is organized as follows:

Room I offers an introduction to ethnology. Then follow rooms devoted to the cultures of the Cora and Huichol (*Room II*), Purépecha (Tarascan) (*Room III*), Otomí and Mazahua from the Toluca valley and Querétaro (*Room IV*), the Puebla groups of the Sierra (*Room V*), Oaxaca groups—including Zapotec, Mixtec, Mixe, Chinanteca, Mazateca, and 15 other groups (*Room VI*), and the Totonac and Huaxtec Indians (*Room VII*). *Rooms VIII and IX* respectively, illustrate the differences between highland and lowland Mayan cultures.

The tribes from the northwest of Mexico include the Seri, Tarahumara, and Yaqui (*Room X*). Their cultures are completely different from those of the more southerly tribes, and their languages as well.

The last section (*Room XI*) contains an overview of the characteristic elements of the Nahuatlan-speaking Indians, numerically the largest group in Mexico, distributed over 13 federal states.

WALK 5: Avenida Insurgentes Sur–*Coyoacán–*San Ángel–*Ciudad Universitaria–*Cuicuilco–**Xochimilco

Subway stop: Insurgentes, Universidad, Taxquena (for Xochimilco)
See map on page 66.

Walk 5 explores the sights along the extensive Avenida Insurgentes. It includes the remarkable Polyforum Siqueiros and a trip to such chic havens for artists and intellectuals as Coyoacán and San Ángel and the rich neighborhood of El Pedregal, and ends at the Aztec canals of Xochimilco.

The Avenida de los Insurgentes, a 30-km.- (18.5-mile-) long north-south artery, is named for the revolutionaries of 1810. After crossing the Paseo de la Reforma, the road leads into the southern section of the city. About 3 km. (2 miles) from the Insurgentes subway station—from which you can get a city bus in just about any direction—is the garden of the *Hotel de Mexico,* whose revolving restaurant offers a panoramic view of the city. In the garden is the peculiar ***Polyforum Cultural Siqueiros** (48), a twelve-cornered building with a theater, art gallery, and permanent exhibition of folk art. The building was designed by David Alfaro Siqueiros (1886–1974); the huge (2,000-square-meter; 6,560-square-foot) mural that adorns the Polyforum was the artist's last work, executed in his customary dynamic, violent style. A sound-and-light show brings the mural to life in a particularly exciting way.

At the next *glorieta* is a soccer stadium and the largest building in the world, the *Plaza México* (49), with a seating capacity of 60,000. (In this capital city, soccer is the main event; each weekend more than 100 teams play in squares along the Zaragoza road.) A little farther on, on the same side of the street, is the circular *Teatro Insurgentes* (50); a mosaic on the façade

by Diego Rivera represents the history of Mexican theater.

A long walk—or short taxi ride—will take you to ***Coyoacán,** once a small town near the capital, now surrounded by Mexico City and an integral part of it. Coyoacán was a rival town to Tenochtitlán, and Cortés encamped here during his siege of the Aztec metropolis. After the conquest, Coyoacán became a resort for Colonial gentry. Now, the little town with its cobbled streets, old houses, and picturesque portals and courtyards is a sort of provincial retreat within the city. It has traditionally been a favorite neighborhood for artists and intellectuals—Mexico City's equivalent of New York's Greenwich Village or the Latin Quarter in Paris.

In the center of Coyoacán is the *Plaza Hidalgo* and next to it, the *Jardin del Centenario* (Centenary Garden), which was laid out on the former atrium of a Franciscan monastery. The *Iglesia de San Juan Bautista* (51) has been rebuilt several times since the 16th century. If you turn left from the church into Calle Hidalgo, you reach the *Museo de las Culturas Populares* (Museum of Folk Cultures) at number 289.

A few blocks from the Plaza Hidalgo is the **Museo Frida Kahlo* (52) at Calle Londres 127. In this house where the artist was

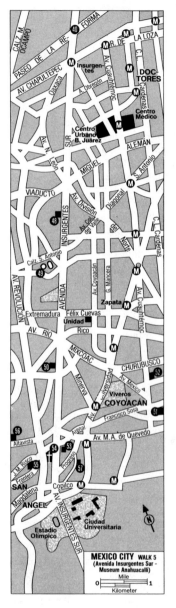

born and lived many years with her husband, Diego Rivera, you will find a collection of her paintings as well as personal mementos. Among her possessions are 18th- and 19th-century Mexican art and pre-Columbian artifacts. Nearby at Calle Viena 45 is the *Museo Leon Trotsky* where he lived in exile from the Soviet Union until his murder in 1940 by agents of Joseph Stalin. The graves of Trotsky and his wife are in the garden. The study is kept as it was on the day of Trotsky's death.

From the Kahlo museum, you can take a pesero—the one with the legend "Metro General Anaya"—to the intersection of Xicotencatl and Viente de Agosto streets. The former Churubusco monastery here is now the *Museo de las Intervenciones.* This museum displays weapons, flags, and other implements of war left behind by the various armies that at one time or another have tried to conquer Mexico or influenced her through armed intervention. Appropriate to its purpose, it is located on the site of the Battle of Churubusco, fought during the Mexican-American War in 1847.

Back on Insurgentes Sur, you will pass the macabre *Monumento Alvaro Obregón* (53) erected at the site of the 1928 assassination of this revolutionary president of the Republic. The monument is grisly, indeed; in a glass enclosure rests the arm of this one-time general— the arm he lost in battle!

West of Insurgentes is ***San**

Ángel, another small town incorporated into the city. At its edge, at the corner of Monasterio and Avenida Revolución, is the former *Convento del Carmen* (54), built in 1617 and now a museum containing religious artworks. On the other side of Avenida Revolución is the *Plaza San Jacinto* (55) and a flower market. Artists show their work here on Saturdays, when the excellent handicrafts market *Bazar Sabado* is also open. The Plaza Jacinto is surrounded by open-air restaurants and Colonial mansions, including the 18th-century *Casa del Risco* (the Cliff House) with its fine collection of 18th- and 19th-century European paintings and furniture and its unusual patio fountain. If you walk up Avenida Revolución several blocks you will come to number 1608, the house containing the *Museo Alvar y Carmen T. Carrillo Gil*. This private collection includes works by Siqueiros, Orozco, and other Mexican and European artists. On Altavista you'll find the *Museo Estudio Diego Rivera* in a building designed by Juan O'Gorman. Once Rivera's home and studio, it now houses changing exhibits. Nearby is the beautiful, Colonial *San Ángel Inn* (56).

South of San Ángel is a wealthy residential neighborhood, *El Pedregal,* where modern houses are built on the rocky lava field created by the eruption of the Ajusco and Xitle volcanoes. The houses are wonderful examples of 20th-century domestic architecture, although it is difficult to get a good view of them from the streets (and tourists on foot are not generally welcome). The layers of lava at Pedregal cover the graves of *Copilco,* which date to about 1500 B.C. An excavated portion of the grave site and a museum (57) displaying Pre-Classical ceramics and stonework are located just east of Insurgentes at Calle Victoria 54.

Between 1950–1955, the *Ciudad Universitaria* (University City) was laid out on the Pedregal adjacent to the Insurgentes. It has more than 80 buildings and sports installations scattered over a wide park.

Be sure to see the **library,** the façade of which was painted by Juan O'Gorman, and the *rector's office,* with murals by David Alfaro Siqueiros. In the southern extension of the university park is the *Sala de Netzahualcóyotl* concert hall.

The *Universidad Nacional Autónoma* (National Autonomous University, or UNAM) is more than 300 years old. Today its enrollment is nearly 300,000 students, including the preparatoria (roughly equivalent to the last two years of high school). Some of the institutes connected with the university are located in other parts of the capital.

In a depression in the lava field, west of Insurgentes, is the **Estadio Olímpico,** the site of the 1968 Olympic Games. You might have noticed by now that in Mexico City no large wall goes

Library of UNAM (Ciudad Universitaria)

unpainted, and the stadium is no exception: Diego Rivera decorated its façade with scenes from Mexico's sports history.

A passage under the Periférico—the highway that skirts the western and southern edges of the city—leads you to the ***Cuicuilco** excavation. From the yard-high petrified mass of lava protrudes a pyramid, the oldest preserved building from the Pre-Classic era. Its round foundation and four wide steps illustrate Indian sacred architecture as it was in the first millennium B.C. An archaeological museum is located nearby.

Across the Insurgentes is the *Villa Olímpica,* where the Olympic athletes bunked in 1968, and on the other side of the Periférico is *Perisur,* a huge shopping center.

Farther south on the Insurgentes is **Tlalpan,* a suburb with the Ajusco volcano as its backdrop. The Colonial charm of this area has been preserved despite the steady encroachment of the city, and it might provide an enjoyable excursion for you.

To reach ****Xochimilco,** a popular weekend destination, you can travel east along the Periférico 10 km. (6 miles) or take a trolley from the Taxqueña subway station. Just past the center of town, with its 16th-century *church of San Bernardino,* is a network of canals that will give you an idea of the Aztec waterways system in Lake Texcoco. Flowers and vegetables still grow on the island gardens, but the greatest attraction is offered by the covered boats. These little barks, decorated with

Xochimilco

artificial flowers, carry sightseers through the canals. So as not to miss an opportunity, merchants selling flowers, tortillas and souvenirs, also ply these waters, and floating mariachi groups will serenade you—for a fee.

You can go back to the city through the Calzade de Tlalpan. Calle del Museo branches off to the left, just after the junction with Avenida Division del Norte. Diego Rivera's ****Anahuacalli museum** is located at Calle del Museo 150. The pyramid-like structure was designed by the painter to house his important collection of pre-Columbian artifacts—especially pottery and Aztec stone sculptures.

WALK 6: *Plaza de las Tres Culturas–**Basílica de Guadalupe–*Tenayuca–*Santa Cecilia

Subway stop: Basílica

Those who still have not satisfied their quest for ancient ruins will find still more excavations of pre-Columbian pyramids in the northern part of the city. Here, too, is the Basílica de Guadalupe, Mexico's holiest shrine.

If you start out from the city center along the Paseo de la Reforma (just where it meets the Avenida Hidalgo), you can detour to the Calle Rayon by turning right at the *glorieta* with the monument to San Martín, liberator of Argentina.

On the left of Calle Rayon is the popular flea market known as *La Lagunilla*. Most of its stalls are now in a modern building, but on Sunday, they spill out into the surrounding streets.

The next landmark you will pass on the Paseo is the *monument to Atahualpa,* the last Inca king. It was given by the town of Cuzco in Peru in exchange for a monument to Cuitláhuac, the next-to-last of the Aztec rulers.

North of the Buenavista railway station is the Tlatelolco district; the large *Nonoalco-Tlatelolco* housing project, which suffered particularly severe damage during the 1985 earthquake, is located here. In pre-Columbian times, Tlatelolco was an independent town; it fell under the authority of Tenochtitlán in 1473 after a fierce battle, but it continued to be an important trading center right up to the Spanish Conquest. The market square, which the Spanish reported on with awe, is now the ***Plaza de las Tres Culturas.** Designed by Mario Pani, this plaza celebrates the "three cultures" that intermingle so neatly here: pyramids of pre-Columbian Mexico stand side-by-side with a Spanish convent church and the high-rise apartment towers of modern Mexico. Visible among the Aztec ruins are the principal pyramid, staircases, walls, and altars, as well as the famous *tzom pantli,* or the "wall of skulls." The *Iglesia de Santiago de Tlatelolco,* built at the beginning of the 17th century and poorly restored, stands in the center of the great square on the site of a 16th-century chapel belonging to the Franciscan convent of Santiago. In the *Colegio Imperial de Santa Cruz,* an old convent building that adjoins the church, the Franciscan monks taught the sons of the Aztec nobility. Bernardino de Sahagún, one of the teachers, was also the great chronicler of the history of New Spain. According to a tablet in the square, the fall of the Aztec empire was "neither a triumph nor a defeat, but the painful birth of the Mestizo people who constitute present-day Mexico."

The Paseo de la Reforma now divides into the Calzada Misterios and the Calzada Guadalupe, both leading to the national shrine of the ****Basílica de Nuestra Señora de Guadalupe,** near the Basílica subway station.

According to the legend, the Virgin appeared on December 9, 1531, in the form of a *moreno,* or dark-skinned woman, to Juan Diego, a converted Aztec. She asked him to have a shrine built to her. But the bishop, Juan de Zumarraga, did not believe Juan Diego and asked him to prove the Virgin's appearance. On December 12, at the height of the dry season, she appeared to Juan Diego again and miraculously caused roses to bloom on a hilltop. Don Diego carried back the roses to show his bishop, but when he opened his cloak to reveal them, they had changed into an image of the Virgin surrounded by a lustrous halo. This is believed to be the image of the Virgin of Guadalupe that hangs above the high altar in the basilica.

Bishop Zumarraga had a shrine built on the hill of Tepeyac, which

Nuestra Señora de Guadalupe

was also the site of an earlier Aztec temple to Tonantzin, the earth mother. From the beginning, the church attracted large numbers of pilgrims.

The original building—the old Basílica de Nuestra Señora de Guadalupe—was built in the 17th century. Today it is unfortunately sinking into the subsoil and has been closed to the public. A new basilica was designed by Pedro Ramírez Vázquez, the architect of the Museo Nacional de Antropologia, and consecrated in 1976. It can accommodate 20,000 worshipers.

Next to the old basilica is the *Capilla del Pocito* (Chapel of the Spring), built in the 18th century by Francisco de Guerrero y Torres. Inside is a spring credited with healing powers where the faithful come to fill bottles with the miraculous waters. On the hill of Tepeyac is the *Capilla del Tepeyac,* built in the 18th century on the spot where Juan Diego's miraculous vision took place.

On December 12, the anniversary of the miracle, convoys of pilgrims with banners and flags bearing pictures of the Virgin converge on the basilica. A high pontifical mass is held, during which the organ tones mingle with the drums and bells of the *concheros;* in Aztec-style feather crowns and costumes, they dance in honor of the Virgin before the holy shrine.

If you leave the shrine on Calle Montevideo and cross the northern arm of the Insurgentes, you reach *Calzada de Vallejo.* It swings northwest and leads, after about 5 km. (3 miles), to the *"**Serpent pyramid" of Tenayuca** in the village of San Bartolo, just outside the city.

This pyramid was begun in the 12th century by the Chichimecs. Like many other Mesoamerican temple pyramids in Mexico, it received a superstructure every 52 years—at the end of an "age;" the last addition to the serpent pyramid was made in 1507 by the Aztecs. The pyramid now stands at a height of 19 meters (62 feet) and measures 62 x 56 meters (203 x 103 feet) at its base, which is decorated with a frieze of 138 serpents. Beside small platforms—two on the north side and one on the south side—are coiled "fire serpents" or "turquoise serpents," which date from the fifth overbuilding.

About 3 km (2 miles) to the north is the *temple pyramid of Santa Cecilia Actitlán,* dedicated to the sun god and the god of rain, Tlaloc. The temple and pyramid have been restored, and are representative of Aztec religious architecture in the late Post-Classic period.

From here you can take the nearby Periférico highway back into the city.

Round Trip Excursions from Mexico City

Quite a few interesting one-day tours are possible from Mexico City, or several can be combined into round trips of a few days. The two cities farthest from the capital—Puebla (140 km.; 86 miles) and Taxco (180 km.; 112 miles)—are certainly worth at least one night's stay. Tour bus trips are available to both cities, but if you prefer to explore on your own, both are accessible by public bus or you can drive there yourself.

Within 200 km. (124 miles) of Mexico City are the central highlands, with their spectacular snow-capped volcanoes, lush valleys, and charming old Colonial towns. The Indians named the fertile plateau around Toluca and Puebla "Anahuac," meaning "where there is water." A few hundred feet lower down is the beautiful valley of Morelos and the tropical paradise of Cuernavaca, Mexico's oldest resort town, with springlike weather year-round.

TRAVEL ROUTE 1: **Mexico City–Tepexpan– *Acolman–***Teotihuacán–Texcoco–**Mexico City (115 km.; 69 miles)

See map on page 88.

The highlight of this round-trip route is the spectacular ancient city of Teotihuacán but the drive also includes several interesting detours to other pre-Columbian and Colonial sites.

If you're in a hurry to get to the pyramids, Expressway 85 D leads directly to Teotihuacán. From Mexico City, pick up 85 D at Insurgentes Norte and head north toward Pachuca. After approximately 25 km. (15 miles), there is a turnoff for the Teotihuacán highway, which leads to the pyramids. (City buses from Terminal del Norte or the subway at Terminal Indios Verde also provide easy access to Teotihuacán.)

For a more leisurely route, exit 85 D at *Tepexpan*, about 34 km. (21 miles) from Mexico City.

Here, in 1949, archaeologists discovered the oldest human skeleton on the North American continent, dating from 10,000 B.C. The town's museum also features the remains of a mammoth elephant from the same period. From Tepexpan, drive 4 km. (2.5 miles) to **Acolman,** an Augustinian cloister built between 1539 and 1571 and restored in 1735. The cloister was constructed over a terrace, probably dating to pre-Hispanic times. Its overall design is Spanish Gothic, with ribbed vaults in the church interior. However, the church façade is pure Plateresque style, which is the Mexican version of Europe's Renaissance style. Two sets of classical columns flank the arched doorway; in between each pair of columns stands a statue of a saint. Echoing this graceful arched entrance is an arched window, flanked by coats of arms from the Spanish houses of Castille and Leon. A striking bell tower rises above the fortified roof. Inside, late–16th-century frescoes survive in the choir room and side altars typify the later Churrigueresque style. A lovely stone cross in the atrium depicts Christ as the Man of Sorrows. Certain details of the cross, such as the skull at its base, suggest it may have been fashioned by Indian artists.

Return to the highway and continue along the road until you reach the circular bypass (Circunvalación) around the archaeological zone to parking areas for Teotihuacán.

***Teotihuacán

See map on page 74.

Teotihuacán is one of the largest and oldest pre-Columbian sites in Central America. Built between 100 B.C. and A.D. 600, the old Aztec city covers more than 11 square km. (7 square miles), an area larger than ancient Rome. In its heyday (A.D. 450–650), Teotihuacán's population surpassed 125,000. The city exercised enormous religious authority and controlled trade throughout Mexico and beyond. Its huge pyramids, spacious plazas, and symmetrical city blocks became a prototype for most later Mexican cities. Then, around A.D. 750, Teotihuacán's center suddenly completely collapsed. Main buildings burned down and most of the city's inhabitants moved away. By the tenth century Teotihuacán had been eclipsed by the warlike Toltecs of Tula. When the Aztecs settled in the Valley of Mexico 600 years after the city's desertion, they named it Teotihuacán—the Place Where Men Became Gods. The Aztecs believed that their world, the Fifth Sun, rose in the last days of this great metropolis, and they revered Teotihuacán as a profoundly sacred place.

By the time of the Spanish Conquest (1519–1521), Teotihuacán was a city of dusty mounds and weeds. It was not until the 1880s that the site was excavated, under the pretext of developing a major tourist attraction. Unfortunately the amateurish efforts of this excavation resulted in the destruction of many early structures. From 1918 through the 1970s, however, renewed digging by competent archaeologists led to major discoveries.

Towering over the city is the ***Pyramid of the Sun,** (Pirámide del Sol) the largest pyramid in the New World, rising 63 meters (206 feet) high. The entire city is bisected by the *Street of the Dead,* about 43 meters (141 feet) wide and 4 km. (2.5 miles) long.

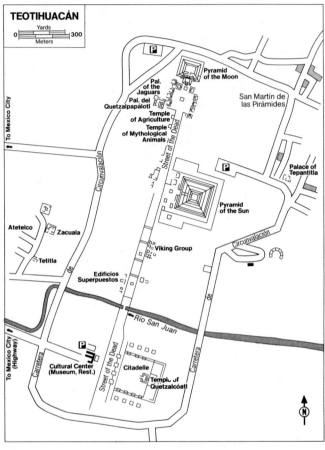

TEOTIHUACÁN

0 ⊢ Yards ⊣ 300
Meters

To Mexico City

Circunvalación

Pyramid of the Moon

Pal. of the Jaguars
Pal. del Quetzalpapálotl

Temple of Agriculture
Temple of Mythological Animals

San Martín de las Pirámides

Palace of Tepantitla

Pyramid of the Sun

Circunvalación

Street of the Dead

Atetelco   Zacuala

Tetitla

Viking Group

Edificios Superpuestos

de

Rio San Juan

To Mexico City (Highway)

Cultural Center (Museum, Rest.)

Street of the Dead

Citadelle

Temple of Quetzalcóatl

Carretera

N

The street was so named by the Aztecs because they believed that the empty ruins on each side were tombs. At the street's north end stands the ****Pyramid of the Moon** (Pirámide de la Luna), approximately 45 meters (147 feet) high. In front of the pyramid's main entrance stretches the *Great Plaza,* with the *Temple of Quetzalcóatl* (the Feathered Ser-

pent), on the right. There is a view east from here of the gigantic Pyramid of the Sun.

Few cities match Teotihuacán's grandiose proportions. The builders of the pyramids and plazas followed a master plan drawn up in the first centuries A.D. and unaltered for generations. Every aspect of the city—from its temples and administrative

Pyramid of the Sun

buildings to its public squares and apartment compounds—was carefully mapped out. Even today, after centuries of erosion and deliberate destruction, Teotihuacán is an overwhelming place.

Depending on where you park your car, you can begin a tour of Teotihuacán at the Pyramid of the Moon, the Pyramid of the Sun, or in the Great Plaza, known as the *Ciudadela* (Citadel). Both pyramids are massive structures, built of air-dried mud brick, called adobe. Their exteriors are covered with hewn stones, laid out in slanting, stepped terraces. A staircase leads to the upper platform, where a temple to the sun or moon once stood. According to ancient belief, these massive shrines symbolized the mountains of heaven: The architects ingeniously positioned the pyramids so that the sun would trace its daily course up and down the terraced steps. There are magnificent panoramic **views of the entire city from both temples, but the Pyramid of the Moon, some 20 meters (65 feet) lower, is an easier

climb, and the view from its platform is nearly as high since it stands on a hill.

In the Pyramid of the Sun, a tunnel, discovered in 1971, leads from the lowest level into a subterranean cave that is divided into walled chambers. These rooms were once thought to be graves, but no signs of burials have been uncovered, so they are now considered an inner sanctuary. From the Pyramid of the Sun, the Street of the Dead leads north to the Pyramid of the Moon. This pyramid stands at the end of its own plaza, and is surrounded by 12 smaller, four-stage temple platforms with an altar in the middle. At the western corner of the plaza are the ruins of a palace noteworthy for its impressive reliefs and frescoes.

From the Pyramid of the Moon, walk west to the restored *Palacio de Quetzalpapálotl* (Palace of the Quetzal Butterfly), so named because its columns display paintings of the Feathered Serpent God, Quetzalpapálotl. It is possible to wander through the courtyards and small rooms of this terraced residence, which proba-

Palacio del Quetzalpapálotl

bly once belonged to a chief priest. The neighboring *Palacio de los Jaguares* has frescoes depicting jaguars blowing into bugle-shaped conch shells or caught in a net held by mysterious hands. A tunnel, its deteriorated walls decorated with green plumed birds, feathered shells, and tropical flowers, leads from here to the *Subestructura de los Caracoles Emplumados* (Buried Temple of the Feathered Snails).

The **Miccaótli** (Street of the Dead) then leads south from the Pyramid of the Moon across large terraces bridged by steps. Flanking the wide street are uniform platforms, built, like the pyramids, using an architectural device known as *talud* and *tablero*—a rectangular inset or ledge (*tablero*) set on a sloping base (*talud*). Much later, others copied and modified the talud-tablero system in building their own cities. But without the original paint to enliven the ledges, this typical Teotihuacán architectural style looks monotonous.

Continue south down the Street of the Dead past the *Temple of Agriculture* and the *Temple of Mythological Animals,* whose magnificently restored frescoes depict an entire menagerie of delightfully imaginative, mythical creatures. On the other side of the street, protected by a roof, a fresco portrait of a large wild cat survives.

Past the Pyramid of the Sun, a little to the west, is a housing complex known as the *Viking Group;* it is named for the American foundation that financed the excavations here. Also west of the street are the *Edificios Superpuestos* (Superimposed Buildings). Additional residences with labyrinthine rooms and inner courts have been discovered farther back from the main avenue. Long ago thousands of small houses and apartment complexes, much like the urban housing common today, must have lined the Street of the Dead and stood between the great pyramids. In many of these surviving structures, well-preserved frescoes provide a glimpse of the once colorful appearance of the sacred city. Note, for example, the *Palace of Tepantitla,* about 500 meters (1,640 feet) northeast of the Pyramid of the Sun, and the complexes of *Tetitla, Atetelco,* and *Zacuala* to the west and outside of the fenced temple district.

At the southern end of the Street of the Dead, cross the San Juan River to a vast area known as the *Ciudadela* (Citadel). Here, the ****Temple of Quetzalcóatl** and the Great Plaza were probably the

Façade of Quetzalcóatl Temple

focus of the entire city. The Temple of Quetzalcóatl consists of two superimposed pyramids; the later version partially covers the earlier structure. To feel the full impact of this temple, wander behind the four-tiered later pyramid and cross the great staircase, where snarling serpents guard the approach to the earlier shrine. Stone images of the Rain God Tlaloc and the Feathered Serpent Quetzalcóatl savagely glare out from the masonry again and again. Remains of faded paint are disquieting reminders of the once terrifyingly vivid imagery.

Near the main entrance, the **Unidad Cultural** houses a museum exhibiting models of the archaeological sites, diagrams, and artifacts excavated from Teotihuacán. The center sells souvenirs, including black obsidian from nearby quarries, the same quarries that flourished thousands of years ago. The restaurant on the second floor offers a good view of the whole city. Another nearby restaurant is located in a cave called *La Gruta.*

If you have time and the energy for a further detour before returning to Mexico City, drive back to Tepexpan and then head south.

After 15 km. (9 miles) you will reach the town of **Texcoco,** once a thriving pre-Columbian community with a population of 30,000. Built on the shores of a great lagoon of the same name, Texcoco quickly grew to rival the nearby Aztec capital of Tenochtitlán during the 14th to 16th centuries. When Hernán Cortés arrived outside the capital, he found support in Texcoco for his plan to conquer the island-city. The fatal ships that carried the Spanish to Tenochtitlán were constructed in Texcoco.

Today Texcoco is a lively market center, only 24 km (15 miles) from Mexico City. On Tuesdays craftspeople from miles around bring in some of the country's finest serapes, rebozos, and heavy wool sweaters to sell at the market. Nearby factories make pottery and glass.

Approximately 1 km. ($^{1}/_{2}$ mile) south of Texcoco on the main road is *Chapingo* and the **Escuela Nacional de Agricultura* (the agricultural school), a former hacienda which houses some of Diego Rivera's most important murals (see page 20). From *Los Reyes,* 23 km. (14 miles) south of Texcoco, several side roads lead back to Mexico City.

TRAVEL ROUTE 2: **Mexico City–**Tepotzotlán– **Tula–*Actopan–**Mexico City (270 km.; 162 miles)

See map on page 88.

This one-day excursion takes in treasures from both pre-Columbian and Colonial periods, from the convents of Tepotzotlán and Actopan to the old Toltec capital of Tula.

Exit Mexico City on Avenida Insurgentes Norte and Calzada Vallejo to Highway 57 D, a toll road. Drive west toward Querétaro for about 40 km. (24 miles) until you reach the turnoff for Tepotzotlán. If you have time for a quick detour, however, exit 57 D earlier at *Cuautitlán*, about 26 km. (16 miles) from Mexico City, and drive 3 km. (2 miles) to the 17th-century *church of San Lorenzo Rio Tenco*, once part of an early Franciscan monastery. The high altarpiece is typically Baroque, decorated with *estípites*—wall pillars that narrow at the base. A richly sculptured stone cross in the atrium dates to 1554. There are also four well-preserved altar paintings by the Flemish master Marten de Vos (1532–1603).

From Cuautitlán, continue on the town road for 8 km. (5 miles) to **Tepotzotlán,** once a major center of religious education. Jesuit missionaries came here to study the Indian languages of Nahuatl and Otomí. The college, founded in 1582, was highly unusual because not only were local Indians involved in the construction, but sons of the Indian elite were educated here. Today the restored church presents an excellent example of Mexican Baroque architecture. The church cloister houses the *Museo Nacional del Virreinato* (National Museum of the Viceroys), whose interesting collection of religious paintings and sculpture dates to the Colonial period; the museum also has exhibits of furniture, jew-

San Francisco Xavier, Tepotzotlán

elry, ceramics, and sacred vessels.

The façade of the **church of San Francisco Xavier,** built along with the convent buildings around 1664, is an exceptionally fine representation of High Baroque Churrigueresque style. The elegant estípites (wall pillars) heighten the tall portal front, and frame the wall panels and niches that hold statues of major historical figures in the Jesuit order. Above the window is a statue of San Francisco Xavier; side niches hold statues of Saint Ignatius of Loyola, Francisco de Borja, Luis Gonzaga, and Estanislao de Kotska. The estípites, popular in Mexican High Baroque, are repeated in the two-storied bell tower built in 1760, and in the gilded altar walls inside the single-nave church. To the right of the nave is the *Loreto Chapel;* of particular note here are the magnificent retable and a model of the modest house in which the Virgin Mary is said to have lived in Nazareth. Adjacent to the chapel is the *Camarín,* an octagonal room decorated with ornate columns, cherubs, and plant motifs. The church and the cloister were carefully restored in the 1960s by the Instituto Nacional de Antropología e Historia.

Before returning to 57 D, drive about 28 km. (17 miles) west along the road to *San Miguel Canadas* to see *Los Arcos de Sitio,* the highest aqueduct in Mexico with multitiered arches up to 60 meters (196 feet) high. The aqueduct spans the Jalpa Gorge for about 40 km. (24 miles). It has supplied water to Tepotzotlán since it was built by the Jesuits in the 18th century. Return to 57 D and continue northwest to the turnoff at *Tepeji de Río.* After about 20 km. (12 miles), a sign in front of a bridge points right to the excavation of the old Toltec metropolis of ****Tula (Tollan),** 85 km. (52 miles) from Mexico City. This popular site is also accessible by city bus from Mexico City's Terminal del Norte, and by numerous private bus tours.

Legends surround the history of Tula, capital city of the Toltec culture that flourished in northern and central Mexico from about A.D. 900 to 1200. The Aztecs recount how Nahuatl-speaking nomads from the north, known as the Chichimecs, arrived at the Valley of Anahuac sometime in the ninth century. They were led

Atlantis columns from Tula

by Mixcóatl, the Cloud Serpent, founder of the Toltec dynasty. Mixcóatl's son Ce Acatl-Topiltzín ("A Reed, Our Prince") moved the capital to Tollan ("Place of the Reeds") in A.D. 968. During Topiltzín's peaceful reign, the Quetzalcóatl religious cult ruled supreme and the arts flourished. But too soon a rival cult arrived that worshiped Tezcatlipoca, the God of the Smoking Mirror, a mysterious deity of the night. They quickly gained dominance, and forced Topiltzín to leave Tollan about A.D. 990. Some say Topiltzín set himself ablaze and rose to the heavens as a beautiful green feathered bird to become the morning star. Another legend holds that he went to sea promising to return. But in view of the prominent impact of Toltec culture on the Mayas of the Yucatán, especially around Chichén Itzá in A.D. 1000, archaeologists have concluded that Topiltzín went there and established a new dominion under the name of the god-king Kukulcán, the Mayan name for Quetzalcóatl.

Under the militaristic reign of the Tezcatlipoca cult, Tollan became the terror of the region, demanding human sacrifices to pacify the gods, and exacting heavy taxes. Weakened by drought in 1156, Tollan fell to the Chichimecs, who burned down the capital in 1168.

Spanish Franciscan Friar Bernardino de Sahagun described the fabled city in his *Historia de las Cosas de la Nueva España* (History of the Things of New Spain), written in the 16th century, but no one believed in its existence until 1938 when Wigberto Jiménez Moreno discovered ruins of the old metropolis. Since then, the city has been systematically excavated and restored.

To reach Tollan, cross the river just beyond the modern town of Tula. Against a blue sky and rolling green hills, the sight of four colossal *Atlantean columns* atop the lofty ****Pyramid of Quetzalcóatl** could convince even the greatest skeptic of the power of the mighty Toltecs. These massive statues, 4.5 meters (15 feet) high, consist of four cylinders each, carved to represent armed warriors adorned in feathered crowns and breast plates shaped like stylized butterflies; the warriors' triangular aprons are knotted at the back and covered by a decorative disk. In his right hand, each warrior holds a spear-thrower, and in his left hand a spear, a pouch, and

a curved sword. Mighty pillars that once supported the roof of the *Temple of the Morning Star* (Tlahuizalpantecuhtli), these stately figures now seem to support the heavens themselves. When the Chichimecs destroyed the temple, they had to roll sections, weighing several tons, down a specially constructed ramp.

Square figures behind the Atlantean columns bear reliefs depicting warriors and piles of weapons; between these reliefs are narrow bands decorated with crocodile heads, an ancient symbol of the earth. On the walls of the pyramid are friezes of jaguars and eagles eating human hearts, symbolizing the two powerful warrior sects, the Jaguars and Eagles. The pyramid rests on a base 40 meters (131 feet) wide. A broad staircase leads about 10 meters (32 feet) up to a platform, where columns have been restored to their original position. A wide porch (*Gran Vestibulo*) in front of the pyramid is filled with pillars, some reconstructed.

To the left of the Quetzalcóatl Pyramid, archaeologist Jorge R. Acosta discovered a complex he named the *Palacio Quemado* (Burned Palace) because of the adobe blocks which had been baked into bricks by the heat of the destroying flames. In the middle court are two Chac-mools— reclining figures with flexed knees. According to legend, the hearts of sacrificial victims were placed in the receptacle on a Chac-mool's indented belly. In the northeast corner of the Burned Palace stand the remains of a bench with a frieze showing a procession of noblemen, or possibly warriors and priests, in relief.

Behind the pyramid the *Serpent Wall* (Coatepantli) stands, 40 meters (131 feet) long and 2.2 meters (7 feet) high; it forms a barrier around the sacred area. Reliefs running the length of the wall depict a human skeleton disappearing into the jaws of a snake. Is this the longed-for triumph of the Feathered Serpent Quetzalcóatl over Tezcatlipoca, the God of the Night? The first of two excavated ball courts lies just behind the Serpent Wall; the second is near the central square, where there are also a small altar and the exposed core of what is presumably the main temple.

Return to the little town of *Tula de Allende,* where there is a 16th-century Franciscan abbey with a fortified turreted church. The church's façade is fashioned in simple Plateresque style.

If time permits, there is a worthwhile side trip to the Augustinian convent of Actopan. Continue northeast for approximately 55 km. (34 miles), through *Tlahuelilpa,* with its open chapel; *Mixquiahuala;* and *Progreso* to ***Actopan.** Located in the Valley of Mezquital, an area inhabited today by Otomí Indians, this town is a good place to buy pottery, woven woolen belts, and cloaks fashioned by the local Indians in the tradition of their ancestors. The town's key attrac-

Fresco in cloister, Actopan

tion, however, is the *Augustinian convent* founded in 1548 and dedicated to San Nicolas de Tolentino. In the open *chapel,* the barrel vaulting (*boveda*) spans 17 meters (55 feet). Wall paintings depict biblical scenes. The portal in Spanish Renaissance style is framed by a double row of Corinthian columns. With its turrets and arches the massive, square bell tower reflects Moorish influence. The Gothic ribbed vault over the entrance and in the choir contrasts with the otherwise Neoclassical interior.

Near the entrance hall (*porteria*) on the right side of the church, the small *Sala de Profundis* contains a large mural representing life in the convent. Here, simple Gothic arches decorate the lower section and smaller round arches fill the upper part of the cloister. The Refectorium has a painted coffer-work ceiling and a reading chancel. In contrast to this structure's many Gothic elements, the staircase leading to the cloister is decorated with Renaissance-style **murals** depicting saints and Augustinian monks and framed with decorative bands of heraldic animals and garlands. A *gallery* reached through the garden has a small exhibit on Otomí folk art.

From Actopan, on the return journey of 121 km. (75 miles) back to Mexico City, it is possible to bypass *Pachuca*. After about 25 km. (15 miles), an access road turns right for the Pachuca–Mexico highway, Route 85.

TRAVEL ROUTE 3: **Mexico City–*Toluca–Ixtapan de la Sal–**Cuernavaca–**Mexico City (350 km.; 210 miles)

See map on page 88.

This route takes you through forested and mountainous country to many of the Indian centers of Mexico. If you have several days to spend, the trip can be combined with Travel Routes 4 and 5. Or, for a shortened version, many travel agencies in Mexico City offer one-day excursions to Toluca and its nearby Indian markets.

Leave Mexico City from the northwest and pick up Highway 130 near Naucalpan. (An alternate route via the toll-free parkway is faster but more congested. Enter the parkway from Paseo de la Reforma.) About 15 km. (9 miles) out of the city is a nature park with the misleading name of *Desierto de los Leones* (Desert of Lions). The park is really an extensive fir and pine forest, and a very popular weekend resort. A pleasant path leads from the park to the remains of a Carmelite convent.

The highway winds its way over the *Paso de las Cruces,* a picturesque mountain pass 3,100 meters (10,168 feet) high, then descends onto the plateau of Toluca. In the distance, snow-covered volcanic peaks of *Nevada de Toluca* rise 4,558 meters (15,000 feet) high.

*Toluca de Lerdo, 64 km. (40 miles) from Mexico City, is the highest city in Mexico, at an altitude of 2,680 meters (8,800 feet). It is the capital of the state of México, and has developed into an important industrial center, with a population of 300,000. Enter the town on the Paseo Tollocan, past a large *equestrian statue* of the peasant revolutionary Emiliano Zapata. Nearby is another monument honoring the Mexican flag. Just a little farther left is the **Museo del Arte Popular* (Museum of Folk Art).

The center of town, laid out in the 19th century, is the *Zócalo,* officially called the *Plaza de los Mártires* (Martyrs Square) in honor of the hundred townsmen who were shot down here in 1812 during the fight for independence.

On the north side of the Zócalo stands the government palace, *Palacio de Gobierno,* built in typical late-19th-century Neoclassical style.

Although the foundation stone for the Neoclassical *cathedral* was laid in 1862, the church was not completed until the 1950s and was only dedicated in 1978. *Portales,* shopping arcades, built between 1832 and 1836, line the rest of the square. Near the center of town is *El Mercado 16 de Septiembre,* once an indoor market. The building's metal frame was prefabricated in Paris around the turn of the century. Its spectacular new stained-glass roof renders it an ideal location for the botanical garden, which features many native plants.

The main reason tourists come to Toluca is to visit the large outdoor **market,* particularly lively on Fridays. Otomí and Matlatzinca Indians come here from the surrounding regions to buy and sell a seemingly infinite variety of items—from vegetables, fruit, pigs, and poultry to handcrafted *rebozos* (woven shawls), *serapes* (men's cloaks), and knitted wool jackets. Unfortunately the traditional ceramic pots and baskets have been largely replaced here by plastic and metal containers.

Three worthwhile side trips can be made from Toluca.

*Calixtlahuaca is 11 km. (7 miles) north of the city. There is a regular bus service from Toluca, or you can drive there. Go about 8 km. (5 miles) on the highway to Querétaro, then turn left onto an unpaved road which leads about 3 km. (2 miles) to the excavation site. Calixtlahuaca was once the center of a thriving Matlatzinca culture, a group driven out first by Toltec and later by Aztec invaders. Although inhabited until the Pre-Classic Period, Calixtlahuaca reached its height between A.D. 300 and 600. The Matlatzincas were known for their distinctive system of terrace-farming on the steep slopes of Cerro de Tenismo, and for their pottery.

The four-storied round **pyramid to Quetzalcóatl,* the Feathered Serpent God, was originally built in a style clearly influenced by the architecture of Teotihuacán. This shrine was actually dedicated to the wind god Ehécatl, a manifestation of Quetzalcóatl. There are three later superstructures. The innermost structure is reached through a tunnel. The later two date to the Aztec period.

On a higher hill are remains of the temple to the rain god Tlaloc, one of several buildings around the main plaza. The staircase reaches only the first of the origi-

Quetzalcóatl Pyramid, Calixtlahuaca

nal four stories and is linked to another temple platform and the Altar of Skulls in a remarkable cross formation. One of the arms of the cross ends in a semicircle decorated with skulls. This complex dates to the Aztec occupation of Calixtlahuaca, when other stone sculptures, such as the statue of the earth goddess Coatlicue, were constructed here. (The Coatlicue statue, as well as one of the wind god Ehécatl, are now displayed in the Museo Nacional de Antropología in Mexico City.)

There are many good roads through the mountainous area of the **Nevado de Toluca,** named for its snow-covered volcanic peaks. To reach the highest summit, 4,558 meters (15,000 feet) above sea level, leave Toluca on Highway 130 southwest toward Temascaltepec. (This highway extends all the way to Zihuatenejo on the Pacific Coast. See page 215.) After about 18 km. (11 miles), bear left on the road to *Sultepec;* after another 8 km. (5 miles), just past the *Raíces* pond, follow an unpaved mountain road that branches off to the left up to the top of the volcano. This gorgeous route climbs through conifer forests and continues up to the desert landscape around the volcanic crater at about 4,250 meters (14,000 feet). From here, it is possible to walk down to two crater lakes, or you can drive there on a narrow road. The best panorama is, of course, from the highest of the crater summits, the *Pico del Fraile* (Friar's Peak). But be careful: at this high altitude, the climb is only safe for those in fit condition.

From Nevado de Toluca, continue south on Highway 130 for about 25 km. (15 miles). Here you will reach a new connection leading another 36 km. (22 miles) to *Valle de Bravo,* a romantic country town on the eastern shore of a reservoir. This retreat, located at an altitude of 1,870 meters (6,133 feet), attracts the city-weary who come to escape the capital's smog and noise, and to enjoy the hilly country, golf, tennis, and swimming. The northern exit from Valle de Bravo leads to the highway back to Toluca.

From Toluca, follow Highway 55 south for about 7 km. (4 miles), then turn off on the access road for about 2 km. (1 mile) to the potter's village of *Metepec.* The multicolored glazed pottery made here by local Indians is both functional and fanciful. Best known are the brightly painted "Trees of Life"

Living Tree from Metepec

candelabras, some 3 meters (9 feet) tall. A Garden of Eden flourishes in their branches, along with Adam, Eve, and the Serpent; delightful flowers, animals, and mythical beings are entwined among the painted leaves. While in Metepec, be sure to visit the *Franciscan monastery* whose massive 17th-century church has a Plateresque façade.

Continue south on Highway 55 for 89 km. (55 miles) to the market hamlet of *Tenango de Arista,* or Tenango del Valle, located at the foot of a rocky plateau. In pre-Hispanic times, this was the site of the fortified town of ***Teotenango,** an impressive ceremonial center said to date to the seventh century A.D. Since excavations began here in 1974, an entire city has been uncovered and restored, complete with temple platforms, residences, stairs, streets, ball courts, and even steam baths. The severe architecture, which combines the influences of late Teotihuacán, Toltec, and Aztec cultures, is attributed to the Matlatzincas who occupied the nearby plateau of Toluca (see page 84). The fragmented remains of a double wall north of the archaeological zone are probably the source of the site's name: Teotenango means "divine wall." In its heyday, the center spanned 21 square km. (12.5 square miles). One of the excavation's most interesting discoveries is a sculpture of a monster eating the sun—a symbolic representation of the solar eclipse of A.D. 1477. The small museum contains a curious Quetzalcóatl statue with a duck's bill, which came from Calixtlahuaca (see page 83).

From Teotenango, there is a choice of two routes—either a detour of 40 km. (25 miles) via *Joquicingo* to *Malinalco,* an Aztec site set in mountainous forests (see Travel Route 5), or a continuation of about 24 km. (15 miles) south along Highway 55 to *Tenancingo,* an agricultural center with extensive peach orchards. Near Tenancingo, in the middle of a lovely forest on a mountain slope, stands the old *Convento del Santo Desierto* (Holy Desert Convent), where Carmelite nuns from the *Desierto de los Leones* arrived around 1800 (see page 82). The story goes that the nuns found the damp climate of their original home near Mexico City unhealthy. Health concerns certainly inspired the Aztecs when they founded the thermal brine bath of nearby **Ixtapan de la Sal,** 146 km. (90 miles) from Mexico City. The name is actually redundant, for the Nahuatl word "Ixtapan" means "place of salt." Today, this fashionable resort draws people from all over the world to its healing, radioactive mineral waters and its elegant four-star spas and hotels. There are public baths (*balnearios*) and even a traditional spa hotel with an old-fashioned bath house and private Roman baths (*baños romanos*). Ixtapan is the most luxurious of all the many thermal spring resorts in Mexico.

From Ixtapan, continue south on 55 past several fascinating stalactite caves: *Grutas de la Estrella* (Star Caves), 161 km. (99 miles) from Mexico City, and the *Grutas de Cacahuamilpa,* 187 km. (116 miles) from the capital shortly past the turnoff to Taxco (see page 92). Both caves are accessible only with a guide. Cacahuamilpa Caves, 1,100 meters (3,600 feet) above sea level, are the largest in Mexico; they cover a distance of more than 12 km. (7 miles). A long path leads through 16 chambers, passing an incredible variety of stalagmite and stalactite formations. Some of these damp cavern interiors soar to heights of 85 meters (278 feet) high.

From the caves, 55 winds past lovely villages and reservoirs, passing the turnoff to *Xochicalco,* an interesting pre-Columbian site 229 km. (142 miles) from Mexico City (see page 91). Near Alpuyeca, pick up Highway 95 north for a direct route of 109 km. (67 miles) back to Mexico City. The highway passes by *Cuernavaca* en route (see below).

TRAVEL ROUTE 4: **Mexico City–**Cuernavaca–**Xochicalco–**Taxco (190 km; 118 miles)

See map on page 88.

This is a route of scenic contrasts—from the garden-city Cuernavaca with its ravishing tropical flowers, to the severe pre-Columbian ruins of Xochicalco, to the picturesque "silver town" of Taxco. Every organized excursion from Mexico City covers this popular route. If you're planning to drive, you need at least two days.

Leave Mexico City on Avenida Insurgentes Sur and pick up either the old toll-free highway marked "Libre" in the suburb of *Tlalpan,* or the toll road marked "Cuota" south to Cuernavaca. Both roads skirt the eastern slope of the extinct volcano *Ajusco* (3,937 meters; 13,000 feet high) and climb about 3,000 meters (9,840 feet). During the ascent, the volcanoes Popocatépetl and Iztaccíhuatl to the east seem to draw closer. After *Tres-Cumbres Pass,* there are excellent views of orchards in the Morelos valley far below. Continue south on Highway 95 to *Cuernavaca,* 85 km. (52 miles) from Mexico City.

**Cuernavaca

Cuernavaca is 1,542 meters (5,000 feet) above sea level. This "town of eternal spring" has been revered for various reasons through the centuries. Cortés kept a summer home here, and it is still a resort favored by many Mexican and foreign officials. It is a beautiful city of flowers and mild breezes. The capital of the state of

Morelos, with a burgeoning population of 209,000, Cuernavaca maintains a thriving year-round tourist business. It offers, among other things, swimming, relaxing mineral waters, and all the luxuries of the leisure life. Bougainvilleas in flaming shades of red and pink grow wild here, lavender-hued jacarandas line the streets, and bananas, mangos, and guayabas dangle from the trees. If you're spending the night, be sure to choose a hotel with a garden.

When Cortés reported his conquest of Mexico, Spain's King Charles rewarded him with Cuernavaca and 29 other cities. After his fall from power, Cortés retired here to live in his fortress-like home, the ***Palacio de Cortés,** built by him in 1530 on what is now the *Plaza de Armas.* The palace was remodeled several times through the centuries, but in 1970 it was restored to its original design. Today it is a regional **historic museum.* During the restoration, the foundation for a pyramid and graves belonging to the Tlahuica Indians were uncovered

Palacio de Cortés, Cuernavaca

in front of the palace. (The Tlahuica, a Chichimec tribe, founded the city during the 12th or 13th century, and named it Cuauhnáhuac, meaning "near trees." The story goes that when the Spanish arrived in 1521 they couldn't pronounce the city's Indian name, so they changed it to the similar-sounding Cuernavaca. The palace's severe façade is interrupted only by two superimposed galleries. From the loggias in the rear is a spectacular view of the valley with the volcanic peaks of Popocatépetl in the background. Frescoes painted by Diego Rivera (see page 20) depict scenes of the Spanish Conquest, the history of the city, and the War of Independence. There is also a well-known portrait of the revolutionary leader Emiliano Zapata leading his white horse by the bridle.

From the palace, walk along Avenida Hidalgo to the ***Cathedral,** part of a Franciscan monastery begun in 1523. In the single barrel-vaulted nave, frescoes dating to the 16th and 17th centuries have been uncovered beneath layers of paint; they portray the friars' missionary voyage to Japan, and the martyrdom of the Mexican saint San Felipe de Jesus. Another frieze dating to the 18th century depicts cherubic angels. Abutting the cathedral is the monastery's large open *chapel,* with its simple vaulting, and the *cloister,* where there are additional wall paintings. In the atrium, the *Capilla de la Tercer Orden* (Chapel of the Third Order) has a Mexican

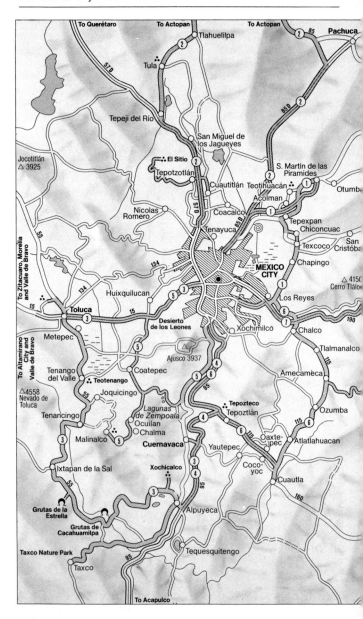

To Tampico

130

Tulancingo

130

N

Lago de la Pueblita

Tepeapulco

Apan

Calpulalpan

Hueyotlipan

119

Apizaco

Ocotoxco

To Veracruz

Tlaxcala

Cacaxtla

Ocotlán

Tepeyanco

cíhuatl
6

Nativitas

Zacatelco

Huejotzingo

4461△
La Malinche

so de Cortés

**Tepanapa-
Pyramide**

119

150 D

Cholula

Tonantzintla

Puebla

To Veracruz
and Tehuacan

5452
ocatépetl

Acatepec

Atlixco

*Presa
Valsequillo*

uaquechula

190

160

Izúcar de
Matamoros

190

To Oaxaca

ROUTES 1–7
(Excursions
from Mexico City)

Miles

0 ⊢⊢⊢⊢⊢ 15

Kilometers

Baroque façade and a carved and gilded altar.

Across from the cathedral on Calle Morelos is the entrance to the *Jardín Borda,* a luxurious 18th-century botanic garden on the grounds of a magnificent mansion owned by José de la Borda, the silver baron of Taxco. When he died in 1778, Borda left the estate to his son Manuel, who lavished much of his fortune on landscaping the extensive terraced gardens. So splendid was this opulent setting that the Emperor Maximilian and his wife Carlota made the estate their summer residence in 1864, where they wined and dined the world's elite.

Nearby, the *Hotel Casino de la Selva* houses a huge mural by David Alfaro Siqueiros (see page 20), and a statue of the painter and revolutionary Dr. Atl (see page 20). About half a kilometer (less than a half-mile) to the east, on Avenida Río Balsas, are the remains of the pre-Columbian cult site of **Teopanzolco,** built by the Tlahuicas when they settled in Cuernavaca. The most important building, a double Aztec-style pyramid, as well as the pottery found at the site, prove that the Tlahuica region became part of the Aztec empire early in the 16th century. Most of the structures here date between A.D. 1250 and 1521. From the platform, you can see the exposed core of the pyramid and parts of its initial structure.

About a mile west of the Zócalo is *Salto de San Anton,* a lovely landscaped park with a picturesque waterfall.

In a valley surrounded by basalt rock mountains is the picturesque Indian village of ***Tepoztlán.** Leave Cuernavaca from the north and follow the old road for about 21 km. (13 miles), or take the highway marked Mexico D.F. north to 115 D and then drive southeast on 115 D toward *Cuautla.* Winding cobblestone streets twist up Tepoztlán's steep town slopes, and the people here still speak the Aztec language Nahuatl. It is a town that blends ancient and modern traditions. At the top of the mountain, 600 meters (1,900 feet) above the town in the rugged *Tepoztéco* peaks, the Tlahuica Indians built a *temple to Tepoztécatl,* god of pulque, a popular drink made from the fermented juices of the maguey cactus; harvest festivals and pulque banquets were once held in Tepoztécatl's honor. It's a steep climb to the base of the two-storied pyramid, all that remains of the former temple. On the western side, narrow stairs lead to a room containing fragmented reliefs with hieroglyphic drawings. The panoramic view from the mountain peak is truly spectacular but only the hardy should attempt this climb in the thin mountain air.

Back down in the village, the main attraction on the plaza is the Dominican monastery, the **Convento de La Navidad de La Virgen Maria,* built around 1580. Although the church façade is richly decorated with sculptures in Plateresque style, the two-storied cloister is strikingly simple. From the corner loggia on the second floor, there is a good view of the mountains. In 1910 the local hero Emiliano Zapata used the monastery to house his troops. Behind the monastery is the *Museo Arqueológico,* where, thanks to the poet Carlos Pellicer Cámara, there is a fine collection of Tlahuica artifacts, as well as Mayan treasures from Jaina Island, off Campeche. On market days local Indians sell handicrafts in the plaza facing the museum.

During the carnival season, Tepoztlán stages a bacchanalean explosion. On Shrove Tuesday masked dancers, known as the Chinelos, perform the Baile del Brinco, an ancient Aztec jumping dance for which they dress as Spanish conquistadors, complete with ludicrous wigs and beards. Another festival held here on September 7 and 8 ostensibly celebrates the birth of the Virgin Mary, but the town takes advantage of the occasion to honor Tepoztécatl and pulque, imbibing generous quantities of alcohol.

From Tepoztlán, 115 D continues southeast to Cuautla. About 10 km. (6 miles) before Cuautla is the *Hacienda of Cocoyoc,* now a hotel (see Travel Route 6). This region south of Cuernavaca is characterized by sugar cane fields, rice paddies, and incredible sweeping meadows filled with multicolored roses.

South of Cuernavaca are the

worthwhile but little-visited pre-Columbian ruins of **Xochicalco**. Follow Highway 95 south to *Alpuyeca*, 109 km. (67 miles) from Mexico City, and then drive another 12 km. (7 miles) northwest in the direction of the "Grutas" (caves). The fortified ruins of Xochicalco sit on a conical mountain overlooking a vast plain. Little is known of the history of this "town of the flower house," because the remains excavated so far can be traced to any number of Indian cultures. Strategically placed midway between the highlands and the south, Xochicalco was clearly influenced by the Teotihuacáns and Tulas of the highlands, as well as by the more southern Zapotecs and Mayas. The site appears to have been settled very early by a Nahuatl-speaking tribe, who in A.D. 700–1350 turned the fortified settlement into an important ceremonial center.

The most beautiful building in Xochicalco, the *Pirámide de las Serpientes Emplumadas* (Pyramid of the Feathered Serpents), stands on top of the hill. Well-preserved flat reliefs along the pyramid's base depict eight enormous feathered snakes flicking their tongues. Between their coils are crouched figures with Mayan features, evidently high-ranking personages. The snake motif alternates with a hieroglyph symbolizing the new fire ceremony. On either side of the staircase, serpents are coiled into a semicircle and enclose hieroglyphs of the calendar.

On the northern slope of the hill are a series of underground chambers that were once part of an observatory. Stairs lead into natural limestone caves decorated with stucco work. One large room contains a light shaft that once may have been used to observe the movements of the sun. Farther on in the middle of the cult center is the ball court; its side walls still bear the stone rings through which the players had to drive the ball after it had touched the ground. Past the court lies one of the residential complexes.

From Xochicalco continue south on 95 to *Taxco*, with a stop at the stalactite cave of *Cacahuamilpa* (see page 86), or, for a faster trip, return to Alpuyeca and pick up 95 D which runs parallel to 95 to Taxco for 20 km. (12 miles) then turns off toward *Acapulco*.

From Alpuyeca, there is a worthwhile side trip to the *Laguna de Tequesquitengo* (Lake Tequesquitengo), approximately 15 km. (9 miles) to the southwest. A road

Xochicalco

circles the lake shore, which is dotted with vacation homes. On the eastern shore, there is a resort of the same name, and about 5 km. (3 miles) north is a hacienda hotel, Vista Hermosa.

At Amacuzac, turn west off the expressway for the Taxco road, a 40 km. (24 miles) winding route through the Sierra Madres to Taxco.

**Taxco

190 km. (117 miles) south of Mexico City with a detour through Xochicalco. By public bus: from the capital's Central de Autobuses del Sur. By car: Highway 95 D south through Cuernavaca.

See map on page 93.

If you were to imagine a fairy-tale city untouched by the 20th century, it would probably resemble Taxco. Sprawling gently over mountain slopes 1,660 meters (5,400 feet) high, Taxco escaped the monotonous Colonial checkerboard pattern of many of Mexico's cities. A charming confusion of narrow, cobblestone lanes twists up, down, and around the hills; multicolored blossoms cascade from the balconies of glistening white stucco houses with red tile roofs. Every other doorway seems to lead to a silver shop. Taxco is the "silver city" of Mexico. It is estimated that half the working population—the city boasts 36,000 inhabitants—makes a living from the booming art of the silversmith.

Although the local Indians knew a silvery metal lay buried in the mountains around Taxco, it was not until the arrival of Cortés that its existence really mattered. While looking for tin to make guns, Cortés struck silver, and soon after founded the mining town of El Real del Telcingo in 1529. The town gradually merged with two other mining communities to form the new town of Taxco in 1581. By the 18th century, the silver mines had long been exhausted, when suddenly an adventurous Frenchman, Joseph de la Borde (later renamed José de la Borda), discovered a new, rich lode of silver. Working this "Veta de San Ignacio" made Borda an incredibly rich man and led to a second economic boom for the town.

Taxco's latest economic boom derives from its status as a tourist mecca, thanks to an unlikely entrepreneur, William Spratling, an American professor from Tulane University, New Orleans. Called Don Guillermo by the natives, Spratling arrived in Taxco in 1930 and opened a silver workshop. He hired goldsmiths from nearby Iguala to make silver jewelry fashioned after old Mexican motifs. His success led to the opening of hundreds of silversmith workshops, whose imaginative products are on sale today locally as well as in many fine boutiques in Mexico City.

The architectural jewel of Taxco stands on the Zócalo. **Iglesia de San Sebastián y Santa Prisca** (abridged by everyone to Santa Prisca church)

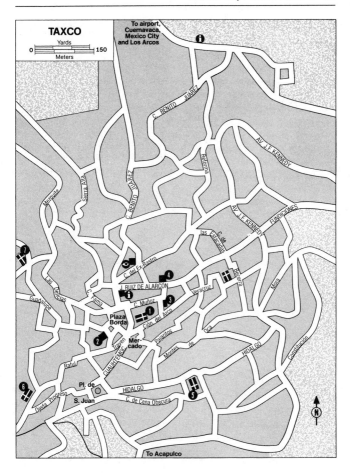

(1) was built by José de la Borda in 1758 in gratitude for his wealth. The silver baron's maxim "Dios da a Borda, Borda da a Dios" (God gives to Borda, Borda gives to God) is realized in this magnificent structure. Built in Churrigueresque style, the church's pink façade overflows with decorations. Above the portal is the papal tiara and a large medallion depicting the baptism of Jesus. Lavishly decorated twin towers frame this entrance, rising 39.5 meters (130 feet) high, and the ensemble is crowned by a blue-tiled dome. The rich interior glitters with 12 gilded altars (*retablos*), abundantly decorated with figures of apostles, saints,

Iglesia de Santa Prisca, Taxco

angels, flowers, and fruit. Above the entrance to the *Capilla de los Indios* (Chapel of the Indians), a painting by Miguel Cabrera (1696–1768) depicts the martyrdom of Saint Prisca, the church's patron saint, who was beheaded in Rome. Other works by Cabrera, some quite valuable, hang in the chapel and sacristy.

Across from the entrance to the Santa Prisca church from the terrace of a small café, you'll have a good view of the *Zócalo*, called the *Plaza Borda*. Like all Mexican towns, the Zócalo sets the heartbeat of local activities; it's a good place to relax on wrought-iron benches, listen to the music from the bandstand, or plan your next foray.

Building regulations in Taxco are strict: any new or renovated structures must maintain the city's 18th-century architectural character. As a result, there is a charming Colonial atmosphere here. Among old Spanish residences of special interest is **Casa Figueroa** (2), located on Calle Guadalupe which winds uphill from the Zócalo. Built in 1767 by Conde de la Cadena, the villa is dubbed the House of Tears because local Indians were forced into slave labor to complete it. In 1943 the artist Fidel Figueroa purchased the house, and with colorful Puebla tiles converted the once dark interior into a gaudy home. The house is now a museum displaying artworks and furniture. A short distance away, above a fountain with a bust of Borda, a small terrace offers a fine view of the Zócalo and church below.

Walk behind the Santa Prisca church and past the *Museo Spratling* (3), now a municipal crafts museum, to Calle Juan Ruiz de Alarcón and the Colonial house, ***Casa Humbolt** (4). Originally the home of Juan de Villanueva, the villa was renamed after the famous German explorer Alexander von Humboldt spent a night here in April, 1803, during his explorations of Latin America. The villa has a Moorish façade and a pretty patio with a fountain; it is now a shop selling wooden crafts, clothing, and handmade furniture.

Near the top of the steep Calle Juan Ruiz de Alarcón is the huge *Casa Borda,* where the silver baron lived. The front of the house is two stories high but the back, built on a slope, rises five stories. The *tourist office* is located here on the first floor.

Of the many churches in Taxco, be sure to see *La Santísma* (5), which may not be the holiest as its name implies, but is certainly the most rustic, with its rough stone walls. Near the church a staircase from Calle Hildago leads back down to the market, which is especially lively on weekends. When it comes to shopping, however, the main interest focuses on the silversmiths—there are well over a hundred *plateros* in Taxco today. Don't expect to find lower prices; no matter where you buy it, silver is no bargain. But Taxco offers the widest selection of original designs. Another local industry that has flourished in recent years

is Colonial furniture-making, thanks again to a suggestion from Spratling.

From the hill of the *Iglesia del Señor Ojeda* (6) or the Iglesia de la Virgen de Guadalupe, there are excellent panoramic views of Taxco and its serpentine streets. The valley station is near the Los Arcos aqueduct, reached by minibuses, called *burritos,* from the Zócalo. The burritos charge low fares to drive passengers up and down the steep town streets and along the "Panoramica" around town.

TRAVEL ROUTE 5: *Lagunas de Zempoala–*Chalma– *Malinalco (115 km.; 69 miles)

See map on page 88.

From Mexico City, Toluca, or Cuernavaca, it is possible to plan a day trip to two pilgrimage sites and an unusual Aztec ruin, a ceremonial center carved into mountain rock. The strong Catholic faith of the people of Mexico—witnessed in the lavish Mexican Baroque cathedrals and monasteries—finds another kind of expression in these pilgrimage sites. Although the architecture here is hardly outstanding, the effect of the shrines and votive offerings can be overwhelming. This itinerary also traverses a national park. It can be easily combined with Travel Route 3 or 4.

There are several daily direct buses to Chalma via Toluca from Mexico City's bus station called T.A.P. (Terminal del Poniente), which is located at the subway station *Observatorio*. If you are planning to drive, the best connection from Mexico City is to take the old Highway 95 toward Cuernavaca to *Tres Marias* (also called Tres Cumbres) about 51 km. (32 miles)

from the capital. There, a lovely road winds west through a conifer forest to the national park of ***Lagunas de Zempoala,** about 66 km. (41 miles) from Mexico City. Located at 2,900 meters (9,500 feet) above sea level, this area was once filled with seven crater lakes. Only three remain today, but they abound with fish and wildlife. This is a wonderful park for fishing, hiking, horseback riding, and camping in the peaceful mountains.

Return to Highway 95 and continue west to *Santa Marta,* about 80.5 km. (50 miles) from Mexico City, then turn left. Continue for 16.5 km. (10 miles) to the pilgrimage station *El Ahuehuete,* named for the large tree that grows at this site. Sometimes called Moctezuma cypress, this ancient tree is more than a symbol of eternal life, for a sacred spring still bubbles up from its roots. The Savior of Chalma is said to have rested beneath its branches, and the spring water is believed to cure all ailments. It is collected in canisters by pilgrims who wear flower wreaths sold here and who decorate their cars with garlands. During feast times, the pilgrims dance on a wooden stage on the hillside. From Santa Marta, continue south to the pilgrimage station of ***Chalma,** about 103 km. (64 miles) from Mexico City. Set in a lush green valley, the land around Chalma has always struck visitors to the area as a gift of God. In pre-Columbian times, a figure of the cave god Oztotéotl is said to have been worshiped in a cave here. Centuries later, in 1537, Augustinian monks replaced the Indian idol with a black Christ on the cross. But it was not until the 17th century that Chalma became the focus of extensive pilgrimages, inspired by a hermit who settled in the cave and promoted a cult in honor of the Christ figure. Between 1680 and 1683 a church

was erected here as a permanent shrine; it has been remodeled several times over the centuries.

From the main road, a path to the shrine winds downhill through narrow crooked streets, past hundreds of booths selling crucifixes, pictures of saints, and *Milagros* (miracles), small metal votives that are offered in gratitude for healing. A flowered gate opens onto the square in front of the church. The faithful leave wreaths at the gate door, then enter and humbly creep on their knees to the altar. A cleansing ritual bath in the river below the church and the adjacent cloister is part of a pilgrimage to Señor de Chalma. It is especially fascinating to visit Chalma during a pilgrimage. Christmas is one such time. It is celebrated in Chalma from December 23 to 26 with singing and dancing, fireworks, and religious services, and draws pilgrims from distant corners of Mexico. Other pilgrimage dates include the lively feast of the Epiphany on January 6, the first Friday in February; Easter; August 28; and September 29, the feast of Michael the Archangel, the town's patron saint. But even if it is not a special holiday, the town is alive with pilgrimage rituals. From Chalma, it is a short drive to ***Malinalco,** 115 km. (71 miles) from Mexico City. This friendly little village of 6,000 people resembles many other small mountain towns with its whitewashed stucco houses and twisting lanes. Hidden on its own

Jaguar sculpture, Malinalco

mountain is the Aztec ruin of *Cerro de los Ídolos*. In 1501 the Aztec ruler Ahuítzotl (1486–1503) began construction on a ceremonial center here, probably used for the initiation rites of elite warriors into the orders of the Jaguar and the Eagles. Expansion of the center continued under Moctezuma II (1480?–1520), and was abruptly stopped by the Spanish Conquest.

The main buildings stand on a terrace about 200 meters (650 feet) above the village. You must climb 400 steps to reach the site but both the commanding view of the valley and the ruins themselves are worth the effort. The most astonishing structure is a round monolithic pyramid, cut into the mountain rock. Flanking the staircase, hewn out of the rock, are two stone jaguars, now headless. The entrance to the round cult room, protected by a thatched roof, forms the shape of the open jaws of a serpent. On each side is a coiled serpent, also carved from the rock, and a warrior's drum. Circling the interior walls is a low stone bench, on which eagle skins frame an artfully stylized jaguar. Another relief of an eagle skin lies on the floor, and behind it, there is a depression, presumably where the hearts of victims were offered to the god Cuauhxicalli. Such artful carving into the rock is all the more amazing since the Aztecs had only stone and wooden tools.

In the village below, the Augustinian monastery dates to 1540; from January 6 to 8 dances honoring the Magi are performed here in the atrium.

You can return to Mexico City via Toluca (see Travel Route 3) or via Santa Marta and Coatepec to the Mexico–Toluca highway.

TRAVEL ROUTE 6: **Mexico City–Amecameca–**Paso de Cortés (Popocatépetl and Iztaccíhuatl)–Cuautla–**Mexico City (270 km.; 162 miles)

See map on page 88.

Even if you don't want to climb the 5,000-meter- (16,400-foot-) high volcanoes, you should take a trip to the Popocatépetl-Iztaccíhuatl National Park to see the impressive scenery and views of the plateau of

Mexico. You can drive up as far as 3,900 meters (12,800 feet) but be sure to go only on a clear day.

Leave the capital on Calzada I. Zaragoza or Calzada Ermita Iztapalapa and pick up the Puebla Cuota (Puebla Highway) which starts about 20 km. (12 miles) from the Zócalo. After about 14 km. (9 miles), turn off for the road to Cuautla. (You can also take the old state road, the Puebla Libre from Mexico City to this point.) You will drive through the old Indian town of **Chalco**, 38 km. (23 miles) from the capital, with a population of 20,000. In pre-Columbian times, Chalco was the center of the allied Chichimec realm, which fell under the rule of Tenochtitlán in 1485. When Cortés led his troops through the town, the Chalca like the other rival groups in the region eagerly offered to help them fight the Mexica Indians of Tenochtitlán. Little did they realize that the devastation of the island-city would also spell their ruin. During the 19th century, the once large lake in Chalco was drained by a canal to Xochimilco (see page 68). From Chalco continue on the road to **Tlalmanalco,** 50 km. (31 miles) from Mexico City. Of note here is the Franciscan monastery, built between 1585 and 1591. In the unfinished open chapel are five richly sculpted arches built in Plateresque style. Farther along the route, at the foot of the volcano range is **Amecameca.** Dominating the eastern horizon, the volcanoes *Popocatépetl* (Smoking Mountain) and *Iztaccíhuatl*

(also Ixtaccíhuatl, White Lady) inspired the Nahuatl-speaking Indians to name the settlement "Place of the Volcanoes." During the 16th century the Dominicans built a church with beautiful Baroque altars and a monastery in the town square. In the eastern part of the little town is the *Sacromonte,* a pilgrimage hill reached on a path lined with the Stations of the Cross. Every year, on March 3, pilgrims climb to the mountain church on top of the hill to honor Señor del Sacromonte—a hermit friar named Martín de Valencia, who lived here. From the summit is a wonderful panorama of the valley of Mexico and its volcanoes. Two kilometers (1 mile) past Amecameca a road turns left to the *Parque Nacional Popocatépetl-Iztaccíhuatl.* After driving 23 km. (14 miles), you reach the ****Paso de Cortés,** at an altitude of 3,580 meters (11,700 feet). A monument here recalls November 3, 1519, when Spanish conquistadors came across the

Reliefs in cloister, Tlalmanalco

pass on their way to Tenochtitlán. In good weather, the view from here extends all the way east to the Puebla valley, and up to the Pico de Orizaba (Orizaba Peak) and the Malinche volcano. From the pass, roads lead to both volcanoes. The easier, and hence more crowded, volcano is Popocatépetl, affectionately called "Popo." Follow the signs for "Popo"; after about 5 km. (3 miles) you reach *Tlamacas Pass* at 3,882 meters (12,800 feet) above sea level. The inns, restaurants, and parking lots here are filled on weekends, and it is recommended that you reserve a night's lodging if you want to stay and climb the volcanoes (call 590-76-94 in Mexico City).

Although the snowy caps at the top of the volcano look near enough to touch, the climb to the highest point, 5,452 meters (17,880 feet), takes from six to eight hours. The best time to set out is between 1:00 A.M. and 3:00 A.M. However, only rugged adventurers in good condition should attempt this climb: The mountain air is thin, and the trail leads through lava rubble, snow fields, and, depending on the wind direction, fumes of sulphur steaming from the crater. But the view into the seething crater is unforgettable. There are several paths to the summit, and it is best to hire a guide.

Scaling Iztaccíhuatl ("Ixta") is even more difficult. It takes about two days to reach the 5,286 meter (17,300 feet) summit. Because this volcano is older, its crater here is no longer visible. From the Paso

de Cortés, continue for about 7 km. (4 miles) toward Iztaccíhuatl to La Joya Inn and the parking area. To return, go back to Paso de Cortés and follow the unpaved road down to Cholula (see page 110).

From Paso de Cortés continue south on Highway 115 (the Cuautla road). After just under 7 km. (4 miles), veer off on a country road to the village of **Ozumba,** 70.5 km. (25 miles) from Mexico City, where there are a 16th-century monastery and an 18th-century church. At the monastery's entrance are some 16th-century wall paintings that have been rather poorly restored; they depict the reception in 1524 of Hernán Cortés by the first twelve Franciscans in Mexico. A short distance away, the road to Cuautla passes through *Nepantla,* the birthplace of the "tenth muse," Sor Juana Inés de la Cruz (see page 22). A memorial stands across from her simple brick house in this quiet village, located 80.5 km. (31 miles) from the capital.

Just before Cuautla is a crossroads, from where it is possible to reach several 16th-century Augustinian monasteries: On the road west to Yautepec (89.5 km., 55 miles from the capital), are the monasteries of *Atlatlahuacan* and *Totolapan,* the latter with frescoes dating from the early Colonial period. About 10 km. (6 miles) from Atlatlahuacan is *Yecapixtla,* with its fortified monastery built in 1540. Shortly before entering Cuautla, a road leads right to the former *Hacienda de Cocoyoc*, now a hotel.

Cuautla, 102 km. (63 miles) from Mexico City, enjoys a mild subtropical climate, thanks to its altitude of 1,290 meters (4,200 feet). Despite its lush plants and exotic flowers, however, the little town is somewhat monotonous, its main attractions being sulphur baths where Spanish colonialists once came to cure their sciatica. Despite its name, which means "Stinking Water," the Agua Hediona is a large, well-maintained outdoor spa with several clear blue pools.

Just under 6 km. (4 miles) south of Cuautla, large sugar cane fields surround the town of *Anenecuilco,* the birthplace of Emiliano Zapata, the revolutionary general whose peasant army dominated the rural south of Mexico for several years (see page 35).

From Cuautla there is a connection to Route 26 which leads to the toll road 115 D and back to Mexico City. You'll reach the turnoff 3.5 km. (2 miles) north of Cuautla. After 10 km. (6 miles) along 26, you'll see the road for *Hacienda de Cocoyoc;* from here, about 3 km. (2 miles) to the right, you'll reach **Oaxtepec,** the old Aztec royal bath. Moctezuma I, ruler from 1440 to 1468, laid out a large botanic garden here. It is said that members of the imperial family were carried here in sedan chairs to bathe in the healing hot sulphur springs. Cortés also visited the soothing waters. In keeping with this long-established tradition, a modern spa was opened in 1964.

Follow State Road 115 D through *Tepoztlán* back to the México-Cuernavaca expressway, Highway 95 D.

TRAVEL ROUTE 7: **Mexico City—**Cacaxtla–*Tlaxcala–**Puebla–*Cholula–**Mexico City (301 km.; 186 miles)

See map on page 88.

This itinerary combines a visit to the Colonial city of Puebla, celebrated for its colorful tiles, with side trips to nearby pre-Columbian ruins and early Franciscan churches. The drive from Mexico City to Puebla (140 km.; 86 miles) takes about two hours. You can tour the town in one day, perhaps also making trips to Cholula, with its massive pyramid-mountain dating to the seventh century, and Huejotzingo, whose beautiful fortified monastery is one of the earliest examples of Plateresque style architecture in Mexico. Ideally, however, in order to explore some fascinating pre-Columbian ruins and several typical Colonial towns, you should plan for a two- or three-day excursion.

From Mexico City, take either Calzada I. Zaragoza or Calzada Iztapalapa to 150 D, the four-lane *Autopista* that leads east to Puebla. As soon as you escape the city smog, you'll see the snow-capped peaks of Popocatépetl ("Popo") and Iztaccíhuatl ("Ixta") rising in the east. Pines and firs line the highway, which leads through the mountain pass that skirts the northern flank of Ixta, 3,150 meters (10,300 feet) high. Continue through the last town in the state of México, Río Frío, remembered as both a carriage stop and a robbers' ambush along the *Camino Real* (Royal Road) that connected the capital and the port of Veracruz. Manuel M. Payno (1810–1894) immortalized this town in his novel *Los Banditos del Río Frío*. From here, the highway descends into the Puebla valley. At *San Martín Texmelucan,* about 94 km. (58 miles) from the capital, pick up Highway 119 north toward Nativitas and Tepeyanco, and take the turnoff to ****Cacaxtla,** 113 km. (70 miles) from Mexico City. This pre-Columbian ceremonial center stands like a fortress on a hill, overlooking the entire Puebla valley up to the distant volcanoes. Just who built these mysterious pyramids and where they came from remains a puzzle. Curiously, the first clues were uncovered by robbers who tunneled through the pyramid walls one night and discovered the remains of pre-Columbian wall paintings. These superb frescoes have now been excavated, and some are quite well-preserved.

From the parking lot, a path leads about 800 meters (2,600 feet) to the excavation site. At the entrance to Building A, a brilliant blue-and-brown *fresco* depicts four male figures, three of them in priestly robes and one dancing. All are framed in a blue decorative band depicting aquatic animals, glyphs, and symbolic ornaments. The oldest fresco, dating to A.D. 75, covers about 22 meters (72 feet) of the base of Building B. It depicts a cruelly vivid battle between warriors of the Jaguars and their opponents, richly adorned in bird ornaments. The figures have Mayan features and are reminiscent of the wall paintings found at Bonampak over 800 km. (500 miles) away (see page 101). Yet the glyphs do not resemble Mayan symbols. An old Indian chronology cites the Olmeca-Xicallanca groups as the area's original inhabitants. But until the glyphs are deciphered and more is known about the relationship of this center with other areas, archaeologists can only guess that Cacaxtla was settled between about A.D. 400 and 1100.

Return to 119, then turn left toward Tetlatlahuaca for about 4.5 km. (3 miles). Here turn left again and continue 11 km. (7 miles) to ***Tlaxcala** (130 km.; 80 miles from Mexico City). The capital of the small state of Tlaxcala, this sleepy provincial town was once the stronghold of a Chichimec group, locally known as the Tlaxcalans. During the 15th century, the Tlaxcalans successfully resisted Aztec expansion, and remained an independent enclave within the Aztec empire. The Tlaxcalans and the Aztecs regularly fought ritual "flower wars" for the sole purpose of obtaining human sacrifices. As a result, the Tlaxcalans had to pay a heavy toll in blood. Cortés, capitalizing on their hatred of the Aztecs, made them his most faithful allies during the conquest of Tenochtitlán.

Today, most of the town buildings have red façades and white door frames, creating a uniformity and monotony that gives the town a closed-in feeling. Only a few buildings remain from Tlaxcala's Colonial past. The *Zócalo*, shaded by large trees, is surrounded by Colonial government palaces and arcades, and by a parish church with a Baroque façade of inlaid Puebla tiles. From the church, cross the Zócalo diagonally to reach the *Plaza Xicoténcatl,* named in honor of the Tlaxcala ruler who initially opposed the Spanish conquistadors. From here, climb to the *San Francisco convent,* built around 1540. Three archways lead to the atrium. This outwardly simple church and tower is resplendent inside—its beautiful dark wooden ceiling, carved in Moorish (*Mudejar*) style, bears inlaid, gilded stars. A staircase leads down to an open *chapel,* one of the oldest of this type in Mexico, with three magnificent arches and Gothic vaults. The convent building now houses the *Museo Regional de Tlaxcala.*

Open chapel (Tlaxcala)

Although no traces of pre-Columbian times survive in Tlaxcala, if you continue along the highway toward Apizaco, about 4 km. (2.5 miles) north, you will reach the ruins of the allied city of *Tizatlán.* Two rectangular altars here decorated with well-preserved frescoes depict the story of the Tlaxcalan wars with the Aztecs. There is also a partially excavated palace in this town.

Only 1 km. (a half-mile) east of Tlaxcala, atop a hill, is the **Santuario de Ocotlán,** one of the most beautiful 17th-century Baroque churches in Mexico. It was built by an Indian architect, Francisco Miguel. The red-brick façade has a rich, white stucco portal featuring columns, figures, and wreaths. Its twin white towers seem to be made of spun sugar. The *Camarín*—the octagonal 18th-century chapel behind the altar—boasts a ceiling on which an Indian artist worked for 25 years.

A few kilometers farther east is *Santa Ana Chiautempan,* center of the Tlaxcalan textile industry, where colorful blankets and *ser-*

Santuario de Ocotlán

sapes (cloaks) are woven and sold at reasonable prices. As you continue along the road, you will see the volcano *Malinche,* or Malintzin, 4,115 meters (13,500 feet) high, named after Hernán Cortés's Indian interpreter.

Continue to *Puebla,* 140 km. (86 miles) from Mexico City.

**Puebla

Puebla (or Puebla de Zaragoza, to do it full justice) is the fourth largest city in Mexico, as well as the capital of the state of the same name. Situated in a high valley some 2,160 meters (7,000 feet) above sea level, it boasts a dramatic setting surrounded by towering volcanic mountains, among them Popocatépetl and Ixtaccíhuatl, both well over 5,180 meters (17,000 feet). Puebla is considered to be one of the jewels of Colonial Mexico, and as such is a must for travellers. Among other things, the city is famed for its *azulejos,* brightly colored ceramic tiles used in murals as well as decoratively in its houses, patios, and 60-odd churches. The *faience* technique common to Puebla originated in the Spanish province of Toledo, brought by settlers from an area known as Talavera de la Reine in the 16th century. In fact, the glazed earthenware made locally is known as *Talavera de Puebla.* While many vestiges of Colonial times remain, the city's economy depends on industry now, especially a large Volkswagen plant, where millions of the ubiquitous "Beetles" continue to be produced for domestic consumption.

Puebla was founded in 1531 under the auspices of Bishop Julian Garces of Tlaxcala as a counterpoint to the nearby Indian city of Cholula. At first it was called Puebla de los Angeles ("town of the angels"), supposedly because of a dream in which the bishop had a vision of a town laid out by angels in a beautiful valley surrounded by mountains. By 1539, the town not only boasted a university but continued to grow rapidly in its dual roles as a stopping point on the road from Mexico City to Veracruz, and as a destination point for goods shipped from Spain's colonies in the Far East through Acapulco and then on into the highlands. A thriving city in Colonial times, it became a focal point of military action in the 19th century. General Scott took the town in 1846 in the course of his victorious march to Mexico City during the Mexican-American War. Sixteen years later, on May 5, 1862, General Ignacio Zaragoza led his troops in a spectacular victory against the French, a battle in which a Mexican force of 2,000 defeated a French force estimated at three times that size, driving them all the way back to Orizaba. This remains the most famous

military victory in the country's history, and to this day, May 5 is observed as a national holiday. (The city had its full name bestowed on it in honor of General Zaragoza.)

The street system of Puebla was laid out by the Spanish in the grid pattern typical of Colonial cities. Since the streets intersect at right angles, a walking tour is easily followed. The center of the city (and the beginning of the numbering

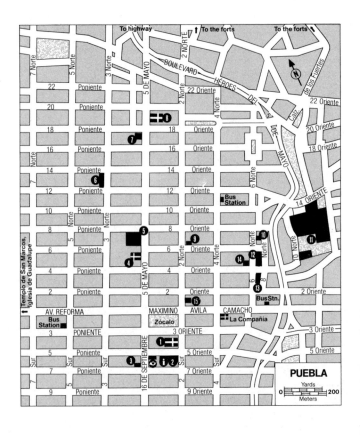

system for the street grid) is the *Zócalo,* also known as the **Plaza de la Constitución.** The central north-south streets, Calle 5 de Mayo and Calle 16 de Septiembre, intersect the major east-west axis, Avenida Avila Camacho and Avenida de la Reforma, at the *Zócalo.*

On the south side of the *Zócalo* is the ***Cathedral of the Immaculate Conception** (1), the second largest cathedral in Mexico (only Mexico City's is larger). The Renaissance-style building was begun in 1575 and not completed until 1649. The portal on the north side of the cathedral features reliefs of the four Spanish Hapsburg kings— Charles V, Philip II, Philip III, and Philip IV. Under the archway can be found their coat of arms. The main portal is a contrast to the rest of the building, reflecting as it does the encroaching influence of the Baroque style. The two tall, graceful towers—the tallest cathedral towers in the country— date from 1678 and 1768 respectively, and the dome is decorated with the *azulejos* for which the town is famed.

The interior of the cathedral is as magnificent as its exterior, with a high altar designed by Manuel Tolsá and José Manzo around 1800, a wrought-iron choir screen by Mateo de la Cruz from 1679, and choir stalls carved by Pedro Muñoz that were finished in 1722. The *Royal Chapel* features a Baroque altar, and onyx, marble, and gilt are the primary decorative materials used throughout.

On the south side of the cathedral is the old *Archbishop's Palace.* The *Casa de Cultura,* the center of Puebla's cultural events, is now housed on the ground floor, and there is a small but popular cafeteria attached to it. On the second floor is the ***Biblioteca Palafoxiana** (2), a library founded by Bishop Juan de Palafox y Mendoza in 1646 and home to a prized collection of rare books. The library is a fine example of the Baroque style, and here, too, *azulejos* are prevalent.

Southwest of the cathedral at Calle 16 de Septiembre No. 505 is the **Casa del Deán** (3), a Renaissance-style structure dating from 1580 and the oldest preserved house in Puebla. Frescoes dating from the end of the 16th century were found inside the house as recently as 1953, and proved to be unusual in their depiction of allegorical themes from a poem by Petrarch (*I trionfi,* 1357) that were illustrated with contemporary Indian symbols.

The **Iglesia Santo Domingo** (4), which dates from 1611, is one of the best examples of Mexican Baroque architecture. In particular, the **Capilla del Rosario* is an astonishing space in which every conceivable surface features carved woodwork, statuary, brightly colored *azulejos,* and an embarrassment of gold leaf. In this temple to the Baroque aesthetic you will find a daily parade of silent worshippers lighting candles and suitably humbled by the awesome surroundings. The statue of the Virgin of the Rosary, patron saint of the Spanish Armada, stands on a high altar, the figures of saints and apostles arranged around her in carved niches.

Just up Calle 5 de Mayo is the *Mercado La Victoria* (5), the primary market for Puebla, which spills out onto the streets. Here you'll find the everyday goods of Mexican life, as fascinating a way as any to obtain an insight into contemporary Puebla. (Puebla is still the place to buy carved onyx.)

On nearby Calle 3 Norte, at the corner of Avenida 14 Poniente, is the ***Santa Rosa Convent** (6), which now contains the *Museo de Arte Popular* and features folk art from the state of Puebla. Its real fame, however, rests on the claim that *mole poblano* was first made in its kitchen. This most famous of Mexican sauces is composed of chocolate, chiles, onions, and upwards of two dozen other ingredients, and can be sampled here at the convent of its origins (see page 13).

The **Secret Convent of Santa Monica** (7), nearby on Calle 5 de Mayo, was founded in 1609 and later dissolved under the reform laws of 1857. In defiance of the secularization reforms, however, it was run secretly until 1934 by several generations of nuns, who used secret doors and passageways to conceal themselves and their activities. It is said that the generosity of several of Puebla's families sympathetic to their cause allowed them to exist, undisturbed, for all those years.

Indeed, there was a secret entrance from the second floor of a private home at Avenida 18 Poniente No. 203 that led directly to the abbess's office. Alas, that entrance was damaged by an earthquake a few years ago, but there's still ample evidence of the secret life here, including a chapel in which the heart of the bishop of Santa Cruz is kept as a relic. Local history has it that the nuns would attend Mass here, which they could overhear as it was conducted in an adjacent church. After the discovery of the nuns, the convent was converted into a museum, which preserved not only the passageways but the fine collection of religious art within the convent's walls.

Across Calle 5 de Mayo is the **Iglesia San José** (8), an 18th-century example of the Baroque style notable for its tiled dome and the use of *azulejos* at the entrance. From here, go south on Calle 2 Norte and then left onto Avenida 6 Oriente, where you'll find the **Museo Regional de la Revolucíon,** or Museo Serdán (9). This was the home of the Serdán family, who struggled against the dictatorship of Porfirio Díaz. Aquiles Serdán, who led an anti-reelection campaign against the dictator, was assassinated in his house in 1910, and his death triggered the downfall of Díaz and the beginning of the Revolution.

Nearby at Avenida 8 Oriente and Calle 6 Norte is the **Teatro Principal** (10), considered to be one of the oldest theaters on the continent. The original structure dated from 1760 but burned in 1902 and was not rebuilt until 1940. If you cross the Bulevar Héroes del 5 de Mayo, you'll come to the ***Monastery of San Francisco** (11). The monastery dates back to the earliest days of Puebla, having been built between 1550 and 1575. Of special interest is the 18th-century façade with its ornate *azulejos* mosaic. The monastery is now a government-run arts-and-crafts center.

Next, walk back toward Avenida 6 Oriente, where you'll find an area known as the **Barrio del Artista** (12). This is the traditional local artists' quarter, but there are now more concessions to tourists than was true in the past. The ***Antiguo Parián** (13), a venerable flea market that dates

Tilework in San Francisco cloister

from the late 18th century, is nearby. Nowadays its business runs more to souvenirs and crafts. Across the street at Avenida 4 Oriente No. 418 is the ****Casa del Alfeñique** (14), known as the "confectioner's house" because of the white stucco decorations that suggest sugar icing on its red bricks and tiles. Besides being a good example of the Poblano style, it also houses the *Museo del Estado,* the regional museum, with examples of local ceramics, period furnishings, and a fine display of Colonial artwork.

The *Casa de los Muñecos* (House of the Puppets) (15) at Calle 2 Norte No. 1, also has a façade worth seeing, this one covered with tiles depicting grotesque half-naked figures representing members of the town council with whom the builder had a dispute. Next door, in the pedestrian zone of Calle 2 Norte, is a fine Art Nouveau façade that once housed a department store. The metal structure of the building was actually brought to Puebla from Paris. Continuing toward Avenida 2 Oriente, two houses from the corner, you'll find a handcraft store called *CREART,* famous for its embroidered textiles from the state of Puebla and surrounding areas. A second shop further down at Avenida 7 Oriente and Calle 16 de Septiembre specializes in ceramics.

Once a flourishing religious center rivaling Oaxaca and San Luís Potosí, Puebla still has some 60 churches dating to Colonial

Casa del Alfeñique, Puebla

times. The ***Iglesia de la Compañía** at Calle 4 Norte and Avenida M. Avila Camacho dates from 1767. This Jesuit church has a Churrigueresque façade and a dome tiled with native blue and white tiles. The sacristy contains a tomb that's said to be that of an Asian princess, Mirrha, who was captured by pirates, kidnapped, and sold into slavery in Puebla, where she languished until she was granted her freedom at the end of the 18th century. In gratitude, she devoted her life to the poor, visiting their homes dressed in a simple cotton blouse and embroidered skirt. The national costume known as *china poblana*, the wide skirt and shawl that is seen throughout Mexico, supposedly originated with her.

At Calle 3 Norte, not far from the *Zócalo*, is the **Museo de Arte José Luis Bello y Gonzalez,** a fascinating private collection of furnishings, paintings, pottery, and wrought-iron.

On a hill in the northwestern part of the city stand two forts: the ruins of the **Fuerte de Guadalupe,** and the **Fuerte de Loreto,** built in 1816, which now contains a small military museum. It was here that General Zaragoza first engaged the French in 1862, and in the museum you'll find artifacts from the battle. The park that now surrounds the forts also contains a monument to Zaragoza, as well as the **Museo del Estado de Puebla,** a state museum noted for its archaeological and ethnic collections.

Puebla is an excellent base for excursions to a number of fascinating towns and sites.

Certainly one of the most popular weekend destinations of Puebla residents is **Atlixco,** just 31 km. (19 miles) south of the city. Surrounded by avocado plantations, this attractive town has markets on Tuesday and Saturday, and a host of attractive buildings, including the *Rosario Chapel* in the parish church on the main square and the Franciscan convent on the Cerrito de San Miguel, where the Feast of Atlixcayotl is celebrated during the last week of September.

From Atlixco, drive 3 km. (2 miles) along the road to Metepec and then turn left for the road to ***Tochimilco.** This mountain village has a fine 16th-century monastery with a Renaissance façade and expansive views of the southern side of Popocatépetl.

Another option is to journey to ***Huaquechula,** with its astounding volcanic landscape and

Franciscan monastery. From Atlixco, take Highway 190 south for 18 km. (11 miles), turn west, and go another 12 km. (7 miles) along a deeply rutted road until you reach the town. The monastery has Plateresque reliefs on the main portal and a Gothic ribbed vault inside.

Still another interesting excursion from Puebla follows Highway 150 southeast from Puebla a distance of about 15 km. (9 miles) to the village of **Amozoc.** There's a fortified Franciscan church in the town, but of special interest are the ornamental smithies where skilled craftsmen create the equipment used by the *charro* riders. Smelting techniques known as *pavona* and methods of encrustation brought from Toledo are used to fashion diminutive silver jewelry such as earrings, cuff links, and buttons shaped like spurs.

If you continue on Highway 150, you'll soon come to the town of **Tepeaca,** about 38 km. (23 miles) from Puebla. In the center of town is a *rollo,* or octagonal watchtower, with distinct Moorish as well as Renaissance features, that was erected in the early 16th century. The Spaniards supposedly used the tower as a public whipping post for their Indian prisoners.

Across from the tower is a house Hernán Cortés supposedly lived in after his defeat at Tenochtitlán in 1520. Also of interest is the massive, fortlike Franciscan abbey that dates from 1530.

Take the unpaved road behind the plaza and head west for 13 km.

(8 miles) until you reach the village of **Cuauhtinchan,** a Chichimec settlement mentioned in the Aztec history *Historia Tolteca-Chichimeca.* The Franciscan monastery with its Renaissance decorative features and two towers was constructed in 1599. The altar is done in Plateresque style and the interior features paintings credited to Juan de Arrué of Colima.

You can return to Tepeaca and take the paved road that runs southwest for 11 km. (7 miles) to **Tecali de Herrera.** In the Náhuatl language *tecali* means "house of stone," and it undoubtedly refers to the landscape, which is rocky and rather forbidding. Once upon a time it was a prime area for transparent onyx, but the supply has gradually dwindled as the quarries have been exhausted. You can still buy the handsome stone from the skilled artisans in town, but you should know that much of it comes from other locales.

Even so, the heyday of Tecali is readily apparent on the façade of the parish church, which is entirely sculpted of onyx. There are also the ruins of a Franciscan monastery nearby and another fine façade, that of the church of the *Convento de Santiago,* which dates from the mid-16th century. The biggest architectural surprise, however, is the round theater that reputedly dates from the mid-16th century as well. Recently restored, there are plans to once again use it as a performing space.

You can return to Puebla on the

road at the Valsequillo reservoir. There is a nearby safari park called *Africam* here, with a variety of exotic animals on display.

From Puebla, follow either Highway 150 D west directly to Cholula or detour south on Highway 190 to **Acatepec** and the *church of San Francisco,* founded in 1560. This church was built in the High Baroque style, typical of the region, known as *Poblano.* Its cheerful façade intersperses blue and yellow Puebla tiles with red brick in patterns that spill over to the columns, ledges, and tower. Inside, the decorations are in gold. Less than a kilometer west of Acatepec is another charming Poblano-style church in the village of **Tonantzintla.** Echoing the playful ceramic exterior of the Acatepec church, the interior of the *church of Santa María* in Tonantzintla is a symphony of colorful stucco ornaments. Over the years, it was decorated by Indian artists who exuberantly blended Christian cherubs and angels with flowers, fruit, and garlands. By contrast, the church's red-brick façade is interrupted only by simple blue and white tiles. Every year on August 15 the church celebrates the feast of the Ascension of the Virgin with music and dancing.

*Cholula is only 12 km. (7.5 miles) from Puebla; it lies on Cortés's route to the Aztec capital of Tenochtitlán. The Spanish conquerors, thinking that the Cholultecs were faithful to the Aztec ruler Moctezuma, lured them into an ambush and massacred between 3,000 and 6,000 people. Recalling his visit, the Spanish conquistador Bernal Díaz de Castillo reported the old Indian town contained as many temples as there are days in the year, a tale

Capilla Real and Tepanapa Pyramid, Cholula

that spawned the legend that there are 365 Roman Catholic churches in Cholula. There are in fact "only" 44. One of them, the *church of the Virgen de los Remedios* (The Virgin of Perpetual Help), stands on the grounds of a much older sanctuary, the ****Tepanapa pyramid.** No more than an overgrown mountain when the Spaniards arrived, the site was used as a quarry for centuries. Although the pyramid is only 54 meters (177 feet) high, its base spreads over 439 meters (1,440 feet), making it the largest pyramid in the world, double that of the Cheops pyramid in Egypt. Inside, archaeologists have discovered several buildings superimposed on each other. The oldest structure dedicated to the Feathered Serpent Quetzalcóatl dates to the Teotihuacán period, perhaps antedating the Pyramid of the Sun there. From the fall of Teotihuacán in about A.D. 650 until the rise of the Toltec 400 years later, this center at Cholula dominated the valley of Mexico. Eventually the Toltec-Chichimecs settled in Cholula, driving the Cholultecs to the Gulf coast.

You reach the various levels of Tepanapa pyramid via an elaborate system of tunnels. There are many wall paintings inside; one depicts a drinking bout, and is drawn in life-size figures; another features butterflies and grasshoppers. There is also a small museum here.

On Cholula's main square stands the fortified *church of San Gabriel,* part of a 16th-century Franciscan monastery. Nearby is the 16th-century *Capilla Real* (Royal Chapel) which, with its many small domes, resembles a mosque. Above its nine naves a vault of 81 arches creates an impressive sight.

From Cholula, follow the old Puebla-Mexico Highway 190, northwest for about 14 km. (9 miles) through a landscape of eucalyptus groves to **Huejotzingo** (192 km.; 119 miles from Mexico City), once the seat of a Chichimec settlement. Strategically located near Puebla on the route to Mexico City, Huejotzingo lies on a fertile plateau at the foot of the volcano Iztaccíhuatl, 5,286 meters (17,343 feet) high. The area was probably settled in the 14th century and quickly grew to rival neighboring territories. Like the Tlaxcalans, the people of Huejotzingo became victims of "flower wars" with the Aztecs, in which ritualistic battles were waged to exact prisoners for sacrifice to the gods. The Huejotzingo formed an alliance with the Tlaxcalans against the Aztecs; when the Spaniards arrived in the area on route to Tenochtitlán, the two tribes short-sightedly agreed to help them. After their victory, the Spanish quickly realized Huejotzingo's influence on the surrounding Indians. They accordingly built one of the first monasteries in the new territory at this strategic site.

Begun in 1525 and completed in 1570, the fortresslike Franciscan *monastery* is an outstanding example of Plateresque style. Note the *capillas posas* (processional chapels) with their pyramidal roofs, as well as the Gothic portals and vaults in the church. The large four-part *retablo* (altar) is decorated with oil panels painted in 1586 by the Flemish master Simon Pereyns. Additional fragments of wall paintings can be seen in the nave and the cloister.

Every year on Shrove Tuesday residents of the town reenact a different kind of ritual from the "flower wars" when they celebrate the capture of the 19th-century guerilla-bandit Augustín Lor-enzo, with costumes, fireworks, and Indian masks.

About 8 km. (5 miles) from Huejotzingo is the monastery of ***San Andrés de Calpan.** Founded in 1548, it features an ornate façade and four *capillas posas* in the atrium. Each is richly carved with flowers and symbols of the Annunciation and the Last Supper.

From Huejotzingo continue north on 190 to *San Martín Tex-melucan* and then pick up Highway 150 D west back to Mexico City, about 94 km. (58 miles) away.

The Central Highlands

The central highlands of Mexico are a diverse area of plains and sierra as beautiful as any region in the country. It's also where you'll find the greatest concentration of Mexico's Colonial heritage. Architecturally, from the fortresslike monasteries of the early Franciscan settlers to the Baroque façades and splendid gilt interiors of the cathedrals in the major towns and cities, this is unquestionably the richest part of the country, and at times you'll feel as if you've been transported back to the 16th, 17th, and 18th centuries. While there are few pre-Hispanic sites in the region, the splendor of the Colonial towns, with their mansions, squares, and patios, more than compensates for it.

The central highlands have an average elevation of 2,000 meters (6,500 feet) in the south and 1,300 meters (4,000 feet) in the north. The Sierra Volcánica Transversal, a volcanic chain of mountains, crosses the country here and boasts the highest peaks in the country, including Popocatépetl, which towers 5,452 meters (17,900 feet) above sea level. (The "smoking mountain" is, as it name implies, an active volcano.) In fact, many of these mountains top out in the *tierra helada* (or "frozen zone"), the above-timberline zone of perpetual snow cover.

The largest city in the region is Guadalajara, Mexico's "second city," which is known for its relaxed pace, its architectural treasures, its numerous murals by José Clemente Orozco, one of Mexico's great 20th-century artists, and its beautiful surrounding countryside.

Also be sure to visit Puebla, the southernmost city of the highlands, located just 140 km. (86 miles) southeast of Mexico City. Puebla (see Travel Route 7) is one of the finest Colonial towns extant, with buildings noted for their brightly colored *azulejos,* or tiles, on both walls and roofs. The city of Morelia (named for José María Morelos, a priest and leader in the struggle for Mexican independence) in the state of Michoacán is also a Colonial gem. It serves as the gateway for nearby Lake Pátzcuaro, where the Tzintzùntzan ruins on its shores, once the ancient capital of the Tarascans, stand as a reminder of past Indian glory.

Guanajuato was built on the fortunes of silver and boasts an extraordinary Baroque cathedral and the infamous Museum of Mummies. The city of Querétaro has managed the remarkable feat of keeping itself on the cutting edge of industrial development while preserving its Colonial heart. Monasteries, mansions, and quaintly lit streets are among the highlights of a visit to this city. Zacatecas sits high in the mountains, another town whose past is inextricably linked with silver mining—a fact that is made abundantly clear by the excessively ornate façade of the cathedral. Dolores Hidalgo lays claim to being Mexico's "Cradle of Independence," the place where Father Miguel Hidalgo declared Mexico's independence from Spain back in 1810. In fact, it was in these towns of the central highlands that the flame of Mexican independence burned brightest during the long, tumultuous years of the 19th century. (Note that if you choose to drive along Travel Route 10, you'll be on the *Ruta de la Independencia*.)

Remember that Travel Routes 8, 9, and 10 can be combined into a longer trip that will take at least 10 days to complete. Even if you can't spare that much time, we urge you to spend some of your visit in the Colonial heartland of Mexico. Even a short trip should allow you ample opportunity to take in the principal sights. For example, from Mexico City, you can travel through Toluca, Morelia, Pátzcuaro, Irapuato, Guanajuato, and then Querétaro. We promise you won't be disappointed. Here in the temperate central highlands, the pace is relaxed, the historical sights unsurpassed, and the travelling among the easiest in all of Mexico.

TRAVEL ROUTE 8: **Mexico City–*Toluca–**Morelia–**Pátzcuaro–**Guadalajara (671 km.; 402 miles)

See map on page 136.

This Travel Route takes you west from Mexico City to Guadalajara, the "city of eternal spring." En route you will have the opportunity to explore the lovely Colonial city of Morelia, as well as other notable sites in Michoacán. The countryside is dotted with villages and towns noted for their various handicrafts, from copper smithing to basket weaving.

The first section of this Travel Route, from Mexico City to Toluca, has been described in Travel Route 3. From Toluca, 64 km. (40 miles) from Mexico City, follow Highway 15 west for 10 km. (6 miles), then turn left and drive 1 km. (half a mile) to the village of *Zinacantepec*. The 16th-century Franciscan monastery here has a Plateresque façade and a large, interesting baptismal font made by Indian artists. As Highway 15 leads into the state of Michoacán, the road becomes more winding and, about 50 km. (30

miles) from the state border, you can turn left to the thermal spa of **San José Purúa,** which lies at the edge of the deep gorge of the Río Tuxpan. About 8 km. (5 miles) past the village there is a well-maintained, older spa hotel situated at the spring. The terrace of the public thermal pool commands a beautiful view of the canyon.

As you continue on Highway 15, you'll go over a high mountain pass, **Mil Cumbres,** which means "a thousand summits"; but even this name cannot do justice to the view it gives of the forested Sierra Madre Occidental. Past Mil Cumbres, you will soon see the Morelia valley and enter Morelia (313 km.; 194 miles from Mexico City).

**Morelia

See map on page 116.

Named for José María Morelos y Pavón, one of Mexico's great leaders during the War of Independence, Morelia is the capital of the state of Michoacán and sits at an elevation of 1,917 meters (6,200 feet) in the Guayangareo valley, through which the Río Grande de Morelia flows. It is truly a gem of a Spanish Colonial city, with unbroken stretches of Baroque architecture lining its streets, arcaded plazas, and broad avenues that will remind you more of Spain than perhaps any other Mexican city. Many of its buildings are constructed of a stone that varies in color from pink to violet, adding to the city's considerable charm. Of course, there are churches, houses, and mansions to be seen (many of the latter converted into banks or hotels), but Morelia is also a university town and as such has a fairly lively cultural life.

In 1530, two Franciscan friars, Juan de San Miguel and Antonio de Lisboa, settled among the Indians at what is now Morelia. By 1537 they had founded a convent and in 1541 they were visited by Antonio de Mendoza, the first viceroy of New Spain, who was enchanted by the surrounding countryside and decided to build a town there. He named it Valladolid, in honor of his hometown in Spain, and soon sent fifty Spanish families to populate the new settlement.

From the beginning, there was a rivalry between Valladolid and the nearby Indian settlement at Pátzcuaro, which had been chosen by the bishop of Michoacán, Don Vasco de Quiroga, as his see. Upon the bishop's death in 1580, however, the prestigious honor was given to Valladolid by a decree of Philip II, and in 1582 the by-then prosperous town was made the capital of Michoacán.

The 17th and 18th centuries saw Valladolid develop into the primary commercial center for the entire region. In particular, the 18th century witnessed the flowering of the town, as the surrounding plantations began to yield great personal wealth to their owners, which resulted, in turn, in the construction of many of the Baroque mansions that still stand on the streets of contemporary Morelia.

It was in the early 19th century that a priest named José María Morelos y Pavón (1765–1815) in charge of two parishes along the coast of Michoacán was offered a military command by another priest, Miguel Hidalgo, during the early stages of the War for Independence. Subsequently, troops under Morelos were successful in wresting control of the states of Michoacán and Guerrero from the Spanish. Morelos then led the first free Congress of the Republic, but was captured by the Spanish after a defeat at the hands of Agustín de Iturbide (who would later crown himself emperor) and was summarily excommunicated by the church and found guilty of treason. He was executed in the town of Ecatepec on December 22, 1815. Soon his fame had grown to the point where he was considered the greatest hero of Mexican independence, and Valladolid was renamed Morelia in his honor in 1829.

With the advent of the reform laws of 1856, church property was confiscated indiscriminately and, unfortunately, some of Morelia's finest ecclesiastical buildings suffered extensive damage as a result. Fifty years later, many of these buildings acquired new façades

thanks to an enlightened populace, and this is what accounts for the sprinkling of Neoclassical and even Art Nouveau touches among the predominately Baroque buildings of Morelia.

Start at the ***Plaza de los Martires** (1), or the Zócalo as it is known locally. It's a pretty setting, with carefully trimmed Indian laurels lining its perimeters, three sides of which have graceful arcades. One of those arcaded sides belongs to the hotel *Virrey de Mendoza,* an 18th-century building with a fine patio.

On the east side of the Zócalo is the ***Cathedral** (2), which is dominated by its two massive towers and a dome covered in *azulejos.* This Baroque edifice, begun in 1640, was over 100 years

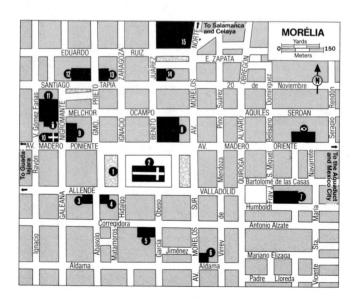

in construction, and wasn't completed until 1744. It was worth the wait: many experts consider it to be the most beautiful in Mexico. The main portal features a relief of the Transfiguration of Christ. The interior, however, reflects the Neoclassical taste popular during the late 19th century, a period when the church was renovated and typical Baroque touches were removed. Of special interest is a 16th-century Christ figure made of dried corncobs, orchid nectar, and sugarcane paste, all of it topped by a gold crown that was donated by Philip II. There is also a superb German organ in the Churrigueresque style and a silver chancel and silver baptismal font suggestive of the relatively considerable wealth of Morelia.

The **Museo Regional de Michoacáno** (3) has a fascinating collection of pre-Columbian archaeological and ethnographical artifacts, furnishings from the Colonial period, and stairway murals by Alfredo Zalce depicting (on the left) those who have had a detrimental effect upon Mexico and (on the right) those who have helped the country. The museum also has a large anonymous painting called *La Procesion del traslado de las monjas* that was done in 1738 and is considered to be a masterpiece. In fact, there is a plaque next to it with an explanation by the great Mexican muralist Diego Rivera detailing its significance to Mexican art.

Across the Calle Abasolo is the **Palacio de Justicia** (4), which houses the Supreme Court of the state of Michoacán. This stately building has a façade redone in a French decorative style, but the interior is in keeping with the Baroque. There is also a famous mural painted by Agustín Cárdenas that depicts the hero Morelos.

Casa Natal de Morelos (5), the house where Morelos was born, was acquired by the city in 1965 and then restored. Documents and artifacts relating to the great man can be seen here, along with narrative murals of his life done by Alfredo Alce. There is a library and auditorium here as well, and the variety of cultural activities includes frequent film showings.

The **Casa de Morelos** (6) (also known as the *Museo de Morelos*) is the house he owned toward the end of his life. Personal artifacts such as his religious vestments and military ornaments are on display, along with various armaments and documents pertaining to the War for Independence.

The ***Casa de Artesanías** (7) is housed in a former Franciscan monastery at the Plaza Valladolid. Here you'll find a permanent exhibition of local arts and crafts, many of which are for sale. The second-floor museum is an especially good one for those interested in tracing the history of the artisan tradition in Michoacán.

The **Palacio de Gobierno** (8) was built in the mid-18th century as a Tridentine seminary, but has housed state offices since

1867. Here, too, you'll find stairway murals by Alfredo Zalce depicting illustrious personages from Mexican history. In the upper gallery, Zalce's frescoes illustrate the history of the town of Morelia, as well as the peoples and landscape of Michoacán.

If you continue three blocks along Avenida Madero, you'll come to the **Colegio de San Nicolás** (9), a Jesuit institution founded by Vasco de Quiroga in 1540 and originally located in the rival town of Pátzcuaro. The college, the second oldest on the North American continent after the College of Santa Cruz in Tlatelolco, which dates from 1537, was moved to Morelia in 1580 at the same time that the bishop's see was transferred.

If you cross Calle Nigromante, you'll come to the **Templo de San Francisco Xavier,** also known as the *Iglesia de la Compañía* (10), a particularly fine example of the rather simple Baroque style to be found in Morelia. Once the Jesuit church for the town, it has been the public library since 1930. Nearby is the **Palacio Clavijero** (11), which was founded in 1660 as a Jesuit school under the direction of Francisco Javier Clavijero. After the school was closed by anticlerical laws, it was used as a prison and storehouse until 1970, when it was enlisted to house state offices, including the tourism office for the state of Michoacán. There is a food and craft market here during the week.

It was Dominican nuns from the Convento de Santa Catarina de Siena who founded the **Conservatorio de las Rosas** (12) in 1590. The conservatory, the first to be established in the Americas, is attached to the *church of Santa Rosa,* a Baroque structure with a unique double doorway that shows the influence of the Renaissance. The Conservatorio was once a girls' boarding school, but since the 1940s has been restored to its original function as a music school, and is home to a well-known young people's choir, the *Coro de los Niños Cantores de Morelia.*

The **Museo de Arte Colonial** (13) at Calle Benito Juárez No. 240, was opened in 1984 and has a fine collection of paintings, religious statuary, incunabula, and early Colonial furniture.

Across the street is the **ex-Convento del Carmen** (14), which dates from 1596. This structure, too, has been recycled, and now serves as the *Casa de la Cultura,* with courses given in theater, literature, music, and folklore.

Just east of the town's center, on the road to Mexico City, you'll see the 253 arches of the *aqueduct,* which was built between 1785 and 1789 to convey water from the nearby hills. The aqueduct runs through what is now a pleasant series of parks along the edge of Morelia.

The **Sanctuario de Guadalupe** is nearby, an 18th-century church that gives new meaning to the word ornate. The **Museo de Arte Contempo-**

Sprawling, modern Mexico City is the largest metropolis in the world.

In Mexico City's Plaza Santo Domingo, scribes write letters for their customers.

The impressive, pre-Hispanic frescoes of Cacaxtla retain their vibrant colors after hundreds of years.

This figure in Santa Maria Tonantzintla is typical of Indian terra-cotta work from the Baroque era.

On All Souls' Day, the Day of the Dead, Mexicans traditionally place offerings, such as these marzipan skulls, on the graves of their dead.

Iztaccíhuatl (left) and Popocatépetl (right) dominate the valleys of Anáhuac and Puebla/Tlaxcala.

The Monument to El Pílipa, located on the Carretera Panorámica, overlooks Guanajuato.

Divisadero provides a breathtaking view of the enormous Copper Canyon in Chihuahua.

Tarahumara women come to Divisadero to sell their woven baskets and wood carvings.

raneo is also in the area, located in the park known as the *Bosque Cuauhtemoc.*

One of the nicest ways to enjoy the marvelous Colonial architecture of Morelia is to sit on the patios of some of the hotels and restaurants scattered across town. The *Hotel de la Soledad* at Calle Zaragoza and Calle Ocampo, a former plantation mansion that was converted to an inn during the 18th century, is especially nice. Another suggestion is *Los Comensales,* a restaurant at Calle Zaragoza No. 148, which has a more intimate but equally graceful patio.

Several interesting excursions can be made from Morelia.

The town of ****Pátzcuaro** (see below), the primary settlement of the Tarascan Indians, is certainly a worthwhile trip and only 62 km. (38 miles) southwest of Morelia. By far the best thing to do, however, is to venture out onto nearby *Lago de Pátzcuaro,* about 4 km. (2 miles) from town. Once there, boats can be hired for trips to the various islands in the 19-km.- (12-mile-) long lake, particularly *Janitzio,* just half an hour away. A lovely fishing village with tile-roofed houses, Janitzio is host to a towering monument to Morelos replete with an inner staircase that leads to the statue's head and affords a terrific view of the lake. If the crowds on Janitzio are too much, go to the island known as *Tecuen,* which is very beautiful and far less populated.

Also be sure to visit *Tzintzúntzan* (the "place of the hum-mingbirds"), the ancient capital of the Tarascans, which is just north of the town of Pátzcuaro along the shores of the lake, and where it is estimated that as many as 40,000 people lived at the time of the Spanish Conquest. Of special note are the terrace and the ruins of the five temples that once dominated the area.

Another popular excursion from Morelia takes you to the Augustinian convents at ***Cuitzéo** and ****Yuriría,** on the way to Guanajuato along Travel Route 10. In particular, the convent at Cuitzéo has a rich, Plateresque façade. The tower dates from the early 17th century and inside are the remnants of what are thought to be the original frescoes. The convent at Yuriría also has an elaborate façade and is unusual in that its style owes more to the Medieval and Gothic traditions than is typically found in the region. At the same time, its fortresslike appearance is a reminder of the Indian raids it was built to withstand.

From Morelia you can continue on Highway 15 through Quiroga (40 km.; 24 miles) and directly on to Guadalajara; or you can take the longer route southwest through Pátzcuaro on the Via Corta, which can be reached from Morelia on Calle Nigromante and Calzada Juárez.

If no other place in Mexico has charmed you, the lovely provincial town of ****Pátzcuaro** with its decorative Colonial architecture will wear down your resistance. It is situated at an altitude of 2,175 meters (7,100 feet) on an idyllic lake near forested volcanic cones; Indian villages dot the lakeshore. *Cerro del Estribo*, about 3 km. (1.8 miles) west of Pátzcuaro's main square by way of Calle Ponce de León, offers the best view of this pleasing landscape.

In pre-Hispanic times, Pátzcuaro was an important center of the Purépecha Indians, who had managed to resist Aztec expansion. But they suffered severe losses during the cruel and abusive conquest by Nuño de Guzmán. Vasco de Quiroga, the Dominican bishop of Michoacán from 1539–1565, who was lovingly called "Tata Vasco" (Little Father Vasco) by the Indians, tried to repair some of the damage caused by Guzmán. The bishop founded some settlements in the area and promoted the local crafts. The villagers here still create the fine pottery, basketwork, wood carvings, copper and lacquer work, embroideries, and musical instruments that became their hallmark under Quiroga's guidance. These crafts continue to find new markets among today's tourists.

Pátzcuaro is a peaceful town of lovely squares and whitewashed, adobe houses with overhanging brick roofs. In the *Plaza de San Agustín* stands a *statue of Gertrudis Bocanegra*. Known as the Heroine of Pátzcuaro for her exploits during the War of Independence, she was executed at the square by the Spanish in 1817. The *Biblioteca Gertrudis Boca-*

negra, a public library in the former *Templo de San Agustín* on the square, dates from the late 16th century and has murals by Juan O'Gorman that depict the history of Michoacán. On Fridays there is a huge market that extends from the Plaza de San Agustín where Indians from all over the lake region sell their wares. Pátzcuaro is known for its traditional Purépecha dances, particularly the *Danza de los Viejitos,* in which masked dancers render a humorous interpretation of the frailties of old age. This popular dance is presented at Indian festivals and in tourist hotels.

Pátzcuaro's main square, the tree-shaded *Plaza Vasco de Quiroga,* is surrounded by two-story homes which hide leafy patios behind impressive façades. Many of these homes have been converted into hotels; note in particular the *Hotel Mansión Iturbe.* The *Palacio Municipal* (the town hall) was also a private home at one time. The *Casa del Gigante,* conspicuous because of its crude brick façade, has lovely decorated windows and a stunning doorway.

Walk from the southeast corner of this square along Calle José María Coss to the 18th-century *Casa de los Once Patios.* This building, which has lost some of its 11 patios, was built as a Dominican convent; it is now a crafts center where you can watch weavers working on wooden looms or lacquer artists making gold-leaf inlays, and buy their products.

From the nearby Calle Enseñ-

Danza de los Viejitos

anza, turn left to the 16th-century Jesuit *Iglesia de la Compañía,* built in simple Baroque style. Cross the Calle Alcantarillas to the *Museo de Artes Populares,* which houses a collection of ethnic art in the former Colegio de San Nicolás Obispo, a seminary founded in 1540 by Don Vasco. It was here that he trained teachers to evangelize and educate the local population in their Purépecha language. Behind the building's brown clay brick walls is a charming garden patio with a well.

The *Iglesia de Nuestra Señora de la Salud,* which dominates the adjacent square to the north, has been altered several times since its founding by Quiroga in 1543. Inside is a 16th-century *Virgen de la Salud,* a Madonna made from

pasta de caña (corn paste), which is a traditional technique used by the Tarascans in their religious art. Processions and Indian dances are held here every year on December 8.

From the center of town it is 4 km. (2.5 miles) to the *muelle* (pier), where you may rent boats on Pátzcuaro's lake. You can take a half-hour trip by motor boat to Janítzio, the largest of the lake's five islands, where the tile-roofed houses cluster along the mountainside under a towering, pompous statue of José María Morelos—one of the heroes in the Independence movement. The island's main source of income was once fishing (which has been replaced by tourism, thanks to the many visitors who come to see the monument) and the knotting of fishing nets is the island's only craft. While in Janítzio, be sure to taste the famous *pescado blanco* (whitefish). The island is also known for its feast of All Saints on November 1, which is celebrated at night in the cemetery with candles and food offerings for the dead.

*Santa Clara del Cobre (officially called *Villa Escalante*), 16 km. (10 miles) south of Pátzcuaro, is the coppersmithing center for the area. The Tarascans exercised this art even in pre-Hispanic times. Copper jars, pots, candelabras, and jewelry are sold under the arcades on the plaza and you can stop at a workshop to watch the artisans practice their craft. A *copper museum* is located at the entrance to the village. The "Feria del Cobre," a large fair with exhibits and crafts competitions, is held in mid-August.

From Pátzcuaro, the route to Guadalajara can be continued either north through Tzintzúntzan and Quiroga or southwest through Uruapan (see page 123). If you wish to go north, follow the road along the lake to ***Tzintzúntzan.** This so-called "place of the hummingbirds" was the metropolis of the Purépechas, as the Tarascans called themselves, at the time of the Spanish Conquest. The origin of the Tarascans, whose language has nothing in common with Nahuatl, is obscure. It is assumed they migrated to the area from the northwest and eventually founded a kingdom under the legendary King Taríacuri at the end of the 14th century. This realm was expanded in the 15th century by conquests ranging all the way to modern Colima and Guadalajara. On a hill above Tzintzúntzan lie the ruins of a *cult center,* a huge

Yácata in Tzintzúntzan

artificial platform, 425 meters (1,390 feet) long, and 250 meters (820 feet) wide, on which stand the remains of five partially restored templelike *yácatas.* This substructure, unusual to Central America, consists of a combination of round and T-shaped components and narrow steps. A wooden temple originally stood on the round substructure. The massive yácata's core is made of loose stones faced with plates of volcanic rock and held together with clay. Two tombs filled with offerings of copper, gold, obsidian, and turquoise were recently discovered at the foot of one of the yácatas. There is a wonderful view from here of Lake Pátzcuaro.

In the town of Tzintzúntzan, visit the carefully restored 16th-century Franciscan *monastery* built in Renaissance style. The frescoes in the cloister depict the evangelization of the Indians. The present-day Tarascans are known for their pottery and basket weaving, offered for sale in the village.

Quiroga, named for Vasco de Quiroga, sits at the northern edge of Lake Pátzcuaro. Woodwork, such as trays and painted chairs, green-glazed pottery, lacquerwork, and other local crafts are sold at the market here. From Quiroga, you can take Highway 15 west toward Guadalajara, past the small town of *Zacapu* with its thermal springs.

If you opt to take the route leading southwest from Pátzcuaro through Uruapan, you'll pass the

Indian village **Tingambato,** with its little-known archaeological zone. The remains here of a *ceremonial center* are built in Teotihuacán style: a pyramid with six steps, platforms with hints of talud-tablero construction, and a ball court. The skeletal remains of 30 people and many grave offerings, mostly pottery, have been found.

The climate begins to warm as you descend from the cool *tierra fría,* the mountainous region, to the *tierra templada,* the subtropical zone.

Uruapan charms visitors with its luxurious gardens and tropical plants. The town has long been renowned for its lacquer work (*maques*), in particular, its inlaid *jícaras* (gourds) and trays. In the center of town, on the main square, is the former Indian hospital *La Huatápara,* now a museum of folk art. The Río Cupatitzio has its source in the nearby **Parque Nacional Eduardo Ruíz** where you'll find pleasant paths along the shore leading to waterfalls.

La Tzararacua is a spectacular waterfall on the Río Cupatitzio, about 12 km. (7 miles) south of Uruapan on Highway 37. Stairs lead down to the cascading water. (From here, Highway 37 continues south to Lázaro Cárdenas and the neighboring beach resort of Playa Azul on the Pacific coast.)

From Uruapan, follow Highway 37 north for 16 km. (10 miles), then turn west onto a gravel road that leads 19 km. (12 miles) to the **Parícutin volcano.** On February 20, 1943, Dionsio Puldo watched in horror as the ground opened in his corn field and emitted a plume of smoke amid subterranean rumbling. What he witnessed was the birth of a volcano which caused an earthquake that was felt throughout Mexico. Within one week the new, firespouting mountain had grown to 30 meters (98 feet), and its sensational spectacle lured scientists and spectators from far and near. Eruptions continued for three years, spewing lava that destroyed several villages and caused thousands of people to be evacuated. The volcano, dormant since 1952, is 2,575 meters (1,600 feet) high and has a crater 250 meters (820 feet) wide and 35 meters (114 feet) deep. To visit Parícutin, you must leave your car in the village of *Angahuan* and travel the last 5 km.

Church tower in Parícutin lava field

(3 miles) on foot or on horseback to the destroyed village of *San Juan Parangaricutiro.* Buried under massive lava flows, only its church tower can be seen above the ocean of gray rock.

Back on Highway 37, 32 km. (20 miles) north of Uruapan is **Paracho,** famous for its hand-crafted wooden products—furniture, toys, and particularly guitars. The *Feria Nacional de la Guitarra,* a large fair, is held every year in August.

Cherán, 13 km. (8 miles) farther, is a large Purépecha village, where the National Indian Institute maintains its regional center. Rebozos (woven shawls) and embroidery are the most notable crafts here.

Follow Highway 37 north for another 27 km. (16 miles) to Carapán where you join Highway 15. Follow 15 west through *Zamora* with its unfinished Neo-Gothic cathedral, and continue past the eastern shore of Lake Chapala. The highway leaves the shore again and continues on to Guadalajara, 671 km. (402 miles) from Mexico City.

**Guadalajara

See map on page 125.

Situated in the Atemajac valley, Guadalajara is Mexico's second-largest city and the capital of the state of Jalisco. The *Tapatíos,* as the local people are known, are strong-willed and independent, traits that are evident in the way they have managed to incorporate the demands of the 20th century into their Colonial city. Streets are broad and public parks are well maintained. The churches and theaters and ornate fountains remain, along with an unhurried sense of pace. Yes, there has been a great deal of modern building in Guadalajara, in particular the Plaza Tapatía, which was completed in 1982 in the heart of the old city, but even with such development, Guadalajara has been able to preserve its remarkable Colonial heritage.

The climate is ideal, as evidenced by the moniker "the City of Eternal Spring." If you don't believe us, hire a horse-drawn carriage and listen to Guadalajara's famous *mariachi* bands sing the praises of their city. The *Tapatíos* have a strong tradition of folk music and dancing, which you will undoubtedly see and hear during your stay. In addition, the crafts of the region, including embroidery, glassware, and papier-mâché, are quite distinctive. You can purchase such items throughout the city. For pottery, however, your best bet is to go to the villages of Tlaquepaque or Tonalá, which are on the outskirts of the city limits.

Guadalajara has the dubious distinction of being founded by Nuño de Guzmán, an unusually cruel and corrupt Spanish conqueror who was also an outspoken opponent of Hernán Cortés. In 1531, he sent Juan de Onate, one of his lieutenants, to a recently conquered area on the Río Santiago; there de Oñate founded Guadalajara, named after Guzmán's birthplace in Spain. The town quickly became the administrative center of a vast area that originally covered the modern states of Jalisco, Colima, Nayarit, Zacatecas, Aguascalientes, and San Luís Potosí. It retained its strong Spanish flavor longer than most new cities, largely because the Indian population in the surrounding area had been so thoroughly decimated. Self-sufficient and actually quite isolated, Guadalajara didn't really begin to expand until the latter part of the 19th century, when it was finally connected by rail to Mexico City.

In the 1940s and 1950s, it began to attract people from other areas of Mexico, and its population grew accordingly. The pleasant climate and the low cost of living also induced many North Americans to retire here, as well as in nearby Chapala, just 43 km. (26 miles) from the city on the shores of Mexico's largest lake.

The most significant feature of Guadalajara is the four plazas that have been set out in the shape of a cross. It's around these squares that you'll find the most important and interesting public buildings.

Start at the **Plaza de Armas** (1), which is marked by a cast-iron bandstand that was prefabricated in Paris, and where the state band plays twice weekly. Across from the square is the **Palacio de Gobierno** (2), the Government Palace, a magnificent Baroque structure that was begun in 1643 and completed in 1744. Inside, you'll find murals by Jalisco's own José Clemente Orozco (see page 20). Perhaps the most famous depicts the Mexican freedom fighter Father Miguel Hidalgo brandishing a torch. Orozco painted with a heavy allegorical hand, often touching upon the problems of excessive militarism and clericalism in his country. You'll also want to see the mural painted by Orozco on the half dome of the building's old chapel, now a meeting room.

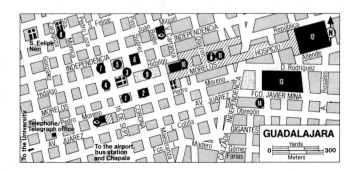

Fresco of Miguel Hidalgo

In the center of the four squares you'll find the ***Cathedral** (3), which also happens to be a good place to orient yourself. Constructed between 1558 and 1616, the building is a mélange of Baroque, Gothic, and even Neoclassical styles. The current towers are not the original ones, which were toppled during an earthquake in 1818. The various chapels boast paintings ascribed to Cristóbal de Villalpando, Miguel Cabrera, and Murillo.

From the front of the Cathedral, you can see the *Plaza de los Laureles* (4), so-called because of the Indian laurels planted there. The nearby **Plaza de los Hombres Ilustres** (5) features life-size statues of the illustrious men of Jalisco who are buried there under the columnar rotunda in a memorial tomb.

The ***Museo del Estado de Jalisco** (6), the regional museum, features archaeological objects from western Mexico, artifacts of the Cora, Huichol, and Tepehuan tribes, and Colonial art, including both European and Mexican paintings from the 17th to 19th centuries. This elegant former Jesuit seminary was built in 1700, and perhaps the most outstanding aspects of its collection

Cathedral, Guadalajara

are the works by provincial artists known collectively as the *Pintura Popular Independiente.* While none of them are known outside of Jalisco (and, in fact, many of the works are anonymous), their sensitive portraiture presents a wonderfully naive depiction of a people and place.

If you cross the Avenida 16 de Septiembre, you'll come to the **Palacio Municipal** (7), or town hall, a modern building that was erected in 1952 but with an attention to Colonial detail so that it would blend in with its surroundings. Of interest here are the period murals inside painted by Gabriel Flores and José Guadalupe Zuno. Just three blocks northwest is the **Iglesia de Santa Mónica** (8), which has a richly carved and heavily symbolic Baroque façade that has unfortunately been left to deteriorate.

If you return to the Cathedral, you'll find the **Plaza de la Liberación** (9) directly behind it. Also known as the *Plaza de los Tres Poderes* (Square of the Three Powers) because the Government Palace, the Chamber of Deputies, and the Court House front on it, the square is the site of a solemn military ceremony every morning when the Mexican flag is raised, and another every evening, when it is lowered.

Across the square from the Cathedral is the imposing **Teatro Degollado** (10), a Neoclassical edifice that was constructed in the mid-19th century during the reign of the Emperor Maximilian. The frescoes inside the dome by Gerardo Suárez picture scenes from Dante's *Divine Comedy.* There is also a full schedule of concerts, theater, and folklore shows that you should take advantage of, if only to see the striking interior.

Adjacent to the theater is the **Plaza Tapatía** (11), a pedestrian mall that links the four squares with the Hospicio Cabañas and the indoor market, and extends beyond the broad Calzada Independencia Sur. Opened in 1982 after a substantial urban renewal effort to clean up the once-dilapidated area, the mall boasts new buildings with expensive, trendy shops at street level, as well as fountains and statues to enhance the parklike feeling it hopes to inspire. It's as fine a place as any in Guadalajara for an aimless stroll and a bit of shopping.

The ***Hospicio Cabañas** (12) was, in fact, an orphanage founded by Bishop Juan Cabañas y Crespo in 1801. There are 23 patios in the building, with the chapel located in the center. The chapel murals were painted by Orozco in 1939, at a point when the entire building was again an orphanage after having served a number of purposes. Not surprisingly, the murals are extraordinary in their blending of Christian and secular imagery, depicting at once both the real and symbolic courses of Mexican history. The dome mural shows the Four Horsemen of the Apocalypse, with the *Hombre de Fuego,* the fiery man of the future, ascending in flames and renewing the human spirit. There are many who consider the murals in the Hospicio to be Orozco's greatest creations. Sketches, graphics, and photo collages relating to the famous painter's work can be found in the numerous other rooms of the Hospicio, which today is home to a cultural institute.

South of the Hospicio, next to the *Plaza de Toros* (bull ring), is the **Mercado Libertad** (13), one of the largest indoor markets you'll find anywhere in Mexico. Locals buy their fruits, vegetables, and herbs here, and you can too, along with a vast array of items geared more to the tourist trade, from leather goods, baskets, and blankets to papier-mâché figurines and a wide assortment of pottery. If you're keen on buying something, you should know that many savvy shoppers forgo this mecca and head instead to **El Baratillo* on Javier Mina (about 15 blocks west of the Mercado Libertad) on Sundays. This free-for-all of a market features a vast array of foods, household goods, and souvenirs, all at terrific prices.

Be sure to visit the **Plazuela de los Mariachis** (14), just around the corner from the Mercado Libertad, when you're in Guadalajara. It's not really a plaza at all, just a narrow street crammed with tables and chairs, but you can sit here and refresh yourself with a drink while competing *mariachi* bands play in the late afternoons. Requests are honored, but be forewarned that the bands expect payment in return.

Next, stroll down the long Calzada Independencia toward the southern part of town until you reach the *Parque Agua Azul,* an oasis of greenery and fountains, a small zoo, and miniature train rides for the children. Situated in the park is the **Casa de las Artesanías,** a terrific place to purchase crafts and folk art from all over the state of Jalsico. Nearby, just across Avenida 16 de Septiembre, is the **Casa de Cultura,** home to the state library and a permanent exhibition of contemporary art. The pavillion of archaeological finds from western Mexico is of special interest.

Walk north along Avenida 16 de Septiembre about 11 blocks and you'll come to the *church of San Francisco,* a mid-17th century structure with an interesting Plateresque façade. The church is built on the foundation of a Franciscan monastery that dated from the 16th century. Just to the west, on Calle Blanco, is the **Templo Aranzazú,** which dates from 1750. Rather unattractive on the outside, the interior is an extravagant example of Baroque ornamentation, with three heavily gilded Churrigueresque altars. You can stroll next door to the adjacent *Jardín de San Francisco* for a moment of rest after taking in the fevered splendor of the church.

Return to the Plaza de Armas and go westward along Avenida Vallarta to visit the *state university,* notable chiefly for the Orozco

The Central Highlands / Travel Route 8 **129**

murals on the walls of its auditorium. These are among the major works in the artist's canon and should be seen by devotees. (Naturally, education is the central theme of these murals.) The *Templo Expiatorio* lies just behind the university. Begun in 1897, the still-unfinished church was designed in the Neo-Gothic style by Adamo Boari, the architect of Mexico City's Palacio de Bellas Artes.

The **Orozco Museum** on Calle Aurelio Ceves No. 27 and Avenida Vallarta is the former studio and residence of the great artist, who died here in 1949. The museum has nearly 90 works on display, including lithographs, drawings, and paintings.

While in Guadalajara, be sure to take in some of the sights in the surrounding areas.

Zapopan, a former Indian-settlement-turned-suburb, is located about 7 km. (4 miles) northwest of the center of the city. If you drive along Avenida 16 de Septiembre, go as far as the traffic circle and then take Avenida Avila Camacho. Zapopan is the site of a Franciscan church, the *Basilica de la Virgen de Zapopan,* that dates from the 17th century and is dedicated to the Virgin of Zapopan, who has been credited with performing many miracles. The walls of the church are covered with the *ex-votos* of supplicants whose prayers have been answered, and Pope John Paul II said Mass here in the open plaza in front of the church on his visit to Mexico in 1979. The statue of the Virgin, a tiny figure with a doll-like head, is brought to the churches of Guadalajara in rotation and displayed for a set period of time. Then, on October 12, it is returned to Zapopan in an impressive pageant that includes dancers and *mariachi* bands.

Adjacent to the church is a small museum that exhibits the folk art of the Huichol and Cora Indians, and offers a variety of craft and folk art items for sale as well.

If you travel north from the city along the Calzada Independencia, you can visit the **Barranca de Oblatos,** an impressive gorge some 630 meters (2,060 feet) deep. The gorge can be viewed from the lookout (*mirador*) at the northern end of the Calzada Independencia, or you can travel down inside it via cable car. Be forewarned, however: it's a very popular place with *Tapatíos* and usually very crowded on weekends.

Of all the towns that surround Guadalajara, perhaps none is better known than ***Tlaquepaque,** once a summer resort and now famous for its artisans and *mariachi* bands, its boutiques and restaurants. While there is a great deal of "tourist" ware, you should be able to find some of the ceramics that the town's reputation is based on. Several small workshops remain where potters work diligently at their craft, but much of the ceramics and glassware the town is noted for is now produced in factories and workshops. Be sure to visit the *Museo Regional de la Ceramica,* located in a charming old mansion at Calle Independencia No. 237. The museum features local pottery from Tlaquepaque, nearby Tonalá, and towns and villages all across the state of Jalisco. While you're there, take a seat at *El Parián,* the central plaza of the town, with its innumerable tables and chairs designed to accommodate your tequila drinking during siesta hours.

The town of **Tonalá,** just 10 km. (six miles) away along Highway 110 or Highway 3 (also known as Avenida Revolucíon), is home to an outstanding pottery tradition that dates back to pre-Hispanic times. The town's carefully painted and polished ceramics first gained notice during Colonial times as a result of the slight odor the finished pieces emitted. Eventually, the locally produced pottery became known as *Loza de Olor,* or "Aromatic Pottery." There is a small ceramic museum in Tonalá, as well, that is located on Calle Constitución in the house of Jorge Wilmot.

About 50 km. (30 miles) southeast of Guadalajara is **Lago de Chapala,** at nearly 86 km. (53 miles) long and 25 km. (15 miles) wide the largest lake in Mexico.

Many of the Americans, Canadians, and Englishmen who have decided to resettle in the pleasant Guadalajara region live near the lake in the towns of Chapala and Ajijic. At Chapala, there is swimming, although the water is not particularly clean, and boats are available for trips to the islands that dot the lake. You'll also find good dining on the large variety of fish from the lake, particularly *pescado blanco,* the local speciality. There is a small crafts market in the town as well. The neighboring community of Ajijic is still somewhat in the shadows of two writers who were temporary residents there, D.H. Lawrence and Ken Kesey. Lawrence wrote his novel *The Plumed Serpent* in a manic, 100,000-word rush here over the course of a mere eight weeks. It is also a town of carefully kept hotels, fine restaurants, and numerous arts and crafts shops, not a few of them run by American retirees.

The town of **Tequila,** the Nahuatl word for the national drink made from mescal, is only 58 km. (36 miles) from Guadalajara and is described in Travel Route 17.

TRAVEL ROUTE 9: **Guadalajara–Aguascalientes–*Zacatecas–*San Luís Potosí (406/473 km.; 244/284 miles)

See map on page 136.

From Guadalajara, this Travel Route arcs north through the old silver city of Zacatecas then east to San Luís Potosí, an important commercial center that has retained its Colonial charm.

Leave Guadalajara via Avenida Alcalde and follow Highway 54 north toward Zacatecas and Saltillo. After approximately 20 km. (12 miles) the road will go through the Río Grande de Santiago gorge and continue through a scenic area of mountains cut by broad river valleys. The surrounding countryside is largely uninhabited until *Jalpa*—168 km. (100 miles) northeast of Guadalajara—which has an 18th-century Baroque *church.* There are two suggested routes from Jalpa to Zacatecas: one via Aguascalientes, the other following Highway 54 due north (see page 135).

If you choose the former, follow Highway 70 northeast from Jalpa another 96 km. (60 miles) to **Aguascalientes,** capital of the small state of Aguascalientes. At an elevation of 1,890 meters (6,200 feet), this former Colonial town with half a million residents enjoys a pleasant climate and is surrounded by vineyards, orchards, and *haciendas* where bulls are bred for fighting. Established by the Spanish in 1575 after decades of brutal fighting with the Chichimecs and other semi-nomadic native tribes, the town

was named *Nuestra Señora de la Asunción de las Aguas Calientes* (Our Lady of the Assumption of Hot Waters) because of the numerous thermal springs in the area (which now attract visitors from the rest of the country as well as abroad). Noted for its pottery, embroidery, and textiles, the city is also known as the *Ciudad Perforada,* or "city with holes," because of the mysterious subterranean passages underneath some of the streets hewn by Indians of unknown origin.

The *Palacio de Gobierno,* in the main Zócalo, is a splendid Baroque building, one of the few left from the 18th century, and was once the palace of the Marques de Guadalupe. The inner courtyard contains colorful murals depicting local sights and industries painted by Osvaldo Barra, a pupil of Diego Rivera.

The twin-towered Baroque *Cathedral,* with its wedding-cake spires, is another relic of the Colonial era. The *church of San Marcos* contains the *Adoration of the Kings,* a painting by José Alzibar, and there's a black Christ and paintings by Andres López in the *church of El Encino.* Another

Patio in the Palacio de Gobierno, Aguascalientes

architectural era is represented by the *Hotel Francia,* built and decorated in the Art Nouveau style in 1916, and popular with locals today.

Turn right at the *church of San Diego* and head to the *Museo de Ciudad,* which features permanent collections of works by Saturnino and Herran, as well as temporary exhibits of other artists. Across the street is the 20th-century Neo-Byzantine *church of San Antonio.* The other museum in town, the *Museo de Guadalupe Posada,* is located a few blocks south of the Zócalo on Calle Colon. José Guadalupe Posada, a local boy born in 1852, was an engraver, cartoonist, and tireless social critic whose work, which is exhibited in the museum, played an important role in turning public opinion against the dictator Porfirio Díaz.

Visitors descend upon the town en masse for the famous *Feria de San Marcos,* a festival in honor of the town's patron saint that's been held every spring since 1604. The fair includes bloody bull and cockfights, as well as art exhibits, poetry competitions, serenades, fireworks, and a large procession. Another lively occasion in Aguascalientes is the *Feria de la Uva,* or grape festival, which is held in mid-September.

A modern thermal pool, the *Balneario Ojocaliente,* stands near the ruins of an older one in the eastern part of town. There are also a number of beautiful parks to run, stroll, or simply relax in.

From Aguascalientes, take Highway 45 north through the

vineyard-covered region that stretches all the way to Zacatecas. The grape vines here require irrigation; blue grapes, harvested in early August, are often used to make brandy. Near Zacatecas, the vineyards give way to a more desolate-looking cactus-and-sage steppe. Turn west onto Highway 49 and drive about 2 km. (1 mile) to the former *Hacienda Trancoso,* a 19th-century mansion, chapel, and mausoleum arranged around a grand plaza. The conical silos of the *Hacienda Tacoaleche,* and a minaretlike tower surmounting its mansion, are visible to the right of the highway.

Continue west on Highway 49 to **Guadalupe**—390 km. (241 miles) from Guadalajara—which is famous for its Franciscan *convent of Nuestra Señora de Guadalupe,* founded in 1707. The convent is now a treasure-laden museum containing a private library and an outstanding collection of religious paintings from the Colonial period (some of which contain intriguing optical tricks). Consecrated in 1721, the church

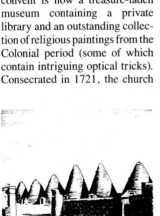

Hacienda Tacoaleche

features a Baroque façade and a high-relief group of the Apostle Luke painting the *Virgin of Guadalupe.* The unattractive tower on the left was added toward the end of the 19th century. The dazzling Neoclassical *Capilla de la Purísima Concepción* inside was the gift of a 19th-century owner of the El Eden gold mine and is decorated with an abundance of gold-leaf. Note also the beautiful parquet floor of mesquite wood, which is laid out in a pattern that incorporates signs of the zodiac with scripture.

From Guadalupe, continue west another 6 km. (4 miles) to ***Zacatecas,** which lies at an altitude of 2,500 meters (8,200 feet) in a narrow gorge at the foot of two large peaks—La Bufa and El Grillo. With its flagstone-paved streets, 18th-century churches and monasteries, and conspicuous absence of modern buildings in the downtown area, Zacatecas has uniquely managed to preserve its Colonial character.

When an unsuspecting Indian presented the Spaniards with a chunk of local silver ore in the mid-16th century, the future of Zacatecas was cast. The Spanish thirst for silver was insatiable, and soon Indians and black slaves were pressed into brutal servitude in the local mines. Granted a charter by Philip II in 1585, the town was built with this seemingly inexhaustible wealth. Nothing lasts forever, though, especially precious metal ore buried in the ground, and gradually the boom times became merely good times, and the good times became not-so-good times as the ore was depleted. Today, Zacatecas is still a mining center, but the nature of the local economy has changed and tourism is now as important to it as silver once was.

Soaring over the Plaza Hidalgo, the splendid **Cathedral,* which was begun in 1612 and completed between 1730–1760, is considered by many to be the finest example of the Churrigueresque style in all of Mexico. Carved from locally quarried red cantera stone (like most of the other Colonial structures in town), the main façade and columns almost seem alive with their exuberant filigreed reliefs. Figures of Christ and the apostles, the four Fathers of the Church, and, in the upper section, God the Father surrounded by heavenly musicians, testify to the blending of European and Indian sensibilities that occurred throughout the country. The dome was rebuilt in 1836. The Cathedral's glories are primarily external, however; the mostly Neoclassical interior, its former treasures removed during the Revolutionary wars and the Wars of Reform, is a barren disappointment.

The *Palacio de Gobierno,* which stands in the center of the adjoining plaza, was built in 1727 for the Conde de Santiago de la Laguna. Today the state capital, the old mansion features fine wrought-iron balconies and a stairwell with a mural depicting the history of Zacatecas. Across the street, the strangely named *Palacio de la Mala Noche* (Palace of Bad Nights) was once the home of a rich mineowner and now houses the state legislature.

The *Teatro Calderón* and *Mercado González Ortega,* both located to one side of the Cathedral, date from the 19th century. The market has been renovated and converted into a shopping center of restaurants and glass-enclosed boutiques, many of which specialize in local crafts and leather goods. The *church of San Agustín,* at one time the greatest sacred edifice in Zacatecas, is now mostly ruins; delicate stonework portraying the conversion of Saint Augustine on the remaining doorway of the side façade is particularly fine, as is the cloister with its Moorish arches.

The new **Museo Francisco*

Cathedral sculpture, Zacatecas

Goitia, located in the former governor's mansion, has a permanent exhibit of paintings by Goitia (1882–1960), which often have revolutionary themes (after studying in Europe, Goitia returned to Mexico to fight alongside Pancho Villa), as well as important works by contemporary native-born painters. The museum is near a well-preserved Colonial *aqueduct* that crosses the end of the peaceful *Parque Enrique Estrada.*

The outstanding art collection of another native son is at the heart of the museum known as *El Universo de Pedro Coronel,* at one time part of a mid-18th-century Jesuit college. Besides the work of Coronel, the museum also features paintings and etchings by Miró, watercolors by Braque, Rouault, Chagall, Léger, and Picasso, a splendid set of original Goya drawings, and a good collection of African and Mesoamerican masks. Next door on Callejon de Veyna is the 18th-century Baroque *church of Santo Domingo,* its plain façade constructed in the form of a "Spanish wall," or *biombo.* Inside, there are finely carved *retablos* in the Churrigueresque style. There's also a beautiful cloister in the former Jesuit college adjoining it.

Dominating the town, and the scene of all its celebratory religious festivals, is the hill called *Cerro de la Bufa,* which is crowned by the 18th-century *Capilla de los Remedios.* A cable car runs from nearby Cerro del Grillo to the top, providing a spectacular view of the town. The *El Eden* mine, which once yielded so much of Zacatecas' gold and silver, now offers tours by mini-train instead (one cavern has even been made into a subterranean discotheque).

If you opt to take Highway 54 between Jalapa and Zacatecas, bear left north of Jalapa on Highway 54 toward Zacatecas. After 45 km. (28 miles) an access road will lead west to the *Presa El Chique* reservoir, a popular fishing and water sports area in the foothills of the surrounding mountains. Highway 54 continues north for another 96 km. (60 miles) to the provincial town of *Villanueva,* where a festival in honor of its patron saint Taddeus is held every October 28. A colorful fair, processions to the *Templo de San Judas Tadeo,* bull and cockfights, and fireworks enliven the proceedings.

From Villanueva, continue north on Highway 54 for 14 km. (9 miles), then turn right at the sign, and drive another 3 km. (1.8 miles) to the archaeological zone of **La Quemada** (or *Chicomoztoc*), where the ruins of a fortified pre-Columbian cult center extend over a barren mountain ridge that overlooks the plain below. Situated in a region that marks the northern edge of the Mesoamerican cultural influence, this settlement probably dates from A.D. 700 and experienced its period of greatest importance in A.D. 900–1000. It was destroyed, perhaps by fire, at the beginning of

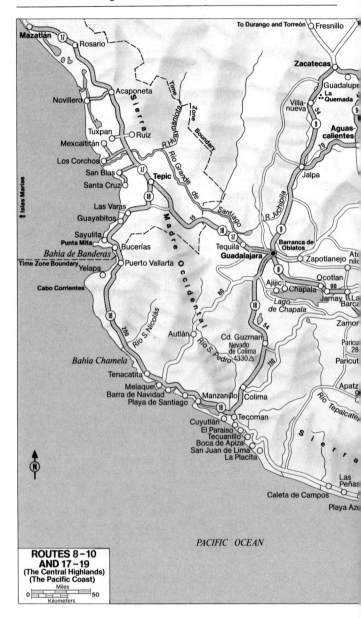

To Durango and Torreón Fresnillo

Mazatlán

Rosario

Zacatecas

Acaponeta

Guadalupe
La
Quemada

Novillero

Villa-
nueva

Tuxpan   Ruiz

Aguas-
calientes

Mexcaltitán

Los Corchos

Jalpa

San Blas   **Tepic**

Santa Cruz

Las Varas

Guayabitos

Santiago

Sayulita

Punta Mita

Bahía de Banderas   Bucerías

Tequila   **Guadalajara**

Barranca de
Oblatos

Time Zone Boundary

Yelapa

Puerto Vallarta

Zapotlanejo

Ajijic   Chapala

Ocotlan

Cabo Corrientes

*Lago
de Chapala*

Jamay

Autlán

Zamor

Cd. Guzman
Nevado
de Colima
4330△

Paricu
28

Bahía Chamela

Paricut

Tenacatita

Apatz

Melaque
Barra de Navidad
Playa de Santiago

Manzanillo   Colima

Cuyutlán
El Paraiso
Tecuanillo
Boca de Apiza
San Juan de Lima
La Placita

Tecoman

Sierra

Las
Peñas

Caleta de Campos

Playa Azu

↑ Islas Marias

Madre   Occidental

Sierra

Río Huaynamota

Rio Grande de

Río Juchipila

Río S. Nicolás

Rio S. Pedro

Río Tepalcate

PACIFIC OCEAN

**ROUTES 8–10
AND 17–19**
(The Central Highlands)
(The Pacific Coast)

Miles
0   50
Kilometers

N

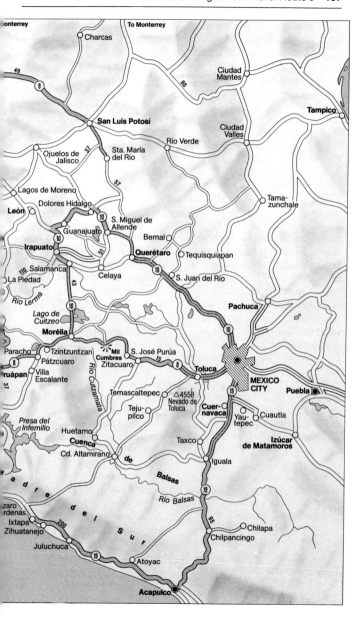

the 13th century. The extant structures are mostly built of adobe brick and layers of small flat stones, which differentiates this site from others in central Mexico. The first complex on the left is called the *King's Palace;* an entrance on the east side of the courtyard leads into the *Great Pillared Hall,* where there are 11 stone pillars, some as tall as 5 meters (16 feet). North of the palace a road leads from a small platform to the *ball court,* an anomaly in this part of the country. The impressive flat-topped *Sun Pyramid* adjoining it has been restored. Higher to the west is a group of buildings called the *Citadel* or *Fortress,* where flights of stairs lead to second and third landings. A five-story structure called the *Temple of Sacrifices* stands in an open courtyard on the third landing. Climbers to the highest level will be rewarded with a splendid view of the entire complex.

Return to Highway 54 and continue to the access road that leads east to Zacatecas (see page 133), 8 km. (5 miles) away. (The road to Chihuahua turns off to the west here, as well; see Travel Route 14.)

From Zacatecas follow Highway 49 east to *Trancoso* (see page 133) and then across a dry plateau to ***San Luís Potosí,** 406/473 km. (251/293 miles) from Guadalajara depending upon which route you take—which sits on a high plateau at an elevation of 1,876 meters (6,150 feet) surrounded by mountains. Capital of the state of the same name, San Luís Potosí is quickly becoming a major commercial center. Despite its urbanization, however, the city, particularly the old section, has retained its beautiful parks and handsome Colonial buildings (most of them built with a red porphyry quarried locally). The area is thought to have been inhabited in pre-Hispanic times by a tribe of Cuachichil Indians. The Spanish under Miguel Caldera began colonizing the area between 1585 and 1590, and with the discovery of silver the town quickly became a rich mining center. By the time Philip IV granted it a municipal charter in 1658, San Luís Potosí was one of the three most important cities in Mexico.

In this "city of plazas," most of the principal sights are found in the downtown area within blocks of each other. The *Cathedral,* built between 1670 and 1740, looms on one side of the central Plaza de Armas, which is also known as the *Jardín Hidalgo.* The exterior has an unusual hexagonal porch with niches for statues of the apostles; inside, one sees a hectic and overloaded clashing of styles. The plaza, with its bandstand, typifies the Colonial *Zócalo.* Opposite the Cathedral stands the 18th-century *Palacio de Gobierno,* now the state capitol, where, in 1867, Benito Juárez briefly ruled the country after his government's expulsion from Mexico City. (Wax figures inside the capitol dramatically illustrate the story of a woman who pleaded in vain for

Juárez to save the Emperor Maximilian from the firing squad.)

The *Plaza de los Fundadores,* one block west on Avenida V. Carranza, is the site where the city was founded. With the exception of the 18th-century Baroque *Iglesia de Loreto,* the plaza is the least interesting in town.

Three blocks south is the *Jardín Guerrero,* a lovely tree-lined square with a fountain, cobblestone streets, and a perimeter of Colonial houses. The *Iglesia de San Francisco,* built between 1710–1719, is on the southwest side of the plaza and boasts a fine Late Baroque façade. To the right of the church, in a two-story Colonial mansion with a patio, is the *Museo de Arte Popular* (with FONART, a government crafts outlet, selling furniture, glassware, weavings, ceramics, and other handicrafts from around the state). Like many of the other old buildings in San Luís Potosí, this one is built of a pinkish-red stone called *tezontle.*

On the southern boundary of the plaza are two 18th-century churches, the *El Sagrado Corazón* and the *Iglesia de la Tercer Orden.* The *regional museum,* on the other side of the square, contains archaeological finds and an exhibit illustrating the development of local crafts, but should be visited primarily to see the *Capilla de Aranzazú* on its top floor, a magnificent example of early 18th-century Churrigueresque architecture. The carved doors are mesquite wood, and the restored interior features rich green and gold stucco ornamentation throughout.

East of the Cathedral is the 18th-century *church of El Carmen,* another splendid product of the Mexican Baroque. Its dome is faced with colored *azulejos* and the façade is covered with intricate stone reliefs. A side doorway within the church, the *Portada de los Angeles,* has a particularly beautiful façade done in a mixed Indian–Churrigueresque style; the elaborate high altar and the golden *Capilla del Rosario* are also noteworthy.

One block south is the severely Neoclassical 19th-century *Teatro La Paz,* designed by the architect Francisco Eduardo Tresguerras, and, across the street, the *Museo Nacional de la Mascara* where

Templo del Carmen, San Luís Potosí

hundreds of old and new masks from all regions of the country are on permanent display.

A pedestrian zone leads from the Plaza de Armas to the colorful *Mercado Hidalgo,* where fruit, vegetables, fish, rebozos, serapes, leather goods, and baskets are sold. The shopping district extends to the Plaza Ponciano Arriaga on Calle Alhondiga, and the large *Mercado de la República* is reached via the shoemakers' street.

Some interesting side trips can be made from San Luís Potosí. **Santa María del Río,** located about 50 km. (31 miles) south of town on Highway 57, is a pleasant little town famed for its beautifully woven *rebozos.* Unfortunately, cheaper machine-made rebozos are replacing the ones traditionally woven by hand. Besides the state trade school near the church, there are now only two workshops where visitors may watch weavers at work. Fine silk cloths are also made here on special order, and local workshops make and sell inlaid cedar chests and baskets, as well. Continue south to reach the thermal baths of *Lourdes* and *El Gogorrón.* About 20 km. (12 miles) east of San Luís Potosí is the ghost town of **Cerro de San Pedro,** where the gold and silver mined in the late 17th century shaped the future of San Luís Potosí. In the *Valle de los Fantasmas,* about 28 km. (17 miles) farther on, the limestone rock of the Sierra de Alvarez has weathered into fantastic shapes.

TRAVEL ROUTE 10: **Mexico City–**Querétaro–**San Miguel de Allende–Dolores Hidalgo–**Guanajuato–**Morelia (553 km.; 343 miles)

See map on page 136.

The most beautiful Colonial towns in Mexico are to be found along this route, which is nicknamed the *Ruta de la Independencia* (Independence Route) as far as Guanajuato.

Take toll road (*Cuota*) 57 D northwest from Mexico City toward Querétaro. Along the way you will pass exits for the Toltec archaeological zone of Tula (see page 79), the basketwork and furniture making center of San Juan del Río, and the Sierra Gorda. Follow 57 D to *Querétaro,* 221 km. (137 miles) from Mexico City.

**Querétaro

See map on page 143.

Capital of the state of the same name, Querétaro has played a leading role in the history of Mexico. A handsome city architecturally, with impressive churches, mansions, and monuments, it nevertheless has a somewhat split personality: Although a busy industrial center, it is at its heart a Colonial oasis mostly free of traffic. Situated at an altitude of about 1,800 meters (5,900 feet), Querétaro has a pleasant, temperate climate, and is a fine place for strolling through well-maintained parks and along pedestrian walkways.

The Spanish founded a town here in 1531 on the site of a Chichimec settlement after defeating a combined army of Otomí and Chichimec Indians. According to local legend, at the climax of the battle the apostle James appeared on horseback in the sky with a lighted cross to award victory to the Spaniards. The Convento de la Cruz (Convent of the Cross) was built on the site, becoming the first Franciscan mission college in America in the process.

During the Colonial period, Querétaro became an important municipal center due to its strategic location between the capital of New Spain and the rich mining towns of Zacatecas and Guanajuato. It also lies at the entrance to the fruitful Bajío region, Mexico's granary. Trade flourished here as a result: Gold and silver from the mines passed through the city as fabrics arrived from Spain and France, silk arrived from Asia, wine was imported from Málaga. A domestic textile industry gradually developed; by 1781 there were 228 looms in Querétaro, most of them used to process wool.

Few Mexican cities can rival Querétaro's special role in the country's history. In fact, the struggle for Mexico's independence began here in 1810 when the mayor's wife, Doña Josefa Ortíz de Domínguez, better known as La Corregidora (*corregidor* means "mayor" in Spanish), warned the rebel leader Hidalgo that his conspiracy had been discovered; Hidalgo then issued his famous call to arms (*El Grito*) that started the Revolution. La Corregidora has been honored as a national heroine ever since.

In 1848, the Treaty of Guadalupe Hidalgo was signed here, ending the war between Mexico and the United States. Yet another dramatic event took place here in 1867 when the ill-fated Emperor Maximilian made his last stand after the withdrawal of French troops from the country; he was ultimately executed along with his

Maximilian Chapel and Juárez Memorial

generals on the nearby Cerro de las Campanas. Finally, Mexico's present constitution was drafted here in 1917.

Today, Querétaro is a bishop's see and a university town, as well as an industrial center, particularly for U.S. firms. Textile companies, grain mills, and processors of the opal found in the nearby hills have been established in a wide manufacturing belt outside of town.

The *Plaza de la Constitución* (1) is a good starting point for a tour of Querétaro, with underground parking available. Across Calle de la Corregidora on the left is the former **Convento de San Francisco** (2), a 17th-century structure that now houses the ***Museo Regional de Querétaro.**

Behind the monastery is the oldest section of town, its picturesque lanes decorated with flowers. Walk along Avenida 5 de Mayo or, to the right of the monastery, Andador Libertad, which is lined with arts-and-crafts shops selling woven goods, embroidered items, and stonework and opal jewelry, to the ***Plaza de la Independencia** (3), also called the Plaza de Armas. This little square, which many believe is the prettiest in Querétaro, has retained its Colonial Spanish symmetry. The modest town hall, built in 1770, is called the *Palacio de la Corregidora* after Querétaro's champion of independence, who once lived there. The high Baroque façade of the 18th-century **Casa*

Escala is far more impressive, however, with artful cast-iron balcony railings and stone decorations around its windows. In the middle of the square is a Colonial fountain with a monument to the Marquis de la Villa del Villar del Aguila, who built the town's aqueduct.

Head east to the *Plaza de los Fundadores,* home to statues of Querétaro's founders. The austere **Convento de la Cruz** (4) was a Franciscan monastery that sent its missionaries to Nueva España's farthest regions. La Corregidora's husband was imprisoned here by royalist forces in 1810, and in 1867 it was the last refuge of the Emperor Maximilian before his execution.

Behind the monastery, turn right off of Avenida V. Carranza and pass the *Pantéon de la Cruz* cemetery, with its monument to the courageous Mayor Domínguez and his wife, on your way to the **aqueduct* (5). Built between 1726 and 1738, it has 74 arches ranging up to 23 meters (75 feet) in height and stretches for a distance of almost 1,300 meters (4,300 feet).

From here, take Calle 16 de Septiembre, a few blocks north of the aqueduct, back into town. The former teachers' seminary, the *Reales Colegios de San Ignacio y San Francisco Xavier,* which dates from 1625, is now part of the Universidad Autónoma. The seminary's main patio was renovated in the mid-18th century, and the church, with its ornate pillars, is

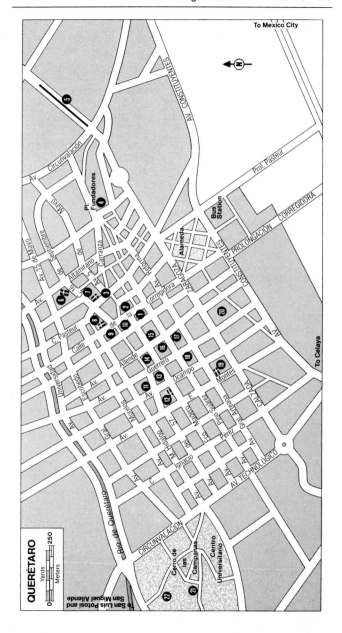

now the *Parroquia Santiago* (6), or parish church.

The next stop is the **Santuario de la Congregación** (7), a once-magnificent old church consecrated in 1680; only a painting by Miguel Cabrera of the Virgin of Guadalupe, a Baroque organ front, and cast-iron railings in the atrium and choir have been preserved, however.

Calle 16 de Septiembre leads to the *Paseo de la Corregidora,* a delightful street lined with 18th- and 19th-century mansions. Here, too, is the *Plaza de la Libertad,* with its monument to La Corregidora. It's also a pleasant place to stop for refreshments, with a number of nice outdoor cafés and restaurants.

At the corner of Calle Corregidora and Calle A. Peralta is another small square that was once the atrium of the **Convento de San Antonio** (8), begun in 1613 by the Franciscans. The church, with its single tower, has lost most of its treasures over the centuries, but the small, serene cloister is still intact.

The **Teatro de la República** (9), inaugurated in 1852, was the scene of two major events in Mexican history. Emperor Maximilian's death sentence was pronounced here in 1867; and 50 years later, it was the place where Mexico's present constitution was proclaimed.

From here you can see the **Jardín Obregón** (10), a tree-shaded square with a music pavilion. Once part of the Convento San

Francisco's atrium, it is now Querétaro's Zócalo. The beautiful *Gran Hotel,* built in the late 18th century to cater to Querétaro's most elegant guests, now offers only spartan accommodations.

West of Calle Corregidora are the 18th-century Carmelite *Convento del Carmen,* at Av. Morelos, and the Capuchin **Convento de Capuchinas** (11), at Avenidas Ocampo and Hidalgo. The latter, which has tall flying buttresses and simple bell towers, is now the state headquarters of Mexico's governing PRI party.

Next, walk south along Av. Ocampo to the **Cathedral** (12), which was begun in 1763. Unlike cathedrals elsewhere in Mexico, it has no plaza. On the other side of the avenue is the former *Palacio de Gobierno* (13), a Neoclassical structure built in the late 1700s as a town house.

From here, walk a short distance on Avenida Madero in the direction of the Jardín Obregón until you come to the **Templo de Santa Clara** (14). The interior of this early 17th-century structure features delicately sculptured and gilded Baroque side altars, a beautiful sacristy door with Churrigueresque carving, and lovely cast-iron railings. In the convent's former atrium is the *Fountain of Neptune,* which was designed in the late 18th century by Francisco Eduardo Tresguerras, the best-known Mexican architect working in the Neoclassical style.

Diagonally across the street is the 18th-century *Hostería de la*

Marquesa (15), a private home built in a kind of "Moorish Baroque" style. Continue on Calle Allende to the corner of Calle Pino Suárez, where you'll find the **Palacio Federal** (16), the government office building and main post office, and once an Augustinian monastery. The Baroque relief decoration of the main patio is particularly beautiful.

At Calle Allende No. 16, past the corner of Calle Pino Suárez, is the 18th-century **Casa de los Perros** (House of Dogs) (17), named for the shape of its water spouts.

The Dominicans built the **Convento de Santo Domingo de Guzmán** (18) at the corner of Pino Suárez and Guerrero, and its severe Renaissance façade is an interesting contrast to the Baroque decoration on the *Rosary Chapel* inside, which was designed by Ignacio Mariano de las Casas. The architect's masterpiece, however, is considered to be the ***Church of Santa Rosa Viterbo** (19) on Avenida General Arteaga. Its slender tower and the double rolls of the flying buttresses are particularly noteworthy. Inside, art connoisseurs will admire the main altar; the Churrigueresque-style altar walls with their gilded carvings, paintings, statues, and cast-iron railings; and the chancel, which is slightly Oriental in style. The monastery buildings now house a school of graphic arts.

The new *market* (20) on Calle Guerrero, south of the wide Calzada Zaragoza, is worth a visit.

To get there, follow Calzada Zaragoza southwest, then take Avenida Technológica to the university campus situated along the Cerro de las Campanas. This is also the site where Emperor Maximilian and his two faithful generals, Miramón and Mejía, were executed on the morning of June 19, 1867, an event that was movingly and brilliantly captured for posterity in a painting by Edouard Manet. On that morning, Maximilian gave each member of the firing squad a gold coin, then said: "Mexicans, I am dying for a just cause, for the freedom and independence of Mexico. May mine be the last blood shed for the happiness of my new home. Long live Mexico!"

Sometime around the turn of the century, the House of Hapsburg ordered a Neo-Gothic chapel built on the site of Maximilian's execution. In 1967, a monument to Benito Juárez was erected on top of the hill, thereby symbolizing the triumph of the Republic over the Empire.

From Querétaro you can visit **San Juan del Río,** 55 km. (34 miles) southeast on Highway 57 D. This is a popular tourist stop due to its pleasant climate and thermal baths. It's also a local center for basket weaving and furniture making. Nearby resort hotels offer horseback riding, golf, and tennis. **Tequisquiapan** is a pretty spa surrounded by vineyards some 20 km. (12 miles) northeast of San Juan del Río on Highway 120. The three thermal baths are named *El Relox, El Centenario,* and *La Peña.* Water sports are also offered here, including fishing in the reservoir.

There are a number of other interesting stops along Highway 120. **Cadereyta,** 50 km. (31 miles) north of San Juan del Río, is a charming Colonial town. One of its 18th-century buildings, the *church of San Pedro y San Pablo* houses a museum of religious art. The cactus farm known as *Quinta Schmoll* is also an unusual attraction that's open to the public. Cadereyta also has a village festival every February 1–2, with a colorful procession, lots of folk dancing, and the requisite cockfighting. Highway 120 continues through the ****Sierra Gorda,** the mountainous region where the Franciscan Junípero Serra (1713–1784) and other monks did missionary work among the Pame and Jonaz Indians in the mid-18th century. The tribes, which had successfully resisted earlier attempts at conquest and conversion, were settled within a few years of Serra's arrival. When he and his fellow missionaries were ordered to California to continue their work, the five mission stations they had established here fell into ruins. Fortunately, they were carefully rebuilt a few years ago, and the Baroque church façades built by the mountain Indians can be appreciated once again in towns such as *Jalpan, Conca, Landa,* and others along Highway 120.

From Querétaro, Avenida Hidalgo leads into Highway 57, which you follow for 30 km. (18 miles) until you reach the turnoff to ****San Miguel de Allende,** one of the few Colonial towns in Mexico to be designated a national monument. (As you drive into town there's a good panorama to be seen from the *mirador,* or lookout, at the Allende monument. It's especially spectacular in early summer, when brightly colored wildflowers cover the nearby hills.)

Lying in a lovely valley on a sloping hillside, San Miguel's charming architecture and agreeable climate have enticed many a transient and expatriate to stay indefinitely. In addition, the artists and craftsmen who flock here, and the many schools and colleges devoted to language and the fine arts, have made it a center of intellectual and artistic life.

There were a number of Chichimec and Tarascan settlements in the valley in pre-Columbian times. Juan de San Miguel, a Franciscan friar, established a mission here in 1542, naming it San Miguel de los Chichimecas; the village was then given provincial town status in 1555. During the ensuing Colonial period, wealthy mineowners and landowners built their houses, many of which still stand. The town was renamed in 1862 for its most famous son, Ignacio Allende, who helped lead the rebellious *criollo* forces in the early stages of the Mexican War of Independence.

The principal landmark of the town, the Neo-Gothic *church of*

San Miguel, which was re-fashioned out of an earlier structure in 1880, rises above the main square. The architect of the renovation, Zeferino Gutiérrez, was an uneducated mason who sketched his preliminary designs (which he based on European cathedrals he had admired in postcards) in the sand with a stick. A much-revered 16th-century statue of Cristo de la Conquista (Lord of the Conquest) fashioned by Indians out of a mixture of cornstalk paste and crushed orchid tubers, is located in a chapel to the left of the main portal. Tombs in the crypt include that of former Mexican president General Anastasio Bustamente (1770–1853), and the *camarín* behind the high altar was done by Francisco Eduardo Tresguerras. The imposing *Casa del Mayorazgo de Canal,* mingling Baroque and Neoclassi-cal features, and with a pleasant inner courtyard, stands at the northwest corner of the square. Two noteworthy 18th-century Colonial buildings, the *Posado de San Francisco* and the *town hall,* can be found just down the street on the north side of the square.

Just north of the Cathedral is the tower of the *Capilla de San Rafael* which Gutiérrez also remodeled in a pseudo-Gothic style. The tourist bureau and a restaurant are located in the former halls of the *Mercado Aldama* nearby.

The house with Baroque ornamentation across the street from the Cathedral is the birthplace of the town's most famous citizen, Ignacio Allende. Several other noteworthy houses surround the square. Visitors are given an opportunity to see many of the town's most attractive houses (most of which are hidden away behind unassuming Moorish-style façades) every Sunday at 11:30 A.M. on special house-and-garden tours that leave from the public library.

Next, turn right from Calle Umaran onto Calle Dr. Hernández Macías and walk one block to the *Convento de la Concepción.* Today, the beautiful tree-shaded cloister houses "El Nigromante," a state-run school under the aegis the National Institute of Fine Arts. The church's splendid dodecagonal dome, which was completed in 1891, was designed by the omnipresent Zeferino Gutiérrez.

Continue walking along Calle Dr. Hernández Macías and then

San Miguel de Allende

turn right on Calle Mesones until you reach the *Iglesia de San Francisco,* a late-18th-century structure with a Churrigueresque façade and tall Neoclassical tower. Another ubiquitous figure in San Miguel, Eduardo Tresguerras, is said to have designed the Neoclassical interior. A small park in front of the church contains a monument to Columbus. On the west side is the 17th-century *Iglesia de la Tercer Orden* (the Third Order was established by Franciscans for laymen who wished to become monks or nuns on a trial basis). The old mail-coach station, *Casa de las Postas,* is also on the plaza.

Two blocks north across Calle Mesones is the *Iglesia de San Felipe Neri,* which was founded in 1712 to replace a *mestizo* church. Nevertheless, its façade of pink stone, and the statues of saints in various niches, exhibit the influence of Indian masons and stone carvers. There are a number of paintings inside, including 33 scenes from the life of Saint Philip Neri, which are attributed to Miguel Cabrera. The *Chapel of Santa Casa de Loreto* to the left of the Neoclassical altar is a copy of the Italian original. Passages on either side lead to an octagonal room called a *camarín,* which contains one Neoclassical and five Baroque altars, the latter noteworthy for the carved and gilded Churrigueresque ornamentation of their *retablos.*

The *Iglesia de Nuestra Señora de la Salud* adjoins San Felipe Neri on the east. Its early Chur-

rigueresque façade has a large conch shell containing the "Eye of God" in its top half, and works by Miguel Cabrera, Antonio Torres, and Tomas Xavier de Peralta can be seen inside. The former *Colegio de San Francisco de Sales,* which now houses a small crafts market, is also nearby. (The regular market is scattered throughout town and takes place on weekends.)

Of course, as you'll quickly realize, the real charm of San Miguel de Allende lies in its narrow cobblestoned streets lined with lovely houses painted in pastel colors. Take some time to wander these streets and experience the ambience of a different culture. At the same time, many hotels, restaurants, and bars have opened in recent years, as well as two art schools and a number of galleries and boutiques, so that the town has acquired a somewhat sophisticated, international flair. Collectors as well as less serious shoppers should keep an eye out for woven straw and hand-embroidered products, tin objects worked by local Indians, and wrought-iron pieces produced in backyard forges.

From San Miguel de Allende, travel north on Highway 51 for 15 km. (9 miles), then turn west and continue for 2 km. (1 mile) until you reach **Atotonilco,** a popular pilgrimage site where the shade next to tree-lined canals and brooks provides a welcome respite from the aridity of the surrounding countryside. The convent here, which was established in 1740, has a much-venerated statue of Christ the Redeemer. The 18th-century *El Santuario de Jesús Nazareno* is filled with frescoes depicting various folk themes (most by Miguel Antonio Martínez de Pocasangre), as well as a number of paintings (including works by Juan Correa). It is also said that the Mexican independence leader Miguel Hidalgo seized a banner with the image of the Virgin of Guadalupe from the church and carried it into battle.

Farther north on Highway 51, you will enter **Dolores Hidalgo,** 326 km. (202 miles) from Mexico City, a lively provincial town at an altitude of 1,990 meters (6,500 feet), which claims to be Mexico's "Cradle of Independence." It was here on September 15, 1810, that Father Miguel Hidalgo, a parish priest, launched the Mexican War of Independence with his famous *Grito* (cry) *de Dolores* (a scene that is now an important part of the annual Independence Day festivities on the Zócalo in Mexico City).

Not surprisingly, the first thing you'll notice on driving into town is a monument to the rebels of 1810. Dominating the *Jardín Hidalgo,* the main square, is the *parish church* (1712–1778) with its Churrigueresque façade. Inside, there are two impressive *retablos* in the same style; the one on the left contains a richly gilded Virgin of Guadalupe. Also on the main square is a bronze statue of Hidalgo, the *Padre de la Patria,* or "father of his country." Hidalgo's

home, the *Casa de Don Miguel Hidalgo,* is just two blocks away and contains historical artifacts of the great man's life.

From Dolores Hidalgo, it's a 54 km. (33 mile) drive southwest on Highway 110 to *Guanajuato* (380 km., 235 miles, from Mexico City).

**Guanajuato

See map on page 151.

This Colonial city has a splendid mountain setting, imposing buildings, and a fascinating history. What may intrigue you most, however, is Guanajuato's street plan—or lack of one. The city's tangled labyrinth includes a street that tunnels underground and another so narrow it is said two people can kiss each other from windows on opposite sides. While in Guanajuato, you'll almost surely want to indulge in the local pastime of meandering the streets, with no particular destination in mind, just for the fun of it.

Set in a narrow valley at an altitude of 2,000 meters (6,500 feet), Guanajuato did not grow according to a plan, unlike most of Mexico's Colonial cities; instead, it followed the fortunes of the surrounding silver mines. Today, this former wealth is evident in its impressive churches and public buildings. Visitors are also drawn to its annual Festival Cervantino, the largest international festival of theater, dance, and music in all of Latin America.

Silver was discovered in the surrounding mountains barely 20 years after the conquest of Cuanaxhuato (Tarascan for "place of the frogs") by Nuño Beltrán in 1529. The settlement grew quickly as camps and fortifications to ward off Indian attacks were built. A college was founded in 1732, and the town gained official status from the Spanish crown in 1741.

By 1800, the surrounding region was producing a quarter of all the silver mined in Mexico. When the War of Independence began, Guanajuato was the site of the first major battle. The victory by Father Hidalgo's rebel army in 1810 was short-lived, however; a year later, the heads of Hidalgo and three of his aides were put on display here by the Royalists. Guanajuato also played an important role during the reform wars of the middle part of the century, when Benito Juárez made the city Mexico's capital for less than a month in 1858.

During the reign of Porfirio Díaz, the local mines were taken over by foreign multinational companies, and the city's buildings from that period—the Teatro Juárez, the Mercado Hidalgo, and the Palacio Legislativo—attest to their profits.

Parking is hard to find in the center of town, and a car can be a handicap. Still, there are a couple of places in Guanajuato where a car comes in handy: to take you up to the ****Carretera Panorámica** for a delightful view of the town, and to drive through ****Avenida Miguel Hidalgo**, the underground street. The avenue was laid out in the 1960s along with a drainage system designed to save the narrow valley from catastrophic floods in the rainy season. Part of the avenue runs above ground affording a view of houses that span or face the riverbed. But the system is constantly being expanded to ease traffic congestion.

Nevertheless, the ubiquitous blue minibuses are still the best means of transportation through the maze of narrow streets in the center of town. Start at the small, triangular-shaped **Jardín de la Unión** (1) the prettiest and most popular of Guanajuato's plazas. The *Posada Santa Fé* here, which

Underground street in Guanajuato

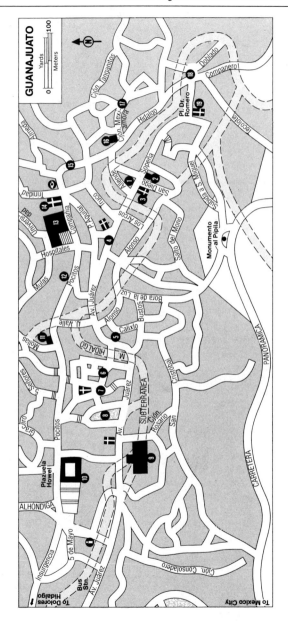

dates to 1862, is the oldest hotel in town. The main building on the plaza is the **Teatro Juárez** (2), inaugurated in 1903 by Porfirio Díaz. Built in the Neoclassical style, it has a columned porch crowned with statues of the muses and an opulent interior. To the right of the theater is the *Iglesia de San Diego* (3), with a richly ornamented Churrigueresque façade dating from 1780.

Continue northwest to the **Plaza de la Paz** (4). About the same size but less crowded than the Jardín de la Unión, it's lined with some of the city's finest buildings, including the former residences of the 18th-century silver barons Pérez Gálvez and Rul y Valenciana. At the upper end of the plaza is the resplendent **Basílica Nuestra Señora de Guanajuato,** a massive Baroque structure built in the late 17th century. Inside the church is a venerated wooden statue of the Virgin given to the city by King Philip II of Spain in 1557.

If you continue your tour along the Avenida Juárez, you'll notice a *Colonial-style house with an eagle emblem* (5) on your left that dates to the early 17th century. Until 1824, it housed the Royal Bureau of Standards, whose job it was to control the weight of silver bars.

Across from it is the beginning of Calle de la Libertad, which leads to the *Plazuela de San Fernando* (6), and from there to the **Plazuela de San Roque** (7). This picturesque little square is the open-air setting for the

Entremeses Cervantinos, comic one-act plays by the Spanish author Miguel Cervantes (1547–1616) that are performed as part of the larger Festival Cervantino.

A staircase leads down to the **Jardín de la Reforma,** or *Jardín Morelos* (8), another square graced with a fountain and tall laurel trees. From here, the Avenida Juárez leads past the *Templo de Belén* (Church of Bethlehem) to the **Mercado Hidalgo** (9), an indoor market that dates to 1910. The iron framework and various elements of Art Nouveau architecture reflect the European taste of the period.

Nearby is one of the city's most important structures, the **Alhóndiga de Granaditas** (10). Built as a granary at the end of the 18th century, the building was used in 1810 by Guanajuato's royalists as a fortification against Hidalgo's approaching army. A miner later immortalized as El Pípila ("the little turkey") set fire to the entrance, losing his life in the process but enabling the rebels to take the warehouse and city—if only for a short time. (A huge monument to the hero now overlooks the town.) There is more grisly history here, as well: The four corners of the Alhóndiga still have the hooks where cages were hung to contain the heads of Hidalgo and three of his compatriots. Now a historic museum, the building also houses a very good exhibit on the history of silver mining.

The ***Casa Diego Rivera**

(11), at Calle Pocitos No. 67, is the birthplace of the famous muralist and a lovely example of the narrow two-story residences typical of Guanajuato. It has been restored and is now a museum with a permanent exhibit of the artist's paintings.

Just down the street at No. 7 is the ***Museo del Pueblo de Guanajuato** (12), a former residence of the Marquis de Rayas, who was knighted for his work in developing the area's silver mining and agriculture. The late 17th-century house features unusual wooden columns in its patio and a Baroque chapel, as well as a fine collection of paintings, statues, and ceramics inside.

Guanajuato's impressive **University** (13) is descended from the Jesuit college founded here in 1732. The main building itself is modern, constructed in 1955 in a Moorish style, but is intended to match the town's Colonial architecture.

Adjacent to the university is the Jesuit **Iglesia de la Compañía** (14), which dates from the mid-18th century; its Churrigueresque façade is decorated with stone ornaments so delicate they seem to have been carved from wood.

A short distance away at the *Plazuela del Baratillo* (15) is *El Agora del Baratillo,* a cultural center housing *Casa de Artesanías,* which displays old and new faïences, as well as other arts and crafts.

For a pleasant walk up from the center of town, take the Callejón de Mexiamora past the *Teatro Principal* (16). As the noise of traffic diminishes, small squares will appear as if by magic, their fountains and balconies bedecked with flowers. The *callejónes* (alleyways) grow ever narrower, until some are little more than stairs that lead to a front door.

To return to the center of town, walk along Callejón Hinojo from the *Plazuela Acosta* to the *Plaza Mexiamora* (17), and from there down to the *Plazuela del Ropero* (18).

The long round trip ends at the Jardín de la Unión after a right turn on Calle Sopeña; on the way, you'll pass the *Iglesia de San Francisco* (19) and the old mint, which is now a hotel.

There are a number of interesting side trips from Guanajuato. Several access roads lead to the 24-km. (15-mile) highway called the ****Carretera Panorámica** that runs along the barren mountaintops, almost circling Guanajuato's narrow valley. Follow it

Former mine in Guanajuato

south to the *Monumento al Pípila,* which commemorates the hero who set fire to the Alhóndiga, and affords the most beautiful views of the town. (Note to photographers: The best light here is in the afternoon.)

Continue east on the highway past the turnoff to the *Presa de la Olla,* a reservoir and park laid out in the mid-18th century. On the north side of the gorge is the old *Mina de Rayas,* still working, and below it the *Mina San Vicente.* The scenic highway ends shortly beyond these two mines.

A bit farther on, along the valley road, is a charming miners' church, the **Templo de la Cata,* with a beautiful Churrigueresque façade.

The ****Iglesia de la Valenciana** lies 4 km. (2.5 miles) from town on the road to Dolores Hidalgo. Built between 1765 and 1788 by the Conde de Valenciana, Don Antonio de Obregón y Alcocer, who was the first owner of the Valenciana mine, it is a jewel of Mexican Baroque architecture, adorned both inside and out with delicate stone sculptures. The three gilded rococo altars are equally rich in ornamentation.

The Calzada de Tepetapa leads from the railway station in Guanajuato to the **Pantéon Municipal** cemetery, a must for those with a taste for the macabre: About 100 mummies are on display here in the *Museo de las Momias,* unintentionally preserved due to some peculiarity of the soil. Follow Highway 110 out of Guanajuato for an unforgettable side trip to the

towering **Cerro del Cubilete,** with an elevation of 2,480 meters (8,134 feet) and a colossal 23-meter- (75-foot-) tall bronze statue of *El Cristo Rey* (Christ the King) astride its summit. To reach it, drive 7 km. (4 miles) toward Silao and then turn right at the sign onto a twisting 19-km. (12-mile) road. The staircase inside the statue climbs 20 meters (65 feet) and provides splendid panoramic views of the fertile plateau of the Bajio and the forested hills of the surrounding countryside. Much visited by pilgrims, the Cerro is also considered to be the geographical center of Mexico.

From Guanajuato follow Highway 45 southeast 20 km. (12 miles) to **Irapuato,** one of the oldest Colonial settlements in Mexico (c. 1547) and the center of what is probably the largest strawberry-growing area in the world. Situated at an altitude of 1,730 meters (5,674 feet), this rapidly growing city has a number of architectural gems, including the *Templo de Guadalupe* and the *Templo de San Francisco.* The latter contains two paintings of the Virgin, one by Miguel Cabrera and the other by Francisco Eduardo Tresguerras. *Iglesia del Hospital* has a Churrigueresque façade dating from 1713, and the *Palacio Municipal* is a Neoclassical structure. The annual strawberry fair begins on April 2, and the town's founding is commemorated with another festival on February 15.

Leaving Irapuato, cross the

direct road (the Via Corta) that runs between Mexico City (327 km.; 203 miles) and Guadalajara (256 km.; 159 miles) and continue another 20 km. (12 miles) on Highway 45 to **Salamanca,** a city that's pleasantly situated on the north bank of the Río Lerma in the middle of a fertile plateau. Best known for its oil-refining industry, the town's real treasure is the *church of San Agustín,* with one of the most richly decorated interiors in Mexico. Begun in 1615, the church has a sober façade, with a carved crucifix under a conch shell at its apex. The interior, on the other hand, is almost entirely covered with painted and gilded paneling. The two side altars dedicated to Saint Anne and Saint Joseph are splendid examples of the Churrigueresque style. Vividly painted scenes from the life of Saint Nicholas de Tolentino decorate yet another side altar. The old parish *church of San Bartolo* is also of interest.

From Salamanca, follow Highway 43 southeast toward Morelia. After passing through the Valle de Santiago, the road follows the western shore of the Laguna de Yuriría, an artificial lake created in the mid-16th century to drain the nearby malarial swamps and now used for crop irrigation. About 50 km. (30 miles) south of Salamanca you'll have the option of a side trip to **Yuriría,** which is another 3 km. (2 miles) east on Highway 116. This old Tarascan town at an elevation of 1,733 meters (5,686 feet) boasts one of the greatest examples of 16th-century architecture in all of Mexico in its *******monastery of San Pablo.* The façade is an unusually rich example of the Plateresque style, with complicated patterns of flowers and foliage and a bird-man motif on the columns flanking the portal. Dominated by a massive tower, the monastery also features a battlemented roof and buttresses (one of its worldly functions was to protect monks and Christianized Indians from the attacks of hostile Indians). In addition, the superb two-story cloister has a monumental open staircase.

Back on Highway 43, head south for 27 km. (17 miles) to **Cuitzeo,** a fishing village on shallow Lake Cuitzeo. The low white buildings in town are all nearly identical, with red painted bases and portals framed by flat stones. Visitors come to see the mid-16th century Augustinian **monastery of Santa María Magdalena,* with its thickly ornamented Indian-Plateresque façade. (The pierced heart above the doorway is the emblem of the Augustinian order.) Inside, there is a large enclosed atrium, and in the cloister, charming water spouts decorated with sirens, doves, and the remains of original frescoes. In 1882 a 4-km. (2.5 mile) dam was built across the width of the lake, which shrinks considerably in the dry season, allowing salt to be harvested from it.

From Cuitzeo, Highway 43 continues south to ****Morelia** (see page 115), 553 km. (343 miles) from Mexico City, where you can connect with Travel Route 8.

Northern Mexico

The border between Mexico and the United States is over 2,600 km. (1,612 miles) long and separates (in theory, at least) two entirely different cultures. Following the jagged course of the Río Bravo (which *norteamericanos* call the Río Grande) from the Gulf of Mexico to Ciudad Juárez/El Paso, the border then zigzags off in ruler-straight lines to Tijuana, just below San Diego, on the Pacific coast. Much of the southwestern part of what is now the United States formerly belonged to Mexico; the boundary is a constant reminder of the permanent loss of much of its territory with the signing of the Treaty of Guadalupe Hidalgo, which ended the Mexican-American War.

Six different types of landscape can be found in the northern border regions of Mexico. In the northeast hard by the Gulf of Mexico you find the lush, low-lying coastal plain. Gradually, as you head west, the plain rises and crumples into the foothills of the Sierra Madre Oriental, and then the mountains themselves. The western slope of the Sierra Madre gives way to a high desert plateau, or *altiplano,* that's studded with sage, mesquite, and cacti. This vast plateau is actually an extremely dry basin lying between the two branches of the Sierra Madre—the Oriental to the east and the Occidental to the west. As you head west and gain elevation, the desert plateau gradually gives way to the northern highlands, which are dotted with green oases fed by rivers rising in the Sierra Madre Occidental. At altitudes above 1,000 meters (3,280 feet) the highlands become grassy prairies where cattle can be pastured. The plant and animal species that live on the *altiplano* must otherwise be able to withstand drought conditions for much of the year. Prickly pear cactus, which can store quantities of water in its fibers, is the most commonly seen vegetation.

This vast desert basin has never been conducive to permanent settlement, although the remains of Casas Grandes, a Pueblo Indian settlement, indicate that in one area of it at least native Americans were able to achieve a high level of civilization. Later, the *altiplano* was sparsely settled by Chichimec tribes, including the Tarahumara, but the latter retreated west into the Sierra Madre Occidental when the Spanish arrived. The raids of other Indian tribes, especially the warlike Apaches and Comanches, kept the Spanish from extending their dominion this far north, and even after Mexico gained her independence, the few outposts in the area remained primarily military garrisons (*presidios*). Only after Mexico's war with the United States were the Apaches forced back behind the newly drawn frontier. Even today, there are few towns of any consequence in this part of Mexico, the important industrial center of Monterrey being the most notable exception.

The rugged mountains of the Sierra Madre Occidental extend about 1,100 km (700 miles) on a northwest-southeast axis from the border, and the landscape is entirely different from the *altiplano*. Here, junipers, oaks, ground plants, and grasses cover the lower slopes, while coniferous forests, mostly pine, are found above 3,000 meters (9,840 feet). In the winter months, the Tarahumara Indians move down to the lower valleys, where the climate is more temperate, moving back to the higher elevations in the summer. (This age-old pattern of migration up and down the mountains may explain, in part, the incredible stamina and lung capacity of these Indians, who partake in ritual runs that can last up to 72 hours at a stretch.)

The western slope of the Sierra Madre Occidental gives way to the broad valleys of the Sonora plains, a narrow strip of land bordering the Gulf of California (called the Sea of Cortés in Mexico). The coast itself is dotted by lagoons and bays surrounded by rocky hills, and is home to the Yaqui Indians, a tribe of fisherfolk and food gatherers. Because of its proximity to Arizona, New Mexico, and California, parts of this once unspoiled coastline are now being developed for international resort consortiums.

Finally, at the westernmost reaches of Mexico's northern border, you'll encounter the harsh, thorny, and radiant splendor of the mountainous Baja California peninsula. The recent completion of Federal Highway 1, the *Carretera Transpeninsular,* which covers the entire 1,300-km. (806-miles) length of the peninsula, has made this once-forbidding place far more accessible to the average person. A long finger of land anywhere from 40–220 km. (25–136 miles) wide, with the Pacific Ocean pounding its western coast and the Gulf of California washing its eastern side, Baja California split off from the mainland and drifted westward some 20 million years ago. Prehistoric cave sites and rock paintings testify to an ancient, now extinct population. Lured by stories of the legendary Queen Califia and her court of pearl-divers, the insatiably greedy Spaniards made repeated attempts to settle here. As always, following in their wake, 17th- and 18th-century mission stations testify to the Jesuits' attempts to convert the native populations to Christianity. Ultimately, thousands of Indians perished from diseases introduced by the invaders, and the Spanish succumbed to the scorching heat, lack of fresh water, rattlesnakes, and otherwise harsh conditions. Today, Baja's Indians (comprised of Cucupa, Kiliwa, and Paipai) barely number a thousand, and it's mostly *gringos* who remain, drawn south by the wild, arid beauty of its desert, its glorious beaches, and the superb fishing.

In Baja California, the stretch along the highway from Tijuana to Cabo San Lucas is described in Travel Route 11. Travel Routes 12, 14, and 15 describe the major car and bus entry points from the United States into Mexico. Travel Route 13 follows the spectacular train route through the Sierra Madre Occidental, and Travel Route 16 runs from the eastern border town of Matamoros across country to Mazatlán on the Pacific coast.

TRAVEL ROUTE 11: Tijuana–La Paz–**Cabo San Lucas (1,725 km.; 1,035 miles)

See map on page 170.

This Travel Route takes you through the northwestern border town of Tijuana and down the full length of the Baja peninsula on Highway 1 to Cabo San Lucas. Baja California is a rugged, wild peninsula, appreciated most by lovers of adventure and natural beauty.

Crass, gaudy, noisy, hectic, and sometimes fascinating, **Tijuana** thrives on its status as the busiest border town in the world, with some 30 million official crossings annually. Mexicans arrive by the thousands every week, lured by the highest minimum wage in the country, as well as its proximity to the U.S. At the same time, more and more U.S. and foreign manufacturers are setting up factories here, attracted by the low Mexican wage scale. Crossing in the other direction, thousands of American tourists, especially Southern Californians, are daily waved through customs to begin their holidays and duty-free shopping. In fact, more Americans visit Tijuana than any other foreign city on earth. As one might expect of the fastest-growing city in North America, however, Tijuana has a surreal feel to it, and won't appeal to everyone.

Tijuana's history is neither old nor particularly memorable. Before the frontier boundaries were established in 1848, the Río Tijuana valley was sparsely settled. In the 1870s, a customs station was set up, and a few shacks sprang up nearby on what, according to legend, was then Aunt Jane's Ranch, or El Rancho de Tía Juana. Far from the center of political power in Mexico, Tijuana did not participate in the Mexican Revolution. The Madero movement, which attempted to instigate a radical social revolution in Mexico, spread to Mexicali and Tijuana in 1911, but was quickly defeated by Federal troops.

Horse racing and gambling began to attract American tourists around the turn of the century, and when Prohibition was legislated in the U.S. during the 1920s, Tijuana boomed. The thirsty stars of Hollywood, only 160 miles to the north, turned the dusty border town into a fashionable mecca, and sea-weary sailors began to make it a port of call. Over the next two decades, Tijuana developed a rather lurid reputation, which it has never quite shed (perhaps realizing that it's good for business). Today, it's the fourth-largest city in Mexico after Mexico City, Guadalajara, and Monterrey.

Whatever it is, Tijuana is *not* a town of great architecture or charming, quiet little streets. The

Cathedral is one of its few notable buildings, and recent development along the Río Tijuana has given the city a somewhat modern look.

The center of action for shoppers is the Avenida Revolución, Tijuana's main drag, and its surrounding streets, where hundreds of souvenir kiosks, craft shops, and food booths line the many arcades and passageways. The *Pasaje del Sombrero* is a particularly lively crafts market where you can hone your bargaining skills. Also on Avenida Revolución, between Calles 6 and 7, is the *Centro Artesanal,* a government-supported arts-and-crafts center.

Once night falls, the noisy, garish life of this city moves into even higher gear. Depending on what your notion of entertainment is, Tijuana offers a wide range of it.

Jai alai, the world's fastest-moving sport (the hard rubber ball travels at speeds in excess of 100 mph), is played every night except Thursday in the Moorish-looking *Fronton Palacio* (Revolución at Calle 7). Originally a product of Spain's Basque country, jai alai is played by two teams of either two or four. Players hurl the goatskin-covered ball with scooped, hand-held baskets called *cestas* against the front wall of a three-sided court, or fronton. The ball may not touch the floor or hit the back wall more than once, and games are played to 21 points. There is also the option of betting on every game.

Bullfights are held on Sundays from early through mid-summer at the *El Toreo de Tijuana* bullfight ring 3.2 km. (about 2 miles) east of Agua Caliente; and from mid-summer until September at the *Plaza Monumentale* ring on the Playas de Tijuana beach. Visiting *toreadors* stay at the *Hotel Caesar,* one of Tijuana's few old buildings, which is located on Avenida Revolución at the corner of Calle 5.

Horse races get under way Saturdays and Sundays at the *Hipodromo* (track) on the Boulevard Agua Caliente; dog races are held here at night from Thursday through Sunday.

Charreadas, or Mexican-style rodeos, are held Sunday afternoons from May to September at the *Plaza Mexico Charreadas* west of Tijuana.

The *Centro Cultural* FONART, located at Paseo de los Heroes at Independencia, is a noteworthy modern building housing an auditorium (*El Omniteatro*) with a circular screen where a multimedia film, *Pueblo del Sol,* explains the history and culture of Mexico. Another popular film shown here takes you on a dizzying "flight" over some of the most beautiful parts of the country. Music and dance performances, including the world-famous Ballet Folklórico, various *mariachi* bands, and theater, are held in the same complex at the *Sala de Espectaculos* performance center and the open-air *Caracol al Aire Libre.*

In addition to all these activities, Tijuana's festival month, the *Feria de las Californias,* runs from August to September and features cultural and sporting events, arts and crafts exhibits, and its share of general merry-making.

Once you've had your fill of this sprawling, noisy frontier town and are ready to explore more of the surrounding countryside, you'll almost immediately find yourself in the hot, desert-like serenity of *Baja California*.

Baja California

This narrow land mass, with the Pacific on one side and the Gulf of California (an arm of the Pacific) on the other, is divided into two states, Baja California Norte and Baja California Sur, with the Sierra de San Pedro Martir range running its 1,300-km. (800-miles) length. Signs of human settlement on the peninsula, most notably rock paintings, date back as far as 7500 B.C., but very little is known of the early Indian cultures that left them. Cortés, seeking the legendary Queen Califía and her court of pearl divers, landed in the La Paz area (on the Gulf of California side) in 1535. Local tribes fiercely resisted the influx of Spaniards that followed Cortés, and, in tandem with the unforgiving climate, were largely successful in discouraging further Spanish inroads. (The Spanish left behind the name "California," in honor of the mythical queen, however.) Jesuit missionaries began to arrive in 1697 and immediately set about converting the natives; fol-

lowed first by Franciscans and then by Dominicans. Baja California was established as a separate political entity in 1804, and was occupied by American troops during the Mexican-American War (1847–1848). When the peace accord was signed and the U.S. troops left, Baja once again was forgotten by all except the few thousand who lived there. That situation remained unchanged until the 1930s, when a handful of Hollywood's movie stars discovered the superb fishing off its coasts.

Since then, Baja has exerted a strong pull on the hearts and minds of visitors, especially those from the States. The land, both barren and beautiful, is nearly all desert, with the exception of a few oases. Ocean breezes cool the western coast, but east of the mountains the desert heat can be unbearable. Tourism is now the principal source of revenue on the peninsula, and there are lavish resorts to be found.

There are two routes you can take from Tijuana. The four-lane toll road, 1 D—called the Ensenada Cuota on highway signs but also known as the Carretera Escenica because of the scenic route it follows—goes directly to Ensenada and ends there. However, this route follows the old highway, Carretara 1, which makes a more leisurely way south from Tijuana to Ensenada, passing beaches and vacation resorts.

Rosarito, 32 km. (20 miles) from Tijuana, has only its beautiful beach to recommend it. *Puerto Nuevo* is a fishing village and a good place to stop for lobster or fresh fish.

El Descanso, 45 km. (28 miles) south of Tijuana on the road's inland side, is a farming town situated near the ruins of an early 19th-century mission. The sand dunes just past *Cantamar* are used as a training and recreation area for motocross drivers and kite fliers. *La Misión* is a peaceful village in a valley just inland from the coast; it's named for *San Miguel de la Frontera,* a nearby Dominican mission that was founded in 1784 and now stands in ruins.

El Mirador, 80 km. (49 miles) from Tijuana, is a good place to stop and enjoy some sweeping views of the desert. About 18 km. (11 miles) farther on is a detour near the fish-packing plant of *El Souzal* that will take you through the Guadalupe Valley to *Tecate* (see Travel Route 12). *Guadalupe,* a Russian colony settled in 1903, was part of the government's efforts to settle Baja California. Although most of the immigrants have long since been absorbed, members of the "Malakan" sect, descendants of the original settlers, still cultivate olives and grapes here. It is also the site of Mexico's largest vineyards.

Ensenada, 108 km. (67 miles) south of Tijuana, has been a favorite with Southern Californians ever since 1930 when Jack Dempsey got involved in an ill-fated scheme to build a lavish casino here. (The plan was dealt a

Table Mountain in Baja California

knockout combination when Prohibition was repealed in the U.S. at about the same time that gambling was outlawed in Mexico.) Lying on the beautiful bay called Todos los Santos, which was discovered by the Portuguese navigator Juan Rodríguez Cabrillo in 1542, Ensenada is the leading port in Baja California. In addition to the cotton and produce of the Mexicali valley that is shipped from here, as well as the commercial fish caught by the local fishing fleet, sportfishing is a key component of the economy, and the city has proclaimed itself the "Yellowtail Capital of the World." There are good (but crowded) beaches north and south of town, but nearly all the hotels are located on Avenida Adolfo López Mateos near the harbor, where there's also a convenient abundance of duty-free shops.

The nearby *Chapultepec Hills* offer panoramic views of the town and the bay. Wine connoisseurs may wish to visit the *Bodegas Santo Tomás,* Mexico's largest winery. On Shrove Tuesday the *carnival* gets under way with a large, colorful procession. The famous 1,600-km. (1,000-miles) *Baja Mil* car race from Ensenada to La Paz is held in early November, while an 800-km. (500-miles) regatta takes place in July.

Leaving Ensenada, continue south on Highway 1 for 10 km. (6 miles), where there is a turnoff to the *El Estero lagoon,* a favorite sun-and-fun spot with the locals. When you reach the farming town of *Maneadero* (now called Sanchez Taboada) 5 km. (3 miles) farther south, detour east and continue another 22 km. (14 miles) to the spit of land at the end of the cove known as **Cabo Punta la Banda,** where, besides the resident sea lions, you can witness a Pacific coast phenomenon. The terrific force of the waves forces water through a narrow blowhole in the rocks, often hurling it 10 meters (33 feet) or more into the air. Because of the thunderous noise, the place is called *La Bufadora,* or "the snorting one."

Backtracking to Highway 1, follow it southeast for 30 km. (18 miles) to **Santo Tomás,** in the valley of the same name, which is known for its wine (the vineyards here are the largest in all of Mexico). The ruins of a late-18th-century church, built as part of a Dominican mission and destroyed by local Indians, stand to the left of the road into town.

Continue south on Highway 1,

which winds inland over the hills to **San Vicente,** another Dominican mission town. South of here the land becomes drier and flatter, and the thermometer rises accordingly. *Colonet* is a supply center for the region's farmers. Two unpaved roads lead west from here to the sea. One takes you 12 bumpy km. (7 miles) to **San Antonio del Mar** and an expanse of beautiful high sand dunes; the other goes 20 km. (12 miles) to **Punta Colonet.** No tourist accommodations are available at either place, but camping is allowed.

Another 11 km. (7 miles) south on Highway 1 will bring you to a turnoff that heads east to the ***Parque San Pedro Martir,** some 98 km. (60 miles) inland. From here, a two-hour drive on a graded dirt road will take you high into the **Sierra San Pedro Martir,* where the meadows and conifer forests provide a striking contrast to the barrenness of the surrounding desert. You'll also find an observatory, the *Observatorio San Pedro,* at the top of the *Cerro de la Encantade,* which at 3,078 meters (10,000 feet) is the highest peak on the peninsula. (A reminder: It's wise to carry an extra jug of water for your car radiator, since many of these mountain grades are steep. In Mexico, an ounce of prevention is worth a pound of cure.)

Returning to Highway 1, continue south to the agricultural center of *Vicente Guerrero,* 276 km. (171 miles) from Tijuana. There is an ocean beach some 10 km. (6 miles) to the west near San

Ramon; lodging can be found at the *Rancho Santa María.*

*San Quintín, 23 km. (14 miles) farther south, is a fishing and market town located in a fertile valley on San Quintín Bay that enjoys a mild, ocean-cooled climate year-round. The first turnoff past the small military base leads to the site of an English agricultural colony that tried to establish itself here in the late 19th century. The old mill is now a motel. Farther south along the bay is a neglected cemetery with English names on the tombstones, another lonely reminder of the many foreigners who tried to settle the peninsula to no avail. A turnoff farther south leads onto a low spit of land separating the inner and outer bays that is dotted with motels and a trailer park. The Santa María and Pabellon beaches, with their thundering waves, stretch along the outer bay; the calmer San Quintín Bay, one of the finest clamming spots on the entire peninsula, is a paradise for fishing and aquatic sports.

The cardón, a species of giant cactus, makes its first appearance near *El Socorro.* These colossal denizens of the desert bloom in July and August, when they bear edible fruits, and can grow up to 18 meters (59 feet) high.

El Rosario, 66 km. (41 miles) south of San Quintín, is divided by a stream into Rosario de Arriba

Candelabra cactus (Cardón)

(the "upper") and Rosario de Abajo (the "lower"); the ruins of the mission built by the Dominicans who founded the settlement, as well as a fine, sandy beach, are found south of the narrow stream.

Past El Rosario, Highway 1 turns east into the peninsula's interior, with its cactus-studded highlands and formidable rock formations. Amateur naturalists will take note of the sun- and heat-blasted vegetation here: yucca trees, organ-pipe cactus, cholla and ocotillo, and the twisted elephant trees (which are actually shrubs with red leaves). Strangest of all, however, are the *cirios,* or "Boojum" trees, their conical trunks topped by little tufts of what look like wild hair. Named after a character in Lewis Carroll's *The Hunting of the Snark,* they are unique to the Baja Peninsula.

San Fernando, 132 km. (82 miles) southeast of San Quintín, lies in its own verdant oasis. Founded in 1769 by Father Junipero Serra (see page 146), it was the only Franciscan mission in the northern part of Baja California during the entire Colonial period. Today, the adobe ruins of the mission stand as mute testimony to the rigorous determination of Catholic priests to convert native tribes to Christianity throughout Baja.

Cataviña, 212 km. (131 miles) southeast of San Quintín, is situated in a natural "park" (a Western term for a broad, level valley), and offers a pleasant rest stop, the hotel *La Pinta Cataviña,* which

was once the main house of a cattle ranch. The shimmering *Laguna de Chapala,* another 56 km. (35 miles) down the road, is more of a mirage than a lake, having dried up long ago. But it does have the *Rancho Nueva Chapala,* which is another pleasant, moderately priced place to stay overnight.

Continue southeast on Highway 1 through the parched desert of the interior until, 305 km. (189 miles) from San Quintín, a road branches off to the east and the **Bahía de los Angeles.** The bay is some 68 km. (42 miles) from the turnoff, but the wait is worth it; it's a beautiful, untrammeled spot with the bare crests of high mountains acting as a backdrop for the many offshore islands strung out along the horizon. The 73-km.- (44-mile-) long *Isla Angel de la Guarda,* the westernmost of the Midriff Islands, shelters the bay from the Gulf of California, and is an ideal anchorage site for sport and fishing boats. There are also two motels and camping facilities in town.

At about the halfway point of the turnoff road leading to Bahía de los Angeles, you'll pass a primitive road that heads south for 40 km. (25 miles) to the **Misión San Borja,** which was established by the Jesuits in 1756 in what had been the Indian settlement of Adac. After the Jesuits were expelled from Neuva España, the Dominicans arrived to complete the stone church and its adjacent convent, which they did in 1802. This road, and one almost equally

Misión San Borja

bad that leads southwest from here for 38 km. (23 miles) before it joins the Carretera Transpeninsular Highway near Rosarito (see below), should be taken only by those with a rugged all-terrain vehicle.

Highway 1 will veer to the southwest after the Bahía de los Angeles, crossing the peninsula to the Pacific coast above Guerrero Negro. A monumental steel eagle, with wings 36 meters (118 feet) tall, some 435 km. (270 miles) from San Quintín will mark the 28th parallel, the border between the states of Baja California Norte and Baja California Sur. You'll also be crossing from the Pacific time zone to the Mountain time zone, so don't forget to set your watches one hour ahead. West of the eagle you'll find an El Presidente motel and a trailer park.

Just 3 km. (1.8 miles) south of the monument is the turnoff for **Guerrero Negro,** where large white mountains of locally produced salt gleam under clear blue skies.

The nearby ***Laguna de Ojo Liebre** is of special interest. About 12 km. (7 miles) outside of town, a sandy road turns south and runs 24 km. (15 miles) to the *Parque Natural de los Ballenas Gris* on the shores of Scammon's Lagoon—named after a 19th-century Yankee whaling captain who discovered this favorite breeding sanctuary of the gray whale. The whales, which weigh up to 25 tons, begin their seasonal migration every autumn from the Arctic to this sheltered spot in the Pacific, where, between the end of November and March, they mate or bear their young after a 13-month gestation period. A hundred and fifty years ago, Scammon attempted to keep the place a secret so he could monopolize the yearly slaughter of whales; others soon found it, however, and the gray whale population was decimated—by the turn of the century some estimates put the number of remaining grays at 100. Today, their numbers are up, thanks in part to the protection they now enjoy here. The best place to see them is from the park in the estuary of San Juan, where some of the bolder whales will come right up to the docks in the morning. An observation tower is also available for viewing the 100 or so whales who make the estuary their home. (Boats are not allowed in the lagoon during the four-month period of the whales' residence.)

South of Guerrero Negro, Highway 1 becomes a narrow obstacle course of deep potholes, and high speeds are impossible. The surrounding region, though it receives scant rainfall, is surprisingly green, thanks to the water pumped from underground sources.

About 23 km. (14 miles) south of Guerrero Negro, you'll come to a road that swings east toward the former gold mining camp of *El Arco,* which is 43 km. (27 miles) farther on. A visit to the mid-18th-century church and ruins of the *Santa Gertrudis mission,* another Jesuit complex that was taken over by Dominicans after the former's expulsion from the colony, will add an additional 37 km. (23 miles), one way, to this detour. It is only recommended, however, for those with all-terrain vehicles.

Back on Highway 1, the road will turn sharply east just before it comes to the oasis of ***San Ignacio,** 140 km. (87 miles) from Guerrero Negro. Here, date palm, fig, and orange trees clustered around a small freshwater lake provide a welcome contrast to the hostile desert. The reconstructed *Dominican church* dates from 1786. In the barren Sierra de San Francisco and Sierra de Guadalupe mountains nearby, several caves containing wall paintings of an uncertain age have been discovered. They are not easily accessible, however, and interested visitors should be in good shape before they locate a guide and mule, and be prepared to spend several days on the expedition. If you're still interested, information can be obtained at the *El Presidente* and *La Posada* motels in town.

From San Ignacio, Highway 1 continues its leisurely route through the desert, passing three towering volcanoes collectively called *Las Tres Virgenes,* before beginning its hair-raising descent to the Gulf of California and ***Santa Rosalía,** 212 km. (131 miles) from Guerrero Negro. This busy little port town was founded in 1880 by a French company that worked the nearby copper mines until 1953. Not surprisingly, the French influence can be seen in some of the houses in the northern part of town. The 19th-century pre-fabricated cast-iron *church* on Obregon at Calle 1 was designed by the same Gustave Eiffel who designed the Eiffel Tower. In addition, there are several fine beaches in town, and a ferry to Guaymas on the mainland. The Transbordadores ferry terminal is on Route 1 just south of town.

Continue south on Highway 1 to **Mulegé,** a verdant, palm-fringed oasis on the banks of the Río Mulegé. The *Santa Rosalía de Mulegé mission,* founded by Jesuits in 1705, sits on a hill to the west of town; services are still held there every Sunday. East of town on another hill is the old territorial prison. There are also several beaches and, of course, good fishing in the Gulf of California. Although this is the area where the finest cave paintings in Baja are to be found, getting to them is difficult. There is a permit-holder in town who, for a fee, will take you in your car (or his) to the private property where the caves are located; from there, mules are required for the final leg of the trip. Further information can be obtained from the *La Casita* and *Serenidad* hotels in town, where you might also consider spending the night after the approximately five-hour drive across the peninsula.

From Mulegé, follow Highway 1 for 45 km. (28 miles) along the fabulous *Bahía de la Concepción* and thrill to the beautiful views of sea, sky, and offshore volcanic islands. The beaches of *Santispac, El Coyote, El Resqueson,* and *Los Muertos,* all with campgrounds, are considered by aficionados to be among the finest in the world. The world's tallest cacti also are reputed to grow in the desert west of the bay.

*Loreto, 412 km. (255 miles) from Guerrero Negro, was founded in 1697 by the Jesuits, thereby earning its distinction as the first permanent Spanish settlement in California. It was the capital of Baja until 1829, when it was leveled by a hurricane, and it was from here that the tireless Jesuits began their exploration, colonization and proselytization of the entire peninsula. The beautifully restored *mission church* is the oldest Jesuit structure on the peninsula; next door, the *Museo de Misiónes* features exhibits detailing the Spanish discovery and conquest of Baja. Nevertheless, despite Loreto's picturesque location on the Gulf of California, with the impressively severe Sierra de la Giganta to the west, and the efforts of the Mexican government to promote it as a major tourist destination, much work remains to be done.

A number of excursions from Loreto to other nearby mission stations offer especially impressive mountain scenery. *San Javier,* which has a well-preserved early-18th-century church with a fine Baroque façade and gilded high altar is 33 km. (20 miles) inland; another 12 km. (7.5 miles) west will bring you to the mission of *San José Comondú.*

Highway 1 south of Loreto follows the shoreline of the Gulf of California, skirting the high, arid mountains of the Sierra de la Giganta. The white stripes on the first hillside outside of the town are formed by millions of shells discarded by former Paleolithic inhabitants of the area. *Nopolo* has several hotels, and there is also a good one at *Puerto Escondido,* 24 km. (15 miles) south of Loreto and reached by a turnoff that heads east from the main highway.

Just past *Ligui,* 40 km. (25 miles) south of Loreto, Highway 1 turns inland and begins to wind its way through the mountains to **Villa Insurgentes,** which lies on a broad plain where agriculture has been made possible by deep-well irrigation. *Ciudad Constitución,* 117 km. (73 miles) from Loreto, has grown rapidly since farming began in the area; today, it exports its cotton from *San Carlos,* 57 km. (35 miles) to the west. A Pacific port town on the Bahía Magdalena that's protected from the open sea by the *Isla Magdalena,* San Carlos is probably the second-best location on the peninsula to observe gray whales in their natural habitat. An added bonus is the large herd of sea lions that live on the *Isla de Santa Margarita* in the bay.

From San Carlos, Highway 1 continues south through an unchanging landscape of light-colored hills and eroded gullies, recrosses the peninsula at its narrowest point, and, eventually, opens up to an exhilarating view of the Bahía de la Paz on the Gulf of California.

In the southeastern corner of the bay is ***La Paz,** 327 km. (196 miles) from Loreto. Until the advent of the transpeninsular highway, ferry service to the mainland, and the subsequent economic boom in tourism, La Paz was little more than a quiet fishing port tucked away amidst a backdrop of cactus-studded hills. From the earliest days of the Colonial period, when Hernán Cortés is said to have landed near the site of the present-day town, repeated Spanish attempts to colonize the area ended in failure. Lured by the extraordinary quality of the pearls found in the bay's oyster beds, the would-be *conquistadors* met with fierce resistance from local Indian tribes, including the Pericue, Cochimi, and Guaicura. Even the indefatigable Jesuits, who founded a mission station here in 1720, finally had to abandon their efforts due to illness and inadequate water supplies. A permanent settlement was not established until 1800; thirty years later, after Loreto was devastated by a hurricane, La Paz (Spanish for "peace") became the capital of all of Baja California. Americans occupied the town during the Mexican-American War, and another American, William Walker, seized the harbor in 1853 in a bizarre attempt to establish an independent state.

Today, there is not much here in the way of architectural or anthropological interest. The local *parish church* dates from the 19th century and the *Government Palace* from the 20th century. There is a *Museum of Folk Art,* as well as a *Museum of Anthropology* that proudly exhibits large photographs of all the Baja California cave paintings you've been unable to see up to this point. What La Paz does have to offer is sun, water, peace and quiet, and duty-free shopping. It is also an excellent base for diving expeditions and deep-sea fishing, as well as for excursions to the nearby islands of *Espiritu Santo, La Partida,* and *Islotes,* all of which teem with sea lions and many different species of birds.

From July to September the La Paz region can be unbearably hot, although evening relief arrives in the form of a dependable ocean breeze called the *coromuel* (a corruption of the name of an Englishman, Cromwell, who used the reliable breezes to aid his privateering). Short, violent tropical storms called *chubascos* frequently deluge the town in August and September. La Paz has always been known for the beauty of its sunsets, and strolling along the *malecón,* or harbor promenade, is a pleasant way to spend the evening.

The best beaches are on the road to *Pichilingue,* the modern ferry terminal 18 km. (11 miles) from town (ferries run from Pichilingue to Mazatlán and Los Mochis). Don't expect long expanses of sand, however, since beaches in La Paz and the eastern Baja in general tend to be nestled in tranquil coves between cactus-covered hills. The *Playa Corumuel* is about 4 km. (2.5 miles) outside of town, next to the beach of the *El Presidente* motel. There's also a good beach, the *Playa Pichilingue,* behind the ferry terminal, where restaurants with canvas awnings serve seafood and provide relief from the intense sun. Excursions in glass-bottom boats are also available from here, and are an excellent way to observe the marine life in these truly beautiful waters.

To begin this last leg of your trip, take Highway 1 south via *San Pedro* past the beautiful Bahía de las Palmas, 105 km. (65 miles) from La Paz, where a sandy road

leads to the *El Cardonal* and *Los Barriles* hotels on the beach. Highway 1 then turns inland, crossing a cactus-covered plain with the Sierra de la Laguna mountains to the west. The road drops down to the glorious southern coast, with its clear turquoise water and endless stretches of beach and headland pummelled by the heavy Pacific surf, and all too soon reaches ***San José del Cabo,** 182 km. (113 miles) from La Paz, one of the two sizeable towns in the area. A fishing village until just a few years ago, San José, with the help of the Mexican government, is now in the business of actively seeking foreign tourists. While it still has its brightly painted houses, town hall, and small pioneer church, it also now has enormous luxury hotels, which have sprung up along the Zona Hotelera on the beachfront. A lush tropical lagoon called the *Estero de San José* is the nesting ground for about 80 species of birds. Surfers ride the waves off *Mirador Point,* 1 km. (half a mile) south of the trailer park, but the heavy surf and violent undertow make swimming in the ocean here, or at any of the beaches, a dangerous proposition.

More hotels can be found on the shores of the rocky bays between San José del Cabo and Cabo San Lucas, the other sizeable town at the end of the peninsula. About 3 km. (1.8 miles) west of San José you'll find the renovated *Hotel Palmilla,* which, like the rest of the cape region, was once accessible

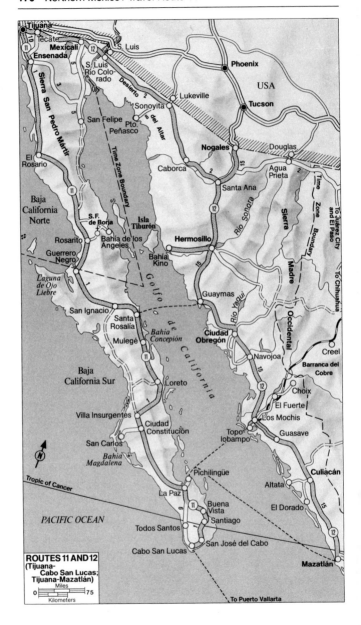

Tijuana
Tecate
Mexicali
Ensenada
S. Luis
S. Luis Rio Colo-rado
Phoenix
USA
Tucson
Desierto
Lukeville
Sonoyita
del Altar
San Felipe
Pto. Peñasco
Nogales
Douglas
Sierra San Pedro Mártir
El Rosario
Caborca
Agua Prieta
Santa Ana
Baja California Norte
S. F. de Borja
Isla Tiburón
Hermosillo
Rio Sonora
Sierra
Madre
Occidental
Rosarito
Bahía de los Angeles
Bahía Kino
Guerrero Negro
Laguna de Ojo Liebre
Golfo de California
Guaymas
Rio Yaqui
San Ignacio
Santa Rosalía
Mulegé
Bahía Concepción
Ciudad Obregón
Navojoa
Creel
Barranca del Cobre
Baja California Sur
Loreto
Choix
El Fuerte
Los Mochis
Villa Insurgentes
Ciudad Constitución
Topo-lobampo
Guasave
San Carlos
Bahía Magdalena
Pichilingüe
Culiacán
Tropic of Cancer
Altata
La Paz
El Dorado
PACIFIC OCEAN
Buena Vista
Santiago
Todos Santos
San José del Cabo
Cabo San Lucas
Mazatlán
To Juárez City and El Paso
To Chihuahua
Time Zone Boundary
Time Zone Boundary

ROUTES 11 AND 12
(Tijuana-
Cabo San Lucas;
Tijuana-Mazatlán)
Miles
0 � 75
Kilometers

To Puerto Vallarta

Fishermen with swordfish

by ship or plane only.

The last stretch of Highway 1 leads to **Cabo San Lucas,** 548 km. (340 miles) from La Paz. This is the very tip of Baja California and the end of the Carretera Transpeninsular, a fact symbolized by El Arco, a natural white stone that marks the point where the turquoise waters of the Gulf of California meet the sapphire blues of the Pacific. The beaches here range from smooth and sandy to wild and rocky; the surf varies, too, from relatively calm to suicidally heavy. Now catering to a luxury tourist class, Cabo San Lucas offers good hotel accommodations, world-renowned deep-sea fishing, and a paradise for divers and snorkelers. Equipment and instructions for the latter can be found at the *Amigos del Mar,* across from the pier, where coral jewelry and local crafts are also sold. Underwater sights include a strange cascade of sand and a section of ocean floor covered with lumps of manganese. Excursion boats, some with glass bottoms, cruise near the headlands in the area for views of the colonies of sea lions and pelicans.

Cabo San Lucas is also the point of departure for the ferry to Puerto Vallarta, a trip that takes 22 hours. If you're planning on taking your car on the ferry and continuing your tour on the mainland, it's recommended that you make reservations early and smile if you find yourself getting bumped to the next boat.

TRAVEL ROUTE 12: Tijuana–Mexicali–Hermosillo–Los Mochis–*Mazatlán (1,818 km.; 1,090 miles)

See map on page 170.

This route follows the Mexican border between Baja and the state of California before traversing inland across the Gran Desierto and then south to the mainland coast of the Gulf of California.

From Tijuana (see page 158) take Boulevard Agua Caliente to Highway 2, which starts out through farmlands, olive groves, and low rocky hills. *Rancho de la Puerta,* 48 km. (30 miles) east and slightly north of Tijuana, is a vegetarian health-and-fitness resort with a variety of sports facilities and a thermal spring, and caters mostly to affluent Americans. *Rancho Cochuma,* a yogic retreat, is located a little farther south.

Tecate, 54 km. (33 miles) from Tijuana, is a farming and industrial center as well as a border town sometimes used as an alternative to Tijuana by travellers who want to return quickly to the United States via Highway 188. (The border crossing here, however, unlike the one in Tijuana, closes every night from midnight until 7:00 A.M.) It was founded in the 19th century after the Guadalupe and Califía valleys were discovered to be suitable, with irrigation, for agriculture, and is now known throughout Mexico (and increasingly in the U.S.) for the beer that bears its name and is its primary industry. On Saturday evenings from May to September fiestas are held on the small tree-shaded plaza downtown.

From Tecate, continue east on Highway 2 as it climbs 1,250 meters (4,100 feet) to a high plateau on which sits *La Rumorosa,* with its strange rock formations and splendid views of the surrounding desert, before descending again. The dried-up *Laguna Saluda* to your right, actually lies below sea level and was once a part of the Gulf of California.

Mexicali, 144 km. (90 miles) east of Tecate, is the capital of Baja California Norte and a prosperous agricultural center with the United States border cutting right through its center. On the other side of the border is its American neighbor, *Calexico,* and you can stroll from one city to the other in a matter of minutes. A dam on the Río Colorado provides essential irrigation to the area, where cotton is the main crop. The vital role of irrigation in the city's development is reflected, oddly enough, in the surprising number of Chinese restaurants in Mexicali, many of them run by descendents of the laborers who were brought in by U.S. entrepreneurs at the turn of the century to dig irrigation ditches. Not surprisingly, the city is more popular with visitors in winter, for the summers can be searingly hot.

A favorite excursion from here takes visitors south into Baja and then on to the fishing and beach resort of *San Felipe,* 200 km. (124 miles) south of Mexicali on the Gulf of California. With the desert for a backdrop, the town is tucked under a high headland that protects it from the open bay. The deep-sea fishing in the Gulf is a popular draw: *Totoaba,* an enormous seabass found nowhere else in the world, and yellowtail are plentiful in the winter and spring months; the local waters are too warm in the summer, however, for most species of sport fish. As one would expect of a resort so close to the huge population of Southern California, San Felipe has all the major amenities, and some of the annoyances, that Americans love:

Boisterous dune buggy and motorcycle enthusiasts can at times make a weekend here resemble something out of *Road Warrior.*

If you forgo the side trip to San Felipe, continue east from Mexicali on Highway 2, crossing the Río Colorado—Baja's border with the state of Sonora—after 72 km. (45 miles). Three km. (2 miles) farther on, you'll pass the town of *San Luis Río Colorado,* which sits amid fields irrigated by water stored behind the Morelos Dam.

Sonora and "Padre Kino"

During Colonial times, the area of modern Sonora and parts of Chihuahua, Arizona, and California were lumped together and called "Pimería." The relatively peaceful colonization of the area in the 17th century was largely the result of one man, the Jesuit known as "Padre Kino" by the Indians he converted. Born Eusabio Francisco Kino in 1641, this intrepid adventurer took part in the expeditions of Admiral Isidro de Atondo to Baja California from 1683 to 1685. Kino, like Cortés before him, became convinced that the Baja was not an island, as was then assumed, but was, in fact, a peninsula.

In his nearly 25 years of benevolent missionary activity, Padre Kino was far more successful in converting the local Indians than the Spanish were. Penetrating as far north as the delta of the Río Colorado at the head of the Gulf of California, Kino founded 25 large missions and several smaller ones, drew maps, and compiled valuable geographic and anthropological studies of the area. With the information he gathered, Padre Kino was able to prove that Baja California was a peninsula, not an island.

From San Luis Río Colorado, follow Highway 2 across the *Desierto del Altar* into a truly vast landscape of barren rocks and hills; after about 150 km. (93 miles), tall cacti and yuccas will begin to appear. The highway runs along the Arizona border for much of this stretch, and once you cross the Colorado River you'll have left the Pacific time zone for Mountain time. From the small border town of *Sonoyita,* 269 km. (167 miles) east of Mexicali, Highway 8 heads southwest for 100 km. (62 miles) to *Puerto Peñasco,* a small fishing village and beach resort on the Gulf. A joint U.S.-Mexico venture now under way to extract salt from the sea hopes to take advantage of Puerto Penasco's location on the Sonora–Baja rail line, as well as its obvious proximity to an endless supply of salt water.

From Sonoyita, Highway 2 veers to the southeast and on to **Caborca,** 149 km. (92 miles) away. A town that grew from one of Padre Kino's Jesuit mission stations (although its church was later rebuilt by the Franciscans), Caborca is sometimes called "Heroica" in honor of its successful defeat of attacking American filibusters in 1857, a victory the town celebrates every April 6. A cotton fair, the *Feria del Algodon,* takes place in November. Also of interest, a road leading southwest from here travels 102 km. (63 miles) to *El Desemboque* on the Gulf, where Seri Indians sell their artwork.

From Caborca, continue east on Highway 2 for 106 km. (66 miles), which will bring you to the town of **Santa Ana.** Lying at an elevation of 687 meters (2,253 feet), the town was a Pima Indian settlement when Padre Kino arrived in 1688. The mission he founded a year later was destroyed and rebuilt several times during subsequent Indian revolts. Today, Yaqui Indians come here during festivals to sell their handicrafts and perform their dances. The *Feria Regional,* held in July, honors Santa Ana, the town's patron saint.

Highway 2 ends here, and Highway 15 goes north through the little mission town of *Magdalena,* where Padre Kino died on March 15, 1711. His final resting spot remained a mystery until 1966, when his skeleton was discovered in the *church of San Francisco Xavier.* Plans are now under way to erect a monument to his memory.

You might want to continue north from here to Sonora's biggest border town, *Nogales,* a drive of 109 km. (67 miles), where buying liquor used to be the biggest draw for visitors from the north. As a port of entry today, the town is always busy, and it's also a major shipping point for winter produce being exported to U.S. markets.

From Santa Ana, take Highway 15 south for 170 km. (105 miles),

with wide-open desert vistas on either side, to **Hermosillo.** Today the capital of the modern state of Sonora, the town was named in 1828 for José Maria González Hermosillo, a leader in Mexico's War of Independence. Originally occupied by Seri Indians, the Spanish, after several abortive attempts, finally settled on the site in 1742 and called the place Pitic ("confluence") because of the nearby confluence of the Río Sonora and Río Zanjon. The *Plaza de los Tres Pueblos* marks the site of the original Indian settlement.

The modern, commercially minded Hermosillo, with its stores and wide boulevards, has little left to remind visitors of its history, and is, quite frankly, a pretty dull place except on weekends, when the *charros* (cowboys) descend from the hills to drink and carouse. The *Museo Regional de Historia de Sonora,* on the campus of the University, houses archaeological and ethnological collections pertaining to the cultures of the local Indian tribes (Seri, Yaqui, Opata, and Pima), including a 12,000-year-old mummified body that was found in a nearby cave. The city also has a 19th-century Neoclassical *Cathedral,* which is located next to the *Parque Infantil,* a grassy oasis four blocks from the center of the city, and a 19th-century *state capital.* The *Madero Park,* with its *mirador,* is located at the top of the Cerro de la Campana.

From Hermosillo, you can follow a road that pushes southwest through hot, irrigated countryside where wheat, corn, cotton, pecans, oranges, and grapes are grown to **Bahía Kino,** 110 km. (68 miles) away and one of the greatest beaches on the Gulf of California. There are two villages here, Old Kino (one of Padre Kino's mission outposts) and New Kino, and their proximity to one another heightens the picture of sharp economic disparity between the original inhabitants of the place, the Seri Indians, and the wealthy Americans who have come in increasing numbers to spend the winter months in one of the seemingly endless luxury condominiums that line the beach at New Kino. The largest island in Mexico, the *Isla del Tiburon* (Shark Island), lies just offshore and has been an uninhabited nature preserve since 1976. A special permit is required to visit, but local boatmen can usually obtain one for you.

The Seri Indians, now numbering no more than 300, are semi-nomadic hunters, fishermen, and food-gatherers who inhabit the coastal region between Bahía Kino and Caborca. Very little is known about their origins, and although they were converted to Christianity by the Jesuits, the Seris still incorporate the sun, moon, and animal demons into their worship. The European influence of the last century is still apparent in the women's clothing, which consists of a high-buttoned corset over a long skirt, head scarves, and necklaces of shells, seeds, or snakeskin. The women still paint their faces in bright colors on special occasions. Woven baskets and figures of animals beautifully carved in ironwood are the traditional crafts of the Seris, and are sold in the vicinity. If you want to take photographs of them, it is proper to ask permission first and payment is expected.

If you decide to skip the side trip to Bahía Kino, continue south on Highway 15 from Hermosillo to **Guaymas,** a drive of 136 km. (84 miles). An active port city mostly known for its deep-sea fishing (marlin, yellowtail, red snapper, sea bass, sailfish), Guaymas boasts good beaches, a beautiful location (the city is situated on a narrow shelf between the sea and a small but impressive range of mountains), and little else to attract the casual tourist.

The bay was first explored by the Spanish in 1535; Padre Kino founded a mission here around 1700; and the town was chartered in 1769. It is also one of the few places in Mexico where the French had an impact in the mid-19th century. One French adventurer, Count Gaston Raousset de Boulbon, even tried to seize Guaymas in order to establish a private colony. He was shot for his efforts. More recent events include the filming of *Catch-22* in the area, and plans are already on the drawing board to intensively develop Guaymas as a major resort in the next decade.

The most popular beach (and the closest to downtown) is *Mir-*

amar, located in the bay of Baco-chibampo, one of Guaymas's two bays. The *Selva Encantada,* or Magic Forest, with its resident parrots, is an enchanted landscape of cactus some 36 km. (22 miles) inland. On the way, you'll pass another of Padre Kino's Jesuit missions, this one called *San José de Guaymas,* with its mid-18th-century church.

Leaving Guaymas, follow Highway 15 east through *Empalme.* The area around here, along the lower stretches of the Río Yaqui, is home to the Yaqui Indians, who live in eight villages—Cocorit, Bacum, Torim, Belem, Vicam, Potam, Rahum, and Huirivis—a few miles south of Highway 15.

The *Yaqui Indians,* numbering over 15,000, were never completely subjugated by the Spanish. Little is known of their ancient origins, but they remained distributed over most of Sonora until the mid-19th century. The government deported many of them to the Yucatán around the turn of the century, but most returned to their tribal homelands. As late as 1927, under their war leader Luis Matuz, the rebellious Yaquis staged periodic uprisings against government authority. Today, they remain autonomous, choosing their own leaders and councils, and pursuing traditional economic activities, primarily farming, hunting, and fishing. Like many other tribes, the religion of the Yaquis freely combines Christianity with age-old Indian beliefs. Magicians and

soothsayers form an important fraternity within the Yaqui social structure, taking part in church festivals but also relied on to ward off evil spirits. Dancing is a prominent feature of Yaqui social and religious rites, the *Danza del Venado* (Stag Dance) being the best known, and wood-and-paper masks, usually representing animals, are a common feature of these traditional dances. Not surprisingly, in a world that is getting smaller, the rhythms of Yaqui music have increasingly inspired and been adopted by contemporary Mexican composers.

Highway 15 continues in a southeasterly direction for 130 km. (81 miles) to **Ciudad Obregón,** a modern agricultural center located 45 km. (28 miles) south of the large irrigation reservoir of *Lake Alvaro Obregón.*

Navojoa, 69 km. (43 miles) farther south, is one of the fast-growing towns in this area of irrigation-farming, and began as a settlement of the Mayo Indians, who still live in the surrounding countryside. Related to the Yaquis, the Mayos number some 28,000 and retain their traditional system of self-government, with village headmen and tribal chiefs, although it's a system that is slowly disintegrating under the relentless assault of modernity. Their first encounters with the Spanish took place in the years between 1530 and 1540, but the warlike Mayos were not pacified until about 1700, when Padre Kino arrived and established a Jesuit mission.

The main religious festivals of the Mayos, which are filled with dancing, are the Día de la Santa Cruz on May 3; the Día de San Juan on June 24; and the Feria de San Francisco during the first week of October.

From Navojoa, you can take a side trip east to *Alamos,* 53 km. (33 miles) away. Now protected as a national monument, Alamos was once a wealthy Spanish mining town. The discovery of gold and silver in 1680 led to such a boom that, 100 years later, the population had ballooned to some 30,000. Incessant raids by the Mayo Indians, a gradual decline in the price of silver as it was replaced by other metals and alloys in industry, and the disruptions of the revolutionary wars all contributed to Alamos's long decline into ghost town status. It was rediscovered after World War II, however, by artists and retirees from the United States, who settled in and began to restore some of the magnificent old Colonial buildings.

The nearest beach along this stretch, *Huatabampito,* lies about 55 km. (34 miles) southwest of Navojoa. There are shorter trips to the Gulf, such as the one to *Agiabampo,* 96 km. (60 miles) southeast of Navojoa on Highway 15, as the road gradually swings closer to the coast.

Continue on Highway 15 into the coastal state of Sinaloa all the way to **Los Mochis,** 159 km. (99 miles) southeast of Navojoa and 5 km. (3 miles) off the highway.

Founded just after the turn of the century by an American, Benjamin F. Johnston, who built a sugar refinery here (now state-owned and one of the largest in Mexico), sugarcane is still the basis of the local economy. In fact, the town is filled with its smell from December to June. The *botanical gardens,* officially called Sinaloa Park, are on the grounds of Johnston's home. Los Mochis is also the starting- or end-point of the spectacular *Chihuahua–Pacific Railroad,* which requires 39 bridges and 86 tunnels to make its way through the Sierra Madre Occidental and across the Continental Divide to Chihuahua (see Travel Route 13). You can also take a train trip from here to the old Colonial town of **El Fuerte** (The Strong One), a distance of 52 km. (32 miles) one way. **Topolobampo,** 24 km. (15 miles) west of Los Mochis on Ohuira Bay, is a fishing village and harbor where ferries depart for La Paz on the Baja peninsula.

From Los Mochis, continue southeast on Highway 15 for 60 km. (37 miles) to *Guasave,* where Mayo dances can be seen during the popular fiesta honoring the Virgen del Rosario, held on the first Sunday of October.

You can pass through *Guamúchil,* 40 km. (25 miles) farther south, the next town on Highway 15, and drive directly to **Culiacán,** 207 km. (128 miles) from Los Mochis and the largest city between it and Guadalajara. Founded in 1531 by Beltrán Nuño de Guzmán, Culiacán, the capital of Sinaloa, is a former mining town that has developed into an important agricultural center, thanks to irrigation. Cotton, sugarcane, and winter vegetables, especially tomatoes, are among the crops grown in the region, as are poppies, which are used in the legal production of opiates. There isn't much of interest for a visitor here except for the 19th-century *Cathedral,* a modern *community center,* and a *museum* that displays items of local origin. The local *bandas sinaloenses* (Sinaloa bands), which combine military marches with Dixieland and Cuban rhythms, are a well-loved part of local and statewide culture.

*Mazatlán ("place of the deer" in the Nahuatl language), 225 km. (140 miles) southeast of Culiacán on Highway 15, is the most important port on Mexico's Pacific coast and one of the most popular beach resorts in the country. Although the town boasts the *El Faro* (the second-highest lighthouse in the world after Gibraltar's) and an aquarium, the *Acuario Mazatlán,* forget about seeing sights of great architectural or historical interest here; visitors come for the beaches and deep-sea fishing. Mazatlán is situated just south of the Tropic of Cancer on a peninsula that juts into a natural harbor and separates its large shrimp fleet and heavy boat traffic from the 16 km. (9.6 miles) of wide sandy beaches that extend northward along the coastal road. The hotels, restaurants, and boutiques begin where the road changes its name to the Paseo Centenario to the Paseo Olas Atlas ("high waves"). Hugging the coast, it becomes the Paseo Claussen near the rock known as *El Mirador,* the place where so-called "death divers" plunge into the sea far below, and then changes its name one last time to the Avenida del Mar. Harbor cruises are available twice a day, and there's also boat service to the *Isla de la Piedra* and *Islas Chivas,* both of which have beaches that are less crowded than the ones on the mainland. Deep-sea fishing yields a bounty of swordfish, tuna, shark, sailfish, and marlin. In addition, the city has two bullfight rings. Finally, there is daily ferry service between Mazatlán and La Paz on the Baja Peninsula, a trip that takes 16 hours.

Highway 40, the mountain road to Durango (see Travel Route 16), begins 25 km. (15 miles) southwest of town. The Pacific coast south of Mazatlán is described in Travel Routes 17–20.

TRAVEL ROUTE 13: Los Mochis–***Barranca del Cobre–*Chihuahua (651 km.; 404 miles by train)

See map on page 186.

The 86 tunnels and 39 bridges of the spectacular Chihuahua–Pacific railway through the gorges of the rugged Sierra Madre Occidental are a fitting tribute to the skills of the Mexican engineers who designed and built it in the years 1953–1961. The trip from Chihuahua to Los Mochis, or vice versa, takes about 14 hours, but in order to fully enjoy the magnificently diversified terrain, you should allow for more time and make several stops along the way. The *Expresso Cañon del Cobre,* or Copper Canyon Express, with its fitful air-conditioning, dining and observation car, is more comfortable than the local, or *mixto,* train. Both trains leave Los Mochis in the morning, and reservations can be made through Aviamex in Mexico City (512 90 97 or 512 90 32). Be sure to buy your tickets at least a day in advance, and be sure to make reservations at hotels along the way, unless you're planning to camp out.

From Los Mochis, the first three hours of the trip are uneventful as the train travels through the coastal plain with its farms and croplands to **El Fuerte,** situated on the Río Fuerte, 82 km. (51 miles) inland. Founded by the Spanish in 1563, the town was destroyed soon afterward by Indians, necessitating the addition of a protective stockade, which eventually lent the settlement its name. An 18th-century church and a scattering of Colonial buildings remain.

The 500-meter (1640-foot) bridge over the Río Fuerte is the longest span on the route. On the other side of the river, the terrain changes dramatically as the train begins its gradual ascent into the mountains, running along the walls of a forested canyon that winds higher and higher into the Sierras. The humid tropical air of the coast is soon dispelled by an influx of fresher, cooler mountain air.

By noon the train reaches **Bahuichivo,** 170 km. (105 miles) from the last stop at El Fuerte, and situated at an elevation of 1,600 meters (5,248 feet). *Cerocahui,* 24 km. (15 miles) away in a peaceful valley, has a

Emblem of the Pacific Train

hotel, the *Misión Cerocahui,* that provides bus service to the Bahuichivo station. The Jesuit mission founded here by Juan María de Salvatierra remains the center of village life, and has a large boarding school as well as a small store that sells baskets and pottery. From here you can also make excursions by foot or on horseback to the *Cerocahui waterfalls,* or travel by hotel bus to the *Cerro del Gallego,* 2,300 meters (7,544 feet) high, with its superb view of the Cañon del Urique. The hotel also organizes trips to an old mining village at the bottom of the gorge.

El Divisadero, another 44 km. (27 miles) east and 650 meters (2,130 feet) higher in elevation, is next up the line. Trains from either direction stop here for 20–30 minutes to let passengers view the magnificent ***Barranca del Cobre** (Copper Canyon), comparable to Arizona's Grand Canyon for sheer majesty. The "canyon" is actually a series of a dozen interconnected gorges containing humid green valleys framed by dramatic rock formations that rise some 2,735 meters (7,500 feet) to their tops. El Divisadero is also where you'll probably get your first glimpse of Tarahumara Indians, since they sell their crafts at this spot. You should consider spending the night, or even a few nights, here. There are a variety of walks and horseback treks to stunning and secluded lookouts, as well as excursions to the bottom, in which

case a guide and camping gear will be needed. The *Hotel Cabañas Divisadero* sits on the rim of the gorge.

The surrounding canyons are the home of some 50,000 Tarahumara Indians, who occupied large areas of Chihuahua before the Conquest, and then retreated into the inaccessible Sierra Madre when the Spanish arrived. The Tarahumaras were followed into their mountain hideouts by Jesuit priests, who converted them to a form of Christianity in which their old Indian religion remained predominant. To this day, the sun and moon are principal Tarahumaran deities, and the peyote cactus is a sacred plant reserved for the elders and medicine men of the tribe. When gold and silver were discovered in the foothills of the Sierras in the late 17th century, newly arrived Spanish soldiers and settlers forced the Tarahumara into forced labor in the mines. Bitter fighting with whites and *mestizos* lasted into the 20th century. Still, the Tarahumara managed to preserve their independence, and today each village is governed by an elected council of three. Traditional dress for the men is a long cotton shirt or cape, a loincloth, and bright red headband; women wear loose tunics and full woolen skirts with belts. Tarahumaran handicrafts include basketweaving, wooden masks, woolen blankets, incense burners, and, oddly enough, handmade violins.

The Tarahumara belong to the Apache family, and refer to themselves as the Raramuri, or "running people," because of their ritual long-distance runs. Teams of Tarahumaras frequently challenge one another to epic races through canyons and rivers, male teams kicking a wooden ball ahead of them, female teams propelling a hoop. Generally barefoot, they are said to be able to run deer to exhaustion. Semi-nomadic, the Tarahumara live in the warmer canyon lowlands during the harsh winters, and move up to the highlands in the summer. The Tarahumara shed their habitual reserve only during the *tesguinadas,* religious ceremonies in which they drink a sacred homebrewed corn beer.

The next stop is **Creel,** 60 km. (37 miles) further east and another 50 meters (164 feet) higher in elevation. Both a lumber center and the most important town in the region, Creel is also a wonderful place from which to explore the Tarahumara canyon country. There are a few hotels near the railroad station and another, the rustic Cabañas Cañon del Cobre (Copper Canyon Lodge) in the mountains, as well as rooms to rent offered by local families. Buses from the station pass *Lake Arareco,* which is set in a beautiful pine wood on the way to town.

The easiest way to see the surrounding country is by taking one of the tours offered by the *Motel Parador de la Montaña* in Creel. The Copper Canyon tour, which lasts about 10 hours, is a good way to explore the beauty of that

vast natural wonder. Another tour is offered to ****Cascada de Basaseachic** (Basaseachic Falls), Mexico's highest, where the water plunges into a pool some 311 meters (1,000 feet) below. The Jesuit *misión de Cusárare,* with its restored mid-18th-century church featuring geometric Tarahumaran wall decorations, can also be visited, as can the mining town of *La Bufa,* a two-day trip there and back.

To see an example of Tarahumaran cave dwellings, follow Mateos past the Motel Pagamar to a fork in the road and turn left. The caves begin a short distance outside of town. One cave, more in the nature of a tourist spot where the Indians sell their arts and crafts, is open to the public.

The last noteworthy stop on the route is **Cuauhtémoc,** 163 km. (102 miles) from Creel, and an agricultural center founded by Mennonites, a religious sect whose origins date back to the

Mennonites in Cuauhtémoc

mid-16th century and who settled here in 1921 after a long search for religious freedom. Mexican President Alvaro Obregón granted them the right to educate their children in their own schools and exemption from military service (Mennonites reject the notion of such service), and with this charter in hand they moved to Chihuahua and soon acquired a vast plantation. About 50,000 Mennonites now live in the area, speaking a Low Saxon dialect or, more formally, an old version of High German, and cultivating small farms and orchards. They are famous for their cheese as well, and have made Chihuahua Mexico's leading producer of oats. Hard-working Mennonite communities have conceded nothing to the amenities of modern life, except the use of tractors and diesel generators for farm work. Motorized vehicles, electricity, and modern appliances are otherwise regarded with suspicion. Goods and property are held communally, and the common good ranks above personal need. Recently, a number of tour operators have made it possible to visit with the Mennonites in their small, well-scrubbed farmhouses. The men, wearing blue overalls and wide-brimmed straw hats, and the women, with their long black skirts, are courteous and curious.

Since the train from Cuauhtémoc is often fully booked, you may find it easier to continue on from here by bus. The last stop, of course, is ***Chihuahua** (see page 184), 651 km. (403 miles) from your starting point in Los Mochis.

TRAVEL ROUTE 14: Ciudad Juárez–*Chihuahua–Torreón–*Zacatecas (1,226 km.; 760 miles)

See map on page 186.

If you cross into Mexico through the border town of Ciudad Juárez, it's a long drive south through sparsely settled country before you get to the heart of Mexico. This travel route takes you to some of the more interesting way stations on the trip south, including the historic town of Chihuahua.

Ciudad Juárez, one of Mexico's largest border cities, is situated, along with its American sister city, El Paso, at the only easy crossing point in the Sierra Madre del Norte. Three bridges spanning the Río Bravo del Norte—or Rio Grande as its called in the States— connect the two cities. Ciudad Juárez itself began as a mission, and was eventually named (in 1888) for President Benito Juárez, who brought his government here during the War of Intervention in 1865–1866. In addition, the folk hero Francisco ("Pancho") Villa made the city his base of operations during the revolutionary years 1910–1921.

The city offers little in the way of cultural monuments, and visitors come primarily for the bullfights, horse and dog racing, shopping, and the nightlife. A *Cathedral* now stands on the site of the original mission church, and a shrine to the country's patron saint, the *Misión de Nuestra Senora de Guadalupe,* dates to the 17th century. The old *Municipal Palace,* located on 16 Septiembre, is the best remaining Colonial structure. The new *Centro Cultural* in the *Parque Chamizal* houses the *Museo Arqueológico,* which provides a good introduction to Mexican history through its collections of pre-Hispanic pottery, statuary, and other artifacts; it also contains an arts and crafts bazaar.

From Ciudad Juárez, follow Highway 45 south through the arid, empty landscape of the Chihuahuan desert past the Samalayuca sand dunes, former haunt of Apache Indians. *Villa Ahumada,* 134 km. (83 miles) south of the border, is an agricultural oasis on the banks of the Río del Carmen.

Near *El Sueco,* there is a connection to Highway 10 which runs west and then north a total of about 200 km. (120 miles) to the important pre-Columbian archaeological site of **Casas Grandes,** which is located 7 km. (4 miles) southwest of the town of **Nuevo Casas Grandes.** Historians and archaeologists continue to study this pre-Hispanic city, which was once called Paquime and shows evidence of influence from two different cultures. The multistoried pueblos are similar to those still seen in the American Southwest, while the many "stepped" pyramids suggest an architectural style more common to Mesoamerica. There is also a partially excavated central market area, a pelota court, and an advanced and ingenious system of indoor plumbing employing hidden cisterns. At its height between A.D. 1000–1200, Paquime was the most important agricultural and trading center in northern Mexico. The city probably came to a sudden, violent end, however, in the 14th century, when Aztec invaders set fire to it. Today, the ancient adobe walls are in constant danger of disintegration, and if you visit, you're likely to see workers patching them.

From Casas Grandes, other archaeological sites in the Sierra Madre foothills may be visited on horseback or by jeep, though they

Cueva de la Olla

are often difficult to find. The once-inhabited cave dwelling known as *Cueva de la Olla* is accessible via the Mormon settlements of *Juárez* and *Pacheco*.

Return on Highway 10 to El Sueco to pick up Highway 45, which will take you to Chihuahua, the state capital.

*Chihuahua

Well situated in a high valley (elevation 1,430 meters; 4,690 feet) and surrounded by the treeless foothills of the Sierra Madre Occidental, Chihuahua was not settled until 1709. The discovery of silver brought people and prosperity, but raids by the Apache and Comanche tribes to the north posed an incessant threat to the settlement. Still, Chihuahua managed to play an important role in Mexico's turbulent history. After his capture by Royalist troops, for example, Miguel Hidalgo y Costilla, the "Father of Mexican Independence," was court-martialed and shot here. American troops occupied the town in 1846–1848 during the Mexican-American War, and again in 1862–1866, during the War of Intervention. Benito Juárez lived here for some time, and it was also here that the successful uprising against the dictator Díaz broke out in 1910. Pancho Villa took the town in 1913 with his army, the División del Norte, and made it his headquarters. After his defeat in 1915, Villa carried out raids from the nearby mountains. He finally made peace with the Mexican government in 1920 and was given a large *hacienda* nearby, but was shot and killed in an ambush three years later.

The Late-Baroque *Cathedral,* which is dedicated to Saint Francis of Assisi and is the most impressive religious edifice in northern Mexico, stands on the **Plaza de Armas,** the city's central square. Built between 1717 and 1826, the façade features statues of the twelve Apostles.

The **Palacio de Gobierno** (state capitol) is located on the nearby *Plaza Hidalgo.* This old Jesuit college (which was rebuilt at the end of the 19th century) was the place where Hidalgo and his lieutenants were captured and executed in 1811; their severed heads were then put on public display in Guanajuato. Inside, murals by Aron Piña Mora depict events in Mexico and Chihuahua's history. Across the street is the **Palacio Federal,** where an eagle inscribed with the word *Libertad* points to the door of the cell where Hidalgo was confined for the two months prior to his execution.

The ***Museo Regional del Estado,** in the former Palace of Justice at the corner of Bolivar and Calle 2, is one of the finest examples of Art Nouveau architecture in all of Mexico. The building contains a number of furnished period rooms and archaeological material from the surrounding area, as well as an ethnological and folk art collection.

*Quinta Luz, at Calle 10 Norte

No. 3014, is the city's biggest attraction. Once occupied by Pancho Villa, it was turned into the *Museo Historico de la Revolución* after the death of Villa's widow, Luz Corral. Inside, there are mementos and souvenirs of this famous bandit and revolutionary hero, including the car in which he was shot and his death mask. (A list of Villa's 23 mistresses and 22 children indicates that his prowess extended to other fields, as well.) The marble mausoleum built for the hero in the Panteon de la Regla stands empty; Villa was buried in Parral, where he died.

Other sights in Chihuahua include the *Capella de Santa Rita,* built in 1731 (a fiesta in honor of Saint Rita, the city's patron saint, is held on May 22). The *church of Guadalupe,* which dates from

Panteón de la Regla, Chihuahua

1826; the *church of San Francisco,* which was erected by the Franciscans between 1721 and 1740; and the ruins of a 5,583-meter- (4-mile-) long *aqueduct* constructed between 1754 and 1864 are also noteworthy.

After your stay in Chihuahua, follow Highway 45 to *Ciudad Delicias,* about 87 km. (53 miles) further south. Founded in 1935 and known for its vineyards, Ciudad Delicias is one of the youngest and most prosperous cities in the state of Chihuahua.

Ciudad Camargo, 144 km. (90 miles) south of Chihuahua, was founded in 1740 as the Franciscan mission of Santa Rosalía and destroyed by Apache Indians in 1797. Today it is a prosperous agricultural center irrigated by the Boquilla reservoir, and local farmers harvest cotton, wheat, beans, and peanuts; ranching is also an important part of the economy. The thermal springs of *Oja de Jabali, Ojo Caliente,* and *Ojo Salado* are located nearby.

In *Ciudad Jiménez,* about 227 km. (140 miles) south of Chihuahua, Highway 45 veers sharply to the west and leads to **Hidalgo del Parral,** a distance of 79 km. (49 miles). This is the town where Pancho Villa retired and where he was murdered in an ambush in 1923; a small museum and memorial tablet commemorate the event. But Parral has been an important mining town since the 17th century, as well. Three churches are particularly notewor-

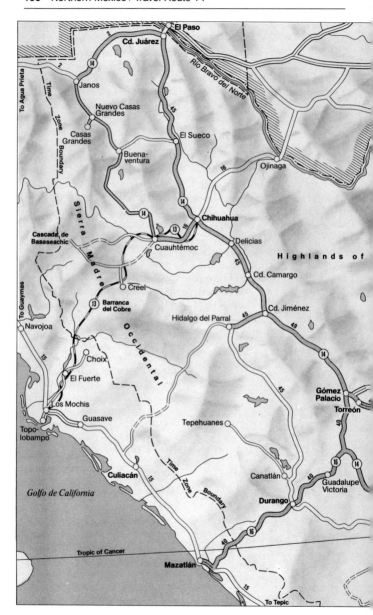

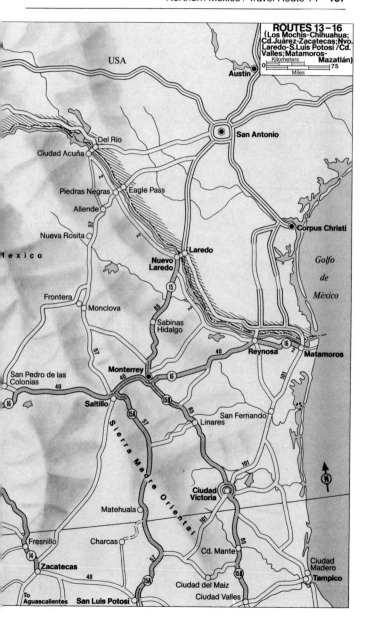

ROUTES 13–16
(Los Mochis-Chihuahua;
Cd.Juárez-Zacatecas;Nvo.
Laredo-S.Luis Potosí /Cd.
Valles;Matamoros-Mazatlán)

thy: the *parish church*, dating from 1710 and with a Churrigueresque altar; *El Rayo*, an 18th-century pilgrimage church with Churrigueresque *retablos*; and the 20th-century *Santuario de la Virgen de Fatima*, built of ore-filled stones in 1953 to honor the patron saint of miners.

Back at Jiménez, follow Highway 49 south, cutting across the northeast corner of the large and thinly populated state of Durango to *Gómez Palacio*. From here it is 6 km. (4 miles) to **Torreón,** 467 km. (290 miles) south of Chihuahua. Located just over the Río Nazas and across the boundary of the state of Coahuila, both Torreón and Gómez Palacio are situated in the *Comarca La Laguna* (Lake District), an area once flooded every year by the river. After a dam was erected in the mid-19th century, foreign companies promoted cotton-growing in the area. *El Torreón* (The Tower) was built to house the supervisors of the project and to protect workers from Indian attacks. Today, the city is mostly an industrial center, with little of interest to the tourist, but it is a convenient overnight stop between El Paso and Mexico City.

Torreón is also a way station on Travel Route 16, which crosses Mexico from coast to coast, and intersects with Travel Route 14. At **Cuencamé,** 109 km. (68 miles) south of Torreón, Highway 40 turns off to Durango; a detour through Durango and Vicente Guerrero is 158 km. (98 miles) longer than the direct route to Zacatecas followed by Highway 49.

The direct route follows Highway 49 south through the state of Durango and into the mineral-rich state of Zacatecas all the way to **Fresnillo,** 333 km. (206 miles) from Torreón, an old silver mining town at an elevation of 2,250 meters (7,380 feet) that was founded by the Spanish in 1554. At *Plateros,* 7 km. (4 miles) north, June 15 is the fiesta day for Santa Niño del Huarachito. The church here was built in 1789 and was formerly dedicated to the *Señor de los Plateros* (Lord of the Silversmiths).

For ***Zacatecas,** 386 km. (240 miles) from Torreón, see page 133.

TRAVEL ROUTE 15: Nuevo Laredo–Monterrey–*San Luís Potosí/Ciudad Valles (752 km.; 466 miles)

See map on page 186.

The trip from Nuevo Laredo, across the border from Laredo, Texas, to San Luís Potosí covers a dramatically changing landscape; from low-lying arid towns near the border only 171 meters (560 feet) above sea level to the verdant foothills of the Sierra Madre, 321 meters (1,052 feet) high.

Nuevo Laredo is an important border town, with extensive agriculture and many processing plants. Although founded in 1867 by San Agustín de Laredo, the treaty settling the Mexican-American War in 1848 made Río Bravo the boundary line between the two countries, placing the town of Laredo on United States soil. But 120 Mexican families refused to take up residence in the foreign country, deciding instead to found a new settlement—Nuevo Laredo—across the river on Mexican territory. Today the town's population has swelled to more than 220,000.

From Nuevo Laredo, follow Highway 85 south toward Monterrey. After about 43 km. (26 miles) you will cross from the state of Tamaulipas to the new state of Nuevo Leon.

Continue south on 85 for about 90 km. (54 miles) to **Sabinas Hidalgo,** a mining town on the Río Sabinas founded in 1693. Silver, zinc, and lead are still mined here, along with bituminous coal. Additionally, farming and a developing textile industry have created a growing population. Today, the town has 25,000 inhabitants.

From Sabinas Hidalgo, continue south on 85 to the state capital of Monterrey.

Monterrey

See map on page 190.

With a population of over 2.5 million people, this is the third largest city in Mexico and the most important industrial center in the north. Located in the valley of the Río Santa Catarina, 538 meters (1,765 feet) above sea level, Monterrey is surrounded in the east and south by the Sierra Madre Oriental mountain range, including the rugged Cerro de la Silla. It is a modern city in a beautiful setting, and has managed to gallop ahead into the technological age while keeping much of its Old World charm.

Founded by the Spanish in 1596, Monterrey did not prosper until the end of the 19th century, when the iron and steel industries set up plants here. Lighter industries, including glass-making, ceramics, and the large Cuauhtémoc beer brewery, soon followed suit. Today, practically every kind of industry—from tractors to construction materials to cigarettes—prospers here. Monterrey is also an important university town, with over 30 institutions, including the prestigious technical school, the Instituto Tecnológico de Monterrey.

In 1980 the *Regiomontanos,* as local residents are called, embarked on an ambitious large-scale modernization project for the town center. Whole streets were bulldozed to create a huge square, the ***Gran Plaza** (1), or Macroplaza. Almost a whole kilometer (half a mile) long, the plaza extends from the modern town hall (2) to the *Palacio de Gobierno* (4), replacing two squares, the Zaragoza and the Cinco de Mayo.

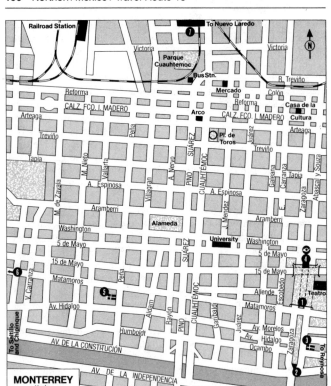

It is enlivened by grassy areas, pedestrian walks (including one right through the town hall), and innumerable sculptures and fountains. At the far end of the square, near the river, is a Baroque *Cathedral* (3) built between 1603 and 1899. Across from this looms a small bright red tower, the Beacon of Commerce, designed by Luís Barragan; it is probably the only tower in the world to flash a green laser beam into the night. Nearby stands the new 1,500-seat city theater *Teatro de la Ciudad*, whose rounded concrete shape adds to the futuristic look of the new city. There is underground parking and a shopping center on the Plaza.

A Mexican flag flies on the *Esplanada de los Héroes*, an open square in front of the **Palacio de Gobierno** (4). Built of reddish sandstone around the turn of the century, this large Colonial building with its stately Corinthian columns and beautiful patio now houses government offices. The splendid reception room is decorated with oil paintings by Anibale Guerini.

Behind the imposing palace, on the other side of the Avenida Cinco de Mayo, is the *Palacio Federal,* the old town hall, now the main post office. In the courtyard, wrought-iron lamp posts and tiled arches are reminders of Monterrey's Colonial past. From the tower there is a panoramic view of the city. At the other end of the Plaza, toward the cathedral, Avenida Padre Mier leads west to the *Iglesia La Purísima* (5), located at the intersection of Calle Serafin Pena. This impressive modern church was designed by Enrique de la Mora y Palomar. Continue along Avenida Padre Mier to the *Cerro del Obispado,* on which stands the **Palacio del Obispado** (Bishop's Palace) (6). Completed in 1790, this solid edifice seems not to have been destined for church use: It has served as garrison, fortress, and military hospital, and is now a museum, the *Museo Regional de Nuevo León.* Pancho Villa, the bandit-revolutionary, hid here during the raids of 1913.

In the northern part of town, at Avenida Universidad and Calle Luís Mora, is the **Museo de Monterrey** (7), an art museum housed in the old vat house of the Cerveceria Cuauhtémoc. The museum's exhibits include a collection of modern paintings by Rufino Tamayo, José Orozco, and David Siqueiros, as well as memorabilia from the old brewery. In new quarters now, the brewery is still very much in operation, producing Bohemia and Carta Blanca beers; it has become one of the largest breweries in Mexico.

There are a number of interesting sights outside Monterrey. About 13 km. (8 miles) south of the center of town is the community of *Garza García,* now considered part of metropolitan Monterrey. Here, you'll find the **Centro Cultural Alfa,** which combines science, art, and technology. Its excellent planetarium is built in the shape of a tilted vat. Behind the center, a toll road begins its climb to the ***Mesa de Chipinque,** a popular resort area with cabins for rent, a hotel, and a restaurant. Located at an altitude of 1,365 meters (4,477 feet), the pine-covered plateau offers a spectacular panorama of the city below.

Planetarium des Centro Cultural Alfa

Southeast of town is the ***Cerro de la Silla** (Hill of the Saddle), the jagged mountain peak named for its distinctive shape. Local folklore recounts how a misguided resident gave the peak its ragged contour by digging around the edges in search of a lost peso. A road leads to the summit 1,800 meters (5,900 feet) above sea level, but a cable car will take you to a halfway point where there is a restaurant.

Take the road to Saltillo (Route 40), about 15 km. (9 miles) to the turnoff near Santa Catarina to get to ***Cañón de la Huasteca,** an impressive gorge with steep walls cut by water.

Another natural wonder further along the same route is ***Grutas de García,** a fantastic cave deep within a high mountain about 50 km. (31 miles) from Monterrey. To get there, take the same turnoff and continue north through Villa Garcia. There is a cablecar to the cave entrance.

Another worthwhile side trip about 40 km. (24 miles) from Monterrey leads southeast on 85 and then along a turnoff near El Cercado to *Cascada Cola de Caballo* (Horsetail Falls), a spectacular waterfall some 30 meters (100 feet) high. A path leads to the falls from the parking lot, where there is a small hotel and restaurant. Horses, donkeys, and carriages can also be rented here.

From Monterrey, two roads lead to Mexico City. The easier way leads through Saltillo and San Luís Potosí, passing lovely Colonial towns in the central highlands. The more difficult drive follows an old road through the mountains via Ciudad Victoria and Ciudad Valles.

Via San Luís Potosí

(*Follow the route marked 15A on the map on page 186.*)

Leaving Monterrey, take the four-lane Highway 40 to *Saltillo* (see page 195). Side trips to Cañón de la Huasteca and the García Caves (see page 192) are not far off the main route. (From Saltillo it is possible to connect with Travel Route 16: Take Highway 54 southwest for 372 km., 230 miles, to Zacatecas—see page 133). Continue south on 57. Shortly before Matehuala, a road turns off to the west, leading through *Cedral* and over a dry steppe to **Real de Catorce,** about 56 km. (35 miles) from Monterrey. This once flourishing mining town lies 2,845 meters (9,330 feet) above sea level. Large quantities of gold and silver were mined from its bare mountains during the 18th century, when the local population soared to 30,000 residents. Today, the near ghost town remains a silent reminder of a glorious Colonial past.

To reach the town, you must follow a poorly paved and then gravel road, which winds up into the mountains. Enter the town through a long tunnel.

Several legends surround the town name, which means "Royal Fourteen." According to the most

Peyote cactus

credible legend, it commemorates 14 soldiers who were killed here during a battle with rebellious Indians. The town comes alive once a year from October 3–6 for the festival of St. Francis; 10,000 pilgrims arrive, among them Huichol Indians who collect hallucinogenic peyote from cactus in the surrounding desert plateaus. Lodging is available in nearby **Matehuala** (576 km., 357 miles, from Nuevo Laredo). An old coach station 1,615 meters (5,297 feet) above sea level, Matehuala became a prosperous commercial center thanks to the wealth from local mines. Today it boasts a population of 35,000.

Return to 57 and continue south to *El Huizache.* Here you can connect with the alternate route by following 80 east, to pick up Highway 85. Or you can continue south on 57 to ***San Luís Potosí** (773 km., 479 miles, from Nuevo Laredo; see page 189). From here, the distance to Mexico City is 420 km. (260 miles).

Via Ciudad Valles

(Follow the route marked 15B on map on page 186)

Leave Monterrey from the southeast on Highway 85. At El Cercado, there is a turnoff to the *Cola de Caballo* waterfall (see page 192). Continue southeast on 85 to *Montemorelos* (314 km., 195 miles, from Nuevo Laredo). Located at an altitude of 432 meters (1,415 feet), this town is surrounded by extensive orange groves. Some oranges are packed in bags and sold on the street but most of the harvest is exported. Another orange-growing area, farther along 85, is **Linares** (366 km.; 227 miles), located at an altitude of 684 meters (2,243 feet). The town, founded in 1712 under the name of San Felipe de Linares, was the bishop's see from 1777 to

Cola de Caballo (Monterrey)

1791, when the see moved to Monterrey. Linares regained its title in 1962 when the pope ordained a second bishop for Nuevo León, and established its see here once again. This provincial town of 50,000 has a city hall and the Teatro Benítez, each with its own lovely square. A large fair is held here in early May, the Feria Regional de Linares, in which local farmers and ranchers exhibit their products.

Continue southeast on 85 through an increasingly lush and subtropical landscape. At the foothills of the Sierra, 520 km. (322 miles) above sea level, is **Ciudad Victoria.** The capital of the state of Tamaulipas, with a population of 100,000, the town is named for General Guadalupe Victoria, who fought in the War of Independence and went on to become the first president of Mexico. Ciudad Victoria is an important crossroads: One route due east leads to the coast through Soto La Marina (171 km.; 106 miles); another route going southeast reaches Tampico (292 km.; 181 miles); and the third major route, Highway 101, extends from the United States border through Ciudad Vic-

toria to Matamoros (308 km.; 191 miles). Continue southeast on 85 to **Ciudad Mante,** the center of a sugarcane industry. Large refineries process the cane between November and April. To celebrate their local industry and economic boom, the 75,000 residents throw a fiesta, the Feria del Azúcar, in early May.

From here, you can pick up Highway 80 to Tampico 155 km. (96 miles) away. Otherwise, continue on Highway 85 through *Antiguo Morelos,* where there is a connection to the alternate route west on 80 through Ciudad del Maíz. After driving 30 km. (19 miles) on 85, a side road leads 11 km. (7 miles) to the impressive *El Salto* waterfall. If you continue south on Highway 85, you reach **Ciudad Valles** (752 km.; 466 miles from Nuevo Laredo). This town, at an altitude of 95 meters (312 feet), is the center of a sugarcane and citrus growing area. There are several good hotels here.

From here, you have a choice of the road to Tampico (see Travel Route 21), or the drive in the opposite direction through the Sierra Madre to Mexico City.

TRAVEL ROUTE 16: Matamoros–Monterrey–Torreón–Saltillo–*Durango–*Mazatlán (1,260 km.; 756 miles)

See map on page 186.

This route crosses Mexico from the Gulf coast to the Pacific coast. The section of the trip that traverses the Sierra Madre Occidental between Durango and Mazatlán is particularly scenic.

Matamoros, lying on the humid coastal plain of the Gulf of Mexico, is separated from Brownsville, Texas, by the Río Bravo (or Rio Grande on the other side of the river), which connects the port with the Gulf of Mexico some 37 km. (23 miles) to the east. There was a small settlement here by 1700; in 1810 the town's name was changed from Congregación de Nuestra Señora del Refugio to Villa de Matamoras, in honor of a priest who was slain in the War of Independence. The American general Zachary Taylor took the city in 1846 and cut it in two, making the Río Bravo the international border, and it was occupied by the French a few years later. Economic development started during the American Civil War, when Southern cotton was shipped out from the nearby port of Bagdad, and arms for the Confederates were shipped in.

The small *Casa Mata Museum* at the corner of Calles Guatemala and Santos Degollado, with its artifacts commemorating the revolutionary period and some Indian pottery and figurines, and the new *Centro de Artesanias* on Carranza near Iturbide are the two tourist sights here. The *Playa General Lauro Villar,* 37 km. (23 miles) east of town at the mouth of the Río Bravo, is the closest beach.

From Matamoros, Highway 101 bypasses Monterrey and connects to Travel Route 15 at *Ciudad Victoria,* 312 km. (193 miles) to the southwest, where there is a turnoff to *Tampico,* a total distance of 503 km. (312 miles). Highway 2 heads due west from Matamoros to **Reynosa,** 98 km. (61 miles) away, an industrial border town on the Río Bravo that was founded in 1765, and from there you can pick up Highway 40 to **Monterrey,** 323 km. (200 miles; see page 189).

From Monterrey, follow Highway 40 in the direction of Saltillo. For a description of side trips from Monterrey to the Cañón de la Huasteca and the Caves of Garcia, see Travel Route 15.

Saltillo, 82 km. (51 miles) southwest of Monterrey, lies in a high valley (1,600 meters; 5,248 feet) surrounded by bare mountains, and is the capital of Coahuila, the third-largest state in the country. First settled in 1575 by Captain Francisco Urdiñola and a party of followers, repeated attacks by nomadic tribes of Indians forced the captain to bring in Tlaxcalan Indians, who had been Cortés's allies against the Aztecs and were granted special privileges as a result. The Tlaxcalans are responsible for turning what had been mediocre pastureland into rich farmland. In time, Saltillo became part of a vast province that included all of modern Coahuila, Texas, and the southwestern part of the United States to the Colorado River. Of course, this territory was divided and Mexico forced to give up the northern sections as a result of the Mexican-American War. Benito Juárez, retreating, as he was so often forced to do, from French invasion forces, set up a temporary headquarters here in 1863.

There are a few noteworthy buildings to be seen among the narrow streets of Saltillo. The *Cathedral of Santiago,* standing on the main square, is a handsome example of the Churrigueresque style. Built from 1746 to 1801, it is also one of the largest religious structures in northern Mexico. Across from it is the early 19th-century *Palacio de Gobierno,* which was remodelled in 1928 and is now a museum dedicated to Venustiano Carranza, a former president of the country. The *church of San Estéban* dates from 1592. The *Alameda* is a lovely square. No. 2 on the main square, *Ateneo Fuente,* with its finely sculpted entrance, was established as a college in 1867 and became the nucleus for the University of Coahuila. More than its architecture, however, Saltillo is known for its hand-woven blankets and *serapes.*

From Saltillo continue south on Highway 40 for 290 km. (180 miles) to **Torreón.** Most of this stretch through the border area of the states of Coahuila and Durango is sparsely populated desert. Only as you near Torreón itself will the irrigated farmland that is the basis of the area's prosperity become apparent. (For a more complete description of Torreón and the adjacent city of *Gómez Palacio,* see page 188.) As you leave Torreón on Highway 40, the terrain will gradually become hillier and the road more winding; the vegetation, however, will remain limited to cactus and dusty sagebrush.

At *Cuencamé,* 109 km. (68 miles) southwest of Torreón, a branch of Highway 49 veers off toward Mexico City via Zacatecas (see Travel Route 14).

From *Cuencamé,* Highway 40 continues on to *Durango,* 155 km. (97 miles) to the southwest and the capital of the state of the same name.

*Durango

Situated on an upland plain to the east of the Sierra Madre Occidental at an elevation of 1,880 meters (6,166 feet), Durango is favored by deep-blue skies and generally mild weather.

The area was first explored in 1551 by the Spaniard Ginés Vas-

Ateneo Fuente, Saltillo

quéz de Mercado, who was looking for a fabled mountain consisting entirely of silver. When he found it and realized his mountain of silver was just a hill of iron ore, Vasquéz turned away in disgust and went off to seek his fortune elsewhere in the Sierra Madre. (Almost four and a half centuries later, the so-called Cerro de Mercado is still an important source of iron ore for the steel industry of Monterrey).

Two years later, a Basque named Francisco de Ibarra discovered silver nearby and founded a settlement on the site of the present-day city that became part of the vast province of Nueva Vizcaya (including the states of Chihuahua and Zacatecas). The local Indians, the Tepehuana, gradually withdrew to the mountains to the west after a series of desperate battles with the Spanish over the next 150 years, and the settlement itself wasn't given its present name until the middle of the 18th century.

Today, Durango is an attractive provincial city thanks to its beautiful Colonial architecture as well as the wild landscapes of the Sierra Madre Occidental that loom above the eastern edge of the city. In fact, the Hollywood film industry has found the scenery and surrounding countryside so evocative, it has been filming westerns here for years, leaving several Wild West "towns" behind in the process.

You should begin your tour of Durango at the peaceful *Plaza de Armas,* where the twin-towered ***Cathedral,** which was under construction from 1695 to 1777, sits in massive splendor. Aficionados of Spanish-Mexican cathedral architecture can follow the evolution of the Renaissance style into that of the High Baroque (Churrigueresque) in its ornately carved portals. The interior features a number of noteworthy paintings from Colonial times, among them a so-called "Gallery of the Bishops," with works by Cabrera and Ibarra.

The **Templo del Sagrario,** located one block southwest of the main square, was built by the Jesuits in the 18th century. The adjacent convent with its attractive cloisters today belongs to the University of Durango's Juárez Institute.

Follow Avenida Piño Suárez west to **Plaza IV Centenario,** a broad square surrounded by arcades that was dedicated in 1963 as part of the celebration of the fourth centennial of the founding of the city. In the center of the square stands a monument to that greatest of Mexican heroes, Benito Juárez. The founding of Durango is celebrated from July 7–17 every year with a large market and festival.

The **Palacio del Gobierno** is located in a Colonial building that dates from the 17th century. This former government palace had its own theater right behind it; today, it's the Teatro Victoria, with a façade from the 19th century.

The **Casa del Conde Súchil,** which is east of the Plaza de

Armas on the corner of Calle Cinco de Febrero and Calle Madero, and dates from 1732, has a manorial corner façade in the Churrigueresque style. Less worthy of fame is its history as a court of the Inquisition.

The **Iglesia de los Remedios,** a small Franciscan church constructed in 1640 and later altered, stands at the top of the Cerro de los Remedios in southeast Durango, and is a good place to enjoy panoramic views of the city, the desert to the east, and the formidable Sierra Madre to the west.

A number of the western sets are located on Highway 45 in the direction of *Hidalgo del Parral,* 10 km. (6 miles) beyond the circle downtown. On your left will be the *Villa del Oeste* (Western City),

complete with saloon, church, and cemetery.

Two km. (1.2 miles) farther on is *Chupaderos,* a gem of a village set off by a resplendent chain of reddish mountains. Time continues to gnaw incessantly at the Potemkin façades on the edge of the village, however. Only the gallows appear permanent.

Before undertaking the long last leg of the route to Mazatlán, find out about road conditions, especially during the rainy season, when there's the additional danger of fog. The trip is best taken in daylight hours when you can easily spot the many potholes that dot the road.

You'll pass a number of villages and small towns on this stretch. *El*

Western village, Durango

Salto, with its modest wood houses covered with corrugated iron and 30,000 inhabitants living at an elevation of 2,600 meters (8,528 feet), depends on the lumber industry for its well-being. Farther on, as you begin the descent, is *La Ciudad,* scarcely more than a logger's camp. You'll cross the border into the state of Sinoloa shortly after that and find yourself face-to-face with fantastic views of the seemingly bottomless depths and rugged heights of the Sierra Madre Occidental.

You'll pass over the Tropic of Cancer 205 km. (127 miles) out of Durango. If you want to linger in the mountains a little while longer,

stop and check out the surprising menu at the small *Hotel Villa Blanca.* In addition to the many German specialties offered up by the German-born owner, coffee and cake are served on the cozy terrace, which is an especially delightful spot for bird lovers. In clear weather, you can see all the way to the Pacific and, at night, the lights of Mazatlán below.

The last stretch of Highway 40 winds down into the hot coastal plain in hairpin curves. Eventually, Highway 15, which follows the coast to Tepic to the south and to Mazatlán (see page 178) to the north, intersects Highway 40.

The Pacific Coast

When we hear of Mexico's Pacific coast, most of us immediately think of Acapulco. But that is only one of Mexico's many western seaside resorts, each with its own special character and devoted following. Sportsmen, café hoppers, and sun worshipers alike will all find their particular paradise somewhere along this broad, seemingly endless sand beach. The climate, of course, is tropical—relieved by sea breezes along the unprotected beaches, but dense and moist in the lush gardens that bloom spectacularly in this hothouse climate.

The season most favored by North Americans is, naturally, winter (officially running from December 15 to Easter), when the heartiest New Englander is ready to become a lizard for just a week or two. But many tourists find the rainy season, which lasts from roughly July to September, a time for romantic escape to a lush land where afternoon showers make the countryside steam and the rains can lash without letup for days on end.

Lower (Baja) California and the coasts of the Gulf of California have already been described in Travel Routes 11 and 12 (northern Mexico). Travel Routes 17 to 20 from Mazatlán follow not only the coast road—which extends to the border of Guatemala—but also take in the most important connecting stretches between Guadalajara or Mexico City and the seaside resorts.

TRAVEL ROUTE 17: *Mazatlán–Tepic–**Guadalajara (531 km.; 329 miles)

See map on page 136.

South of the seaside resort of Mazatlán lie the swamps and lagoons of tropical Mexico, along with the quiet, relatively untrammeled beaches for which Mexico's Pacific coast is famous.

From Tepic, it is possible to travel up into the surrounding mountainous territory of the Cora and Huichal Indians (see page 201), whose societies have been less affected by modern Mexico than those of most other Indian groups in the country.

Travel Route 17 can be combined with Travel Route 18, omitting Mazatlán, into a round trip from Guadalajara.

From Mazatlán (see page 178) follow Federal Highway 15 southeast 25 km. (16 miles) to the turnoff where you can either go east on Route 40 into the Sierra Madre Occidental in the direction of Durango (see Travel Route 16), or continue south.

Rosario is located on the banks of the Río Baluarte, 68 km. (42 miles) from Mazatlán on Highway 15 toward Guadalajara. It is not a particularly interesting town except for its late-16th-century *Iglesia de Nuestra Señora del Rosario* (church of the Virgin of the Rosary) in which the exquisite 18th-century altar and gilded retable indicate the wealth silver mining once brought to the region. About 30 km. (19 miles) west is the fine sand beach of *El Caimanero*—but watch for high surf—and the lagoon of the same name.

From *Escuinapa,* 91 km. (56 miles) southeast of Mazatlán on 15, another road leads west through the swampy plain to the coast and then south 20 km. (12 miles) farther to the palm beach of *Teacapan,* at the southern tip of the state of Sinaloa. At Teacapan, the local motel offers guided trips into the surrounding jungle and to La Pantilla beach across Teacapan Lake.

Return to 15 and continue southeast to **Acaponeta,** a small town (population 25,000) that was founded in 1584 by the Franciscans. Nearby, in the virtually inaccessible Sierra del Nayar, live many groups of Cora Indians; their settlements can be reached only in one-day trips by horse or small plane. One road—a trail really—exists for cross-country vehicles, leading to *Huajicori* (18 km.; 11 miles from Acaponeta). The Cora Indians are small farmers living poorly on the produce of the arid soil—corn, beans, squash, and tropical fruits. They also hunt deer, puma, and coyotes.

The jagged Sierra del Nayar was first discovered by the Spaniards in 1581, but Indian uprisings continued well into the 19th century. In the 17th century the Coras also resisted the establishment of Jesuit missions. They retain many of their old beliefs today, but have strangely admixed them with Catholic elements: They pray to the stars and water in addition to the Christian saints, and they celebrate both their old fertility ceremonies and Catholic festivals with ritual dances. On Good Friday, for example, the men, in black body paint, fight mock armed battles with sticks. The woven bags worn over the shoulder are the really striking feature of Cora costume, though the clothing of the women is individually designed with fine flower motifs.

The access road of Highway 15 from Acaponeta to the beach of *Novillero* (36 km.; 22 miles) is asphalted only as far as *Tecuala* (13 km.; 8 miles); it extends toward the sea from Agua Brava Lake, where a ferry can be boarded.

Continuing on 15, at *Rosa Morada* (196 km.; 122 miles south of Mazatlán), a rough wagon road leads 12 km. (7 miles) to the Cora village of San Juan Batista, where you can see the quite remarkable Holy Week dances.

About 20 km. (12 miles) farther south on 15, a branch road leads west to **Mexcaltitán,** which can be reached via a paved road 31 km. (19 miles) long. Launches leave frequently for Mexcaltitán. The town is well worth a visit, particularly since some archaeologists claim that it is the original home of the Aztecs. Its streets, which turn into canals during the rainy season—thus also giving this poor fishing village the reputation, otherwise quite undeserved, of being "Mexico's Venice"—are laid out just as the Spanish described Moctezuma's city: Four parallel pairs of streets lead from the square in the four directions of the compass, meeting in an outer ring like the spokes of a wheel. Mexcaltitán Lake, at the outlet of the Río San Pedro, is a paradise for waterfowl.

Farther south on Route 15 is the branch road that leads 8 km. (5 miles) to *Santiago Ixcuintla,* a center for the cultivation of tobacco and home to many Cora Indians. Eight km. (5 miles) farther on, a second branch road leads northwest to *Mexcaltitán Lake* (25 km.; 16 miles), going to *Sentispac* and then over a gravelly dam, from which you can see crab fishermen, waterfowl and Zebu cattle standing in the low waters, and continue on to Mexcaltitán.

If you don't go to Lake Mexcaltitán from Santiago Ixcuintla, then it is a 40-km. (25-mile) trip from the main road to *Playa Los Corchos,* a sandy beach with a palm-thatched restaurant that is practically empty during the week.

Return to 15 and continue southeast past mango, banana, and papaya plantations to the San Blas turnoff.

San Blas (36 km.; 22 miles from the turnoff) might be described as every North American's vision of Old Mexico. It is a popular seaside resort of palm trees and mansions gone to seed, modest and musty hotels, and cantinas that may inspire you to become sad, lonely, drunk, and philosophical.

In Colonial times, San Blas was a busy port. After independence, the British and Americans made it a sort of colony for their import-export trade, running roughshod over the federal authorities. A Colonial church, now in ruins, some deserted Spanish fortifications, and the disused customs house mansion loom as reminders of San Blas's more adventuresome past. Boat excursions from here tour around the *Islas Tres Marías*—a penal colony! Or take a motor boat to the clear springs of *La Tovara* or through the mangrove jungle teeming with tropical vegetation and wildlife.

Instead of continuing to Tepic via Highway 15, you can drive south from San Blas along the coast past *Los Cocos* and *Miramar* beaches to Santa Cruz where you take the turnoff east for 51 km. (32 miles) to Tepic.

The Federal Highway 15 winds up the mountain—in almost switch back fashion—until it reaches **Tepic** (286 km.; 177

miles from Mazatlán), the capital of the state of Nayarit. Tepic sits at an altitude of 915 meters (3,000 feet), surrounded by sugar plantations and forested hills. *Sangangüey,* an extinct volcano (2,243 meters; 7,357 feet) that looms in the southwest gives Tepic both its character and its name: In the Nahuatl language, Tepic means "hard stone," and due to past volcanic action, basalt is abundantly present in the region.

The town was founded in the mid-16th century. Perhaps its most notable achievement was in sheltering the famed missionaries Eusebio Kino and Junípero Serra. It was from the town's *Convento de la Cruz* that these men departed to found missions and convert Indians far to the north. Legend has it that the church (dating from 1744) was built where it is because the grass on the site grew in the form of a cross. It is still a favorite pilgrimage destination for the Cora and Huichol Indians.

Tepic's *Museo Regional* features anthropological and local history exhibits; it is worth seeing if you are interested in the indigenous cultures of Mexico's west coast. For those with an even deeper interest in these cultures, it is possible to penetrate the mountain homeland of the Huichol Indians either by plane or by car on roads leading to the edge of Huichol country. There are, however, no facilities for visitors, so you must plan a same-day return.

From Tepic continue about 34 km. (20 miles) southeast along 15—crammed at this point with slow-moving trailer trucks that are tempting but dangerous to pass. A turnoff to the left leads 11 km. (7 miles) to *Santa María del Oro,* near which is hidden an attractive crater lake, where you can swim. Farther south on Highway 15 is *Chapalilla* and, as the road continues, you pass through the eerie black lava fields deposited by the *Ceboruco* volcano (2,164 meters; 7,098 feet), which last erupted in the late 19th century. After about half an hour's drive, you'll reach **Ixtlán del Río** (population 20,000; elevation 1,042 meters; 3,418 feet), a town offering inexpensive roadside food service, and not much else. Near Ixtlán—out of town and to the left—is a large archaeological site, the most important in northwest Mexico, yet nowhere nearly as large as Teotihuacán or the Mayan ruins. A temple to Quetzalcóatl in his manifestation as God of the Winds (Ehécatl) stands on a high round platform and a building supported by columns, all connected by a paved processional road. The site dates from the 7th or 8th century A.D.

From Ixtlán, continue east on 15 as it passes from the state of Nayarit to Jalisco. Avoid the temptation to pass on blind curves; it is terribly dangerous, and in any case, the road does eventually open up again for safer passing. Along this stretch, you will pass *Magdalena,* famous for its opals. Some are sold along the road, and of course, better selections are found in the town itself. To get a good stone at a good price, however, you have to bargain and know what you're looking at.

From Magdalena, continue to **Tequila,** (population 15,000) where Mexico's national liquor originated. The blue agave maguey plant, from whose pulp tequila is made, grows in great plantations along the roads. Indeed, tequila is made only from this one variety of maguey plant, which grows here and only in one other location nearer to Guadalajara. The maguey was sacred to the Aztecs who also prepared an alcoholic drink from its core. Distilleries in the area are generally open to the public: the old *Herradura plant* outside of town, or in

town the *Tequila Sauza* or *Tequila Cuervo* plants, plus many others. Processing times are irregular, but you're sure to find at least one distillery operating.

A relatively unexplored *archaeological zone* lies about 42 km. (25 miles) south of Tequila where a road forks west 15 km. (9 miles) to *Tala.* The site is made up largely of overgrown ceremonial and sports structures—playing fields, courts, platforms, etc.—and is dated to the Pre-Classic period (A.D. 200–300).

Return to 15 and continue to ****Guadalajara** (531 km.; 329 miles from Mazatlán), see page 124.

TRAVEL ROUTE 18: Tepic–**Puerto Vallarta– Manzanillo–*Colima–**Guadalajara (765 km.; 474 miles)

See map on page 136.

The varied appeal of the resorts lining the Pacific coast is nowhere clearer than along this particularly popular and attractive stretch between Puerto Vallarta and Manzanillo. Puerto Vallarta, once a sleepy and virtually inaccessible little town, now draws the same glamorous and high-spending crowd that Acapulco always has, while smaller towns like Colima, Guayabitos, Compostela, and Bucerias draw middle-class Mexican and North American families on budget holidays, as well as "loners," who simply want quiet and plenty of sun. The beaches generally are broad and sandy, and the scenery along the drive lush and dense. Here, in this popular and populous section of Mexico, you are still about as close to a tropical paradise as you are likely to find anywhere.

Colima, which can be reached by heading inland from Manzanillo, offers two very good museums, some spectacular views of the still-active Nevado de Colima volcano, and an unhurried, quiet village life.

From *Tepic* (see page 202), Route 200 winds easily down the coast through hilly country dotted with sugar cane plantations. *Compostela* (population 20,000), 37 km. (60 miles) south of Tepic, was founded in 1531 by Nuño de Guzmán, and it remained the bishop's see and capital of the province of New Galicia for several years until those functions were moved to Guadalajara in 1560. The town itself has not much to recommend it for a stopover, but it has a quiet charm and an authenticity lacking in many of the more popular places.

From *Las Varas,* follow Route 200 south along the coast as it runs close to the sea; this is one of its loveliest stretches, bordered as it is by the lush tropical vegetation of southwest Mexico: palms, bananas, mangoes, and wonderfully fragrant lemon groves. An unpaved road leads 9 km. (6 miles) to *Chacala Bay.*

Guayabitos (95 km.; 59 miles from Tepic) is a manicured, quiet seaside resort perfect for long stays and short budgets. Its accommodations are largely trailer parks and small hotels and bungalows that rent inexpensively by the month. No discos, no fine dining—and no hassle!

About 30 km. (18 miles) farther along the road, through fruit plantations and tropical forests, a turn-off leads 3 km. (2 miles) to *La Sayulita,* a small fishing village with wonderful seafood restaurants and a pretty sand beach along a well-protected bay. Hotels here are reasonably priced, just as they are in nearby *Punta Mita* (22 km; 14 miles off Route 200) or at *Playas de Guanacaxtle.*

Bucerías, the gateway to Puerto Vallarta, provides you with your first taste of the gracious style of resorts on this particular part of the west coast. The town of Bucerías itself is graced by a lovely promenade lined with bougainvillea and is surrounded by an exclusive and very beautiful golf course and the *Nuevo Vallarta marine complex,* a recent development of canals and luxurious villas whose residents can anchor their yachts at their doors.

Note that you are now entering the state of Jalisco and another time zone, Central Standard Time. You must set your clocks ahead one hour once you cross the Río Ameca.

**Puerto Vallarta (175 km.; 109 miles from Tepic) is one of Mexico's most popular resorts, although only 25 years ago it was virtually unheard of. Then, it was a dream of quiet isolation. Lying on the large, u-shaped *Bahía de Banderas,* with wide, sandy beaches, it offered seaside living without telephones or even very many cars. Cobbled streets, tile and stucco houses, and lots of small, lazy restaurants created a pleasing atmosphere. The world was hidden by dense jungle to the north and the Sierra Madre to the south, and if someone just had to get in touch with you, a telegram was the only way—and that office remained open just a very few hours a day.

All this changed rather abruptly in 1962, when the film *The Night of the Iguana,* starring Elizabeth Taylor and Richard Burton, was made here. After that, the tourists never stopped coming. By 1967, a real highway was built into town, telephones were installed, and all along the beach dazzling hotels popped up. By 1970, Puerto Vallarta's airport had become an international jet port, and Acapulco had a real rival. Today, Puerto Vallarta has a population of 100,000.

The quiet, the isolation, the ineffable charm of the old Puerto Vallarta has, of course, been irretrievably lost. Like Acapulco, it exists now for the crowds, the fun, the dollars. But bay, jungle, and mountains tend to keep the town from feeling overgrown, and there still can be found an atmosphere of seaside stillness in some parts of town.

The beaches offer the customary diversions: parasailing, surfing, and just plain swimming. On land, there are horseback rides into some wonderful mountain country, as well as an 18-hole golf course, hunting, and polo games played on donkey-back!

Puerto Vallarta's grand new hotels stand mainly north of town along the highway to the airport, although some moderate to expensive hotels have also been built in the southern end of the town. In the town itself, there are some moderate and even inexpensive hotels. All are quite comfortable, and you are never more than minutes from the beach.

Strolling through town can be one of Puerto Vallarta's most attractive occupations, for the town has managed to retain some of the lazy pace it once had and the charm of its southwestern architecture. The *Malecón*—a beach-

Guadalupe church, Puerto Vallarta

front promenade—provides a lovely, fresh seaside stroll, and the town streets and small *Zócalo* offer flower-hung balconies near the *Guadaloupe Church*, open-air shopping, restaurants, bars, and boutiques. A small island in the Río Cuale, which runs through the town, has a complex of shops that should also be visited.

Manuel Lepe (1936–1983), a "primitive" painter, worked here, and if you take a meal at the *Capistrano restaurant,* you will get a good view of the scene he painted over and over again.

From Puerto Vallarta, follow Highway 200 southeast toward Manzanillo, taking in some beautiful views of the rocky coastline and the famous *Los Arcos,* three rock arches rising from the water.

Along the road are several small, isolated beaches, among them *Mismaloya,* where Richard and Liz are rumored to have begun their romance, and *Yelapa,* which can be reached only by boat.

Beyond the *Boca de Tomatlán,* the mouth of the river that has cut deep into the mountains, the road leaves the coast and proceeds through vegetation that slowly becomes less tropical, giving way to pine forests. You'll reach a plateau at *El Tuito* where there are tilled fields, and dense bushy forests. Gravel roads lead off to still more isolated beaches and bays. To the left looms the Sierra Madre.

The landscape becomes more arid here, but at the Río San Nicolas lowland, a lovely green oasis appears. And some 10 km. (6 miles) farther on, a turnoff leads roughly 3 km. (2 miles) to the beaches of *La Fortuna* and *Perula.* The road cuts through mango plantations for about 2 km. (1.2 miles) and to the right you can turn off to *Chamela* on a quiet bay protected by a number of projecting islands where hotels and campgrounds can be found. *Club Méditerranée* operates *Playa Blanca* here, and they charge hefty entry fees and keep strict visiting hours to discourage day-tripping on their domain. But just here at the turnoff you can visit *Careyes Beach* and stay, if you wish, at the luxurious hotel at *Tenacatita* called *Los Angeles Locos* (The Mad Angels).

Just east of Tenacatita on Highway 200 there is a turnoff to Gua-

dalajara (Federal Highway 80). Nearby you'll encounter two resorts that have long been popular with Mexican vacationers but that are now in the process of becoming "international" and, therefore, far more costly and less quiet: *San Patricio Melaque* and *Barra de Navidad.* It's still possible to rent rooms and dine inexpensively in either place, and to watch the construction and dredging that means another Puerto Vallarta in the making. It was from Barra de Navidad in 1564 that the transpacific expedition headed by López de Legazpi departed. That expedition led to the Spanish conquest of the Philippines, and the route Legazpi took remained the Manila galleon route for over 250 years!

Just past Chihuatlán you cross the Río Chacala, which also forms the border between the states of Jalisco and Colima. You are heading now straight for Manzanillo, whose airport is off a side road 5 km. (3 miles) away. On the last 40 km. (25 miles) of Highway 200 before it enters the city several luxury hotels and clubs have been developed. The most famous is *Las Hadas* (The Fairies), located on the peninsula in Bahía de Manzanillo: It is a white, Mediterranean-style hotel-and-bungalow complex. Eccentric and dreamlike in its design, Las Hadas was also thoughtfully planned to preserve this region's lushness and serenity. Plants, flowers, and lawns separate the bungalows from each other and from the 200-room hotel, the condominiums, golf course, and yacht club. Utterly self-contained, and cut off from industrialized Manzanillo, Las Hadas does give you the feeling that you could be anywhere—but at the same time, this "anywhere" is as much of Eden as most of us are likely to see.

Manzanillo itself isn't terribly interesting. It is a highly commercialized and industrialized town, and a busy port, but for all that not unattractive. If you choose Manzanillo as your base, beaches and rural scenery are well within the reach of short day trips, and the Zócalo provides some lively entertainment in the evening.

There are other easily accessible beaches farther along Federal Highway 200 as it follows the 50-km.- (31-mile-) long *Laguna de Cuyutlán* behind Manzanillo. A side road leads 7 km. (4 miles) to the small, attractive, seaside resort of *Cuyutlán*. Nearby *Playa Paraíso* is reached from *Armería*.

Shortly past Armería, 200 intersects with Highway 54, which leads north toward Colima and Guadalajara. (You can continue on 200 to pick up Travel Route 19.) You will leave tropical vegetation behind as you ascend into the Sierra, covered with bush and magueys.

*Colima (555 km.; 344 miles from Tepic) is an attractive town that is the capital of the state of Colima. It lies at an altitude of 458 meters (1,502 feet), just beneath the still-active *Volcán de Fuego* (3,960 meters; 12,989 feet) and the larger volcano *Nevado de Col-*

ima (4,330 meters; 14,202 feet). Colima is large, with a population of 100,000. All the important public buildings—the *Cathedral* (1894), the *government offices,* and the *town hall*—stand on the town square. They are connected to each other by Moorish arches.

Colima contains one of Mexico's great museums, the *Museo de las Culturas Occidente,* which is known especially for the clay figures depicting the life of the Indians of the region. The *Museo Nacional de la Danza y la Máscara y el Arte Popular del Occidente* at the university (Instituto de Bellas Artes) is dedicated to folk dances, masks, and art.

Via Corta becomes Federal Highway 29, leading toward Guadalajara. The road leaves the state of Colima and returns to Jalisco, then winds through a ravine and travels through deep valleys. A turnoff becomes a country lane leading 27 km. (17 miles) to the *Parque Nacional Volcán de Fuego* (Fire Volcano National Park), whose volcano last erupted in 1957; smoke and sulfur vapors still fill the air.

Highway 29 continues through the *Atenquique valley* and then a road branches off to the *Nevado de Colima* which can be reached in about three hours by car, but only if you are careful to follow instructions, stay on the main road, and not wander onto one of the many fire trails.

Highway 29 runs into Highway 54 and continues to Guadalajara. On the way, you can visit **Ciudad Guzmán,** at an altitude of 1,507 meters (4,923 feet), with a population of 80,000. The city was severely damaged by the 1985 earthquake, but its old Colonial streets still contain many lovely buildings and arcades dating from the Spanish period. This was the birthplace of one of Mexico's great painters, the muralist Clemente Orozco; some of his paintings as well as archaeological artifacts are displayed in the small *museum* in town.

Highway 54 leads along the reedy bank of Laguna de Zapotlán. Beyond *Sayula*, it follows the flat lake of the same name and Laguna de Zacoalco.

Federal Highway 80, coming from Barra de Navidad, connects with Federal Highway 54 just west of Acatlán de Juárez, and shortly after the connection, the four-lane highway begins the 34 km. (20 mile) approach to *Guadalajara* (see page 124).

TRAVEL ROUTE 19: **Mexico City–**Acapulco–**Zihuatanejo–Ixtapa (671 km.; 416 miles)

See map on page 136.

Despite the competition offered by several newer spots, Acapulco continues to be the most popular of Mexico's seaside resorts. If you don't fly directly to Acapulco, it takes about five hours by car to reach the resort from Mexico City. But it is possible and certainly worthwhile to extend the trip by making several excursions en route. Acapulco is glamorous, fast-paced, and expensive; for a quieter stay by the sea, the Zihuatanejo–Ixtapa resort area offers a harmonious combination of the traditional and the modern.

Depart Mexico City from the south on Highway 95 toward Cuernavaca. Along this toll road are the interesting cities of **Cuernavaca* (see page 86), **Xochicalco* (see page 91), and **Taxco* (see page 92) which is 40 km. (25 miles) west of the highway. Follow 95 to **Iguala** (population 70,000), 180 km. (112 miles) from Mexico City, at an elevation of 730 meters (2,394 feet). It was in Iguala that the Three Guarantees (also called The Plan of Iguala) were issued by Agustín de Iturbide and Vicente Guerrero on February 24, 1821.

This document was Mexico's "Declaration of Independence" (see page 34). It is possible to drive directly to Zihuatanejo from Iguala by following 51 southwest to *Ciudad Altamirano* and then continuing south on 135. At *Iguala*, 95 narrows and continues south.

Xalitla (219 km.; 136 miles from Mexico City) and other villages in the vicinity are known for their handicrafts. Traditional clay vessels, painted with mineral colors, are manufactured here. A more recent handicraft is paintings on *papel amate,* the bark paper prepared in the old style by Otomí Indians in the Puebla Sierra (see page 224). Painted *papel amate* began to be used for wall decorations and other small items, all of which have become favorites among souvenir hunters in Mexico. These *papal amate* creations as well as the traditional clay vessels are sold in booths along the street.

Continue south on 95, winding through the valley of the Río Balsas, where organ cacti stand as straight as candles. Cross the bridge and continue past the village of *Mezcala.* About 10 km. (6 miles) farther on begins *Cañon del Zopilote* (Vulture Canyon), 20 km. (12 miles) long. After passing through *Zumpango del Río,* a flowering tropical landscape on the banks of the Río Zopilote, you reach **Chilpancingo** (280 km.; 174 miles from Mexico City; population 50,000). The capital of the state of Guerrero, it is situated at an elevation of 1,360 meters (4,460 feet). The town's name is derived from the fighters for independence who came from this mountainous region. The city was founded by the Spanish in 1591 as a way station on the Asia trade route between Mexico City and the port of Acapulco. In 1813, the national congress convened by José María Morelos proclaimed independence in the parish church here, although victory for the insurgents was still many years away (see page 34).

A long but worthwhile side trip from Chilpancingo leads northeast along the road to Tlapa, which is only partially paved, through the mountain villages of *Sierra Madre del Sur,* the homeland of the Nahua and Tlapaneca Indians. In the vicinity of *Chilapa* are the *caves of Acatlán,* where pre-Columbian rock paintings dating to 900–700 B.C. were discovered in 1968. At *Tlapa,* 179 km. (107 miles) from Chilpancingo, the road—which is scarcely passable in the rainy season—turns north for 40 km. (25 miles) to *Olinalá,* where attractive and popular lacquered works are manufactured.

Return to Chilpancingo and continue south on 95. After about 11 km. (6.5 miles), a turnoff leads east 37 km. (23 miles) to *Colotlipa,* a village in the *Juxtlahuaca National Park,* where you can visit a splendid stalactite cave. The cave is interesting not only because of its geological formations but also because of the Olmec rock paintings found within it. The round trip takes about two hours. Return to 95 and continue south.

Tierra Colorada (344 km.; 213 miles from Mexico City), with its many small restaurants, offers a good opportunity to relax. From here on, the vegetation becomes more and more luxuriant, and tropical heat and moisture rise from the nearby coast, to which the road winds down. At *Las Cruces,* which belongs within the municipal area of Acapulco, you can pick up Highway 200 heading southeast toward *Pinotepa Nacio-*

nal. A last ascent on Highway 95 to the coastal mountains follows, from which a view suddenly appears of the splendid bay of Acapulco.

**Acapulco

See map on page 212.

This resort, the most important in Mexico, is at least as well known throughout the world as any of Mexico's larger cities and important cultural centers. It has always had about it an air of exclusivity; visions of a pampered international jet set invariably come to mind whenever the city is mentioned.

Until the 1960s, Acapulco truly was the near-private domain of the rich and famous. But that decade saw the number of tourists soar from fewer than a hundred thousand (93,000 in 1954) to the some 3 million who are now estimated to visit it annually. Inevitably, the resident population grew as well: In 1930, there were only some 6,500 inhabitants; today, the population has swelled to a quarter million.

When the Spanish discovered its bay in 1521, Acapulco was a fishing village inhabited by Nahuatl Indians. The Spanish made the well-protected bay the port from which they set out to explore—and exploit—the South Seas. By the end of the 16th century, after the discovery of the Philippines, their Pacific trade began to move to and from Acapulco's natural harbor. Goods arriving from the South Seas reached Acapulco and were trans-shipped overland to Veracruz, on the east coast, from where they were shipped by sea to Spain. The profitable South Seas trade attracted British and Dutch pirates, who preyed on the richly loaded Spanish galleons off Mexico's coast. To protect their shipping, the Spanish eventually fortified Acapulco's harbor. After 1779, however, new travel routes between Spain and the Philippines around the Cape of Good Hope rendered Acapulco far less important.

Acapulco would wait more than a century and a half before seeing her star rise again. But rise it did in the 1950s, when the first through-road from Mexico City was completed. No longer a haven from piracy but a tropical retreat from the cold and the mundane, Acapulco once again drew wealth and the wealthy to her natural harbor. In the 1970s, when an international jet airport was completed, the real tourist invasion began, diluting the exclusive nature of the already famous resort. North Americans, of course, make up most of the foreign tourists, but a surprising two-thirds of Acapulco's guests are Mexicans.

The *Las Playas Peninsula*, which encloses the bay in the west, is Acapulco's oldest tourist complex, defined by elegant villas and old, often restored, hotels, like the famous *Caleta*.

More moderately priced older and smaller hotels are found in the center of the city and along the coast road, Costera Miguel Alemán—named after a president of the Republic (1946–1952) who was a tireless promoter of Acapulco. The road's six lanes separate the more modest hotels from the luxury towers along the beach itself. Newer hotels—among them, the deluxe *Acapulco Princess* and the *Pierre Marques*—have been built on the eastern side of the bay, along *Revolcadero Beach.*

The coastal mountains that surround Acapulco—giving it the "amphitheater" form to which it is so often compared—is home to the poorest of Acapulco's year-round residents and to the immi-

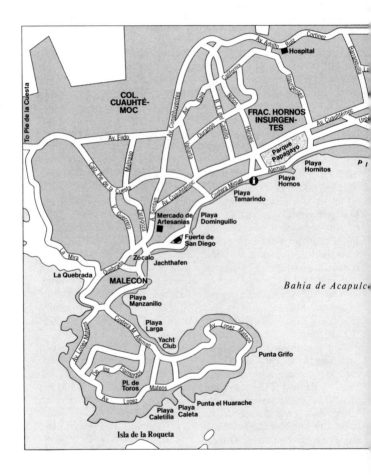

grants who continue to crowd into the city in the hopes of finding work. Here, huge, impoverished slums of wood and corrugated metal huts look down on the fabled hotels, discos, restaurants, and beaches of Mexico's Pacific jewel.

Beaches. Acapulco offers some of the world's most appealing, varied, and spectacular

beaches, with water temperatures perfect for swimming all year. Rough surf or calm, thronged or practically deserted, your perfect beach lies somewhere along Acapulco's coast, and there's always plenty of room, even where the crowds are thickest.

The calmest beaches, enclosed by steep rocks, are those on the *Las Playas Peninsula;* of these, *Playa Caleta* and *Playa Caletilla* are among the most attractive and were once the center of action in Acapulco. From Caleta, you can take glass-bottom-boat excursions to *La Roqueta Island,* a perfect place for swimming, diving, and dining.

For those seeking more challenging surf, the beaches in the broad inner area of the bay have higher breakers—but it's wise to check the surf and tidal conditions posted on the boards by the hotels: The surf can get rough, and the tides tricky, and even the most intrepid should be careful.

Close to the city, *Playa Los Hornos* and *Hornitos* are local favorites, while the luxury hotels are chiefly built along the *Condesa* and *Icacos* beaches, lively and well stocked with vendors, restaurants, and tourists.

High up on the east cape, at the *Las Brisas* bungalow hotel, there are many small private pools for the guests, as well as jeeps that provide transport to the hotel beach. Just behind the cape and between the shell beach at *Puerto Marqués Bay* and the large *Revolcadero* sand beach, you can wander by the other great luxury hotels, such as the pyramidal *Hotel Princess,* and along the 18-hole golf course. In the high, rough surf of the Revolcadero Beach, a surfing competition is held yearly.

Swimming and surfing are only two of the many aquatic amusements available at Acapulco's many beaches: Snorkeling, diving, waterskiing, fishing, and sailing will bring you out into the water, and parachute sailing will bring you out over it. If you're determined to stay dry, however, hundreds of dealers in arts and crafts, T-shirts, and straw hats will divert you, while, for a few pesos, small boys demonstrate their musical and acrobatic skills.

Sights. Acapulco is not a city of great public monuments and fine period architecture; it is a city built for its harbor and the sea beyond, and it is these grand vistas that you must take time out to enjoy.

Take a trip along the beach—mornings on the eastern elevations above the Las Brisas Hotel; afternoons from the western hill overlooking the city, or from a perch on the peninsula. Sunsets, lovely at any point along the coast, are probably best enjoyed at the *Pié de la Cuesta* beach (located about 15 miles out of town on the highway leading south to Zihuatanejo), with its high waves cresting against a brilliant orange sky.

Indeed, *Pié de la Cuesta* is worth a day's stay. It is relatively unpopulated, and rustic hotels and restaurants line the wide beach where the surf is as dramatic as it is dangerous. You can rent a hammock, have a meal, ride horseback along the beach, or use the pool at the marvelous little *Ukae Kim Hotel.* For freshwater swimming and smooth waterskiing, cross the street to the "beach clubs" on *Laguna La Coyuca,* a nature reserve whose tropical wonders can be explored by *Safari Tour.*

Once the sun has set, Acapulco offers perhaps its most brilliant show: the city itself lit for the evening, spread out glittering and delicate toward the sea. You can enjoy this from just about any high spot, but most comfortably, of course, with drink in hand from one of the hotel terraces on the mountain.

You won't find great architectural monuments to explore in Acapulco, or any particularly moving displays of Mexico's rich past. Perhaps the closest thing to urban "sightseeing" is offered by the *Parque Papagayo,* a 52-acre plot along the Costera. Dedicated to children, the park boasts a medley of odd but entertaining diversions: a life-size replica of a galleon like those that once harbored here, a racetrack with child-size Cam Am cars, a replica of the *Columbia* space shuttle, and bumper boats. The aviary is for everyone, with hundreds of species of birds that can be glimpsed from shaded walkways.

CiCi (Centro International para Convivencia Infantil) is an amusement park for children. It features dolphin-and-seal shows, a swimming pool with waves, water toboggans, and other water-oriented rides and amusements.

Surely the most intriguing sights—and something you should not miss—are the divers at *La Quebrada,* who plunge 40 meters (130 feet) into water 1.5 meters (5 feet) deep! They can be watched outside or from the terrace of the *Mirador Hotel.* The divers perform this nerve-shattering display daytime and evening.

The *Zócalo,* the main square, offers quiet, shade, and a good view of the somewhat elaborate *Cathedral. San Diego Fort,* built to protect the harbor in the 17th century, is now a museum dedicated to the pre-Columbian past of the state of Guerrero. The *Mercato*

Cliff divers, Acapulco

de Artesanias downtown offers handicrafts and souvenirs. While it panders unabashedly to tourists, some very talented artisans work here, and many of them will paint ceramics to your specifications.

At least as famous as Acapulco's beach life is the nightlife—restaurants, nightclubs, and discos abound.

The trip west from Acapulco to Zihuatanejo (245 km.; 152 miles), a fast-developing seashore resort, takes about three hours by car and a good four hours by bus. There are a few small towns and villages along this stretch of Route 200, bordered by palm groves and lakes (Pié de la Cuesta and Laguna de Coyuca; see page 214). A road turns off at *San Jerónimo,* an attractive town with tile-covered roofs, leading by way of *Laguna de Mitla* to the beaches of *Paraíso Escondido* (Hidden Paradise). *Piedra Tlacoyunque* is a lovely isolated beach that can be approached from San Luís San Pedro. Continue to ****Zihuatanejo** (population 30,000).

Just a few years ago, Zihuatanejo was a small fishing village lying on the bay of the same name. Adventurous local and foreign travellers knew of it as a place with a lovely beach and virtually no guests, and they kept the secret pretty much to themselves. But then the Mexican National Trust Fund for Tourism Development, enriched by petrol dollars, saw potential in the miles of unspoiled, palm-lined beaches both in

Zihuatanejo and neighboring Ixtapa; it succeeded in creating a dual resort as glamorous as Acapulco and as charming as Puerto Vallarta.

Villa del Sol is Zihuatanejo's answer to Acapulco chic: Duplex rooms—often booked a year in advance—seaside bar and restaurant, tennis courts, and the usual water sports are all available here. *Sotavento*, which is one of the town's earliest super-hotels is still among the best, with 70 rooms on a hillside overlooking the bay.

**Ixtapa, close neighbor to Zihuatanejo (only 10 km.; 6 miles away), lies on Bahía de Palmar where most of its better hotels are clustered. Somewhat more chic and up-to-date than Zihuatanejo, it is also the more carefully planned of the two resorts. Dramatically nestled between two projecting rocky capes, *Punta Ixtapa* and *Punta Carrizo*, Ixtapa was planned brick-by-brick to satisfy the most demanding tourists in the most comfortable way possible. It worked.

While Zihuatanejo still has its municipal market, which is the focus of the local life, Ixtapa has a carefully planned pedestrian center, with bars, restaurants, and boutiques, all easily accessible by the shoeless, carefree tourist. Deluxe hotels, like the *Camino Real*, the *Ixtapa Sheraton*, and the *Krystal*, as well as the *Aristos, Dorado Pacifico, El Presidente,* and others, offer the best of resort-hotel living, while the naturally beautiful setting of both Zihuatanejo and Ixtapa remind you constantly that you've undoubtedly found your tropical paradise.

A short taxi ride separates the two towns, and since each has its special charms, you should plan to visit both while you're in the area.

You can now travel directly to Zihuatanejo from Mexico City by Route 135, the new shorter road that goes by way of Toluca and Ciudad Altamirano.

It is possible to connect with Travel Route 18 from here: Follow Highway 200 up the coast about 455 km. (282 miles) to the turnoff to Manzanillo or Colima. En route, you will pass *Lázaro Cárdenas* (where Mexico's important steel plant Las Truchas is located) and the small seashore resort of *Playa Azul* in the state of Michoacan.

TRAVEL ROUTE 20: **Acapulco–Tapachula– Guatemala (1,042 km.; 646 miles)

See map on page 244.

Travel Route 20 takes you southeast along Mexico's Costa Chica to the Guatemala border. The character of the region changes dramatically; there are villages that were settled by African slaves, secluded seaside resorts, Indian settlements, and ancient archaeological sites.

Leave Acapulco from the east along the **Carretera Escénica (Scenic Highway) 15 km. (9 miles) to the south. Then there is a turnoff to *Puerto Marqués* (see page 213) as you approach the Acapulco International Airport.

The **Costa Chica,** as the coastal region here is called, has an interesting character, formed in large part by its harrowing place in New World history. It was along this portion of coast that African slaves who were able to flee from the port of Huatulco (see page 218) settled. Despite pursuit and often violent capture and punishment, many slaves did manage to elude the Spanish authorities, and their descendants still live in many settlements along this southern stretch of coast. Follow Highway 200 east through the town of *San Marcos,* noted for its salt production in the nearby lake. About 112 km. (69 miles) from Acapulco, you'll cross a bridge over the Río Nexpa, where a small road turns off to Laguna La Fortuna, a favorite fishing spot. Nearby *Cruz Grande* is a village of huts situated near Laguna Chantengo, which also has good fishing. Attractive beaches are close by, in the fishing village of *Marquelia.*

Continue east on 200 to *Huehuetán,* where a road proceeds north 16 km. (9 miles) to **Ometepec,** where the Amuzgo Indians live. A partially explored archaeological site here has so far yielded a stone head with Olmec features, as well as ceramics in the style of Monte Albán III, zoo-morphic basalt sculptures, and stelae with carved reliefs (found in graves in a neighboring site, there-after called *piedra labrada* or "worked stone").

Cuajinicuilapa (234 km.; 145 miles from Acapulco) is the last village in the state of Guer-rero. It has the curious look of an African village, and indeed, the straw huts still built here are inhabited by descendants of Bantu slaves brought to the area by the Spanish in the 16th century. Between Cuajinicuilapa and the sea lies the town of *San Nicolás,* also called Guerrero Negro because of the dark skin of the native population.

Cola de Palma, 8 km. (4.5 miles) away, is a well-explored archaeological site (actually at *El*

Ciruelo). Here you can see several terraces from the Classical period, measuring 60–80 meters (197–262 feet) long and 3 meters (9 feet) high, as well as figures of the gods cut in quartz and some large anthropomorphic basalt statues, most of which have now been donated to museums.

A turnoff (Route 125) to Oaxaca by way of Tlaxiaco is reached at the town of *Pinotepa Nacional*. After 2 km. (1.2 miles) on this stretch, a road leads 25 km. (16 miles) to the Mixteca village of *Pinotepa de Don Luís*. Until recently, the Mixteca women wore only skirts—which are still woven here—that hung to their ankles but left their upper bodies exposed.

Pinotepa Nacional is located back on 200 in the Mixteca coastal region (*Mixteca de la Costa*). It is populated not only by Mixtecas but also by Amuzgo Indians, other mixed Indians, and blacks. The Sunday markets—and especially the colorful Easter celebrations—draw all these populations together in town.

Continue east along 200 to *Jamiltepec* (316 km.; 196 miles) and *San Pedro Tututepec*, towns inhabited by Mixteca Indians and Chatino Indians, whose language is related to Zapotecan. They are farmers who are also known for their highly finished crafts, especially embroidery. Somewhat farther south is *Bahía de Chacahua,* which together with *Laguna de Pastoría* has been established as a national park largely for its coastline of tropical forest and wildlife.

**Puerto Escondido (429 km.; 266 miles from Acapulco; population 5,000), the "Hidden Harbor," is a small fishing village in an inlet, which has recently been developed into a seaside resort. Its appeal is primarily to the young, and there are many simple and attractive midpriced hotels. On *Carrizalillo* and *Bacocho beaches* the sea rolls toward shore in foaming breakers, while from the flat beach at *Puerto Angelito* you can walk far out into still, clear water. Laguna de Maniatepec offers the calm and peace of a freshwater setting.

If you wish, you have a choice of two tortuously winding roads that lead north from Puerto Escondido and *Pochutla* (a town further east on 200) through the Sierra Madre del Sur to Oaxaca. From Pochutla, a road also leads south for 10 km. (6 miles) to ***Puerto Ángel** (population 3,000), a small fishing village with its own following of seaside tourists. Clear water shimmers in an infinity of blue shades in a quiet bay. A luxury hotel on the hill overlooking the town and bay as well as small guest houses along the dusty village streets offer rooms, and there are hammocks on the beach. Fish restaurants offering the day's catch set up tables along the beach front.

Huatulco, a little northeast of Puerto Ángel has been a secret passed among campers for years. But now under FONATUR, a new vacation center is being developed here, with plans for 1,300 hotel rooms to be ready by the end of the decade. The project also encompasses Bahía Santa Cruz, 19 km. (12 miles) farther on.

Highway 200 from Puerto Ángel to **Salina Cruz** (695 km.; 431 miles from Acapulco; population 30,000) has only recently been paved; there are few settlements along it, and consequently few gas stations.

The name Salina Cruz is derived from the production of salt here. This port on the Gulf of Tehuantepec, which dates from the beginning of the century, was recently expanded to permit the docking of oil tankers that are filled from the pipeline running from Minatitlán to Veracruz. Fishing and crabbing—age-old activities here—led to canning industries being established in this highly industrialized town. While it is possible to swim at *Playa Ventosa* (Windy Beach—which it most certainly is!), it is rarely a pleasant experience.

The Panamerican Highway (Federal Highway 190), coming east from Oaxaca runs together with 200 just 18 km. (11 miles) north of Salina Cruz at **Tehuantepec** (population 25,000) The town spreads out on a hilly, tropical landscape, which was already inhabited in the pre-Columbian period. The conquistadors built their ships here, and a number of churches date from the Colonial period, though they are of no particular architectural beauty or significance. The region is known for its festivals, at which the women wear richly adorned costumes: New Year's Day; the church

fair of the San Sebastian district and the *Laborio* on January 15–22; the San Juan festival in the Guichevere and Atotonilco districts on June 10–26; the patron saint festival in the San Pedro district on June 22–30; and the Resurrection of Mary in the Santa Maria district on August 17th.

About 15 km. (9 miles) west of town, you'll find a track that leads 6 km. (4 miles) to a path that will take you eventually to the archaeological site of **Guiengolo,** a Zapotecan refuge dating to the later Post-Classical period. The path will take about an hour's climbing along a rocky, scrubby hillside rising about 400 meters (1,300 feet) before you are rewarded with the impressive ruins. Its ceremonial center is laid out on an artificial platform—similar to that of Monte Albán at Oaxaca—which is 430 meters (1,410 feet) high; it includes temple pyramids and a ball-playing field. The remains of the palace built in the form of a labyrinth with about 400 rooms are also found in the complex, which is fortified with stone walls all the way around.

Juchitán lies about 26 km. (16 miles) east of Tehuatepec on Route 190. Like Tehuatepec, it is also famous for the festive dress of the Tehuanas, which is worn on the festival of San Isidoro, May 24; the August Vigil on August 13–16, which also includes flower processions and night dances; and the Pine Vigil on September 3. The market is also lively.

From Juchitán, it is only 7 km.

(4 miles) to *La Ventosa*, where the Interoceanic or Transisthmus Highway 185 turns north toward the Gulf of Mexico. At Tapanatepec, Highway 190 splits away from Highway 200 and turns north in the direction of Tuxtla Gutíerrez (see Travel Route 29, page 264).

Follow 200 across the border of the states of Oaxaca and Chiapas and through the town of *Arriaga* to **Tonalá** where side roads lead to the bathing beaches of *Paredon* (12 km.; 7 miles), *Mar Muerto* (Dead Sea), and *Puerto Arista* at Laguna La Joya Lake (17 km.; 11 miles); at Puerto Arista there are remains of a pre-Columbian settlement, as well as the archaeological zone of *Tonalá Viejo*, about 13 km. (8 miles) northwest of the small town.

The following stretch of 200 is monotonous, and the coastal plain thinly settled. The Sierra Madre de Chiapas extends to the left. An attractive mountain drive turns north at *Huixtla* (984 km.; 610 miles from Acapulco), which passes close to the border crossing into Guatemala at *Ciudad Cuauhtemoc* (111 km.; 69 miles). From Huixtla, 200 continues east to **Tapachula** (population 80,000), located near Tacaná Volcano (4,100 meters; 13,448 feet). This town is the commercial center of the fertile Soconusco area, where coffee is the principal crop. German settlers moved here at the end of the 19th century, and their descendants and some place names still indicate their strong influence on the region.

*Izapa (1,037 km.; 643 miles from Acapulco), an important archaeological site, lies along both sides of the road leading to the Mexican border. Largely hidden by cocoa plantations, remnants of a ceremonial center are located here, dating from 600 B.C.–A.D. 600. What remains of the architectural work, however, are chiefly foundations and overgrown mounds. Far more interesting are the stone stelae, masterfully cut, and the altars, thrones, and other monumental elements.

Puente Talismán (1,042 km.; 646 miles from Acapulco) is located at the border of Mexico and Guatemala, which is formed by the Río Suchiate. It is about 300 km. (186 miles) from here to Guatemala City.

The Gulf Coast

Largely because its climate is less reliably warm and dry during the winter months, Mexico's Gulf coast has never attracted the international tourist set that the Pacific coast has. Along its virtually endless stretch of beaches, only a few small resorts have managed to take hold, and these are far more popular among Mexicans than among foreign tourists. For most of this century, the Gulf coast has meant oil—and it is generally this profitable, and polluting, industry one thinks of when the Gulf is mentioned. There is, however, a rich agricultural industry along the coast. Extensive sugarcane fields alternate with plantations growing pineapples, papayas, and mangoes, as well as citrus fruits.

The most important petroleum deposits in Mexico are located south of Veracruz at Coatzacoalcos and Minatitlán. The relentless exploitation of these deposits, with little regard for the environment, has meant considerable pollution all along this part of the coast. Waterways have been contaminated by petroleum, by the dirt and chemicals used in building the roads and factories, and by the refining associated with the oil industry. The air is often fouled by fumes from the refineries in the area. The fate of modern Mexico is certainly tied inextricably to the petroleum industry, but as you pass through the oil fields and refineries, you realize that mining the black gold has cost dearly.

The most common route for foreign tourists is along the Gulf coast toward the Yucatán. There are only a few archaeological sites worth visiting in this abundant and well-watered landscape, but they include the especially important ruins of the Totonac city of El Tajín. In both Jalapa, the state capital of Veracruz, and Villahermosa excellent museums house the ceramic art of the Totonaca people and the monumental stone sculptures of the early Olmec high culture.

The drive through the mountains of the Sierra Madre Oriental to the harbor cities of Tampico and Veracruz offer exciting scenery. If you have the time and inclination, cut-offs from the main roads lead to the villages of the Huasteca Indians. Here, stimulated by tourism, many of the old crafts are still practiced and offered for sale.

The following routes describe the stretch along the coast between Tampico and Villahermosa, as well as the approach to the Gulf from Mexico City.

TRAVEL ROUTE 21: **Mexico City–*Pachuca–Tamazunchale–Ciudad Valles–Tampico (636 km.; 394 miles)

See map on page 232.

This is not the shortest route to Tampico (that would lead from Pachuca by way of Tulancingo), but it is by far the most scenic. The mountain landscapes are breathtaking, but be warned that the winding roads can be treacherous unless you're experienced at this sort of driving.

Along this route you might want to visit the Augustinian monasteries at Actopan and Ixmiquilpan. The archaeological site at Tamuín is also an interesting side trip.

Federal Highway 85, a toll road, runs north from Mexico City to ***Pachuca** (population 130,000; elevation 2,430 meters; 7,790 feet).

Pachuca is the capital of the state of Hidalgo. It is a pretty little mining town founded by the Spanish as Real de Minas de Tlahuiliapan. Bartolomé de Medina discovered amalgamation here in 1557; this was a process for obtaining gold and silver from ore with the aid of mercury (the process has now been replaced by cyanide leaching or by a combination of both processes).

At the entrance to the city, you are greeted by the *Atlantis column* from Tula, site of the ruins of the Toltec empire. Along Avenida Juárez is a monument to independence with a statue of Hidalgo, and at this traffic circle you will find the **Casa de las Artesanías** of the state of Hidalgo. Attractive articles woven by the Otomí Indians are sold here.

At **Plaza Juárez** stands one of the many monuments to Benito Juárez found throughout Mexico. The *Palacio Legislativo* and the *Teatro Rebolledo* are also located here. Follow the Calle Matamoros to the **Plaza de la Independencia,** the main square in town, where the chimes of the high clock tower imitate Big Ben's! Four marble sculptures in the plaza represent independence as it was won in 1810; freedom secured in 1821; reform, initiated in 1856; and the constitution, ratified in 1857.

Calle Hidalgo leads to the former **San Francisco Monastery,** which was completed in 1598; it became a missionary college in 1732. The building currently houses the *Casa de la Cultura* as well as the regional *historical museum.* The church attached to the monastery dates from the 17th century. Other structures dating from Colonial times are the houses of the mining barons, for example, **Casas Coloradas** constructed from reddish rock by Count de Regla in the 17th century. Today, the Casas Coloradas house the *Palace of Justice*. The fortress-like **Casa de la Caja** also dates from the 17th century. It was used to store the "Quinto Real," or "Royal Fifth," the portion of the mining proceeds owed to the Spanish crown. The Casa de la Caja is located at 106 Calle Venustiano Carranza; it is now owned by the State Mining Association.

Sightseeing tours of the mining works are conducted free of charge, but you must reserve for the tour in Mexico City (Compañía Minera del Real del Monte y Pachuca, Calle Memphis 104, Col. Ampliación Clavería, Atzcapozalco).

From Pachuca, you can visit **Real del Chico.** Take Federal Highway 105 toward Tampico about 8 km. (5 miles) to a turnoff. The turnoff road to this picturesque mining site leads 19 km. (12 miles) through a national park whose bizarre rock formations attract experienced climbers. Overnight accommodations are available at the Miguel Hidalgo hostel, but only on Friday and Saturday nights.

Continue north on 105; 10 km. (6 miles) from Pachuca, is the famous mining site of **Real del Monte**, renamed *Mineral del Monte*. The projecting towers of the silver mines, called "La Rica," "La Purisima," "La Dificultad," and "Dolores," can still be seen above the town's red corrugated iron roofs.

About 3 km. (1.5 miles) farther on, a side road branches off, leading 12 km. (7 miles) through the attractive village of *Huasca* to the former ***Hacienda San Miguel Regla** which has been converted into a fashionable hotel. This hacienda, which was used for silver processing, was built in the 18th century by the immensely wealthy mine owner Pedro Romero de Terreros, Count de Regla. The water reservoirs at the hotel also formerly belonged to the hacienda.

Also in the vicinity is the privately owned **Hacienda Santa María Regla,* which stands at the bottom of a ravine into which a waterfall tumbles. The massive Augustinian monastery of *Atotolnilco el Grande,* 15 km. (9 miles) to the north of Pachuca on 105 is a typical 16th-century building.

From Pachuca, follow 85 to ***Actopan** (136 km.; 84 miles from Mexico City; population 15,000), at an elevation of 2,070 meters (6,790 feet). The **Augustinian monastery* (see Travel Route 2, page 77) here has unusual ****wall paintings**. In the nearby mountains are magnificent rock formations that look like organ pipes, and indeed are called *Monte de los Organos*. Also in the vicinity are rocks for climbing, locally referred to as *Los Frailes* (The Monks), reached by a carriage road in the direction of San Jeronimo. **Ixmiquilpan** (184 km.; 114 miles from Mexico City; population 30,000) on the Río Tula is known for its ***Augustinian monastery.* Construction on the monastery began in 1550; it was patterned after the monastery at Actopan, though it is somewhat smaller. A massive tower rises between the church and the monastery portal. The open chapel with its broad arch is also still standing. Especially interesting are the remnants of 16th-century Indian wall paintings in the church, which depict a battle between Otomí Indians and Aztecs in the pre-Columbian codex style. There is also an attractive Gothic ribbed vault over the presbytery.

Valle de Mezquital, as this valley is called, is inhabited by Otomí Indians. The settlements of this relatively large group (now numbering about 300,000) are widely distributed in the states of México, Hidalgo, Guanajuato, Querétaro, Puebla, Tlaxcala, and Veracruz. Their lifestyles, clothing, and craftwork differ by areas. As with many of the Indian groups in Mexico, there is a commingling of Catholicism and animistic customs in the beliefs and practices of the Otomí.

The landscape hereabouts is dry: Maguey, cacti, and thornbushes are the natural vegetation. But here and there broad valleys appear with agriculture maintained by irrigation. At *Tasquillo* (207 km.; 128 miles from Mexico City on Highway 85), for example, there are vineyards and fruit orchards.

Shortly after Tetzú you'll come upon an impressive gorge. The bridge over the deeply cut Río

Tula marks the beginning of the most scenic stretch of road through the forested Sierra Madre Oriental. The views of the mountain peaks are spectacular—that is, when they are not obscured by fog, which also makes driving these winding roads hazardous. About 80 km. (50 miles) from the gorge, Highway 85 gradually descends from an elevation of 2,300 meters (7,544 feet) into warm, subtropical lowlands full of luxuriant plant life. **Tamazunchale** (388 km.; 241 miles from Mexico City; population 18,000) is only some 200 meters (656 feet) above sea level, located in the rich valley of the Río Moctezuma in the state of San Luís Potosí. Coffee, sugar cane, and tropical fruits are cultivated here. The town's 16th-century chapel is its only noteworthy architectural feature. You should, however, wander over to the *Balcón de Moctezuma,* an observation point which provides a fine view of the green river valley. Continue north on 85 to **Ciudad Valles** (see page 194), where it is possible to connect with Travel Route 15 to the northern border.

From Ciudad Valles, Federal Highway 70 leads east to Tampico. A turnoff some 20 km. (12 miles) farther on leads to *Taninul* (3 km.; 2 miles), a sulfur bath and hotel. The archaeological site of El Tamuín lies about 8 km. (5 miles) south of the village of *Tamuín*.

El Tamuín was a ceremonial center of the Huasteca people between A.D. 900 and 1500. Only a part of this extensive site has been excavated so far. Several hills made of earth are symmetrically distributed on a broad platform 5 meters (16 feet) high. A small temple rises in the center; it was connected by narrow platforms to two round altars whose preserved frescoes depict a religious procession.

Some of the most beautiful Huasteca sculptures were discovered in these excavations, including the famous "tattooed" relief statue of a youth bearing a child on his back as a sun symbol. It has been interpreted as representing a Quetzalcóatl priest; the original statue is now in the Museo Nacional de Antropología in Mexico City.

Nearby, at *El Aserradero,* are the imposing Huasteca pyramids of *Tantoc,* which have not yet been fully excavated.

Continuing on Highway 70, you'll come to **El Ébano,** a town that serves the oil workers of the area. In the vicinity there is a Huasteca round adobe temple from the Pre-Classical period.

Tampico (636 km.; 394 miles from Mexico City; population 300,000) is located on the north bank of the Río Pánuco, 10 km. (6 miles) from its estuary in the Gulf. Tampico is an important export harbor and a center for the processing and freezing of fish. But most of all, Tampico is an oil town, whose now faded prosperity came from the oil wells first drilled here in 1907.

Tampico, like Veracruz, has retained its rough, colorful, and crude port-of-call character, and if it's "atmosphere" you've come looking for in Mexico, you'll find it here. Rough seamen gather on the *Plaza Libertad,* while in *Plaza de Armas* the burghers of Tampico stroll under the palms in front of the regal *town hall,* a monument to the city's one-time prosperity. Whichever plaza you choose—and it does somehow seem as if you have to make a choice—you'll find here something of the Mexico depicted in old movies—colorful, exuberant, flashy.

Tampico's history goes back a long way. It was settled first by the Huastecas, probably as early as 1000 B.C. By the 15th century, the Aztecs had made the area a military colony, and the Huastecas were compelled to pay tribute to their new rulers. In 1516, the Spanish arrived at the mouth of the Pánuco, and within a few years they had conquered the Huastecas. Alonso de Olmos, a Franciscan, founded a mission in 1532 from which the settlement of San Luís de Tampico grew. Pirates constantly harassed the settlement, however, and in 1683 they destroyed it.

Following independence, Tampico was resettled in 1823, but the harbor became important only in the 20th century, when oil was discovered nearby. Then the boom began, and Tampico quickly developed into a major commercial center and port.

The *Museo de la Cultura Huasteca* (Museum of Huastecan

Culture) has an important collection of ceramics, sculpture, jewelry fashioned from precious metals and tortoise shell, musical instruments, weapons, and costumes—many of which are still worn by descendants of the Huastecas who live in the isolated mountain hamlets of the Sierra Madre Oriental. The museum is located about 7 km. (4 miles) north of the center of town in the suburb of *Ciudad Madero*.

Pollution has taken its toll on the once-rich rivers near Tampico, but good fishing is still possible in some of the branches of the Pánuco and Tamesí rivers. The *Miramar* and *Altamira* beaches (about 15 km.; 9 miles north of the city) on Laguna de Champayan offer good swimming.

The distance from Tampico to Matamoros, on the northern border of Tamaulipas is 500 km. (310 miles). You can also pick up Travel Route 25 (see page 235) in a southerly direction along the Gulf coast.

TRAVEL ROUTE 22: **Mexico City–Poza Rica– *Papantla–***El Tajín–*Veracruz (550 km.; 341 miles)

See map on page 232.

El Tajín is an important archaeological site of early Totonac culture, and a visit here makes it worthwhile *not* to select the shorter route, via 150 D, to Veracruz. Along the route you can also make side trips into the Sierra Madre Oriental mountains to isolated Indian villages, whose arts and crafts are widely admired.

From Mexico City follow Highway 85 north past the pyramids of *Teotihuacán* (see Travel Route 1) in the direction of Tulancingo. The highway runs along a plateau with extensive maguey plantations.

After some 55 km. (34 miles) there is a turnoff leading east for 21 km. (13 miles) to *Ciudad Sahagún*, a new industrial city where automobiles and railroad equipment are manufactured. Some of the old haciendas in the vicinity have been well maintained or restored, for example, the *Hacienda San Miguel*

Ometusco, with its 19th-century murals, or the *Hacienda Xala*, which is now a hotel. Both haciendas can be reached from the road to Otumba.

The *Hacienda Los Arcos*, known for its manufacture of pulque, a fermented drink made from agaves, is on the stretch of Highway 85 leading to the Gulf. About 15 km. (9 miles) away, you'll come to the turnoff to *Singuilucan*, which boasts an Augustinian monastery built in 1540 and a Baroque church from the 18th century. After another 12 km. (7 miles) on 85, you reach the junction with Route 130.

Tulancingo (116 km.; 70 miles from Mexico City; population 70,000) at an elevation of 2,220 meters (7,282 feet), is a textile center. Its wool products are displayed at a large annual market, which is held during the Fiesta de los Angeles on August 2. From Tulancingo a road leads to an Augustinian monastery built in 1569 at *Acatlán.*

About 12 km. (7 miles) farther along 130 a turnoff leads left for 12 km. (7 miles) to *Metepec*, from where *Tenango de Doría* can be reached. The people of this Otomí village make gaily colored embroidery, often decorated with grotesque animal motifs.

A short distance farther on the left of highway 130, a poorly maintained road leads 28 km. (17 miles) to *Honey* and **Pahuatlán,** a *mestizo* settlement surrounded by Indian villages. The Otomí Indians in the village of *San Pablito* still manufacture *papel amate,* traditional painted Indian bark paper. The women sit in front of their huts and beat the bark to flatten and smooth it. Their costumes are pre-Columbian; they wear a *quexquémitl,* a poncholike garment made from wool and then embroidered, over a wraparound skirt. The *San Carlos* is a new, small hotel in Pahuatlán that blends in well with the surroundings.

Also in the same area of Highway 130 is the road (Route 119) south to *Apizaco* by way of *Zacatlán* (40 km.; 25 miles from

Highway 130). This area is well known for its cider, made from the apples that grow in the cool mountain region of the Sierra Madre Oriental.

Return to 130 and continue to *Huauchinango* (population 30,000). This town's lower elevation of 1,470 meters (4,822 feet) is responsible for the delights of its sub-tropical climate and its dazzling floral bounty is opulently displayed at the flower festival held here at the end of February.

In *Xicotepec de Juárez* (population 31,000; elevation 1,060 meters; 3,477 feet), the comfortable hotel *Mi Ranchito* is situated on a hill in the center of lush gardens. Xicotepec de Juárez is a coffee-growing center, and you'll notice immediately the great change in climate here. The pleasant, temperate climate quickly becomes warm and humid as you enter the tropical forests.

About 85 km. (51 miles) from Xicotepec, you'll come to *Poza Rica* where 130 connects with Federal Highway 180, which leads north 58 km. (35 miles) to *Tuxpan* and on another 195 km. (117 miles) to *Tampico* (see Travel Route 25).

Poza Rica (population 200,000; elevation 60 meters; 197 feet) means "rich pool," and it is indeed just that: a rich petroleum deposit in the coastal plain. Two pipelines transport oil from the refinery here to Mexico City and Salamanca. At night high gas flames turn Poza Rica into a ghostly place, and yet only 20 km. (12 miles) south is another world in another time, *****El Tajín** (295 km.; 183 miles from Mexico City). One of the most interesting archaeological sites in Mexico, this was the ceremonial center of a Gulf coast culture during the Classical period, which began around 200 B.C. and reached its apex between A.D. 100–900 under the influence of the Toltecs. The city was devoted to the cult of Tajín, god of lightning and hurricanes.

El Tajín's most important feature is the famous *Pirámide de los Nichos* (Pyramid of the Niches), with a square ground plan of 36 meters (199 feet) and a height of 18 meters (59 feet). It is divided into six platforms, each with projecting horizontal cornices. A total of 365 niches are carved into the tiers. They symbolize the days of the year. Originally, they were blue with red frames inside; now, the colors have faded, but the play of light and shadow still make this an impressive structure. The purpose of the niches remains a mystery. They may have contained altars, funeral urns, or figures.

On the highest section rises a flat, covered temple. The inside chamber measures only 5 by 5 meters (16 by 16 feet). A broad stairway—which cannot be climbed—leads up one side of the pyramid. It is bordered by two ramps with winding ornaments. Five small platforms with recessed structures are located in the center of the stairs.

Many other monuments are grouped around squares on various levels of the hilly terrain. Only some have been exposed and reconstructed.

There are many *ball courts* at El Tajín, and some think that the game originated here and may have included human sacrifice. On the two reconstructed ball courts, flat reliefs have been preserved on the lengthwise walls that indicate the ritual character of the games. The detailed scenes on the six stone tablets at the *Juego de Pelota Sur* (South Ball Court) are particularly impressive. Seen from the east, the first scene on the right represents the sacrifice of a player. The other motifs lend themselves to various interpretations.

The main architectural characteristics of El Tajín are inclines, horizontal bands, and projecting ledges. The pyramids and residences were decorated with niches, intricate fretwork, and diamond-shaped patterns. The terrain rises to the northwest to a terrace with the so-called *Tajín Chico* group from the Post-Classical

Pirámide de los Nichos, El Tajín

period; this includes a two-storied palace with an inner courtyard.

The *Edificio de las Columnas* (Building of Columns), farther uphill to the northwest, is hard to reach, especially in the rainy season. It is nonetheless impressive. The pyramid's name is derived from the portico at its eastern, narrow front. The massive columns found here, with diameters of over 1 meter (over 3 feet), have been reconstructed and set up in front of a temporary museum at the entrance to the archaeological zone. The flat reliefs depict events from the life of an Indian ruler. In the dark museum hall are interesting relief tablets and stone statues found during excavations.

In the parking lot behind the entrance is a tall metal mast, which the daring *voladores* (fliers) use for their acrobatic flights on weekends. Performed by Totonac Indians, the aerial dance stems from an ancient ritual (see page 11). They "fly" from a high mast on Corpus Christi Day (which falls in May or June) in nearby (16 km.; 10 miles) ***Papantla** (population 40,000), a town lying amid tropical green hills and *barrancas* (deep river beds). The Totonacs who live here are descendants of the builders of El Tajín. On holidays the Totonacs wear airy, white costumes: simple knickerbockers, shirts, and dark shoes or sandals for men, and muslin skirts and

Voladores

lace scarves for the women. The region has long been known for growing vanilla beans, which are used to make figures of spiders and scorpions, as well as vanilla essence and liquor. These items are sold in stores along the road between Papantla and *Gutiérrez Zomora*. The main road (180) continues to **Tecolutla**, a small beach resort on the Gulf coast. Three large, old hotels are located on the beach, as well as other more modest lodgings. A toll bridge spans the mouth of the Río Tecolutla in the direction of Nautla and **Veracruz* (550 km., 341 miles, from Mexico City, see page 238.)

TRAVEL ROUTE 23: **Mexico City–**Puebla (–*Cuetzálan)–*Jalapa–*Veracruz (424/642 km.; 263/398 miles)

See map on page 232.

The anthropological museum of Jalapa is one of the most important in Mexico, second only to the national museum in Mexico City. This Travel Route offers a direct route to Jalapa from Mexico City and a longer, more leisurely circuit by way of Cuetzalán. You will need two days if you intend to visit Cuetzalán in the Sierra Norte de Puebla and Teziutlán.

The route to Puebla (see page 103) is described in Travel Route 7. From Puebla, follow Highway 150 D northeast. If you are driving to Cuetzalán, you will exit the highway at *Amozoc* for Highway 129; if not, you will exit 22 km. (14 miles) past Amozoc for Acatzingo and Highway 140, the direct road to Jalapa. In **Acatzingo** (179 km.; 111 miles, from Mexico City), there is an early 16th-century *Franciscan monastery*. Its church, with Gothic vaults and Medieval-looking baptismal font, is quite impressive. The road crosses the plateau between the volcanoes of *La Malinche* (4,461 meters; 14,275 feet high) and *Pico de Orizaba* (5,747 meters; 18,850 feet high), whose snow-covered summit is visible only in good weather. The *Laguna de Alchichica* is a crater lake of volcanic origin. Continue on 140 to *Perote* (see page 23).

If you take the longer route via 129, near *Tepetlaxco*, on the left, is La Malinche volcano (its Indian name is Matlalcueyetl). In *Tequixquitla/El Carmen*, a road turns right past the flat *Laguna Totolcingo* to *Zacatepec,* where there is a connection to the direct road (140) to Jalapa. Continuing on 129 past *Oriental,* you will be driving across a barren plateau where storms whip up sand dunes during the dry season. Agaves, from which pulque is made, are grown here. Don't miss *Acuaco,* just before Zaragoza; From Acuaco, a beautiful *mountain road* leads west for 53 km. (33 miles) through *Zacapoaxtla* to **Cuetzálan** (population 5,000; elevation 1,020 meters; 3,345 feet). This pretty town has a Sunday market to which the Nahua Indians come from the surrounding countryside to sell handicrafts, such as embroidered blouses, woolen scarves, and woven belts. The women wear lovely costumes of white woven gauze *quexquémitl* over embroidered blouses, and purple woolen head coverings, called *copetes,* that are wound like a turban. During the festival of the patron saint, held on October 4, there are quetzal dancers and performances by the voladores (see page 11). From Cuetzálan it is about an hour's walk (or you can drive a very bumpy road) to the ruins of a Totonac cult site near *Yohualichan.* A group of stepped niche pyramids in the El Tajín style have been uncovered here.

Return to Acuaco and continue along Highway 129 through *Zaragoza* (285 km; 177 miles from Mexico City) and past *Tlatlauquitepec* (elevation 1,930 meters; 6,330 feet) on the eastern slope of the Sierra. The mountains here are often covered by mist or rain clouds, even in the dry season. Near *Teteles,* a narrow road leads about 10 km. (6 miles) to *Hueyapan,* noteworthy for the wide, long woolen scarves that are embroidered in bright colors here. Back on the main road, **Teziutlán** (elevation 1,990 meters, 6,527 feet) is a small mountain town with a population of 30,000. A Colonial parish church and a few Colonial houses are situated around the main square.

At Teziutlán, Highway 129 continues 94 km. (58 miles) to *Nautla* on the Gulf coast (see page 236), or you can take Highway 131 past *Altotonga* to *Perote* where you can rejoin the main road (140) to Jalapa.

Perote, 267 km. (165 miles) from Mexico City (population 20,000; elevation 2,465 meters; 8,085 feet) is in the state of Veracruz, at the foot of the *Cofre de Perote* (4,120 meters; 13,510 feet). It is possible to drive almost to the summit of this volcano. Perote is known for its fort, the *Fuerte de San Carlos,* which was built toward the end of the 18th century and was later used as a prison.

From Perote the road begins a quick descent—almost 1,000 meters (3,280 feet) in 50 km. (31 miles)—to the green hills that surround ***Jalapa** (320 km.; 198 miles from Mexico City; population 200,000; elevation 1,400 meters; 4,592 feet), the capital of the state of Veracruz and the center of a large coffee-growing region. The old part of Jalapa still has some pretty cobbled streets; the white 18th-century Cathedral, which has since been altered, towers above the rest of the town.

By far, Jalapa's most interesting attraction is the ****Museo de Antropología,** which has extensive collections of artifacts of the Gulf coast cultures. Of particular note are monumental Olmec stone sculptures and charming terracottas from the early Totonac cul-

Totonac sculpture

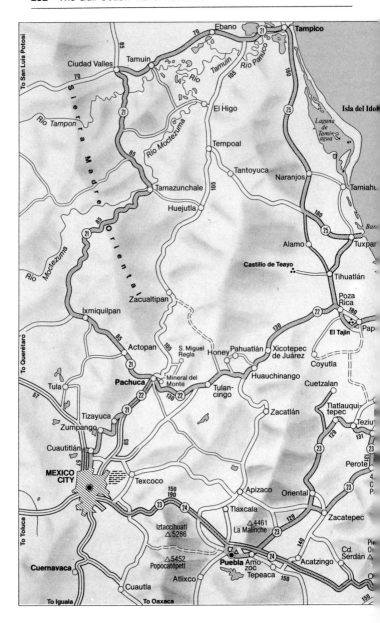

ROUTES 21–25
(The Gulf Coast)

Miles
0 ⊨⊨⊨⊨⊨⊨ 30
Kilometers

Golfo de México

pan

tiérrez
mora
Tecolutla

22

129

Nautla

Martínez
de la Torre
coyan

25

180

ga

Palma Sola

22

Jalapa

23

Zempoala

Cardel

23

Veracruz

22

140

Coscomatepec

24

25

Fortín
Córdoba

24

150

180

Villahermosa

Mendoza

ture, which include the familiar smiling faces and the finely worked pottery vessels and stone and clay sculptures of the Huastecs. Modern objects used by descendants of these ancient civilizations complete the exhibit. A new museum has been under construction since 1986, and will soon take over these exhibits.

The road (140) from Jalapa east to Veracruz is well paved. Follow it 59 km. (35 miles) to *Tamarindo,* where tamarind trees grow and their pods are sold on the street. From here, the 40-mile toll-free road to Veracruz turns right. In *Cardel* the new road joins 180 and proceeds to **Veracruz* (424 km.; 263 miles from Mexico City, see page 238.)

TRAVEL ROUTE 24: **Mexico City–**Puebla–Orizaba–*Veracruz (428 km.; 265 miles)

See map on page 232.

If you are going to the Yucatán Peninsula from Mexico City and do not want to make too many stops along the way, you should take this fast route to Veracruz.

Exit Mexico City on either Avenida Iztapalapa or Avenida Zaragoza and then follow the toll road, 150 D to *Puebla* (see Travel Route 7). After Puebla, the highway has only two lanes and climbs more than 1,000 meters (3,000 feet) in serpentine curves. It passes **Orizaba** (population 150,000; elevation 1,285 meters; 4,215 feet), which lies in a wide valley. From here there is a view of the highest mountain in the country, the *Pico de Orizaba,* or Citlaltépetl, whose summit, at 5,747 meters (18,850 feet), is usually covered in clouds. Orizaba is an important industrial center, known primarily for its large brewery.

The town has tried to preserve some of its Colonial heritage, and indeed in the center of the town the churches—*San José de Gracia,* once part of a Franciscan monastery; *El Calvario,* a Neoclassical building by Manuel Tolsá; *del Carmen;* and the massive parish church, the *Parroquia*—all serve as reminders of Mexico's Colonial past. Sister Alférez, a nun who was famous among the colonists because of her bold adventures in warriors' clothing, is buried in the Baroque *San Juan de Diós* church.

Continue north on 150 D, now a lovely mountain road, to *Tehuacán,* a distance of 83 km. (51 miles), where it is possible to connect with Travel Route 27 to Oaxaca (see page 251). Follow the road to **Fortín de las Flores** (population 20,000). It was once a way station between Mexico City and Veracruz during the Colonial period, guarded by a small Spanish bastion. This pretty town is surrounded by the lush tropical vegetation that inspired its name, "Fortress of Flowers." Coffee and sugarcane are grown in the region. The town holds an annual flower festival from April 15 to 17.

Almost 300 km. (186 miles) from Mexico City, 150 leads to **Córdoba** (population 120,000), the center of this tropical farming area. The town is named for the Spanish viceroy Diego Fernández de Córdoba, who ordered it built in 1618. It was here, in the *Casa Ceballos* on the main square, that the last viceroy, Juan O'Donojú, and Agustín de Iturbide signed an agreement granting independence to Mexico on August 24, 1821; the Spanish king Ferdinand VII, however, did not immediately accept the treaty. Continuing on 150, **Yanga** (population 3,000) bears the name of an African who landed in Mexico with a slave transport in 1579. He escaped and fled to the mountainous region around the Pico de Orizaba, where he gathered more escaped slaves as well as *mestizos* and Spaniards fleeing from the law. The group lived by attacking travelers between Veracruz and the interior. Yanga was captured by Spanish troops in 1609, and was pardoned for his crimes. With some of his followers, he settled this village; blacks are still the majority here.

Ciutláhuac (elevation 400 meters; 1,312 feet) is the next village on the road. From here, there is an unpaved road of about 10 km. (6 miles) to a 15-century Aztec pyramid.

On the road (145) that turns off 150 at *La Tinaja* you can drive through *Tuxtepec* and pick up either the short road to *Villahermosa* (450 km.; 279 miles away) or the road to the *Gulf of Tehuantepec* (345 km.; 214 miles away), and from there to *Chiapas* (see Travel Route 28).

Continuing along 150, near *Paso del Toro* (Bull's Step), the coastal road 180 turns right to *Villahermosa* (see Travel Route 25). Highway 180 in the opposite direction will take you along the coast, past the fishing villages of *Boca del Río* (River's Mouth) and *Mocambo*, with its wonderful beaches, to **Veracruz* (428 km.; 265 miles from Mexico City, see page 238).

TRAVEL ROUTE 25: Tampico–*Veracruz–Villahermosa (961 km.; 596 miles)

See map on pages 232 and 244.

This is the route to take if you're driving from the north—Matamoros, Nuevo Laredo, or Monterrey—and you want to proceed directly to the Yucatán. The route follows the Gulf, and there are abundant opportunities to sunbathe and swim along the way. You should plan to take a side trip to El Tajín (see page 228).

Exit Tampico (see page 225) from the south and cross the Río Pánuco, which forms the border between the states of Tamaulipas and Veracruz. *Villa Cuauhtémoc* on the south shore was built at the site of San Luís de Tampico, founded in the 16th century and

later abandoned. The town's old name, Pueblo Viejo (Old Village), survives in the nearby *Laguna de Pueblo Viejo*. From *Tampico Alto* (17 km.; 10 miles from Tampico), there is a side road that parallels the main road, 180, running along the *Laguna Tamiahua* through several fishing villages. Salt has been harvested in this area since pre-Columbian times. In **Naranjos** (111 km.; 69 miles from Tampico) rejoin 180, in the heart of the Faja de Oro (Golden Belt) where oil has been drilled since 1913.

Near *Alazan* you can drive straight through *Alamo* on side roads toward *Poza Rica,* which is 24 km. (15 miles) shorter than following 180 through **Tuxpan** (191 km.; 118 miles from Tampico; population 50,000). This small port city lies some 11 km. (7 miles) above the mouth of the Río Tuxpan. There are facilities for water sports here, and the *museum* to the right of the *Cathedral* has a lovely collection of pottery and decorative items from the Huastec culture. A small road from here to the coast ends at the fishing village of *Tampamachoco* where there is a wonderful beach, the *Barra del Norte.*

To the south is *Tihuatlán* (225 km.; 139 miles from Tampico), where the road from Alamo joins. From here, you can take a 17 km. (10 mile) side trip west to **Castillo de Teayo.** There is a three-storied **pyramid* here called Castillo by the Spanish. A steep staircase leads to the uppermost platform, on which a masonry temple has been preserved. Stelae, reliefs, and statues indicate that there was an Aztec garrison in this area, but the temple itself seems to be older. It may, in fact, have been built by Toltec immigrants, after the decline of

Tolla in the 12th century, on the site of an earlier Totonac ceremonial center.

Back on 180, Travel Route 25 follows Travel Route 22 between Poza Rica and Tecolutla. Of particular note is the side trip to the archaeological site of ****El Tajín* (see page 228).

Almost 3 km. (2 miles) before Nautla, a tortuous road turns off Highway 180 into the mountains, leading 94 km. (58 miles) to *Martínez de la Torre* and *Teziutlán* (see page 231). *Nautla* lies at the mouth of the Río Nautla at the Gulf of Mexico. There are lovely beaches on the *Barra de Nautla,* and small seafood restaurants line the coastal roads. Unfortunately, it's hard to get a good view of the Gulf as you're driving since palm groves stand between the sea and the road. Near *Vega de Alatorre* (359 km.; 222 miles from Tampico), at the end of the Laguna Grande, a side trip leads 3 km. (2 miles) to the beach of *Las Higueras.* There is a 10-km.- (6-mile-) long beach with fine sand near the village of *Palma Sola.* At the *Laguna Verde,* you'll find Mexico's first atomic power plant. **Villa Rica** (422 km.; 262 miles from Tampico) is where the Spanish laid out their first port in 1519, called Villa Rica de Veracruz. In 1524 the town site was moved to the mouth of the Río Hutzilapan (where La Antigua is now located, see below), and finally to its present site in 1589.

Continue along 180 to **Zempoala** (440 km.; 273 miles from

Tampico) which can be reached by a side road that swings inland for almost 3 km. (2 miles). At the edge of the small village are the interesting ruins of an old Totonac settlement. The Spanish received a friendly welcome in Zempoala in 1519. The "fat cacique," as the Spanish called the chieftain Chicomacatl, allied himself with the newcomers to throw off Aztec rule. But in the event, he was powerless to prevent his Spanish "allies" from destroying the statues of Indian deities and idols in the temples. A year later, the once prosperous town was in ruins, destroyed in the fighting between Cortés's troops and a punitive expedition sent out from Cuba. During the archaeological exploration of the pre-Columbian town, twelve walled temple districts were found; it is likely that dwellings were grouped within these structures.

The road to the right of the entrance to the village is marked and leads to the greatest and best-preserved ceremonial site. Surrounded and protected against floods by a wall about 1.2 meters (4 feet) high, crowned with crenels, is the *Gran Pirámide* (Great Pyramid), partially hidden by palm trees. The *Templo Mayor* is the main temple on the broad north side; to the left is the *Templo de las Chimeneas* (The Chimney Temple), with its crenelated top platform. Because there were few stones in the coastal flood plain, the builders used clay, sand, and lime for the core and stones from the river to cover their sanctuaries, which are laid out with stepped terraces and broad staircases.

On the broad plaza there are several small buildings. Especially interesting are the round pyramids with rectangular stepped terraces, which stand next to the Gran Pirámide, and the circular structures with crenels, which perhaps were platforms for performing ritual dances.

The little museum at the entrance to the complex displays some of the small ceramic skulls, called *caritas,* that decorated the *Templo de las Caritas* (Temple of Small Heads). The temple itself is located a short distance to the east of the walled area.

Back on 180, a road leads east to the beach of *Chachalacas,* where there are several hotels. You can also reach this beach by crossing the junction of the road to *Jalapa* near *Cardel* (see Travel Route 23). The toll road to Veracruz begins here at Cardel. **La Antigua** (455 km.; 262 miles from Tampico; population 5,000) is the old Veracruz, the second port founded by the Spanish in 1524 near the mouth of the Río Huitzilapán. On the shore stands the small 16th-century chapel dedicated to Santo Cristo del Buen Viaje. A small wooden statue of Santo Cristo brought to the New World by Cortés is now in the parish church on the plaza. The *Casa de Cortés,* allegedly Cortés's house, is now a ruin.

Continue on 180 to Veracruz

(480 km.; 297 miles from Tampico).

*Veracruz

See map on page 240.

It is in Veracruz that modern Mexican history really began, and up through this century, Mexico's violent encounters with Europe and the United States were centered in this tough but still dignified port city—the first city established on the American mainland by Europeans. Cortés landed just north of Veracruz in 1519, burned his boats to ensure that the fainthearted would not turn back, then began his march west to the Aztec capital. The city was bombarded by the Spanish during Mexico's War of Independence. Seventeen years later, Veracruz was again attacked, this time by the French. Then, in 1847, American troops occupied Veracruz during the Mexican–American war. In 1860, the French returned, with their candidate for emperor, Maximilian. Finally, in 1914, the United States again bombarded Veracruz during the stormy period following the Revolution of 1910.

In addition to receiving the bombs of her would-be American and European conquerors, Veracruz has also received their refugees, since for a long time it was Mexico's principal port of entry. In the 20th century, Mexico's revolutionary sympathies led her to welcome political exiles from fascist Europe, and in so doing developed a certain European flavor that mingles nicely with the Caribbean atmosphere of this, perhaps the liveliest of Mexican cities.

Not far from the harbor—still one of the most important in Mexico—is the ****Zócalo** (1), the town square, and the international heart of the city. Everyone meets in the Zócalo, the local people, tourists, and sailors from everywhere. It's a place for hard drinking late into the night, for promenading afternoons or evenings, and for sampling the café life of this cosmopolitan port early in the morning or well past midnight. Birds sing in the trees by day, but evenings are given over to the strolling musicians, marimbas, trios playing portable harps and miniature guitars, and strident mariachi groups all of whom compete for attention. The crowds seem as if they'll never tire and have nowhere else in the world to go. The pitch is always high in

Zócalo, Veracruz

Veracruz, and it reaches its greatest intensity during Mardi Gras, the week before Lent—a celebration that easily rivals the festivities in New Orleans or Rio de Janeiro.

A short distance away from the Zócalo is the *Malecón,* Veracruz's waterfront boulevard, where you can watch the ships loading and unloading, or simply stroll and shop at the souvenir stores in the *Mercado de Artesanías* (4). Nearby is the **Aduana Marítima** (3), the customs office.

From the Malecón you can take a boat to the island fortress of **San Juan de Ulúa** (5), constructed in 1582 by the Spanish as protection against the British and Dutch pirates who lay in wait for the rich galleons setting sail for Spain. The buildings here now date mainly from the 17th century, however. It was from this fortress, by the way, that the Spanish and the French were able to conduct their bombardment of Veracruz, practically leveling it during the War of Independence. Boats also leave from the Malecón for the *Isla de Sacrificios,* so-called by the Spanish because they found traces of human sacrifices there. Today, there are several good seafood restaurants, and the harbor's lighthouse stands rather majestically here.

Successive bombardments and simple neglect has left little of Veracruz's Colonial architectural heritage. The *Baluarte de Santiago* (6), built in 1746, is one of the few buildings remaining from that period. The *parish church* on the Zócalo, an unpretentious Colonial structure now elevated to the status of cathedral, dates from 1734; the *town hall* (2) facing it dates from the 19th century. The city's **Museo de la Ciudad** (7) houses historical and archaeological collections that are, unfortunately, badly maintained and of little importance. The oldest structure in the city, the *Iglesia del Santo Cristo del Buen Viaje* (8), is located at *Gutiérrez Zamora Park.* It was built in the 16th century but is not particularly interesting architecturally.

Although there is a beach in town, *Villa del Mar,* the best beach, *Mocambo,* is found just outside the city limits. The best hotels are here, too, among them the *Mocambo* and the *Torremar.* Farther south, at the fishing village of *Boca del Río,* is the *Hosteria Suiza,* a wonderful Swiss restaurant in a beautiful setting.

Exit Veracruz on the coastal road, 180, toward Villahermosa. Along the way, there are good beaches at *Mocambo* and the fishing village of *Boca del Río.* Past *Salinas,* the coastal road runs on a narrow spit of land between the sea and a lagoon fed by the waters of the Río Papaloapan and its tributaries. Near the fishing village of *Alvarado* the spit is interrupted by a toll bridge. About halfway to *Lerdo de Tejeda* (20 km.; 12 miles from Alvarado) where sugar cane from the surrounding plantations is processed, you can pick up Highway 75 through the marshy

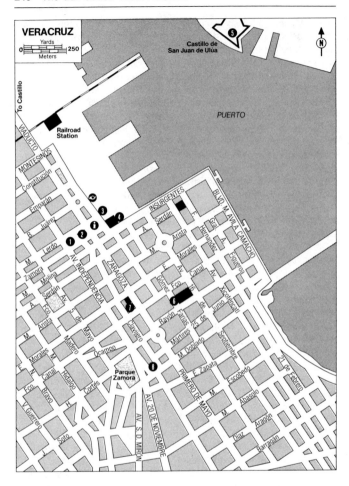

coastal plain, dotted with lakes, and proceed to *Tuxtepec*. The trip to Oaxaca from there through the Sierra de Juarez, barely 350 km. (217 miles), offers completely different scenery.

Continue on 180. In *Angel R. Cabada* is the roadway to *Tres Zapotes*, through *Zamora*, one of the Olmec archaeological sites. There is little of interest here except the **museum*.

Santiago Tuxtla (620 km.; 384 miles from Tampico; population 20,000; elevation 285 meters; 934 feet) lies in the valley of Río Tuxtla. On the main square stands a colossal Olmec head which was found near the town. Other Olmec items from the area are exhibited in the small *museum*. **San Andrés Tuxtla** (population 45,000) is an important commercial center, and a shipping point for the tropical fruit and tobacco grown in the region. The *San Martín* volcano, at 1,738 meters (5,700 feet) is the highest mountain in the Sierra de los Tuxtlas, a small mountain chain rising up from the coastal plain.

Highway 180 passes by ***Lago de Catemaco,** a large crater lake, 11 km. (7 miles) long and at its widest 8 km. (5 miles) across. It is picturesquely nestled between green hills. At its western shore is the fishing village and popular resort of **Catemaco** (population 35,000). Along the town's dusty main street are frame houses with terraces, most of which rent rooms at very modest prices. On the shore promenade there are motels, and on the road to Veracruz is the comfortable *Hotel Finca*. The restaurants here will catch a fish for you and cook it on the spot. You can also rent boats for trips to nearby islands, the most unusual of which is the "monkey island," on which a horde of Indian macaques have been introduced for research purposes.

The *Virgen del Carmen,* a painting of the Virgin in a village church, is said to perform miracles. The same is said of the many *curanderos* (healers) and *brujos* (magicians) of Catemaco. Commerce in miracles and cures is widespread in the state of Veracruz, particularly in the Tux-

tla region, and many visitors come here seeking some sort of divine intervention.

In *Acayucan,* 180 intersects with Federal Highway 185, called the Transistmica, which crosses the isthmus of Tehuantepec. Continue along 180 through **Minatitlán** (768 km.; 476 miles from Tampico) and **Coatzacoalcos.** This is a region given over to the oil industry. You'll encounter tank trucks and derricks as you travel the terribly crowded roads, which, though they skirt the towns, simply cannot handle all the traffic they bear. In this area it's wise to avoid public transportation on the weekends because the planes and buses are filled with oil workers going to other parts of Mexico to visit their families. Oil production for the whole region is concentrated in the river port of Minatitlán and conveyed from there in pipelines; exports are shipped from the harbor of Coatzacoalcos.

Just past the bridge over the Río Tonalá, which forms the boundary between the states of Veracruz and Tabasco, is a turnoff leading 3 km. (2 miles) to **Villa la Venta** where, in the midst of this busy oil region, lies the archaeological zone of *La Venta,* the name of the Olmec culture here (see page 26). As it is, the zone is not worth visiting since most of the interesting sculpture has been moved to museums, primarily the one in Villahermosa (see below).

From Cárdenas, Highway 187 leads north for 36 km. (22 miles) to ***Comalcalco,** a small town with a pre-Columbian ceremonial site, which is considered to be the westernmost outpost of Classic Mayan culture. Its most peculiar feature is the use of brick for building, necessary because of the lack of stones in the area. The monuments that remain here date from the Late-Classic period, that is, from the sixth to the eighth centuries. Fragments of a stucco coating with reliefs are preserved. *Temple I* of the northern group is impressive; it is a step pyramid 20 meters (65 feet) high. The *Great Acropolis* is equally impressive; it is a giant artificial platform 35 meters (115 feet) high on which the remains of a palace are visible next to a few temple ruins. A tomb in the Palenque style (see page 275) was discovered underneath one of the temples; it is decorated with nine stucco sculptures. Items from the graves and other finds are exhibited in the *museum* at the entrance.

If you travel north some 20 km. (12 miles) on 187, you'll come to *Paraiso,* and it is truly a tropical paradise. From here the road leads to the nearby beaches of *El Limón* and *Puerto Ceiba.*

Back on Highway 180, you'll enter *Villahermosa.*

Villahermosa

Villahermosa (961 km.; 596 miles from Tampico; population 150,000) is the capital of the state of Tabasco. It is, as its Spanish name says, a pretty town, though it is in the tropical zone and therefore hot and quite humid. But suffer the heat just a bit and visit the two museums here; they have important collections of objects from Mexico's pre-Columbian past. As you enter the town on the Boulevard Grijalva, there is a sign to the access road to the ***Parque La Venta,** an open-air museum at the *Laguna de las Ilusiones.* Among the sculptures moved here with great difficulty from La Venta (see above) are several altars and stelae and some colossal Olmec heads with negroid features. The largest is 2.70 meters (9 feet) high and weighs 40 tons.

The excellent new ***Museo Regional de Antropología** stands on the banks of Río Grijalva and is part of the modern research center called CICOM (Centro de Investigaciones de las Culturas Olmeca y Maya). The museum is also called *Museo*

Olmec Colossal head

Carlos Pellicer, in memory of the poet who was the director of this archaeological collection for many years.

A tour of the museum begins on the upper floor with an overview of the ancient Mexican cultures and representative examples from the Pre-Classic period. The lower floor is given over to the Olmec and Mayan societies and contains typical stone statues and fine jade jewelry of the La Venta culture. Among the Mayan objects are lovely ceramic figures from the cemetery island of Jaina on the west coast of the Yucatán.

Selected pieces from these two cultures are exhibited in a special location on the balcony. These include a Mayan *drinking vessel* with finely painted decoration, named for Carlos Pellicer; a precious *potsherd;* and the *Urn of Teapa,* a Mayan piece from the Late-Classic period, found in Tabasco, that is shaped like a sitting priest. You can also see a jadeite *dagger* from La Venta with the traits of a jaguar man engraved on it.

The artifact store of CICOM sells basketry and leather goods, including pocketbooks, shoes, and belts of snakeskin, crocodile leather, and sharkskin—and a special drink, cocoa wine.

Ethnic art from Tabasco is on display at the **Museo de Cultura Popular,** at Calle Zaragoza 810. One room is given over to Indian dances, and exhibits the costumes, masks, and musical instruments that accompanied them. Other showcases contain objects from the daily life of the ethnic groups of Tabasco, including a detailed facsimile of a Chontal hut.

The *Plaza de la Constitución* is the center of town, which was founded in 1593. On the plaza stand the *Palacio de Gobierno* and the *Cathedral,* dating from 1614. Guanábana and ceiba trees line the plaza, and the *Café del Portal* provides a good place just to sit and watch the action. A pedestrian mall called *Zona Luz* is also quite lively, day and night, and it's here you'll find the post and telegraph offices, banks, stores, and inns. The restaurant ship *Capitán Beuló* sails the Río Grijalva, and excursions on it are available from Villahermosa.

The Mayan ruins at *Yaxchilán and *Bonampak (see page 277) in the jungle of Chiapas can be reached by charter plane from Villahermosa, Tuxtla Gutiérrez, San Cristóbal, Palenque and Tenosique. From Palenque there are also trips by land to the ruins. In fact, you should spend a night in Palenque (see page 275) in order to visit the ***ruins in the jungle.

The Southern Highlands

Stretching from Oaxaca to Chiapas, the southern highlands encompass two mountainous regions that converge abruptly at the low isthmus of Tehuantepec. In addition, several mountain chains seal off a central basin in the state of Oaxaca. Unfortunately, the pines were cut from these mountains long ago, and even the grass that grew in their place has disappeared, the result of heavy grazing. Today, all that remains are stony hills crisscrossed by eroded gullies and dotted with thorn bushes and cactus.

Despite this inhospitable landscape, the broad plateau on which the Colonial city of Oaxaca sits has been densely settled since pre-Columbian times. The Zapotecs and Mixtecs have left impressive ruins in the

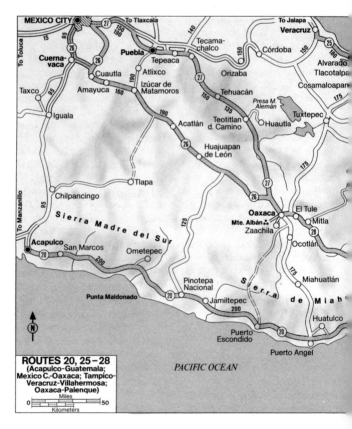

ROUTES 20, 25 – 28
(Acapulco-Guatemala;
Mexico C.-Oaxaca; Tampico-
Veracruz-Villahermosa;
Oaxaca-Palenque)

area at Monte Albán, Mitla, and Yagul, exquisite reminders of their glorious past, and Indian languages and traditions are still very much alive. Unlike Indians elsewhere in Mexico, who may seem withdrawn and wary of foreigners, the tribes around Oaxaca, mostly of Zapotecan stock, are outgoing and friendly. Other Indian groups—the Mazatecs, Popoloca, Mixe, Chinantecs, and Chontal Indians among them—live in greater isolation in the remote Sierra Madre del Sur and are correspondingly less comfortable with strangers.

It is the state of Chiapas, however, that can lay claim to the greatest number of Indian tribes today. Here, an estimated two million descendants of the once-powerful Mayas still live in the junglelike highlands, protected by their very remoteness, as well as by the hot, humid weather and roads that are impassable in the rainy season. These obstacles not-

withstanding, the ancient Mayan sites of Palenque, Bonampak, and Yax-chilán receive flocks of visitors every year. Interestingly enough, the modern Mayas in Chiapas speak a variety of languages that are not mutu-ally understood, and in spite of centuries of contact with *mestizos,* espe-cially in the local markets, each group is very conscious of its own traditions.

The differences in peoples and cultures in this region are matched by the varied climatic zones and scenery—all of it greatly influenced by altitude. The Sierra Madre de Chiapas lie more or less parallel to the Pacific coast and is home to the Chuj Indians, as well as the smaller tribes of the Mame and Kakchiquel, whose range extends into the Soconusco region of Guatemala, famous for its large coffee plantations. Adjacent to the coastal mountain range is the relatively dry valley of the upper Río Grijalva, which cuts its way into the lowlands of Tabasco through the *sumidero*—Spanish for "drainpipe"—a deep, narrow gorge.

The pretty Colonial town of San Cristóbal lies in the middle of a lime-stone plateau. The surrounding pine-forested mountains and valleys are peopled by the Tzotzil Indians, the largest ethnic group in Chiapas, as well as Tzeltal and Tojolabal Indians. To the north is the hilly country of the Sierra de los Lacandónes, also piled on top of a bed of karstic lime-stone. The tropical rain forest here, called the *selva,* is home to the mod-ern Lacandón Indians, the last Mexican tribe living in close harmony with nature, and one whose way of life is as threatened by civilization as is the rain forest on which they depend for their existence.

TRAVEL ROUTE 26: **Mexico City–Cuautla–Izúcar de Matamoros–***Oaxaca (523 km.; 324 miles)

See map on page 244.

Full of sinuous curves, this route is only a little longer than Travel Route 27 and a challenge for driving enthusiasts. It offers magnificent mountain scenery, some marvelous monastical architecture in Yanhuitlán and Tep-oscolula, and a stop at the potters' village of Acatlán de Osorio, where the fragile tree-of-life figurines are fashioned of clay and painted in wonder-ful colors.

If you have a lot of time, you can follow Travel Route 6 to **Cuautla** and take a side trip to the *Paso de Cortés* to see the majestic snow-capped peaks of Popocatépetl and Iztaccíhuatl. If your time is lim-ited, drive out of Mexico City on the road to Cuernavaca; after about 69 km. (43 miles) you'll come to a toll road that turns off toward Cuautla. Approximately 77 km. (48 miles) from the capi-

Indians dressed in brightly colored costumes come to Oaxaca from the surrounding mountains to participate in the great folklore festival.

Tulum, on the Caribbean coast, is one of many Mayan sites in the Yucatán peninsula.

Vacationers from Mexico, as well as foreign visitors, flock to Acapulco.

Hats are in abundant supply in the market at Ocotlán (Oaxaca).

Pre-Hispanic, Colonial, and modern buildings are the models for these tombs in Hoctún (Yucatán).

The archaeological zone of Monte Albán lies above the Oaxaca valley.

A ceiba tree has slowly reclaimed the so-called "House of Cortés" in La Antigua.

Towering cacti are common features of the landscape south of Tehuacán.

Festival in San Andrés Larraínzar in Chiapas.

Blue shawls, sometimes worn on the head, are part of the traditional clothing worn by the women of San Juan Chamula.

The Lacandones, who live in Chiapas, may be the last living descendants of the Mayas.

The masterful skill of the Palenque stone masons is evident in this bas-relief of the smoking-god in the Templo de la Cruz.

Hot chilis and other fresh produce are plentiful in marketplaces like this one in Chalma.

tal, you'll reach ***Tepoztlán** (see page 90). Continue for another 21 km. (13 miles) until you reach a turnoff on the right for the Hacienda Hotel in **Cocoyoc** (see page 100), or take the turnoff on the left to **Oaxtepec,** about 3.5 km. (2 miles) farther on (see page 100).

From *Cuautla* (see page 100), pick up Highway 140 toward *Izúcar de Matamoros.* After 19 km. (12 miles), you'll come to a side road that leads to the archaeological site of **Chalcatzingo.** (There is a turnoff for the ruins about a mile past the roads to the villages of Jonacatepec and Tepalcingo.)

Chalcatzingo lies in the fertile valley of the Río Tenango and is surrounded by basalt mountains. Near the town at the foot of the slopes of the *Cerro de la Cantera* are the ruins of a sanctuary dating to the middle Pre-Classic period, about 1000–600 B.C. With the exception of two pyramids and a partially excavated ball court, few buildings remain, but there are fine painted petroglyphs in Olmec style preserved on rocks, on stone stelae, and in the interiors of caves. The various motifs suggest that they're the work of a fertility cult, as does a relief of the rain god on the summit of the 305-meter- (1,000-foot-) mountain. From here, there is also a breathtaking view of distant Popocatépetl to the north.

Just southwest near the thermal spa of *Jonacatepec* lies *Las Pilas,* with its talud-tablero stone structures dating to A.D. 500–650. During excavation archaeologists uncovered an extensive network of canals that had been used to bring water to the fields from springs in the mountains. Grave artifacts found in the canals resemble objects from Teotihuacán and seem to reflect the existence of a water cult, yet nothing similar has been discovered anywhere else in the vicinity.

Returning to Highway 140, you'll go through *Amatitlanes,* locally famous for its thermal waters. Continue another 3.5 km. (2 miles) to reach **Izúcar de Matamoros** (*azucar* is Spanish for "sugar," a reflection of the extensive sugarcane fields in the area). This small town of 25,000 is known for its two large families of potters whose thriving business produces multicolored chandeliers that are sold as souvenirs in the capital. There is also a 16th-century Dominican *monastery* and an impressive 16th-century *fountain* in town.

From Izúcar de Matamoros, it is another 89 km. (55 miles) to **Acatlán de Osorio,** a pottery-making village with a population of about 10,000. Over 100 workshops are devoted to producing the clay figurines and tree-of-life sculptures for which the town is justly famous. The fanciful animals and hand-painted designs may be imitated elsewhere, but none can match the refreshing, imaginative flair of these gaily colored sculptures. In keeping with traditional Mexican techniques, local potters also shape earthenware pots and dishes, then polish or paint them in many colors rather than using glazes. The studio of potter Heron Martínez is located on the left near the village entrance.

As you continue on southward toward Oaxaca, you'll drive through the strange, dry cactus landscape typical of the Mixtec region between Puebla and Oaxaca and leave the state of Puebla crossing into Oaxaca. Just across the state line is *Huajapan de Léon,* a trading center for hats and other articles woven in palm fiber. From here the road curves upward again as you begin to climb the rugged foothills of the Sierra Madre del Sur.

The mountain villages and highland valleys in this region are clearly Mixtec territory. Although their origins remain somewhat mysterious, codices and *lienzos*—historical scenes from the period after the Conquest recorded on cloth—recount the rise and fall of three distinct Mixtec empires in the centuries before the arrival of the Spanish in 1521. Some archae-

ologists believe the Mixtecs settled in the area around Oaxaca as early as the seventh century. By the 15th century, they had pushed into the Valley of Oaxaca, driving the Zapotecs from their ceremonial centers in the process. To this day, their descendants fashion pots and jewelry using the same motifs that have been passed down through the generations. And in more remote areas of the mountains, ceremonial customs honoring such deities as the wind god are still observed by the local Indians.

About 370 km. (231 miles) out of Mexico City, at *Santiago Tejupan,* you'll come to a road that leads to **Coixtláhuaca,** the capital of the Mixtec kingdom of Mixteca Alta and a major trading center until the Aztecs subjugated the region in the middle of the 15th century. Buildings and graves excavated here date to the last two centuries before the Conquest. After the arrival of the Spanish, Dominican friars erected a monastery on the site of a Mixtec ceremonial platform. The façade of the church, built in 1546, is done in the *Plateresque* style, and was crafted by local Indian artists. There is also an open chapel with a Gothic vault and an 18th-century high altar worth visiting.

If you drive 13 km. (8 miles) out of *Yucura* in the direction of Pinotepa Nacional, you'll pass another architectural jewel of the Colonial period, the church of **San Pedro y San Pablo Teposcolula,** which was built with

Yacatecuhtli, Mixtec god of flight

materials from a ruined 16th-century monastery. The niches of its façade feature a number of large statues, and the open chapel, which was built in 1570, has a hexagonal presbytery with two colonnades that's an exceptional example of pure Renaissance style.

About 120 km. (75 miles) northwest of Oaxaca is **Yanhuitlán,** an Indian village located in a valley with heavily eroded soil. In the distance overlooking the valley is a 16th-century Dominican *monastery* built right on top of the ruins of an ancient Indian pyramid. The pyramid has broad stairways on three sides. The main façade of the church dates to the 17th century, but the side portal is from an earlier period. Inside, Gothic ribbed vaults span the large nave. In the apse, the carved and gilded altar is decorated with a variety of sculpture and paintings. There is also a remarkable 16th-century fresco dedicated to Saint Christopher in the stairway leading to the upper floor of the cloister.

Continuing toward Oaxaca, you'll pass **Nochixtlán** and **Chachoapan** 11 km. (7 miles) from the highway on an unpaved road. Both villages were once part of the Mixtec kingdom of Tilantongo. Remains of a pre-Columbian cult site have been discovered on a mountain near Chachoapan.

About 35 km. (22 miles) northwest of Oaxaca at **Telixtlahuaca,** Highway 190 joins Travel Route 27 from Tehuacán. For other noteworthy detours before entering the city of Oaxaca, see page 259; a description of the charming capital of Oaxaca can be found on page 251.

TRAVEL ROUTE 27: **Mexico City–**Puebla–Tehuacán–**Oaxaca (490 km.; 304 miles)

See map on page 244.

If you want to visit the Colonial town of Puebla, with its colorful tile façades and lavish Baroque churches, plan a two-night stopover. This will allow you to visit both the town and the fascinating pre-Columbian ruins in the surrounding countryside.

Once you reach Tehuacán—the halfway point between Puebla and Oaxaca—you can switch over to Travel Route 26 by taking Highway 125 south to Huajuapan de Léon. This relatively short crossroad will allow aficionados of Colonial church architecture to compare the Franciscan monasteries of Puebla with their Dominican counterparts in the state of Oaxaca—all of them set in an austere but magnificent cactus-and-shrub landscape.

For the 133-km.- (83-mile-) route to *Puebla*, from the capital, follow Travel Route 7.

On leaving *Puebla* (see page 103), take Highway 150 east toward Tehuacán. There are several interesting stops along the way: *Amozoc*, a town of noted silversmiths located 16 km. (10 miles) out of Puebla; *Tepeaca*, a market town; and the Franciscan monasteries of *Cuauhtinchan* and *Tecali*, known for their onyx workshops and quarries (see page 109).

Continuing southward on Highway 150, you'll come to a turnoff for Highway 140 that leads east to *Jalapa* (see Travel Route 23). A 14-km. (9-mile) side trip from here takes you to the medieval Franciscan monastery of *Acatzingo* (see page 230).

Back on Highway 150, you'll pass **Tecamachalco,** situated 2,500 meters (6,724 feet) above sea level. On the left will be the ruins of a Franciscan abbey. The

church, completed in 1557, has been totally neglected, its altar now a nesting spot for birds. Yet surprisingly, the ceiling frescoes painted on the Gothic cross-ribbed vault over the choir gallery in 1562 by Juan Gerson are remarkably well-preserved.

There is a rather charming church with a yellow-glazed tile dome at **Tlacotepec.** From here on, stretching away from either side of the highway, you'll see agave plantations and yucca trees until you reach **Tehuacán.** Located 251 km. (157 miles) from Mexico City, this provincial town of 75,000 people is one of the best-known thermal spas in all of Mexico. Many of the fashionable hotels, including the *Hacienda Spa Peñafiel* and *Hotel El Riego,* have seen better days, but they're quite reasonably priced and serve nicely as romantic reminders of the spa's past splendor.

The town developed around a Franciscan monastery in the 17th century. The monastery church, *Iglesia de la Conception,* with its tile dome, and another local church, *Iglesia del Carmen,* both date to the 18th century. Some of the most fascinating town treasures, however, can be found in its small archaeological museum— namely, the ancient ears of corn that were discovered at nearby Coxcatlán.

From Tehuacán, you have the choice of taking either a mountain road through a surreal cactus landscape to Huajuapan de Léon, 120 km. (75 miles) away, or the main

Corn granary (cuescomate)

highway to Oaxaca, which passes the Dominican monasteries described in Travel Route 26.

Travel Route 27 follows Highway 131 across the Valley of Tehuacán, which has been irrigated since pre-Columbian times. In fact, there is evidence that corn was cultivated here as far back as 7,000 years ago. Along this route, you'll pass turnoffs for a number of interesting towns and villages, including *San Gabriel Chilac,* a town known for its embroidered textiles and the elaborate Feast of the Dead it celebrates on November 2; the Nahua village of *Altepexi,* where reeds are woven into handsome baskets; and *Coxcatlán,* where the oldest cultivated corn in Mexico was found (see above). The highway then crosses into the state of Oaxaca at *Teotitlán del Camino;* from this village, centuries-old footpaths lead to the mountain villages of the Mazatecs, who still practice ancient Indian rites and healing ceremonies along with their Roman Catholic faith.

Near Cuicatlán—about halfway to Oaxaca—the road crosses the Río Grande del Sur several times. The next 50 km. (31 miles) wind up into the mountains from a starting elevation of 750 meters (2,460 feet) to a pass 2,150 meters (7,052 feet) above sea level. Just beyond this pass and the village of *Telixtlahuaca,* Travel Route 27 joins Travel Route 26 (about 454 km.; 284 miles from Mexico City).

Near the town of *Huitzo* are several onyx mines, as well as a 16th-century Dominican monastery. Local workshops in the town offer carved onyx in the form of chess pieces, bookends, and ashtrays.

In this same area where the Mixtecs once flourished, the Dominicans built a massive monastery at *San Pedro y San Puebla Etla.* Further on, just before the outskirts of Oaxaca, there is a turnoff to the potters' village of *Atzompa* (see page 263). Continue to *Oaxaca,* a starting point for visits to several fascinating archaeological sites, as well as a number of Indian villages in the surrounding mountains. For a panoramic overview of the valley of Oaxaca, take the road toward Mitla and then follow the signs to the scenic lookout called *Mirador* on the *Cerro del Fortín.*

**Oaxaca

See map on page 252.

Surrounded by the rugged peaks of the Sierra Madre del Sur, Oaxaca lies on a vast plateau at an altitude of 1,542 meters (5,084 feet)—a magic city frozen in time, part Colonial, part Indian. Cut off from the central highlands of Mexico by the mountainous terrain, here flourished great Indian civilizations hundreds of years before the birth of Christ. Today, the breathtaking ruins of Monte Albán, Mitla, and Yagul just outside town make the area one of the richest archaeological zones in all of Mexico. Most *Oaxacanos—*

usually outgoing and talkative—
are descendants of the Zapotec
and Mixtec tribes, and are quick to
assure you that their ancestors
were peace-loving rather than warlike people. Oaxaca in any case is
still an important trading center
for the widely scattered Indian villages in the surrounding valleys
and mountains.

A favorite retreat in Colonial
times, this sleepy provincial city
of 240,000 retains much of its Old
World charm, thanks in large part
to the fact that the inner city has
been designated an historic district—in keeping with architectural tradition, no building may be
more than two stories tall. Once
upon a time, the elegant Colonial
houses fashioned out of porphyry
taken from local quarries inspired
the fairy-tale name for Oaxaca—
"the jade city." Today's more
modest buildings are made of
adobe brick plastered over and
painted in light pastels. Like many
Colonial Mexican towns, cast-iron
railings adorn windows, narrow
balconies, doors, and ledges, and
multicolored flowers tumble from
balcony flowerpots, offering a hint

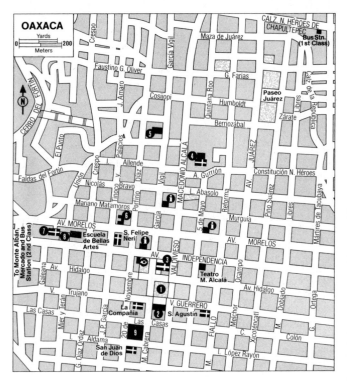

of the soothing patio oases that lay behind closed doors.

Isolated and boxed in by mountains, the town has been largely overlooked by industry—making it all the more attractive for visitors. It is a city that follows the traditional rhythms of Indian life, repeated for centuries. The inviting Zócalo at the center of town becomes the focus of evening activities as music wafts from the bandstand, couples stroll along the flower-lined paths, friends gather to chat, and laughter spills from the outdoor cafés surrounding the plaza. On Saturdays Indian traders from miles around offer seemingly unlimited quantities of fresh food, baskets, clothing, and the fine black pottery for which the region is famous.

By the time the Spanish arrived in Oaxaca, the high point of Zapotec and Mixtec civilization had passed and these tribes found themselves under the domination of the Aztecs. Reconnoitering the region in 1521, a group of *conquistadors* took over a strategically located Aztec military base at the foot of the Cerro del Fortin and founded their own garrison named Antequera. Three years later, the status of the settlement was changed to that of a city and renamed Oaxaca (a Spanish corruption of the Nahuatl word meaning "place covered with trees"). After a struggle for power between Hernán Cortés and the representatives of the crown, Cortés was given the title of Marquis of the Valley of Oaxaca, and he and his engineers began to lay out the settlement in the classic grid pattern that the Spanish employed throughout Mexico.

Soon a bishop's see as well as a commercial center, Oaxaca quickly became an important city in the colony of New Spain. The local industry of silk processing flourished along with the manufacture of a popular red dye made from the cochineal bugs that were found in the nopal cactus. And so things remained through the centuries until, with the onset of industrialization and modern communications, Oaxaca's economy began to decline. Today, the city is one of the poorest but also one of the loveliest provincial capitals in all of Mexico.

The ***Zócalo** (1) (also called the *Plaza de Armas*), with its tall shade trees, music pavilion, sidewalk cafés, and restaurant arcades, is a popular meeting place not to be missed. On its south side stands the *Palacio de Gobierno,* or Governor's Palace (2), built in the neoclassical style.

The low, solid **Cathedral** (3) stands at the northwest corner of the Zócalo. Started in the middle of the 16th century, Oaxaca's Cathedral took almost 200 years to complete. Today, Corinthian columns, innumerable statues, and ornamental reliefs decorate its Baroque façade. Inside, paintings from the Colonial period hang in the sacristy, the chapter room, and the side chapels. The old wooden clock, a gift from the king of Spain to the people of Oaxaca, still faithfully keeps time, a fitting reminder of the town's Colonial heritage.

The most beautiful church in Oaxaca, however, is the ****Templo de Santo Domingo** (4), five blocks to the north of the Zócalo. Once part of the huge fortified complex of a Dominican convent, the severe façade of this 17th-century church masks a luxurious interior. Walls, ceilings, and domes are lavishly decorated with gold-leaf and glossy colored stucco ornaments. On the ceiling above the entrance is a gilded genealogical tree showing Saint Domingo de Guzmán, the founder of the Dominican order, at the head of a many-branched vine from which 34 smaller statues sprout. The elaborate interior ornamentation culminates in the dazzling *Rosary Chapel,* which was built between 1724 and 1734. The main convent building, which was used as a barracks until recently, now houses the ****Museo Regional de Oaxaca,** or state museum. The museum is home to three distinct collections—archaeological, ecclesiastical, and ethnological. In the upper cloister is its most valuable exhibit, priceless Mixtec treasures, including imaginatively worked jewelry, death masks, and art objects of gold, jade, turquoise, and other semi-precious stones, discovered in Grave 7 at Monte Albán in 1932. Other finds from Monte Albán, as well as artifacts from additional Zapotec and Mixtec sites in the area, are also on display.

The religious art and memorabilia of the Dominican order date from the Colonial period. In contrast, the ethnological exhibition focuses on the various present-day Indian tribes in Oaxaca, showing their modern costumes, utensils of daily life, and religious customs.

One block northwest of the monastery at Calle García No. 609 Vigil is the **Casa Museo de Benito Juárez** (5). Born in 1806 in a village near Oaxaca, Juárez is said to have worked in this house as a servant in his youth before becoming a lawyer and going into politics.

On the way back to the *Zócalo,* be sure to stop at Avenida Morelos No. 503 to visit the ****Museo de Arte Prehispanico de Mexico Rufina Tamayo** (6). Thanks to the generosity, nationalistic pride, and keen eye of the Mexican painter Rufino Tamayo, this is one of the truly outstanding collections of ancient Mexican art in the country, spanning a period from 1250 B.C. to the 16th century. Located in a beautiful Colonial house, the five galleries are arranged by culture—Olmec, Totanac, Zapotec, Mixtec, Mayan, Nayarit, and Teotihuacán.

If you continue on the Avenida Morelos a short distance westward, you'll come to the ***Basílica Menor de la Soledad** (7), which is dedicated to the *Virgen de la Soledad,* the patron saint of Oaxaca. The Baroque façade, built in 1695, imitates the shape of a partially folded triptych, and the niches between columns are filled with beautifully sculpted statues. A relief over the doorway depicts the Virgin kneeling before the cross, and her statue stands in a glass case inside the church. A *museum* of religious art is attached to the basilica as well.

The small square below the church has been transformed into a peaceful garden café called the *Jardín Sócrates* (8). On one side of the café is the former Capuchin *monastery of San José,* now the *Escuela de Bellas Artes,* or art school.

Among the other interesting churches in Oaxaca are those of *San Felipe Neri,* with its Plateresque façade and gilded carved altars; *San Juan de Díos,* which is preferred by Indians; and the *church of San Agustín.*

Oaxaca is still very much a city of regional markets. The huge weekly market on Saturday draws Indians from the mountains on the backs of mules, their wares stuffed in sacks, as well as traders from afar with trucks waiting to be filled with Oaxaca's regional treasures. Because of a lack of space, the market is now held at the western edge of town instead of in the center, its traditional location.

Equally picturesque is the **Mercado Benito Juárez** (9), held every day in the old market building one block south of the *Zócalo.* Here, food and lovely Indian handcrafts are on sale side-by-side with the inevitable 20th-century plastic baskets and other paraphernalia.

The **Guelaguetza,* a famous Zapotec festival, has recently been extended beyond the third and last Mondays in July that were its traditional dates (check with your travel agent for the most up-to-date information). In addition, a large open-air theater called the *Auditorio* has been built on the Cerro del Fortín in the northwestern part of the city to accommodate the large audiences that flock to see the dances by various Indian groups from the surrounding areas.

****Monte Albán**

If you're an archaeology buff—and in Mexico it's hard not to become one—Oaxaca is a dream come true, with all kinds of fantastic ruins waiting to be explored just beyond its city limits.

Foremost is Monte Albán, one of the most impressive archaeological sites in all of Mexico. Leave Oaxaca heading south along the Veinte de Noviembre, cross the Río Atoyac, and turn right after the bridge, continuing for about 9 km. (5.5 miles) along a winding road in the direction of the ruins. Monte Albán is also easily accessible by bus (try to get a seat on the right side for the best views of the mountain as you make the climb to the site).

Rising 396 meters (1,300 feet) above the town of Oaxaca on an artificially flattened mountain are the ruins of a holy city once inhabited by more than 40,000 people. Here in this city in the sky, colossal gray-stone pyramids stand regally atop a vast green plaza with

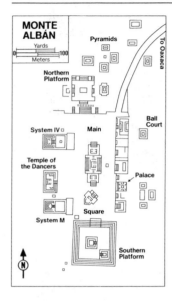

MONTE ALBÁN

Yards
0 ——— 100
Meters

Pyramids

To Oaxaca

Northern Platform

Ball Court

System IV

Main

Temple of the Dancers

Palace

System M

Square

Southern Platform

N

later known because of their lofty residence).

From A.D. 900–1200, the period known as Monte Albán IV, the complex was in decline. By the time the mountaintop site was taken over by the Mixtecs, during its last phase before the Spanish Conquest (a period known as Monte Albán V), the area was being used only as a cemetery. Oblivious to its noble past, the Mixtecs emptied Zapotec graves to bury their own dead and laid out new tombs, creating a grandiose city of the dead.

Today, the entire area of Monte Albán covers an area of about 39 sq. km. (15 square miles). Although only a small portion of the entire archaeological zone has been exposed so far—an area of 200 meters by 305 meters (656 feet by 1,000 feet)—Monte Albán creates an unforgettable impression.

an almost too-perfect blue-and-white backdrop.

Although the very first settlers of the area remain shrouded in mystery, scholars believe that people, possibly Zapotecs, had definitely settled in the valley of Oaxaca some eight centuries before Christ. This tribe then leveled off the mountaintop in order to build a huge ceremonial center; archaeologists refer to this period from 800–300 B.C. as Monte Albán I. Over the next three centuries, the site was expanded, and then reached its greatest flowering in the years between A.D. 100–900, the period known as Monte Albán III, which has been unquestionably attributed to the Zapotecs (or "Cloud People," as they were

Golden amulet (Monte Albán)

At the entrance to the left is the **Ball Court,** which dates to the classic Zapotec period known as Monte Albán III. The sides of the court lack the stone rings that other pre-Columbian people such as the Toltecs used to play the game, and it is unlikely that the Zapotecs, a pacific people, ever played the game as mercilessly as their Mesoamerican counterparts.

The first of the adjacent pyramids, all dating to Monte Albán III, has an inner stairway leading to the top, and was connected with the group of buildings in the center of the plaza by a tunnel so that priests could move from building to building in secret. Along the east side of the plaza are several platforms; one platform-building, called the **Palacio,** was undoubtedly the foundation for the priests' dwelling. A cruciform grave was discovered under the inner patio that supports the remains of walls.

In the center of the plaza are four buildings, three of which are connected. The main building has a wide eastern-facing staircase leading to a two-room temple. The two buildings on either side of it are almost identical, with staircases leading to temples on the north and south.

Standing apart at a 45-degree angle to the main axis, the fourth building does not fit in with the overall symmetry of the complex. Unlike the others, its ground plan resembles the bow of a ship pointing southwest. At the side opposite the angle, a staircase leads to the upper platform of the building,

where there is a curious tunnel. Other tunnels of this type were usually built as part of some astronomical structure, yet here the sky isn't visible at all. Nevertheless, figures and hieroglyphs have been cut into stone slabs on the widest wall. The oldest part of the building is estimated to have been built toward the end of Monte Albán II—that is, before the Christian era.

At the southern end of the plaza looms the large **Southern Platform.** If you're up to it, you can climb the monumental staircase—40 meters (131 feet) wide—to the top for a spectacular view of the entire zone, particularly beautiful at sunset. Although many of the important relief stelae found here have been removed to the National Museum of Anthropology in Mexico City, Stela 1 remains intact at the northwestern corner of the Southern Platform, its rows of hieroglyphs hanging above an image of a jaguar sitting on a hill and wearing the headdress of the rain-god Cocijo.

Walking north, you'll come to a large rectangular structure consisting of two buildings connected by a patio. Here stand two other stelae, numbers 12 and 13, both of them also covered with number glyphs. Next to them on the southwestern side of the plaza is perhaps the most fascinating monument at Monte Albán, the ***Edificio de los Danzantes,** or Building of the Dancers, which is named for the stone slabs bearing reliefs of human figures

Relief on Edificio de los Danzantes

depicted in strange, contorted poses. Once part of a high terrace wall, the slabs now lean against the foot of the two-story building, which has been rebuilt several times over the centuries. These carved figures date to early Monte Albán I, approximately the fifth century B.C. Clearly the glyphs—of which only the numbers have been deciphered so far—indicate that these early Monte Albán inhabitants had both a system of writing and a calendar. Whether the figures are dancers, slaves undergoing torture, or sketches of clinical case studies from a medical school remains an enigma.

The large **Northern Platform,** covering an area 250 meters by 200 meters (820 feet by 656 feet) is reached by another wide stairway. On either side of the stairs are cult rooms containing graves and decorated with hieroglyphic reliefs. At the top of the platform, the stumps of columns 2 meters (6 feet) thick stand guard in double rows, silent reminders of what was once a great hall. A stair leads down to the **Patio Hundido,** or Sunken Court, where there is an altar at the center.

From the Northern Platform, a path leads northwest to **Grave 104,** with its well-preserved wall paintings dating to about A.D. 500. Below this grave is another, **Grave 172,** in which a skeleton and various artifacts have been preserved as they were found. The famous **Grave 7,** which was discovered by Alfonso Caso in 1932, lies a little outside the actual ceremonial site. You can follow a path from the main street to this Mixtec burial site, but most of the treasures—including almost 500 objects decorated with gold and precious stones—are exhibited in the Museo Regional de Oaxaca. (See page 254.)

A word of advice for the insatiably curious: Oaxacanos are especially proud of their Zapotec heritage, and there are many excellent guides (some of whom were actually present at the original digs!) whose archaeological information will astound you. If you're lucky enough to travel here in the off-season, be sure to get a local guide for a private tour—it's relatively inexpensive and will make a world of difference.

Other Sights Near Oaxaca

When you're finally ready to leave Monte Albán, descend the mountain toward Oaxaca. You'll see a turnoff to the right toward the village of **Cuilapan.** There on a hill are the eerie remains of one of the largest *Dominican monasteries* in Mexico. Started in 1555, only the church was ever finished. The simple Renaissance façade of the now roofless basilica is flanked by two round towers, and behind them are two incomplete rows of massive columns. At the rear wall of the basilica is an interesting slab bearing glyphs that date to the Mixtec period. The monastery was deserted in 1663 when the monks moved to Oaxaca.

Cuilapan is also known for its once-flourishing cochineal industry, the red dye made from the insects found in nopal cactus plants. (More recently, Pope John Paul II stopped in the village as part of his eight-day trip in 1979, drawing thousands of villagers from the surrounding hillsides.)

If you continue south on the same road about 17.5 km. (11 miles) you'll reach the rustic village of **Zaachila,** where it is thought that Zapotec rulers once sought refuge from the advancing Mixtecs. In 1962 archaeologists discovered two tombs under a broad artificial platform on a hill behind the church. *Grave 1* can still be visited: its façade bears two stone jaguar heads, and the inner walls are decorated with stucco figures, including two owls with outspread wings in the antecham-ber and human figures in the main chamber. On the rear wall is a figure wearing a headdress that resembles a snake's jaws; the figure's body is covered with a turtle-shell breastplate. Much of the Zapotec ceramics and later Mixtec jewelry uncovered in the excavations of this grave and *Grave 2* are now housed in the National Museum of Anthropology in Mexico City.

Another excursion out of Oaxaca sure to be of interest leads southeast on Highway 190 through the wide Tlacolula Valley in the direction of *Mitla.* About 11 km. (7 miles) down the road is *Santa María del Tule,* home to a truly spectacular botanic speci-men—a 2,500-year-old sabine tree (*Taxodium mucrunatum ten*) that towers 49 meters (165 feet) and is reputed to have the *greatest girth of any tree in the world.* While undeniably a tourist stop, it is nonetheless worth a short pause to walk around this venerable object.

Another 17.5 km. (11 miles) in the same direction will bring you to a turnoff to the village of *Tlacochahuaya,* which is another 1 km. (half a mile) down the road. The 16th-century church, with its charming Indian wall paintings of angels, birds, and flowers, and its elaborate Baroque altar, is a small architectural jewel.

Continue on the road another 19 km. (12 miles) to **Dainzú;** after 1 km. (half a mile), turn off to the right and you'll find yourself at the ancient site of the same name. Here, archaeologists discovered 50 sandstone slabs that once decorated the façade of a large pyramid. The slabs bear reliefs, most of them depicting ball players in dynamic poses, reminiscent of the *danzantes* at Monte Albán and probably dating to 800 B.C. They may even prove to be Olmec works, which would make them older than the dancing figures in Monte Albán.

Some of the buildings at Dainzú are also similar to those at Monte Albán, particularly the building with four terraces, vertical walls, and a platform on top with an entrance to an inner tomb. Farther away, a small, partially restored ball court dates to a later, more classical period. However, only a small part of this ancient site has been excavated.

Returning to Highway 190, there is a turnoff on the left to *Teotitlán del Valle,* a village of 5,000 people, only 21 km. (13 miles) from Oaxaca. Situated at an altitude of 1,800 meters (5,900 feet), this village is known for its handmade goods woven on domestic looms. In the past, local weavers fashioned *serapes* and *rebozos,* the classic Mexican shawl; today they're just as likely to make blankets and wall coverings for export. In addition to old Indian motifs, weavers now base their patterns on paintings by Picasso, Miró, and other internationally celebrated modernists.

A short drive farther on, just 27 km. (17 miles) from Oaxaca, is **Lambityeco,** a Zapotec cult center that flourished from the seventh through ninth centuries.

Here, under a pyramid, archaeologists have uncovered several earlier structures, including the patio of a residence with tombs underneath it. The entrance to the tombs is decorated with expressive three-dimensional stucco portraits of a man and a woman. Other realistic human figures, which are in stark contrast to the usually religious and ritualistic Zapotec art, were found on a stucco frieze in the same inner court.

The old Zapotec town of *Tlacolula* is another 3.5 km. (2 miles) down the road. Its Baroque church contains a lovely chapel, the *Capilla del Santo Cristo,* whose lavish stucco ornaments rival those found in the church of Santo Domingo in Oaxaca. The magnificent cast-iron gate, which depicts the crucifixion and dates to the Colonial period, also merits a second look. On Sundays the town is host to a colorful regional market.

About 2 km. (1 mile) off the road to the left (about 33.5 km., 21 miles, from Oaxaca) in a countryside dotted with cactus, lies ***Yagul.** Settled by the Zapotecs during the early phase of Monte Albán (about 800–300 B.C.), this ceremonial center reached its zenith between A.D. 900–1200 (Monte Albán IV). Today, a fortress city set on top of a mountain and overlooking three levels of palaces and temples is all that remains of this once-flourishing site, but what a stirring legacy it is.

On the lowest level is the *Patio de la Triple Tumba,* located between four temples. On the left stands a statue of a toad, symbol of the Zapotec rain god. Below the platform in the center of the court are three tombs with sculptured façades; in one tomb, the stone carvings are chiseled into the shape of human heads.

The next level contains the *Ball Court*—the largest in the valley of Oaxaca. Like others in this region, it lacks rings on the sides of its walls. Next to the Ball Court is a complex with a long, narrow room, the *Sala del Consejo,* or Council Chamber, and a court surrounded by more ceremonial buildings. This structure and the labyrinthine palace to the north on the third level—called the *Palacio de los Seis Patios* because of its six inner courts— were presumably changed by the Mixtecs. The climb to the fortification at the top, though steep, is rewarded by a marvelous view of the entire valley.

On leaving Yagul, return to the main highway and continue toward **Mitla,** about 41.5 km. (26 miles) from Oaxaca and only 3.2 km. (2 miles) beyond Yagul. The first thing you'll notice about these famous pre-Columbian ruins is a large, modern-looking artisan market with about 100 booths at the entrance to the site. Despite its obvious commercial aspect, the center does offer an excellent sampling of local weaving, including rugs and clothing.

Located high on a hill, the ruins of Mitla, with their intricate stone mosaics, are unique in Meso-american architecture. Add this to the fact that Mitla is one of the easiest archaeological sites in Mexico to explore, and your visit here should be a rewarding one.

Although it was the Aztecs who gave the town its name (meaning "place of the dead"), the site was first occupied thousands of years before the Christian era. The Zapotecs from nearby Monte Albán spread out to the neighboring areas of Mitla and Yagul sometime during the first century after Christ, and transformed Mitla from a simple farming settlement into a major ceremonial center. The buildings that are visible today, however, are the work of the Mixtecs, who pushed the Zapotecs out around A.D. 900. Like its neighbors, Mitla fell before the superior firepower of the Spanish *conquistadors* in 1521.

The excavated area covers five architectural complexes spread out over both banks of a small river. The most important is the *Grupo de las Columnas* (Group of the Columns), which is laid out around two rectangular patios, with three halls around each patio. The first patio gives you a spectacular view of the *Hall of Columns,* with its exquisite fretwork façade. Inside, the stairway leads to a room 38 meters by 7.5 meters (125 feet long by 25 feet wide) that features six huge pillars, each 3 feet in diameter. From this room, a crooked passage with a low roof leads into a smaller inner court, called the *Patio de la Grecas*

Patio de las Grecas, Mitla

(*grecas* is Spanish for "meanders"), which is itself encircled by four narrow rooms.

Here you'll find the mosaic gems for which Mitla is justly famous. Resembling lacework in their delicacy, the elaborate geometric patterns made from cut stones laid into the wall form as many as 14 variations, labyrinthine designs alternating with cross shapes, zigzags, and Greek-key motifs. (These labyrinthine patterns have been dubbed "step-meanders," and are a form of ornamentation commonly seen in Mesoamerican pottery, textiles, and jewelry.) In addition, the heavy stone slabs framing the doors and passageways are astonishing engineering feats for a people who did not know the use of the wheel.

Next, cross the second large patio, which is known as the *Patio of the Crosses.* Although less well preserved than others at Mitla, the fine pillared doorways and underground tomb should not be missed. At the north side of the tomb stands an isolated pillar, known locally as the *Column of Life.* Legend has it that visitors can calculate how long they will live by hugging the column and measuring the distance between their hands.

In the center of the so-called *Northern Complex,* the Spaniards built a church. But mosaic designs from pre-Columbian days still remain on the old Indian walls, and a fresco survives in an inner court on the north side. There is also a small archaeological museum, the *Museo de Arte Zapoteca,* next to the *La Sorpresa* restaurant.

Before leaving the Oaxaca area, there are four artisan villages worth visiting for their handcrafts. Only 6 km. (4 miles) down Highway 190 in the direction of Mexico City is a road on the left that leads to **Santa María Atzompa,** just another 4 km. (2.5 miles) from the turnoff. This village is known for its green-glazed pottery fashioned into animal shapes. Called *chivos de chia,* or cress animals, these small vessels are made of porous clay and then planted with cress seeds. Similar green-glazed pottery is also made in **Magdalena Apasco Etla,** 29 km. (18 miles) farther on Highway 190. **San Bartolo Coyotepec,** another pottery village located 14.5 km.

(9 miles) south of Oaxaca on the road to Puerto Angel, is known for its finely polished black-fired pitchers and lamps. Another kind of craft—weaving—is the focus of attention in *Santo Tómas Jalietza,* 16 km. (10 miles) further down the same Puerto Angel road.

TRAVEL ROUTE 28: **Oaxaca–Tehuantepec–Tuxtla Gutiérrez–**San Cristóbal de las Casas–***Palenque (817 km.; 506 miles)

See map on page 244.

Starting high in the bare mountains of the Sierra Madre del Sur, this route takes you down to the Gulf of Tehuantepec, then up into the rolling Indian hill country of Chiapas, and finally back down into the tropical rain forest of the Chiapan lowlands.

On Highway 190 traveling from Oaxaca to Tehuantepec, you'll pass Teotitlán del Valle and Mitla, day excursions easily reached from Oaxaca (see page 251). After 50 km. (31 miles), the road leaves the valley of Oaxaca and begins to wind its way through the sparsely settled Sierra Madre del Sur; spectacular views of the valley below will crop up with breathtaking regularity.

About 200 km. (125 miles) south of Oaxaca is *Tequesistlán,* a green palm oasis situated on the river of the same name. Together with the Río Tehuantepec, the Tequesistlán supplies the water for the *Presa,* or Benito Juárez Reservoir, which you'll see off to the left.

South of the highway is the virtually impassable area populated by the Chontal Indians, which extends all the way to the Pacific coast. The Chontals live modestly off their farming and the sale of hammocks and baskets.

About 243 km. (152 miles) from Oaxaca, you'll come to a turnoff on the left that leads to the archaeological zone of *Guiengola* (see page 219). For the 131 km. (82 miles) after Tehuantepec, the route is the same as Travel Route 20 (see page 219).

In *Tapanatepec,* 381 km. (238 miles) south of Oaxaca, Highway 190 leaves the coast and heads inland across a hilly landscape, then climbs into the mountains again. You'll come to a road on the left that turns off across the fields toward the *Aguacero,* a deep gorge reached by a staircase that leads to a waterfall almost 3.5 km. (2 miles) away; the descent into the gorge only takes 15 minutes, but you should allow 25 minutes for the climb back out.

Just outside **Tuxtla Gutiérrez,** you'll pass a turnoff for the airport. Soon after, you'll enter the young, modern capital of the state of Chiapas itself. Situated 530 meters (1,738 feet) above sea level, Tuxtla Gutiérrez lies in a hot, humid valley where sugarcane and a variety of tropical fruits flourish. Although there are no outstanding architectural attractions here, the city does have a regional museum, the *Museo del Estado,* with a fine archaeological collection. In addition, the botanic garden and *zoo* in the northeastern section of town feature jaguars, caymans, and many species of exotic birds. The *Bazaar Ishanal* at Boulevard Belisario Dominguez No. 950 specializes in Indian handcrafts. In the same building, the *tourist office* has information on air taxis to Bonampak (see page 277); reservations must be made at least two days in advance.

From Tuxtla Gutiérrez follow the signs for **El Sumidero.** A mountain road will take you 22.5 km. (14 miles) north (exit on Parque Madero) to a magnificent rock terrace 1,235 meters (4,054 feet) high with several scenic lookouts and a restaurant perched above the grand gorge of the upper Río Grijalva (also called the Río Chiapa). This ancient natural lookout is known as *Los Chiapas* in memory of the Indian from the town of Chiapa who is said to have jumped from it in 1527 to escape enslavement by Spanish *conquistadors.*

Today, the motorboats on the river below look like nutshells, but they become real and inviting enough when you reach *Balnearo Cahuare,* a resort below where there is swimming.

Boating and swimming are also available in the nearby town of **Chiapa de Corzo,** located on the banks of the river. (From here you can take a two- to three-hour excursion into the canyon and the site of Indian Chiapa, an old cult center that has been partially excavated and restored.) The Spanish built their first settlement in the area here in 1528, and the large brick Moorish-style fountain on the plaza was built soon after. The same material was used to construct the Dominican *monastery of Santo Domingo* between 1554 and 1572, but the church has been remodeled numerous times since then. In the small *Museo de la Laca* on the *Zócalo* are exhibits of lacquerwork from Chiapa and other Mexican towns, as well as a fine Chinese lacquerwork display.

Mask from Chiapa de Corzo

The region is best known, however, for its painted black gourds decorated with brightly colored flowers. Equally interesting are the colorful masks worn in Indian dances during the great Festival of Saint Sebastian, which is celebrated from January 19–22.

From Chiapa the road winds upward. Some 565 km. (353 miles) out of Oaxaca, there is a turnoff on the left that will take you to Villahermosa, another 256 km. (160 miles) away. The route to Villahermosa runs through a varied mountain landscape that made headlines in 1982 when the volcano Chichonal suddenly erupted. As a result, San Cristóbal was covered with a light layer of knee-deep ash that stopped all traffic for several days. (Scientists also thought the cloud of ash that rose from the volcano would affect the local weather, but this has not yet been proven.)

The narrow road continues to spiral its way upward, occasionally offering magnificent views of the broken limestone summits of the surrounding mountains. The long uphill climb will eventually end at *San Cristóbal de las Casas* 615 km. (384 miles) from Oaxaca.

**San Cristóbal de las Casas

See map on page 267.

Located in a quiet mountain valley at an altitude of 2,100 meters (6,900 feet), San Cristóbal is a lovely Colonial town that seems to exist in a time warp, blending Indian traditions within a Hispanic framework. Surrounded by pine-forested mountains whose peaks rise above 3,000 meters (9,500 feet), the town goes through a daily unveiling, but once the morning mist has cleared, the whitewashed walls of the one-story houses positively shine in the pure highland light. Days can be hot, and the nights cold.

The charm of San Cristóbal lies not so much in its architectural wonders as it does in the arrangement of its low houses with their slightly protruding red-tiled roofs. Behind the wrought-iron window gratings and heavy wooden doors lie splendid patios and inviting, shady colonnades decorated with flowers; in recent times, some of the grander structures have been converted into hotels.

The town is divided into several quarters, or *barrios,* each with its own church. The main attraction and pulsating center of San Cristóbal is the colorful market to which the Tzeltal and Tzotzil Indians flock from their mountain villages in traditional costume to buy and sell, primarily fruit and vegetables.

The town is indebted to the moderate highland climate for its location. In 1528 a group of Spaniards under the leadership of Diego de Marzariego settled on the banks of the Río Grijalva at the site of what is now Chiapa de Corzo. But the hot, humid climate did not agree with them, and so they moved up into the high, cool

Indian woven design

valley of San Cristóbal later that same year. To assist them in their war against the local Indian population, the Spaniards brought in Indians from the central highlands and settled them in the *Barrio de los Mexicanos*, the Mexican Quarter. Until the 19th century, the town was called Ciudad Real; the current name honors its first bishop, Bartolomé de la Casas, who tried to protect the local Indians from Spanish exploitation and persecution.

Capital of the province of Chiapas until 1892, when it was replaced by Tuxtla Gutíerrez, San Cristóbal developed into a trading center during the Colonial period. But because it had no products to export and communication networks were poor, the town never grew beyond its role as a regional center. With its large Indian population, San Cristóbal remained a world unto itself.

The building of the Pan-American Highway in 1950 brought an abrupt end to this isolation. The combination of its rugged yet peaceful setting and the ever-present influence of its native Indian cultures at first made San Cristóbal particularly attractive to backpack explorers. In fact, several stayed and eventually opened their own handcrafts stores, as well as cafés and restaurants featuring natural foods. Nevertheless, apart from the growing number of tourists whom the new highway has lured into the highlands, San Cristóbal's image as a provincial Colonial town has hardly changed.

The **Plaza 31 de Marzo** (1) is the main square, or *Zócalo*, and is named for the date the town was founded. Around it stand the town hall with its tourist information bureau, a number of old patrician homes, and the **Cathedral** (2), the first church built in San Cristóbal. Inside are paintings from the 17th through 19th centuries, including the main painting on the *Altar del Perdon* by Juan Correa and a painting of Mary Magdalene by Miguel Cabrera.

Next to the Cathedral is the massive *church of San Nicolás* (3), a parish church built early in the 17th century and restored in 1815.

Across the square at the corner of Avenida Insurgentes is the **Casa de Mazariegos** (4), former home of the town's founder and now the hotel *Santa Clara*. One of the oldest private houses in town, its lovely doorway features a pair of Castilian lions carved of stone.

The most imporant sacred building in San Cristóbal is the ***Templo de Santo Domingo**

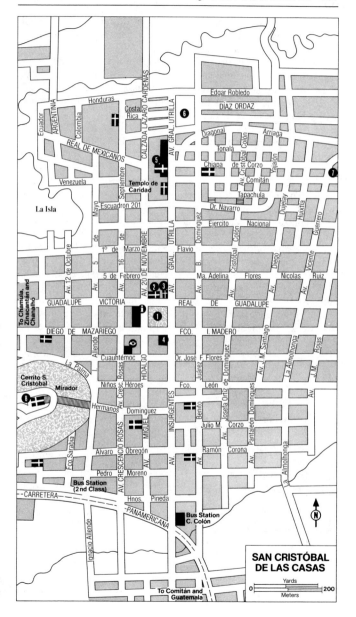

SAN CRISTÓBAL
DE LAS CASAS

Yards
0 ———————— 200
Meters

(5), the church of the Dominican monastery five blocks north of the Zócalo. Started sometime between 1547 and 1560, the façade dates to the 17th century and is done in the Mexican High Baroque style. Over the portal between twisted Ionic columns is a double-headed eagle—the coat of arms of the Hapsburg Emperor Charles V. The church's interior is richly decorated with gilded wooden altars and an artistically carved Baroque pulpit. The monastery complex of which it is a part has been converted into a combination cultural center and sales outlet for high-quality crafts, primarily textiles, from the Indian cooperative of *San Jolobil.*

The nearby **mercado** (6) attracts Indians from the surrounding mountains throughout the week, except Sundays. The

colorful costumes of these villagers reflect the mixed Indian heritage of the two largest Mayan groups in the region, the Tzotzil and Tzeltal tribes. (A reminder: these proud highland Mayas do not like to be photographed. Despite what will probably be a strong temptation, respect their feelings.) Part of the market is now held in a modern, somewhat stifling hall, but don't let these inevitable changes discourage you; the lively atmosphere and local color should not be missed.

Several blocks east of the Templo de Santo Domingo at Avenida Vincente Guerrero No. 33 is **Na Bolom** (7), the home of Danish archaeologist Franz Blom and his wife, Swiss photographer Gertrude Duby. Fittingly, for a couple who devoted their lives to studying the Lacandón Indians of the highland rain forests, their house bears the Tzotzil name meaning "house of the jaguar." When Blom first arrived in the Yucatán in 1919, the region was virtually unknown to white men. During the 1940s, the couple began to explore the Chiapas highlands, worked with the Lacandón Indians, and eventually helped prevent the extermination of that tribe. Over the years, the Blom home in San Cristóbal became a sanctuary for scholars working in the Yucatán and Chiapas, their extensive library a home away from home. Since her husband's death in 1963, Mrs. Blom has continued to open her doors, and guest rooms are available, as are

Templo Santo Domingo

arrangements for meals. Now in her eighties, Mrs. Blom generously shares her remarkable photographs of a fast-disappearing way of life in some of her home's rooms, which are open to the public.

For a lovely view of the whole town, go to the *Cerrito de San Cristóbal* (8), where you'll find a church by the same name. This is also the main site for the festival of the town's patron saint, which is held from July 17 to July 25. (There is also an excellent view of San Cristóbal from the hill on which the church of Guadalupe is situated.)

If you want to see more of the Indians who come to the San Cristóbal market, you should visit at least one of their villages located in the plush green rain forests of Chiapas. The most interesting time for a visit is during market or festival days, but of course this is also the most crowded. Getting there, however, is easy—minibuses, called *collectivos,* leave from the *Zócalo* or adjacent side streets at regular intervals. You can also get there by taxi, rented car, or organized tour. And you must obey the prohibition against taking photographs, above all in churches. (If you do not, you may find yourself physically compelled to do so.)

The road to the Tzotzil village of **Zinacantán** is now paved. Leave San Cristóbal from the northwest corner of town and follow the main highway until you come to a turnoff on the left for San Juan Chamula. You'll hit Zinacantán at about the 9.6-km.-(6-mile-) mark out of San Cristóbal. On festival days, particularly those of San Sebastian (January 18–20) and San Lorenzo (August 8–11), the men's costumes, with their pink *rebozos* over short white trousers and flat straw hats decorated with brightly colored ribbons, are especially striking.

Continue on the same road until you reach ***San Juan Chamula,** a ceremonial center belonging to the Tzotzils about 13 km. (8 miles) from town. The large wooden crosses on the Calvary hill at the village entrance are not only Christian, but also ancient Mayan symbols. (A cut in the vertical beam covered by pine branches forms the ancient Mayan sign, the cross with equal-length arms representing the four directions of the compass.) The village church with its beautifully painted portal can be visited for a fee, but taking pictures is strictly forbidden. Inside, the church is distinguished by its soft carpet of aromatic pine needles.

Parish church, San Juan Chamula

Sunday is market and court day. The dignified town council, appointed at the end of each year in a traditional ceremony, meets at the corner of the main plaza. Carnival is celebrated in a similarly carefree manner, with a liberal imbibing of homemade spirits one of its chief characteristics. Other important festival dates include the festival of Santa Cruz on May 3; the festival of the village's patron saint San Juan from June 22–24; the festival of Santa Rosa on August 30; and the festival of Our Lady of the Rosary (*Nuestra Señora del Rosario*) on the first Sunday in October.

An unpaved road will take you from San Juan Chamula to other mountain villages with equally interesting festival traditions: *San Andrés Larraínzar* has a colorful carnival and feast for its patron saint on November 29; *Mitontic*, which is on the road to Chenalhó and has its own 16th-century church, has a carnival and feast of San Miguel on May 6–8, and the feast of Jesus of Good Hope (*Jesús de la Buena Esperanza*) on August 6.

Several Tzeltal villages also celebrate festivals throughout the year. *Tenejapa*, located 27 km. (17 miles) north of San Cristóbal, observes the feast of Saint James the Apostle (*Santiago Apostól*) on July 24. The potters' village of **Amatenago del Valle,** 39 km. (23 miles) from town on the road to Comitán, is known for the embroidered skirts, or *huipiles*, worn by its women on festival days, including those of Saint Peter on April 28–30, Saint James the Apostle on July 25, and Santa Lucía on December 13.

On the way to Amatenago, you can take a side trip to the *Grutas de San Cristóbal*, the dripstone caves 9.5 km. (6 miles) out of town. Shortly past the caves themselves is the turnoff to Ococingo and Palenque.

If you're interested in exploring further afield, take the Pan-American Highway in the direction of Guatemala to **Comitán,** a small town 86 km. (54 miles) southeast of San Cristóbal. Situated some 1,520 meters (5,000 feet) above sea level, this peaceful town of 40,000, with its modest white houses and patio gardens still looks much as it did in Colonial days—so much so, in fact, that novelist Rosario Castellanos used the setting in his *The Nine Watchmen* to capture the mood of an older, less modernized Mexico.

Although the next destination may seem fictional on account of its fairy-tale landscape, the cooling waters of ****Lagunas de Montebello,** a region containing 60 to 70 small lakes hidden in the rain forest that extends eastward all the way to Guatemala, are delightfully real. To get there, continue south from Comitán for about 16 km. (10 miles) to the turnoff. Then, after driving another 29 km. (18 miles), you'll come to the turnoff to the excavations of **Chincultic*, a former Mayan ceremonial center set in dense tropical jungle between two

Indian farm in Chiapas

lakes. From the top of either of two pyramid temples, you can look into a water-filled crater, the Cenote Agua Azul, into which the ancient Maya threw offerings. Unfortunately, only the relief stelae found here remain at the site (other artifacts are now in the museum in Comitán). There is, however, a 50-meter- (164-foot-) long ball court near the entrance to the zone on the left.

Return to the road and continue another 8 km. (5 miles) until you reach the entrance to the *Lagunas de Montebello National Park.* In the park itself, there are roads to seven of the over 60 lakes. Their different colors—from emerald green to deep blue and even red— are due to the depth of the water and the soil on their bottoms. The water is cold, but you can swim at Lake Montebello, the largest one, if you don't mind icy conditions.

Lodging is available at Lake Tziscao.

From Comitán, it is 83 km. (52 miles) to Ciudad Cuauhtémoc, an important border crossing to Guatemala. In the same direction, Highway 190 takes you south to Tapachula (see page 220), the last major city before Guatemala.

San Cristóbal can also serve as a starting point for unusual excursions by air taxi into the rain forest of Selva Lacandona, where you can visit the Mayan sites of *Bonampak* and *Yaxchilán*, the Lacandón settlements of *Lacanha* and *Naha*, and ***Palenque***, which is also accessible by highway.

The drive from San Cristóbal to Palenque is still rather primitive—potholes are a given and during the rainy season sections can be all but impassable. If you do decide to drive, leave San Cristóbal on Highway 190 heading toward Comitán (see page 270). After 11 km. (7 miles) take the fork on the left to Ocosingo. Along the way you'll pass the Tzotzil village of *Huixtan,* followed by *Oxchuc,* a Tzeltal village. After 90 km. (56 miles), the green valley of the Río Jatate will open to reveal **Ocosingo,** a Tzeltal village.

The signs on the right just before the Mayan ceremonial center are misleading. You'll probably need to ask directions to *Toniná, about 14.5 km. (9 miles) farther east, where a guard accompanies visitors through the partially excavated ruins. The buildings here are grouped on five terraces carved out of a hillside and fortified with a wall. (A model in the visitors' center shows what this cult center looked like in its heyday from A.D. 600–800.) Two of the ruined temples on the uppermost terraces have been preserved and offer fine views of the valley below. One of the temples has a roof comb and stands on a pyramid base. Nearby, archaeologists have discovered a grave containing a monolithic sarcophagus. On a ledge below the grave are two stone altars, one with a carving of an alligator head, the other with a jaguar head. Behind them is a palace with labyrinthine passages partially built into the hill. There is also an enigmatic large stone ball inside a cave whose entrance is framed by entwined stucco ornaments. At the foot of the hill, in the middle of a pasture, are the outlines of an ancient ball court. And scattered around the site, relief stelae and marvelous sculptures worked in the round, unusual for Mayan art, lean against trees in the open.

If you continue on through the surrounding tropical rain forest toward Palenque, you'll pass the spectacular falls of **Agua Azul,** Spanish for "blue water," where the water cascades down over broad limestone terraces into deep blue basins. Nearby, unpretentious restaurants and camping sites inviting swimmers are attractions too good to pass by.

About 810 km. (506 miles) out of Oaxaca, you'll reach ***Palenque* (see page 275), where you can connect with Travel Route 29 for the drive through the Yucatán peninsula into Mayan country.

The Yucatán

What sets the Yucatán peninsula apart from the rest of Mexico is not only its relatively flat terrain but also its distinctive culture, which is a direct outgrowth of its Mayan heritage—of which we only have an incomplete knowledge. Because of a decree of the Spanish missionary Father Diego de Landa, almost all written Mayan records were burned in July of 1562. His order to destroy such records was carried out so faithfully that only three or four Mayan "books," called codices, survived. As a result, factual information about the Mayas and the history of the Yucatán peninsula remains limited.

Justifying his actions, the Franciscan monk once called the burned records, mostly hieroglyphs, "superstitions and lies of the devil," but when he was recalled to Spain to stand trial for his fanatical conduct, he drew up as part of his defense a detailed account of the people he was accused of oppressing.

Eleven years later, after he was acquitted, Father de Landa was made a bishop and returned to the Yucatán. His account of the customs and history of the Maya, titled *Relacion de las Cosas de Yucatán* (*An Account of Things Pertaining to Yucatán*), was placed in official archives in Madrid and then virtually ignored for 300 years. Discovered in 1863, it has since become the main source for students of Mayan history by virtue of the fact that very few stories recounting the origin of the race, explaining their migrations, or detailing their ancient rites and customs have survived oral transmission intact through the generations.

Three Mexican states—Yucatán, Quintana Roo, and Campeche—along with the northern border areas of Belize and Guatemala make up the Yucatán peninsula, an area characterized geologically by its flatness, with elevations rarely exceeding 300 meters (1,000 feet) and the massive limestone shelf underlying it. This karstic terrain is dotted with sinkholes and crisscrossed by ravines. After a rainfall, water collects in *aguadas,* natural tublike ponds, or seeps into the porous limestone, forming underground rivers and lakes. When the surface collapses, as it does in spots, a *cenote,* or open well, is formed. (The original Mayan word for "cenote" was *dzonot,* but the Spanish corrupted the spelling to its present form.)

The Mayas, recognizing that without water there could be no life, regarded these cenotes as sacred. To appease Chac, the Mayan rain god (whose likeness appears on innumerable gargoyles and masks found at the many Mayan archaeological sites), sacrifices were made. Gold, jade, and human beings (in some accounts, usually young virginal maidens) were among the things thrown into these sacred cenotes.

Although most of the Mayas were conquered by the Spaniards by the middle of the 16th century, one group resisted, retaining its autonomy for another 150 years. When Mexico finally won its independence from Spain in 1821, intense fighting broke out between the Mayas and the land-owning oligarchy of the peninsula, which was made up of whites and local *mestizos*. This, in turn, led to the political separation of the Yucatán from the rest of Mexico. It was not until early in the 20th century, and the first shots of the Mexican Revolution, that the Yucatán was successfully reunited with the rest of the Mexican republic.

Until chewing gum became popular in North America around the time of its first U.S. patent in 1869, only one product, sisal hemp, was grown in any abundance and exported by Yucatán plantation owners, its sword-shaped leaves used in the manufacture of rope and mats. With an increase in the demand for chewing gum, however, the resin, or chicle, of the sapodilla tree (*Achras zapota*) became a viable export as well. But prosperity was short-lived. Techniques for making sisal and chicle from synthetic substances were not long in coming, and with them the demand for low-paid Mayan workers to pick sisal leaves or collect resin dried up.

Today, the largest industry of the Yucatán is tourism, fostered mainly by the development of highways in the 1950s and by the more recent expansion of air and cruise ship service. The main destinations are the Mayan ruins at Uxmal, Chichén Itzá, Tulum, and Cobá, all in Mexico, and Tikal in Guatemala, and the beach resorts of Cancún, Cozumel, and Isla Mujeres.

The following three Travel Routes describe the major sights to see in the Yucatán peninsula.

TRAVEL ROUTE 29: Villahermosa–***Palenque (–*Bonampak–*Yaxchilán)–Campeche–***Uxmal–*Mérida (557 km., 354 miles)

See map on page 279.

Villahermosa, capital of the state of Tabasco, is a convenient jumping-off point for the Yucatán region. This Travel Route takes you from there to some of the most fabulous Mayan ruins in Mexico. At the end of the route, you can explore Mérida, the capital of the Yucatán.

From *Villahermosa* (see page 242) there are two major routes to choose from: an inland route to Campeche that takes you through Francisco Escárcega, or the coastal route (see page 281) along the Gulf of Mexico. The first route, though longer, is actually faster than the second, which is scenic but requires repeated interruptions to board a succession of car ferries that take you across the mouths of various rivers. If you plan to drive around the entire peninsula, you should consider taking the scenic coastal route at this point. In either case you'll want to see Palenque, a beautiful Mayan ceremonial center surrounded by jungle. The first route will get you there in short order, but you'll have to endure a rather lengthy stretch of monotonous scenery while doing so. If you take the coastal route, you'll bypass Palenque for the time being and have it to look forward to on your return trip.

Assuming, however, that you're going directly to Palenque from Villahermosa, leave the city via the toll bridge over the Río Grijalva and take Highway 186 toward *Francisco Escárcega*. At Catazajá, 115 km. (71 miles) from Villahermosa, the road to Palenque will swing right and then divide after another 28 km. (17 miles) at the entrance to the village of Palenque. From here it is 8 km. (5 miles) to the excavation site, which is open from 8:00 A.M. to 5:00 P.M.

***Palenque

Palenque, which lies at the foot of a chain of karstic foothills in the state of Chiapas, was an important ceremonial center for the Mayas during the 200 years between A.D. 600–800. The question that has never been answered satisfactorily is why the site, like other Mayan towns of the Classic period, was abandoned suddenly in the ninth century.

The rain forest, or *selva,* that has encroached on the ruins for centuries, along with the region's high humidity, have seriously damaged many of the site's finely cut façades. The best preserved and most beautiful are the façades of the so-called ****Palacio,** or Palace, a group of buildings that stands on a large artificial platform accessible by two broad stairways and surmounted by a tower, which at one point was probably an observatory several stories high. The pillars marking the entrance to the Palacio, at least those that remain, are decorated with stucco reliefs. On the west façade are four scenes depicting religious ceremonies in which two people are officiating. Four of the panels on the eastern façade show priests in ceremonial robes flanked by two crouching, subservient-looking figures. The interiors of the long narrow rooms are decorated with a variety of stucco masks, medallions, and garlands. In the largest of the four inner courtyards is a stairway covered with hieroglyphs, its sides protected by large male stone figures, which, judging from their humble posture, probably are representations of Mayan slaves. Behind the Palacio are the remains of a tunnel built with large stone blocks to channel water from the nearby Río Otolum.

The ****Templo de las Inscripciones,** which is named for the hieroglyphic texts on a wall of one of its rooms, sits atop an elongated 21-meter (69-foot) pyramid and is reached by a steep stairway. The temple has a narrow room in

Templo de las Inscripciones

front with five portals and three chambers behind the portals. Fragments of stucco reliefs can be seen on the entrance pillars.

In 1949, the Mexican archaeologist Alberto Ruiz Lhuillier discovered a stairway under a floor plate that led 25 meters (82 feet) into the pyramid. After four years of excavation, the stairway was uncovered and at the bottom an enormous crypt was found, a reconstruction of which can now be seen in the National Museum of Anthropology in Mexico City. The crypt was covered with a heavy stone slab decorated with a bas-relief showing a man sitting on the mask of the earth god, his knees drawn up against his chest. In the crypt, which measures 9 meters by 4 meters (30 feet by 13 feet) and stands 7 meters (23 feet) high, was a monolithic sarcophagus. Inside, the skeleton of a male was found covered with jade orna-

ments and jewelry intended for his journey into the next world.

According to the hieroglyphics in the temple, the pyramid was the burial place of the priest-king Pacal, who had ruled over Palenque from A.D. 615–683, and the discovery of his tomb was the first evidence that pyramids had served as burial places in Mesoamerica as well as in Egypt.

To the southeast is a complex of four temples arranged around a courtyard called the **Group of the Cross.** Three of the temples were built at about the same time, the end of the seventh century, and are named for the dominant motifs of their interior panels: the *Templo del Sol* (Temple of the Sun), the *Templo de la Cruz* (Temple of the Cross), and the *Templo de la Cruz Foliada* (Temple of the Foliated Cross). The fourth temple, known simply as *Temple XIV,* is smaller than the others and was built at a later date. (It's not considered a great architectural achievement and tends to break the harmony of the original group.)

Scenes of homage are depicted in the reliefs on the rear walls of each chamber in the three main temples. The sun god, symbolized by a shield with two crossed lances, occupies the place of honor in the Templo del Sol; the Templo de la Cruz Foliada has a relief of a corn stalk with leaves and ears in the shape of human heads; and the Templo de la Cruz is distinguished by its relief of a stylized cruciform corn stalk (the panel can be seen in the National

Relief in Templo del Sol

Museum of Anthropology in Mexico City).

The Templo del Sol is also remarkable for its well-preserved roof comb, a superstructure built in the shape of a pierced wall—a motif that once was incorporated into most of the buildings in Palenque.

Walking past the rear of the Palacio, you'll soon reach the northern part of the excavation, where you'll find what's left of a deteriorated ball court and, to the left, two temples: the small *Temple X* and the **Templo del Conde** (Temple of the Count), named for the Austrian travel writer Jean Frederic von Waldeck, who lived in it in 1832. Built around A.D. 650, it is the oldest building so far excavated at the site.

Situated on a long terrace in the northeastern section of the zone

are five temples generally referred to as the **Northern Group.** Nearby is a small museum in which local finds (stelae, ceramics, stucco fragments, and tomb artifacts) are exhibited.

If you decide to spend the night in the vicinity, there are lodgings available at a variety of price ranges in the town of Palenque and on the road to the excavation site itself.

An unusual but somewhat difficult side trip takes you to ***Bonampak**—once a small Mayan dependency—149 km. (93 miles) from Palenque deep in the dense Chiapan rain forest. To get there overland will require a four-wheel-drive vehicle, which can be rented along with a driver-guide in Palenque. You can also make the trip by small plane, at the same time visiting the hidden Mayan site of *Yaxchilán* on the Río Usumacinta.

The ruins at Bonampak are not particularly significant from an architectural standpoint, but one in particular, the ****Templo de las Pinturas** (Temple of the Murals), which was first shown by a Lacandon Indian to an American in 1946, contained murals that were like nothing else in Central America and which eventually yielded considerable information on the life of the Mayas. Because they had been protected over the centuries by a limestone "varnish" that had formed quite naturally, the colors of the murals were brilliant when first uncovered. Once they'd been exposed to the humid air, however, the colors began to fade. Sadly, the murals are hardly recognizable today, but you can see what they once looked like at the National Museum of Anthropology (Mexico City) where faithful reproductions are on permanent display.

The trip to Bonampak can still be rewarding, however, for there's a certain mysterious allure to the sight of buildings standing on a terraced hill in the lush jungle valley of the Río Lacanja. At Bonampak, a large plaza spreads out before them, and in its midst is a 6-meter- (20-foot-) high stela that has been restored. The relief on it, with a glyph signifying the year A.D. 785, shows a priest-king in full ceremonial robes. Two additional stelae along the stairway to the terraced hill also depict people in regal, authoritarian poses.

The building on the right on the first broad platform is the *Templo de las Pinturas,* for which Bonampak ("place of the painted walls" in the Mayan language) was named. Usually, the three rooms that contain the murals are closed, but if you're lucky enough to get in, those in the room on the left show preparations for a war ceremony; the murals in the middle room show battle scenes and sacrifices of captives; and the third room is decorated with scenes of victory celebrations.

*Yaxchilán, once a major Mayan ceremonial center, is about 55 km. (34 miles) by air taxi from

ROUTES 29–31
(The Yucatán Peninsula)

Miles
0 |——————————| 50
Kilometers

N

Golfo

de

México

*Bahía
de
Campeche*

29B

Puerto Real
Cd. del Carmen
Frontera
29A
180
29B
**Villa-
hermosa**
186
Río Usumacinta
29A
Palenque
Ruinas
Pichucalco   **Agua Azul**
Chilon
Ococingo
S. Cristóbal de
las Casas   **Bonamp**
Chiapa de
Corzo   Amatenango
Comitán
To Ciudad Cuauhtémoc

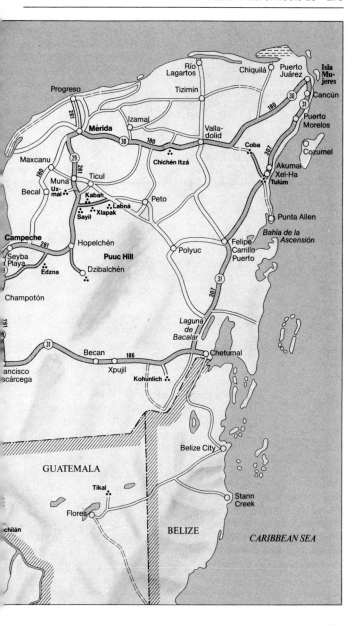

Bonampak, and is almost entirely surrounded by the meandering Río Usumacinta, which forms the border with Guatemala. Here, the Mayas left fine reliefs on stelae, altars, and doorposts, but the lush green jungle with its exotic flowers has overpowered the ruins, and traces of the life that once animated the site remain mostly hidden. Instead, what you'll notice immediately will be the incessant chirping of birds mingled with intermittent shrieks from monkeys. If you take an air taxi or other small plane, you'll only have a couple of hours to take everything in, so if you want to see the most beautiful details of the ruins, ask the guard at the site for a tour.

Yaxchilán was one of the great cultural and administrative centers of the lowland Mayas, especially during the Classic period from A.D. 300–900. Only a part of the site has been excavated and restored, however, most notably the 300-meter- (980-foot-) long plaza along the river with its complement of buildings. The remains of two ball courts are also visible nearby.

Higher up along the hilltop are a number of palatial structures, elongated and low-slung, and usually with three entrances each. The upper parts of the façades were once decorated with stone figures plastered over in stucco and crowned by fencelike roof combs similar to those found in Palenque. The most beautiful example is the *Palacio del Rey* (Palace of the King) on the hilltop nearest the river. Most of the reliefs on the doorposts here, as well as on other structures and the approximately 30 freestanding stelae, depict historical motifs. By deciphering the glyphs, scholars have been able to determine the succession of the priest-kings whose deeds are depicted.

When you finally return to Highway 186 after your side trips to Palenque, Bonampak, and Yaxchilán, you'll find that the road runs through the humid plains of the valley of the Río Usumacinta, with its many lagoons and marshes home to an abundance of heron and its lush meadows still used as pasture. About 21 km. (13 miles) from Catanza there is a turnoff to the right that will take you southeast to the villages of *Emiliano Zapata* about 10 km. (6 miles) away and *Tenosique,* some 68 km. (41 miles) farther, where flights to Bonampak and Yaxchilán are less expensive than they

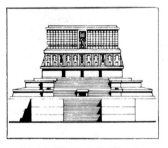

Model of Quetzalcóatl Temple, Yaxchilán

are from the larger cities of the Yucatán. If you stay on Highway 186, you'll come to a toll bridge across the Usumacinta in another 10 km. (6 miles).

From *Francisco Escárcega* (372 km., 230 miles from Villahermosa), a way station with a small restaurant and hotel, Highway 186 continues due east to Chetumal (see page 313), while Highway 261 branches off in a northerly direction toward Campeche. At *Champotón* near the Gulf of Mexico, Highway 261 joins Highway 180 (see page 282)—the alternate route from Villahermosa. What follows is a description of this coastal route.

After a drive of 75 km. (46 miles) from Villahermosa through marshy country on Highway 180, you'll reach a ferry (the Spanish word is *transbordador,* but locally it's called a *panga*) that crosses the confluence of the Usumacinta and Grijalva rivers just before they empty into the Gulf. (The Grijalva is the largest river in Mexico, carrying fully a third of its runoff waters into the Gulf.) On the far bank lies *Frontera,* a city of 15,000 and the main port of the state of Tabasco.

The next ferry, 97.5 km. (61 miles) from Villahermosa, crosses the narrow Río San Pedro y San Pablo, an arm of the Usumacinta, which here forms the boundary between the states of Tabasco and Campeche. In the swampy area along the coast,

you'll be able to spot cattle—some of them Zebu—standing chest-deep in the water. The crossing itself only takes five minutes and is made frequently.

Zacatal, 167 km. (104 miles) from Villahermosa, is the ferry landing on the shores of the **Laguna de Términos,** a huge inlet of the Gulf that's 72 km. (43 miles) long and up to 42 km. (25 miles) wide. When the first Spanish expeditions sailed from the island of Cozumel to explore the coast of the Yucatán, they assumed it ended here at this lagoon.

The ferry from Zacatal crosses a channel to the fishing town of *Ciudad del Carmen* at the western tip of the *Isla del Carmen* every two hours between 5:00 A.M. and 11:00 P.M., and in the opposite direction every two hours between 4:00 A.M. and 10:00 P.M. (While waiting to make the 30-minute crossing, try the freshly caught fish that's offered for sale near the ferry dock.)

The 42-km.- (25-mile-) long island road, which is sometimes washed out, passes through a small village and crosses a lagoon amid thick tropical vegetation and a number of dunes. The channel between *Puerto Real* on the eastern tip of the island and the fishing village of *Isla Aguada* on the mainland is now spanned by a bridge—the Puente de la Unidad—that is more than 3 km. (2 miles) long and saves you a fourth ferry ride (but not, alas, the toll). After the bridge, the highway runs along a beautiful stretch of sandy beaches lined with coconut palms for some 105 km. (65 miles) until you reach **Champotón** at the mouth of the Río Champotón. The town, a rather unremarkable fishing village spread out over both sides of the river, does boast the remains of a fort erected in 1719 to protect it against pirates. It's also the place, as mentioned above, where Highway 261, the inland route from Villahermosa, joins Highway 180.

Lerma, a fishing village with a marina, is near the outskirts of **Campeche,** a city of about 120,000 and the capital of the state of the same name. For the best view of Campeche with its hexagonal town walls, turn right past the entrance to the Camino Escenico and follow that road to the fort on the hill.

Campeche was founded in 1540 by Francisco de Montejo, "the Younger," and flourished as a port during the Colonial period. To protect it from marauding pirates in the 16th and 17th centuries, the entire town was placed behind ramparts. Today, visitors can walk on some of the preserved portions of the massive wall which surrounds the *Old Town.* The Old Town is also the location of the *Zócalo* and the *Cathedral,* which was begun in 1540 but not completed for 165 years.

The *Museo de Historia,* or archaeological museum, which contains local finds and documents relating to the history of the town, as well as a collection of weapons, is located in the *Baluarte de la Soledad,* one of the many bastions in the city. Others, such as the *Baluarte de Santiago* and the *Baluarte San Carlos,* house the botanical garden and a crafts center, respectively. Both are on Calle 8.

Northeast of the center of town is the 16th-century *Monastery of San Francisco,* which is noteworthy for the fact that Hernán Cortés's grandson was baptized there in 1562.

Once you're ready to leave Campeche, continue out of the city on Highway 180. There will be turnoffs on the left after 10 and 30 km. (6 and 19 miles) to *Via Corta,* the fastest route to Mérida. Although it's 50 km. (31 miles) shorter than Highway 261, it won't take you to the most interesting archaeological sites in the region.

A road in the village of *Cayal,* 15 km. (9 miles) past the junction of 180 and 261, turns off on the right and runs for 18 km. (11 miles) to the partially exposed ruins of ***Edzná.** Judging from the extant remains, it must once have been a huge settlement that prospered right through the Classic period. The predominant architectural style is plain and unadorned, but over the centuries it assimilated elements of styles such as the Río Bec, the Chenes, and the Puuc, with the predictable result that archaeologists have been confounded in their attempts to accurately date the various structures.

Excavations are concentrated in

the old religious center, where the buildings surround a large plaza measuring 170 meters by 100 meters (560 feet by 328 feet). One complex of buildings, the *Gran Acropolis,* rests on a platform that is reached by a broad limestone staircase. Dominating this particular grouping is the 31-meter- (102-foot-) high ***Templo de los Cinco Pisos* (Temple of the Five Stories), a four-story priests' dwelling topped by a sanctuary with a 6-meter- (19-foot-) high roof comb. Stone pillars in the Río Bec style once supported the entrances to the rooms on the lowest floor, while monolithic pillars with Puuc-style capitals were used on the uppermost floor.

The other buildings in this group are considered less important. In the center on a base stands *La Picota*, which looks like a pillory but was probably an altar.

South of the acropolis is the terminus of the main canal of an extensive system that was used to drain swampy, low-lying areas, and wasn't discovered until the 1970s.

East of Cayal, the road crosses a broad plain where grain, sisal, and fruit are grown. In *Hopelchén,* with its fortified 16th-century church, archaeology buffs can take a side trip south to the ***Chenes area,** so-named for the Mayan suffix *chen,* which appears in the names of many towns and villages, and means "fountain." Characteristic of the style of architecture that developed in this region after the seventh century

are temples and palaces with façades richly decorated in stone. Huge, stylized masks, their mouths open and often forming entrances, are its dominant motif.

At various points along the road to *Dzibalchén,* access roads lead to the excavation sites of *Dzehkabtún, Dzibiltún,* and *El Tabasqueño.*

From Dzibalchén, a road runs northeast about 20 km. (13 miles) to *Iturbide,* where the archaeological zone of *Dzibilnocac* is situated. Though one of the largest in the Chenes area, it remains little more than a ruin due to the fact that the Indians in the nearby village insist on using its stones for their own purposes. Only the outline of the former 70-meter- (230-foot-) long temple-palace with its three pyramidal towers is worth seeing.

Nine miles southwest of Dzibalchén is the small ceremonial town of *Hochob.* A three-part temple-palace on the north side of the site has a façade that is considered the prime example of the Chenes style and has been reconstructed in the open area of the National Museum of Anthropology in Mexico City.

The neighboring *Río Bec* zone to the south also has mask façades influenced by the Chenes style, but its temple cities are more easily reached from Highway 180, which runs between Chetumal and Francisco Escárcega.

Returning to Highway 261, which runs north from Hopelchén to Mérida, you'll find that the jungle stretches far and wide on both sides and the road through this sparsely settled region carries little traffic. Shortly before you reach *Bolonchén de Rejón,* there's a turnoff on the left to the **Grutas de Xtacumbil-Xunán* ("the cave of the hidden woman," a name derived from local legend), which is a network of dripstone caves and cenotes.

At the border to the state of Yucatán, an arch spans the road. It is also the symbolic gate to the hilly landscape of the Sierrita de Ticul, whose summits run northwest to southeast and known as the ****Puuc region.** *Puuc,* the Mayan word for "hill," has been borrowed from this region to label the style of architecture associated with it.

During the period of A.D. 800–1000, the region (the center of which is Uxmal) was densely populated, with a number of ceremonial centers of varying size. Invariably, the architecture of these centers was distinguished by its smooth walls and square doorways in the lower levels of buildings, while the upper levels, often separated by a ledge, were lavishly decorated. The basic patterns of the friezes were predominantly geometric, and masks of the rain-god Chac, usually located above entrances and in corners, were commonplace. As the Classic period of Mesoamerican culture wound down, façades broken up by broad entrances with round supporting columns, which included false columns used for dec-

oration, came to characterize the Puuc style.

As you approach Uxmal, there are several other interesting, though not so extensive, archaeological sites off Highway 261. One of these is ***Sayil,** where the Late-Classic style of decorating the lower parts of a temple's façade is very much in evidence. The only building completely excavated, however, is the ****Palacio,** with its two upper levels recessed from the ones below it. The palace's western side has been reconstructed, and its middle level is broken up by wide column-supported entrances that alternate with narrow doors. In the frieze running above the doors are carvings of Chac masks, along with a diving figure framed by stylized serpents. From the top level (which is reached by a stairway), you'll get a good view of the dense bush in which other buildings stand, among them the *mirador,* or lookout, with its tall roof comb. A trail leads from the *mirador* to a stone idol with a large phallus.

Five miles away is the excavation site of **Xlapak,** where a Classic Puuc-style temple designated simply as "Structure I" has been restored. The decorations on its façade begin above the entrances and continue across to a ledge of small columns and a frieze mostly made up of meandering lines. The temple also has towerlike superstructures decorated with Chac masks featuring protruding noses.

Yet another group of pre-Hispanic ruins, in this case connected

The Palacio in Sayil

by a ceremonial street of limestone, or *Sacbé* (the Mayan word for "white road"), can be found in ***Labná.** At first glance, its *Palacio* appears as a haphazard complex situated on a large terrace. The façade of the eastern section is decorated with groups of three

Arco de Labná

false columns, large meanders, and a variety of masks. In the southeast corner is a Chac mask with open serpent's jaws swallowing a human head.

The southern group at Labná is dominated by a temple-pyramid with a roof comb. But the best-known structure at the site is the ****Arco de Labná,** a large gate with a corbeled arch. Two rooms adjoin the arch, which is 16 feet high and 10 feet deep, and typical Mayan huts appear in the friezes above the entrances to the rooms.

*Kabah, which is only four miles away, is known for the ****Codz-Poop** (Palace of the Masks), a 147-foot-long structure with two parallel rows of rooms. The palace itself is built on a low platform, which in turn stands on a large terrace. The lower part of the temple's façade is covered with innumerable masks, but most of their protruding, curled noses have broken off.

The simple palace in the northeast is an interesting contrast to the heavily decorated facade of the Codz-Poop. The upper part of the building seems to have been built over the now mostly destroyed lower story.

Only a heap of stones remains of the large pyramid on the other side of the road. Other structures in the western part of the zone are also in ruins, but there is a well-preserved tower gate with a corbeled vault on hand. Presumably, it once marked the beginning of the 20-km.- (12-mile-) long processional route to Uxmal, which is another limestone *Sacbé.*

One other spot in the vicinity, *Mul Chic,* just west of Santa Elena, is worthy of attention, although its prize possessions, its frescoes, are in Mérida, where they are preserved in the *Museo de Arqueológia.*

***Uxmal

Uxmal is one of the most stunning examples of Mayan city building. The style is classic Puuc—a name derived from the surrounding Puuc hills—which is a "lacier" style of ornamentation than that found at Mayapán (see page 29). There are also wide variations in the actual structures themselves, some of them pyramidal, others rectangular or nearly square.

Most scholars believe Uxmal to have been founded in Mesoamerica's Classic period, which dates from the sixth century. The builders are believed to have been Mayas who moved north from the region of Petén in what is now Guatemala, and their most spectacular achievements are dated to the ninth and tenth centuries.

Lacking natural wells—the cenotes associated with so many Mayan sites—the people of Uxmal had to rely on rain water, which was collected in large cement-lined reservoirs and cisterns (*chultunes*). The development of cement had another telling effect on the grand style of Uxmal: It permitted its builders to go beyond the limitations of usual cut-stone construction and span wider spaces using a pointed, or corbeled, arch. As a result, the Mayas were able to build palaces with huge interior spaces and wide entranceways.

The ruins are dominated by the 30-meter- (124-foot-) high ***Pirámide del Adivino** (Pyramid of the Magician), which you encounter shortly after entering the grounds. Built on a unique oval foundation, the existing pyramid is the end result of five buildings erected one on top of the other over a span of more than 300 years. According to legend, the work was done in a single night by a magician, a Mayan chieftan with supernatural powers. (Some versions of the legend portray the builder as a dwarf, other versions say he was the son of a witch.)

On the west side of the pyramid, portions of the foundation of the first temple are visible at the structure's base. Apparently, it was one of four small buildings surrounding a courtyard, which was later covered over as the present pyramid took shape. Placed atop this original pyramid was a second temple, which can still be reached by a tunnel that's approached from the middle of the stairs on the existing structure's east face. Next to its rear wall is the third temple, which consists of three rooms but can't be seen from the outside due to the fact that it's entirely encircled by the fourth temple. (It can, however, be reached by climbing a steep stairway on the west face of the existing structure.) What distinquishes this fourth temple from the others is the fact that it's entered through the mouth of a Chac mask, a characteristic of the Chenes style of construction found farther south in Campeche. At Uxmal, the fourth temple is one of only two or three buildings that share that distinction.

The fifth temple—at the top of the existing structure—can be reached by the stairs on the east face of the pyramid or by way of two narrow sets of stairs on either side of the temple below it. As daunting as the climb to the fifth temple may appear, the effort is well rewarded, for it's from this one-room rectangle decorated on the outside by latticelike stonework that the best overall views of the entire Uxmal complex will be found.

A word is in order here about climbing pyramids. You'll more than likely see other visitors scampering up steep flights of stairs, and you'll probably be tempted to do the same thing. At the pyramids in Mexico, however, especially those built by the Mayas, you should be aware that the climb is not as easy as it looks. The steps are narrow and do not conform to the pitch that most of us are accustomed to. But going up isn't the hardest part.

Getting down presents an even bigger problem, and unless you try it yourself, you're not likely to appreciate just how difficult the descent can be. At some pyramids, a rope or chain has been installed to assist visitors in getting up and down. Trying to negotiate the steps of a pyramid that does not offer the extra assurance of a rope, however, can give you an acute case of vertigo. It's a good idea to test the angle of descent yourself by climbing five or six steps and, before going higher, turning around to see if you feel comfortable coming back down.

Northwest of the Pirámide del Adivina is the ***Cuadrángulo de las Monjas** (Nuns' Quadrangle), so-called because of its 88 cell-like cubicles, which were probably the living quarters of administrators but which reminded the conquering Spaniards of nuns' quarters. The huge courtyard, which is entered through a corbeled arch in the center of the building on the south, is surrounded by four long buildings,

Cuadrángulo de los Monjas and Pirámide del Adivino

each built in a different period of Uxmal's development. Following the Puuc style, the lower façades of the buildings consist of smooth walls, but higher up, above the doors, runs a three-dimensional frieze of carved stone in styles that vary from building to building but combine to create a harmonious total effect.

A closer look reveals that the worship of Chac, the rain-god, was an integral component of the

Chac mask, Uxmal

Mayan religion. On the southern building, Mayan huts and Chac masks are interspersed in the frieze, and above the ledge on the northern building (the oldest in the quadrangle) rise four towers, each with four Chac masks placed one above the other. Friezes containing a pattern of thatched-roof huts and serpents continue the design on the towers.

On the eastern building, the serpent pattern is continued, with two-headed serpents placed side by side to form trapezes. The heads of owls are also incorporated into the frieze. The fourth building, on the west, offers the most complicated and perhaps most artistic frieze, with the ubiquitous Chac masks interspersed with slinking snakes, carved thrones, and a variety of geometric designs.

South of the quadrangle are the remains of a *ball court*, through which a path that leads to another complex of buildings has been etched by a parade of visitors. The first one you come to is the so-called **Casa de las Tortugas** (House of the Turtles), a building of great simplicity that is named for the figures of turtles carved into the frieze on the upper ledge of the building. According to Mayan mythology, turtles played a significant role (along with Chac) in their existence, for when there was a drought the turtles supposedly grieved for the Mayas, their eyes filling with tears, which in turn fell as rain. Also carved into the frieze are a series of small round columns resembling a bamboo fence.

As interesting as the Casa de las Tortugas is, it's dwarfed by the ****Palacio del Gobernador** (Governor's Palace), which commands attention from the huge platform (about 15 meters; 50 feet high) on which it stands. The palace is about 107 meters (350 feet) long and has two wings attached to it by corbeled arches, and you can get inside to inspect its 20 or so rooms from an entrance on the east side of the building. The palace, which many experts consider the best example of pre-Hispanic architecture in the Western Hemisphere, is distinguished by a complex frieze containing hundreds of Chac masks, serpents, and geometrical designs, and standing 3 meters (10 feet) high. Above the palace's central entrance is a figure, probably a chieftan, in a feathered headdress.

On the terrace in front of the palace is a sculpture of a three-headed jaguar carved from a single block of stone. This *Altar of the Jaguar* was part of a much larger observatory complex, with the main door of the palace looking out on the altar and an unadorned single column that guides the eye to the rising of Venus above the main pyramid at Nohpat, a nearby Mayan site.

The ***Gran Píramide** to the southwest of the Governor's Palace is distinguished by a wide stairway that leads to a temple crowning its top. The temple, decorated with Chac masks and parrots, was one of four temples that originally formed a rectangle on top of the pyramid (a rectangle similar to the Cuadrángulo de las Monjas). If you climb to the temple, you'll discover that you can enter one of its rooms by stepping on the snout of a Chac mask.

In the complex of buildings a bit to the west of the Great Pyramid is one that's unusual for the design on its roof comb. The triangular markings with openings that remind one of a pigeon house have given the building its present name: **Palomar** (the Dovecote). It, too, is one of another group of four buildings that formed a quadrangle predating the Cuadrángulo de las Monjas.

If time permits, you'll want to look at some of the other sights in Uxmal and its environs. While still in the zone, you can follow a path southeast to the *Pirámide de la Vieja* (Old Woman's Pyramid), which is in ruins but which legend says was the home of a sorceress, the mother, in fact, of the magician who was supposed to have built the huge pyramid that dominates the area around the entrance to the zone. On the way to the Pirámide de la Vieja, you'll pass the *Templo de los Falos* (Phallus Temple), where fragments of phallus-shaped stone sculptures that may have been water spouts can be discerned.

Much farther south, and reached by another footpath, is a large corbeled archway that marks the beginning of a 17-km. (10-mile) paved causeway that passes the ruins at *Nohpat* and ends in *Kabah* at a similarly large and impressive arch.

Closer to the center of the Uxmal zone (west of the ball court) is the *Grupo del Cementerio* (Cemetery Group), so-named because of the skull and crossbones that decorate the small platforms in the inner courtyard. On the *Platforma de las Estelas* stands a group of eroding stelae ranging up to 10 feet in height.

Visitors who are able to stay overnight at Uxmal have an opportunity to witness one of the best sound-and-light shows anywhere in the world. Spectators sit on folding chairs on a terrace overlooking the Cuadrángulo de las Monjas and listen to a recorded narrative with musical accompaniment of the history of the site while various buildings and pyramids are illuminated. The total effect is truly spectacular. There are two shows nightly (check with your travel agent for last-minute changes in the schedule), the first in Spanish at 7:00 P.M. and the second in English at 9:00. And although the show itself only lasts 45 minutes, the memories of it will last a lifetime.

Continue on Highway 261 to Mérida, 557 km. (335 miles) from Villahermosa (810 km., 486 miles, if you took the side trip to Palenque).

*Mérida

See map on page 292.

Those who come to the Yucatán primarily to see the pyramids and other architectural achievements of the Mayas will most likely make Mérida, the capital of the state of Yucatán, their base, and a wise choice it is. Situated in the northwestern corner of the peninsula only a few feet above sea level, Mérida has an international airport, many fine hotels and restaurants, an interesting cathedral, several museums, and one of the largest marketplaces of any city in Mexico. And it's within easy driving distance of the major Mayan sites.

Established shortly after Campeche, Mérida was the second Spanish settlement on the peninsula. The subjugation of the Mayas in the area had been entrusted to Francisco de Montejo, one of Cortés's *conquistadors,* but it was Montejo's son, Francisco de Montejo el Mozo ("the Younger"), who founded the settlement in 1542 after his father, who had failed to subdue the native population, relinquished his command. Built on the site of the crumbling and nearly deserted

Mayan town of Tiho, El Mozo named the settlement "Mérida" because the spot reminded him of the ruined Roman city in Spain of the same name.

Today, Mérida is distinguished by its buildings of limestone, which account for its nickname, "the White City." Not surprisingly, white is also the predominant color worn by the majority of the population, a fact that can be attributed to the climate of the region, which is generally hot and humid. For women, the most common items of apparel are the *huipil,* a rectangular-shaped blouse with lace trimmings and usually embroidered with flowers, and a long, gathered skirt. For men, the basic garment is the *guayabera,* a loose-fitting shirt with large pockets at about waist level instead of at the chest, and worn outside of long white pants in place of a jacket.

Before leaving for the ruins, spend some time getting to know this charming city. One of the best ways is to take a ride in a *calesa,* a high-wheeled horse-drawn carriage that is quite typical of Mérida, as well as a few other Yucatán towns. Or you can simply enjoy a stroll along the tree- and shrub-lined paths of the *Zócalo,* here called the ***Plaza Mayor** (1), which is in the center of town

Plaza Mayor, Mérida

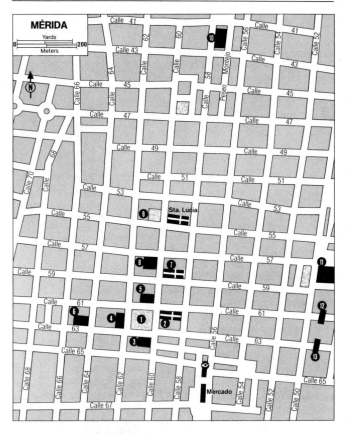

opposite the *Cathedral* (2) at the intersection of Calles 60 and 61.

Like most of Mexico's Colonial towns and cities, Mérida is laid out in an almost perfect grid. The streets once had names, but today all the downtown streets are numbered: Even numbers are used for streets that run north and south, odd numbers for those running east and west. In the heart of town, traffic is one-way only, alter-nating directions on every other street.

Opposite the plaza on the north and west are the main government buildings, the *Palacio de Gobierno* (5) and *Palacio Munici-pal* (4). On the south is *Casa Montejo (3), the former residence of the elder Francisco de Montejo, and on the east side is the Cathedral.

Along the staircases and inner

balconies of the *Palacio de Gobierno,* which was built in 1892 on the site of a former mansion used to house Spanish officials, are murals by Fernando Castro Pacheco (most of them painted between 1971 and 1973) depicting the history of the Yucatán.

Noteworthy at the Moorish-style *Palacio Municipal,* which dates from 1542 but was rebuilt in 1735 and again in the mid-19th century, is the clock tower (dating from 1633), with a double tier of arches running across its façade.

If the *Casa Montejo* is open (the hours have been known to be erratic, but it's generally open during banking hours), don't miss the chance to see the interior of one of the first Spanish houses built in Mérida. Its design, with a well, a cistern, and a double patio, was intended to cope with the problems of water and ventilation in a tropical climate. Note also the tile and marble floors, which were made from ship ballast.

If the house isn't open, you'll have to content yourself with viewing its impressive exterior: an exquisitely carved, two-story Plateresque façade created by a master Mayan mason using blocks from Mayan ruins. The coat-of-arms of both the Montejo family and the Spanish royal family crown the massive double doors, and larger-than-life Spanish knights standing on the heads of defeated Mayas line both sides of the entryway.

The **Cathedral,** or Convento de las Monjas (6), which was built between 1561 and 1598, is a huge, fortlike structure lacking the Churrigueresque embellishments that characterize so many other Mexican churches, but having two notable distinctions nevertheless: It's the largest church on the Yucatán peninsula as well as the oldest cathedral in Mexico (though it wasn't the first one started; work on the Cathedral in Campeche was begun somewhat earlier, but the structure wasn't completed for more than 100 years).

After touring the area around the plaza, stroll down Calle 60 at least as far as Calle 57, where the *University of Yucatán* (8) sits on the site of a Jesuit college founded in 1618. On the way, just before reaching Calle 59, you'll come to a small park, the *Plaza Cepeda Peraza.* As you continue northward, take time to study the *Iglesia de Jesús* (7), built by the Jesuits in 1618 and sometimes referred to as the Church of the Third Order, just across the street.

Next to the church is an even smaller park, the *Parque de la Madre,* which boasts a copy of the Monument to the Mothers, a statue by the Frenchman Francis Lenoir (the original is in the Luxembourg Gardens in Paris).

As you pass the *Teatro Péon Contreras,* built in the Neoclassical style with Italian marble between 1900 and 1908 and restored in 1982 for musical and dramatic performances, you'll get a nice look at the Moorish-style buildings of the university across the street, which date from 1938. Should you be in the vicinity after 9:00 P.M. on a Friday, you can listen to a selection of Mexican folk music performed in the courtyard. Such "serenades," as they are called, are common throughout the city and are generally offered free of charge.

If you're still in the mood for walking, continue a block north to the *church of Santa Lucía,* which was built in 1575 for black slaves to worship in. Across the street is another park, the *Plaza Santa Lucía* (9), which was the terminus of the stagecoach line in Colonial days. In fact, the hooks used to tether horses are still visible on the period columns supporting the plaza's arched portico. Serenades are offered here on Thursday evenings, as well.

Next, your walking tour of Mérida should take you to the *Paseo de Montejo,* a small-scale facsimile of the Champs-Elysées lined with Victorian mansions that was planned early in the 20th century when the city was prospering on account of the henequen boom. (Henequen is the fiber of the agave plant, and is used for making ropes and fabrics.) To get there, continue up Calle 60 to Calle 47 and then head eastward for two blocks.

On the west side of the Paseo de Montejo two blocks north is the ***Museo de Arqueología** (10), which occupies the basement of what was once the *Palacio Cantón,* or governor's mansion. Some of the jade and gold relics in its small but fascinating collection were found in the Sacred Cenote of Chichén Itzá. Among the pieces are stone statuettes, pottery, carvings, and utensils.

At the other end of town southeast of the main plaza is the sprawling indoor **Mercado Municipal* where you can wander past stall after stall of almost every kind of merchandise imaginable, from food and clothing to live ducks and color TV sets. Of course, locally made sisal products such as hammocks, Panama-style hats, and floor mats, and garments such as *guayaberas* and *huipils,* are much in evidence, hanging on racks and suspended from hooks. Sandals, belts, pocketbooks, and other leather products can also be found in abundance.

The surrounding area—Calle 56 between Calles 65 and 67—is dotted with restaurants and bars. One of the favorite local specialties is fresh shrimp, served in a tall tulip glass with cocktail sauce and a lime wedge.

The 18th-century chapel and adjacent buildings of *La Ermita de Santa Isabel* (Hermitage of Santa Isabel) on Calle 64 south of the city have been restored to present a picture of what the Jesuit founders intended for their retreat. The garden next to the chapel features a collection of sculpture taken from various Mayan sites. The *Convento de la Mejórda* (11), at Calle 57 and Calle 50, is housed in an even older building, a 17th-century Franciscan monastery.

The Moorish-style *Arco de San*

Juan, which is south of the Plaza Mayor at Calles 64 and 69, is part of the wall that once surrounded the central part of Mérida. In the 17th century, when the wall was built by the Spanish, there were a total of seven decorative arches connecting its various segments. Today, only two other arches, both east of the city on Calle 50, are still standing: the *Arco de Dragones* (12) at Calle 61, and the *Arco del Puente* (13) at Calle 63.

Also east of town, at the *train station* on Calle 55 between Calles 46 and 48, you'll find evidence of more recent Yucatán history— the peninsula's first locomotive, which has been placed on permanent display.

At *Centennial Park,* on the other side of the city at the intersection of Calle 59 and the Avenida de los Itzaes, is Mérida's zoo, which is noted for its collection of tropical birds and wildlife typical of the Yucatán peninsula. There is also an amusement park on the grounds, with a variety of rides and stalls selling food and trinkets.

When you finally decide it's time to see more of the area surrounding Mérida you'll have a choice of directions in which to head—north to *Progreso,* the port town on the Gulf of Mexico with a mile-long pier and a wide, fairly clean beach; southwest to ***Uxmal* (see page 286), the site of extensive Mayan ruins (particularly impressive at night when they're illuminated); south to *Mayapán,* where the architecture of

what was once a leading Mayan center is interesting but considered inferior to most other Mayan sites; or east to ***Chichén Itzá* (see page 297), one of the largest Mayan sites, with excavations even more extensive than those at Uxmal.

Farther east is the peninsula's once-pristine Caribbean coast, which in recent years has been developed into a major tourist destination, the centerpiece of which is Cancún.

En route north on Route 261 to the beach at Progreso you'll have the chance to visit ***Dzibilchaltún,** a Mayan site that is said to predate the Christian era by about 800 years and was inhabited until the Spanish arrived in the 16th century. Thanks to its proximity to coastal salt flats, Dzibilchaltún prospered for centuries by selling salt to neighboring Mayan communities, and grew to the point where it sprawled over 20 square miles— about the same size as present-day Washington, D.C.

In 1590, the Spanish built a small chapel at the site, which is about all that remains, the original temples and buildings having been destroyed by the *conquistadores,* with many of the stones later used to pave the highway between Mérida and Progreso. Nevertheless, the remains of a causeway, 18 meters (60 feet) wide and 2 km. (1.5 miles) long, connecting the temples and other buildings to a central well, the 48-meter- (147-foot-) deep *Cenote Xlacah,* gives some idea of the huge scope of the original city.

To the east of the causeway is a reconstructed temple, the *Templo de los Siete Munecas* (Temple of the Seven Dolls), which was built about A.D. 500 and once served as a solar observatory. Over the centuries the temple was renovated, and in time a larger temple was built over it. After many years that temple was demolished, and the earlier one consecrated anew. In the process, seven figures of deformed people were buried in the floor, giving the temple its present name. A small tunnel was added to provide priests with a means of communicating with the buried spirits, which were supposedly helpful in curing the sick. The temple is also unusual in that it has windows, something not found in most other Mayan temples.

In addition to the temple, many artifacts, including pottery shards, jewelry, and human bones, were found in the site's cenote, some of which are now in the collection of the small museum that is maintained at the site.

Continue on Route 261 to *Progreso* (12 km.; 20 miles from Mérida), the expanding port city for Mérida. About 1.5 km. (3 miles) east lies *Chicxulub Puerto*, a popular Gulf coast beach that in no way compares with its counterparts on the Caribbean side of the peninsula.

At **Mayapán** (47 km.; 28 miles south of Mérida), which is approached through a rather formidable jungle, the architecture is considered mediocre and lacking in originality, but scattered about are sculptures of feathered serpents and other bits of temple decoration, and one building near the center of the site looks remarkably like a small-scale version of the renowned central pyramid known as El Castillo (Spanish for *castle*) at Chichén Itzá.

TRAVEL ROUTE 30: *Mérida–***Chichén Itzá–**Cancún (320 km.; 192 miles)

See map on page 279.

The main attraction on this Travel Route is the famous Mayan ruin of Chichén Itzá where you can easily spend a whole day exploring. On the way to the ruins are Izamal and Valladolid, two small Colonial towns.

The road to Chichén Itzá from Mérida isn't particularly scenic, passing as it does mainly through scrubland, the occasional thinly forested area, and some thicker junglelike undergrowth, but there are sisal plantations (as there are all the way to Puerto Juárez in Quintana Roo), as well as a few towns that merit a visit, if you're willing to make a short detour or two.

Take Highway 180 east from Mérida (see page 290). At *Tahmek,* about 40 km. (25 miles) east of Mérida, you'll come to a turnoff for the Henequen Hacienda, on the grounds of which is *Aké,* the site of some minor Mayan ruins, the most notable of which is a colonnade called the *Palacio.* The detour is about 12 km. (7 miles) one way. (Aké can also be reached by way of Tixkokob, which is on the road to Motul and actually makes for a slightly shorter drive.)

Near *Hoctún,* there's a road that heads north to *Izamal,* 24 km. (15 miles) away. Take time in Hoctún, however, to visit the colored tombstones shaped like buildings that stand in the cemetery.

*Izamal, which sits atop an old Mayan settlement, preserves the Mayan name but little else of the original site. Before the arrival of the Spaniards, it was visited regularly by Mayas on their pilgrimages to worship Itzamna, the sky god (sometimes credited with being the creator of the universe) and Kinich-kakmo, the sun god. Starting sometime around 1540, the *conquistadors* and their Franciscan entourage tore down most of the pyramids and temples and replaced them with buildings of their own, most notably a church and a monastery called **San Antonio de Padua,* using the remains of the large Mayan temple of Popol-Chac as their foundation blocks.

Some of the original structures of Izamal have been uncovered recently, however, including the pyramid dedicated to Kinich-kakmo, which was one of the largest pyramids in the Yucatán at one time. Ironically, its stairway now leads to a cross instead of a temple.

Rejoin Highway 180 and continue heading east. You'll pass a number of hotels that offer lodging to visitors to nearby *Chichén Itzá.*

***Chichén Itzá

See map on page 298.

Just as an overnight stay is recommended at Uxmal, it is even more advisable at Chichén Itzá (Mayan for "the place of the well of Itzá"), where more buildings have been restored and there is, as a result, more to see.

Mayas traveling north from Guatemala are believed to have founded Chichén Itzá about A.D. 450, but the city did not become important as a place of worship and pilgrimage until about A.D. 800. The ascendancy of Chichén Itzá was rather short-lived, however. About A.D. 1000, groups of Indians from Tula in central Mexico brought their high degree of culture to the area, and the city flourished in a Post-Classic renaissance. But within 200 years Chichén Itzá had been surpassed as the leading city in the Yucatán by Mayapán. By the time the Spaniards arrived, the site had been almost totally abandoned.

There are two main sections of the present archaeological zone, which is divided by a road that's closed to through traffic. (It was once Highway 180, the main trans-peninsular route, but now

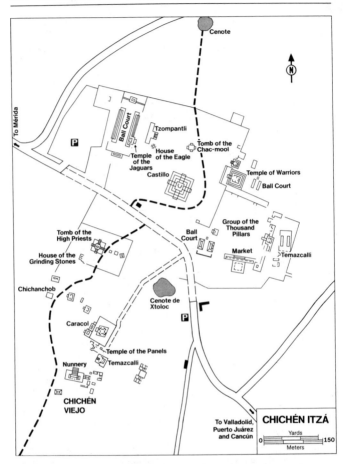

it's merely an access road off the rerouted highway.) North of the road, the predominant architectural influence is Toltec, which is characterized by the often-photographed figure of Chac-mool in a reclining position with an offering bowl on its lap. Pillars fashioned in the shape of warriors and the worship of the feathered serpent Quetzalcóatl—which to the Mayas was Kukulkan—are also characteristic of the Toltec influence.

The pyramid of Kukulkan, called ***El Castillo (the castle), is the tallest structure at the site and dominates its surroundings. The pyramid itself rises 24 meters (79 feet) from its platform to the temple at the top, and staircases—

each with 91 steps—on all four sides of the pyramid lead to the temple. The total number of steps—91 multiplied by four, plus the common step to the temple platform on top—equals 365, the number of days in a solar year. At the top, fronting the temple, is a portico with two columns carved in the shape of feathered serpents, and on the northern side of the pyramid the steps end in serpent heads.

Twice a year, at the equinoxes, a remarkable phenomenon occurs in connection with the steps. Then, at the precise moment of equal day and night, the sun casts a huge shadow on the steps, creating the effect of a giant reptile descending the stairs. If you can't time your visit to Chichén Itzá to coincide with either equinox, you can still witness a good imitation of this spectacle during the nightly sound-and-light show.

While the Castillo was being restored, archaeologists working on it discovered that what appeared to be the main pyramid had, in fact, been built over a smaller pyramid, one that contained in its temple a stone Chacmool figure as well as a stone bench carved in the form of a jaguar. The jaguar is painted red and encrusted with jade, pieces of which are used for its eyes and spots. The entrance to the stairway leading up to this jade jaguar throne (for that's what scholars believe its function was) is on the north side of the pyramid, but is only open at certain times of the day. After checking the posted hours and returning later, if need be, you'll have to climb a steep staircase through a narrow passageway illuminated by a string of naked light bulbs to reach the inner chambers.

East of the Castillo is the

Castillo and Caracol, Chichén-Itzá

**Templo de los Guerreros
(Temple of the Warriors), which is distinguished by its gallery—two rows of columns in front of the pyramid carved in the shape of warriors. Apparently, they once supported a roof. A Chac-mool sculpture stands in front of the temple on the platform that supported the structure, which can be reached by climbing another steep set of stairs. The roof of the forecourt of the temple was once held up by stone columns carved in the shape of serpents standing erect, their jaws open. The serpent heads now lie on the ground. In addition, Chac masks and birdmen are carved into what was once the façade of the temple.

Only a few relics remain in the interior of the temple. In one room

Chac-mool, Templo de los Guerros

is a stone table that was supported by short columns, and there is evidence that many of the walls were painted and the pillars and doorposts were decorated with carved representations of warriors.

The pyramid supporting the temple, like the pyramid of El Castillo, is built over a smaller pyramid, and the design of both pyramids is strikingly similar to the Temple of the Morning Star in Tula (dedicated to the god Quetzalcóatl, who is portrayed in carvings as both a feathered serpent and as Venus, the morning star, see page 79).

Just beyond the Temple de los Guerreros is a large complex, mostly in ruins, showing evidence of fallen columns and now called the **Grupo de las Mil Columnas** (Group of the Thousand Columns). It appears to have once been a huge plaza surrounded by colonnaded halls on three sides and by a market on the fourth.

One of the sights that everyone who visits Chichén Itzá makes an effort to see is the **Cenote Sagrado** (Sacred Cenote), which can be reached by following a wide paved path (*sacbé*) that was used by the Mayas for ceremonial processions. The sacbé, 6 meters (20 feet) wide and 29 meters (98 feet) long, leads north and west from the Templo de los Guerreros to the cenote, an almost round natural well some 27 meters (90 feet) in diameter. On the bottom of the cenote, which remains filled to a depth 11 meters (35 feet), divers have recovered a variety of offerings to the rain-god Chac: ceramics, precious stones, copper, gold and silver, and the partial skeletons of 50 people who were sacrificed during times of drought or other distress, such as epidemics.

Southwest of the Cenote Sagrado is another fascinating reminder of Mayan life, the ****Ball Court,** one of seven at Chichén Itzá. Nearby are the trio of structures known as the *Central Platforms.* The *Platform of Venus* is decorated with carvings of serpents along its stairways and, in sunken regions of the platform itself, representations of Quetzalcóatl as Venus in the form of man, bird, and serpent.

Just beyond the Platform of Venus is the *Tzompantli* (Platform of Skulls), a square structure decorated with the skulls—placed on poles—of victims who were sacrificed. Also adorning the base of the platform are scenes of eagles eating human hearts and a warrior

with writhing serpents emanating from his sides. The eagle theme is repeated in the adjacent smaller platform called the *Casa de los Aguilas* (House of Eagles).

The gigantic Ball Court is set off lengthwise by walls 8 meters (26 feet) high. In the center of each wall is a stone ring through which a ball had to be "shot"; players, however, were only allowed to use knees, hips, and elbows. At the base of each wall is a sloping stone bench decorated with carved scenes depicting religious themes associated with the "game." One panel, for example, shows players in stunning attire, the first of whom holds the decapitated head of an opponent. (Scholars have surmised that the decapitation of winners was tied to fertility rituals.) At both ends of the court are temples on low platforms. The east wall serves as the base for the *Templo de los Tigres* (Temple of the Jaguars). As one would expect, the frieze on the temple depicts roaring jaguars, and inside are what is left of murals that depict battle scenes.

Finally, at the rear of the east wall below the Templo de los Tigres is a smaller building, the interior walls of which are completely carved with flat reliefs of warriors. A stone jaguar stands between the entrance pillars, which are also covered with carvings.

If you have followed the route described above, you will have covered the northern section of Chichén Itzá in a somewhat coun-

Ball court, Chichén Itzá

ter-clockwise fashion, and should be ready to explore the southern section, which lies across the two-lane road that formerly served as the main highway between Mérida and Valladolid.

The first major sight you'll come to in the southern section is the *Usario,* also known as the *Tumba del Gran Sacerdote* (Grave of the High Priest), so-named for the fact that burial chambers containing valuables such as jade, copper, crystal, and shells, as well as human skeletons, were uncovered inside. The pyramid has been left unrestored and is not nearly as impressive as El Castillo in the northern section, but indications are that it was once the equal of El Castillo and that a paved causeway connected the two. Serpent carvings on columns scattered about are still visible, and it's also possible to discern where the four stairways that led to the temple at the top were.

Next you come to the *Casa Colorado,* a platform with rounded corners and an unadorned temple that apparently was built over a ball court similar to the one in the northern section. The Casa Colorado is believed to date from the seventh century, but the ball court is even older and presents a puzzle for scholars, for it had long been presumed that the Toltec influence didn't appear at Chichén Itzá until about the tenth century.

The most unusual building in either section of the zone is ***El Caracol,** or the Snail, which is the oldest towerlike structure in

the Yucatán and was evidently an observatory, for it has four doors facing the cardinal points of the compass. Above each door is a carved Chac mask, and a narrow passageway spirals in snail-like fashion up to the upper floor of the tower. The entire structure looks a bit strange: It was originally built on a rectangular platform, which was later buttressed by the addition of a circular platform; later still, a temple was added at the base, giving rise to the comment by the archaeologist J. Eric Thompson that it "stands like a two-decker wedding cake on the square carton from which it came."

To the south is the **Edificio de las Monjas** (the Nunnery), a designation from the Spaniards, who were reminded of their own convents by the combination of structures. One building, called the Annex, boasts a façade completely covered by huge Chac masks, and the frieze on another nearby building called the *Church* continues this Chac-mask motif.

About 137 meters (150 yards) east of the Nunnery is the *Akab-Dzib,* a palacelike building done in Classic (relatively plain) Mayan style. In Mayan, the name means "obscure writing" and refers to the fact that the hieroglyphic inscription on the lintel over an inner doorway seems to be indecipherable.

The ruins of still another building, the *Templo de los Retablos* (Temple of the Sculptured Lintels), lie between the Church and

El Caracol. The remains consist mainly of scattered pieces of columns and sculpture, and its name refers to the carvings on the outside of the north and south walls. Although eroded, the almost cartoon-like Mayas in seated positions can still be made out.

From the Nunnery, a path leads to a little-explored section of the zone called **Chichén Viejo,** or Old Chichén, where the buildings, hidden by jungle, are inhabited mainly by iguanas. Diehard enthusiasts may wish to hire a guide to help them find the so-called **Templo de la Fecha** (Temple of the Dates). About all that remains of it, however, is a door lintel bearing the glyph for the year A.D. 879, the only fully decipherable date at the entire site.

South of the Templo de la Fecha are the *House of the Phalli*—named for the carvings found on an interior wall—the ruined *Temple of the Four Lintels,* and the completely restored *Temple of the Three Lintels,* which, except for its decorated base, is done in plain Puuc style. Be advised that you'll have to hike a considerable distance over an overgrown path to reach either temple, but if you make the effort, you'll have covered just about all there is to see at Chichén Itzá.

With your tour of one of the world's most fascinating archaeological sites complete, it will be time to move on. As you travel east from Chichén Itzá on Highway 180 toward the Caribbean coast of the peninsula, you'll pass numerous Mayan villages. Straw- or palm-covered huts, usually with rounded walls made from wooden slats or cane, and high thatched roofs, are the norm in these villages. Their construction is deliberately airy due to the intense heat, and you'll probably be tempted to stop during the afternoon, or even to stay overnight, in which case you can rock yourself to sleep on a hammock.

Whether you interrupt your trip for a brief stay in one of these villages or not, consider visiting the ***Grutas de Balankanché,** a sacred cave dating to the Toltec period (A.D. 900-1300), which is only 1.5 km. (3 miles) from Chichén Itzá. Stumbled upon accidentally by a local tourist guide in 1959, the cave was found to contain a number of chambers filled with ceremonial artifacts, including a variety of ceramics, incense containers, and *metates* (grinding stones). Many of the objects bore the face of the Toltec rain-god Tlaloc, and all were left as they had been found. (An added attraction are the stalactites in the central altar room, but unless you're limber enough to crawl into this deep grotto, you won't have a chance to see them.)

Returning to Highway 180, you'll soon come to **Valladolid,** a former Colonial outpost just 41 km. (26 miles) east of Chichén Itzá. Founded in 1543 by a member of the Montejo family and then moved two years later to the site of the Mayan town of Zaci, its present site, Valladolid has a population of 30,000, the usual central square, a large 16th-century church, and an enclosed marketplace where, as in Mérida, a wide variety of foodstuffs, handcrafts, and manufactured products are offered for sale.

The bakeries in Valladolid are also outstanding, especially for the sweet bread called *pan dulce,* which almost tastes like cake, and the town is favored by budget-conscious travelers, who like its generally less expensive restaurants (compared to those in Chichén Itzá, Mérida, or Cancún).

Just outside of town is the *Zaci Cenote,* which is hidden in a large limestone cave. There are stairs that lead down to a viewing platform, and it's also home to a species of blind fish the Maya call *lub.*

The Franciscans, who built the church and monastery of *San Bernardino* in Valladolid, built another monastery at about the same time in *Tizimín,* 51 km. (32 miles) north of Valladolid. The Feast of the Epiphany, a popular event for residents and visitors alike, is celebrated there.

To the south of Valladolid, Highway 295 heads to *Felipe Carrillo Puerto* in the neighboring state of Quintana Roo, but most travelers at this point will continue east on Highway 180 toward Cancún.

In *Nuevo X-Can,* 61 km. (38 miles) east of Valladolid, you'll find a turnoff to the right that will take you 19.5 km. (31 miles) to *Cobá.* Part of the road is paved; the rest is gravel but well maintained. Along the route you're likely to see any number of wild parrots in the junglelike growth on either side of the road.

Depending on your itinerary and the time of day, you may choose to take this shortcut to Cobá, continue on to Tulum, and then work your way farther south to Chetumal or back north to Cancún. If it is approaching dusk, however, you're best advised to stay on the main east-west highway and proceed to Cancún. Highway 180 is fully paved, well marked, and much easier to travel in the dark than the partially paved and totally unmarked cutoff route. Bear in mind, though, that this alternative can be a time-saver in returning to Mérida, for it allows you to avoid backtracking between Cancún and Nuevo X-Cán.

Whatever your final decision, the next important stop, whether you're mainly interested in Mayan ruins or state-of-the-art leisure, is Cancún (320 km.; 192 miles from Mérida), the computer-generated resort on the Caribbean coast of the state of Quintana Roo.

TRAVEL ROUTE 31: **Cancún–**Tulum–Chetumal– Francisco Escárcega (646 km.; 390 miles)

See map on page 279.

Idyllic palm beaches with romantic villages, sparkling turquoise water, clear fish-laden lagoons, and hidden ruins of the great civilization of the Mayas—these are but a foretaste of the eastern route along the Yucatán's Caribbean coast. The archaeological highpoint is Tulum and its dramatic location on a coral cliff. The last portion of the Travel Route, through the Mayan region called Rio Bec, completes the circuit of the Yucatán peninsula.

**Cancún

See map on page 307.

Until the 1970s, there was hardly anything at Cancún but powdery white sand. Today, there is a string of modern luxury hotels attracting some 750,000 visitors a year to a narrow offshore sandbar that's connected to the mainland by a causeway. In more ways than one, Cancún now rivals Acapulco, the long-established resort on Mexico's Pacific coast, as the premier luxury resort in the country. It has the same types of hotels that cater to the jet set, and the same kind of nightlife. It offers a variety of water sports as well as golf and tennis. Its range of boutiques is second to none. And Cancún has a nearly perfect year-round climate, with an average of 243 sunny days a year—54 more than the average for Acapulco.

Besides all that, Cancún is within easy reach of Tulum, Cobá, and Chichén Itzá, the most important Mayan archaeological sites on the eastern half of the Yucatán peninsula. Vacationers who choose to spend a week or more here have no reason to fear boredom, for in addition to sampling all the attractions of the resort itself, as well as those nearby on the mainland, there are also two interesting islands just off the coast: Isla Mujeres and Cozumel.

Historically, Cancún differs from most other resorts in a significant way: It was, in a sense, conceived by a computer and then built in a relatively short span of time at the instigation of the Mexican government, with government-sponsored participation by private investors. The story goes something like this: Toward the end of the 1960s, in the days before the discovery of huge oil reserves under the Bay of Campeche, Mexico found itself trapped in the classic deflationary scenario that plagues so many developing countries. Its exploding population was spurring the demand for imports, exports were shrinking, and the subsequent balance-of-payments shortfall put downward pressure on the value of the peso, which only served to exacerbate the situation. Increasingly, tourism seemed like the answer to the country's problems (and, in fact, today it's Mexico's second-largest industry, after oil). After evaluating various locations that might have been suitable for a beach resort, government experts, aided by computer technology, selected Cancún. The work crews and heavy machinery moved in rapidly, and an international airport was started. The state of Quintana Roo did its part by developing roads, sewers, and utilities. Within five years, the state had set up the entire infrastructure, including an 18-hole golf course, a convention site and shopping center, the airport, and a town to house workers and provide facilities for service personnel, and—*voilá*—Cancún was born. In the decade or so since the first guests began arriving, the wisdom of the developers and experts has been borne out. Cancún is the second most popular resort in the country, and in time appears destined to eclipse its rival, Acapulco.

Cancún's mainland town was originally planned for 50,000 inhabitants, but with the population of the unplanned, fast-growing outlying areas added in, it's now reached twice that size. The municipal buildings are located downtown on 50 acres. The central business district was established on both sides of the Avenida Tulum, and at its northern end is the *Mercado de Artesanias,* a government-sponsored crafts center where a wide variety of woven, carved, and other handmade articles are on sale.

The hotels on the beach are all in the first-class or luxury category; most of them are located on the sheltered east-west section of the 22-km. - (13-mile-) long sandbar, which is bathed by gentle waves. But the stretch of sandbar running north-south is also being built up, despite the fact that its beaches are dotted with rocks and reefs, and pounded by the surf. (Most of the new buildings are condominiums, and owners rent their units out to visitors for terms ranging from a week to a year.)

As you can imagine, aquatic sports of all kinds are a passion at this beautiful Caribbean resort, and the snorkeling and diving along the coral reefs are world-class. Besides the abundance of colorful, exotic fish, Cancún's transparent waters are the final resting place for a number of 17th-century Spanish galleons and 20th-century German U-boats. If you're curious about the secrets of the sea but don't want to get wet, you can take a guided tour of the reefs and wrecks in the minisub *Aquascope,* and pretend—at least for a day—that you're another Jacques Cousteau.

Wind surfing and sailing in the lagoon are safe, the only dangers being the water- and jet-boat skiers. Boats for sport fishing are also for rent, and there's good fishing north of Cancún near the

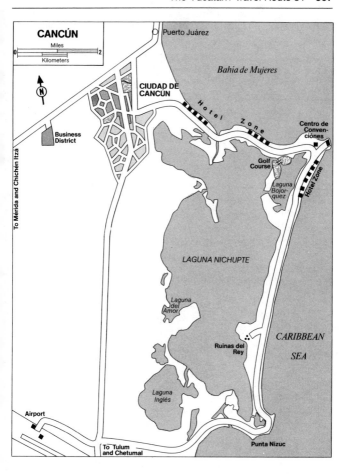

CANCÚN

Miles

Kilometers

N

Puerto Juárez

Bahía de Mujeres

CIUDAD DE CANCÚN

Hotel Zone

Business District

To Mérida and Chichén Itzá

Centro de Convenciónes

Golf Course

Laguna Bojorquez

Hotel Zone

LAGUNA NICHUPTE

Laguna del Amor

CARIBBEAN SEA

Ruinas del Rey

Laguna Inglés

Airport

Punta Nizuc

To Tulum and Chetumal

island of Contoy, which also happens to be a bird sanctuary. Parasailing seems to be the latest rage these days, but if you prefer to keep your feet on the ground, there's tennis, an outstanding golf course, and enough shopping for two vacations.

For archaeology buffs, the Mayan ruins of *El Rey* are located between Punta Cancún and Punta Nizuc. A number of small pyramids and their temples, along with 50 graves, have been uncovered so far. In addition, a small anthropological museum has been set up in the convention center to accommodate these local finds, and is open from 10:00 A.M. to 2:00 P.M. and 5:00 to 8:00 P.M. Also of interest is the CEDAM maritime museum in the main building of the apartment block on Paseo Kukulkan, where objects from the sunken Spanish galleons are on display. Its hours are 11:00 A.M. to 8:00 P.M.

For evening entertainment, you need not leave the beach area: Hotel restaurants and discothéques, of which there are many, are open to everyone.

If you plan on staying for any length of time in Cancún, you may wish to take a side trip or two to any of a number of nearby places of interest. A bus leaves for *Chetumal* every two hours or so and stops at the Mayan ruins of *Tulum* and the *Xel-ha Lagoon.* You can also make a day trip to *Chichén Itzá* by bus or rental car. And there are several ways to reach the neighboring islands of *Cozumel* and *Isla Mujeres.*

The passenger ferry to Isla Mujeres leaves from Puerto Juárez, 5 km. (3 miles) north of Cancún; the car ferry, which takes the local bus as well, leaves from Punta Sam, another 5 km. (3 miles) farther north. Unless you fear leaving your car on the mainland, however (and there really is no reason to worry), there's no point in taking an automobile to Isla Mujeres: The island is so small, and the main business and resort area so concentrated, that you can easily get around on foot

or rental motorbike (a necessity for the trip to the southern tip of the island to see the small Mayan temple that stands in ruins).

The car ferry to Cozumel leaves from Puerto Morelos, 32 km. (20 miles) to the south, and the passenger ferry from Playa del Carmen, another 27 km. (17 miles) farther south. The Aliscato hydrofoil, which leaves from the latter, practically flies to Cozumel. Several yachts, some with glass bottoms, also make the trip.

Isla Mujeres

Judging from its name, Isla Mujeres, or the "isle of women," one might guess that this small offshore island is a paradise for romance. And, in a sense, it is, even though its name is derived from the clay statues of women that were found here in 1517 by the Spanish seafarer Francisco Hernández de Córdoba.

Today, Isla Mujeres has become an extremely popular vacation alternative for budget-conscious travelers, especially Mexicans from other parts of the country, thanks to its smaller and much more reasonably priced hotels. First "discovered" by tourists in the 1960s, it has remained a haven for travelers who shun glitzy luxury hotels ever since.

The island itself is 8 km. (5 miles) long and only 1.5 km. (1 mile) wide at its widest point. Coconut palms line its beaches and lagoons, which are the equal of Cancún's. *Playa Cocos,* on the western side of the island, is a pleasant, peaceful beach, while the eastern side is subject to heavier surf. Another option is to rent a bicycle or motorbike and head south to *El Garrafón Bay,* where the offshore coral reef is a major attraction for snorkelers and divers. The huge colonies of fish do not seem to be bothered by either the snorkelers or the excursion boats that make all-day trips out to the reef.

A turtle farm and the ruins of a pirate hideout, the *Hacienda Mundaca,* are among the other attractions on the island, and behind the lighthouse on the southern tip lies the Mayan ruin, which dates to the Late Classic period, and which scholars think may have been an observatory dedicated to the moon and fertility goddess, Ix-chel.

**Cozumel

While Isla Mujeres, just north of Cancún, is small and unassuming, there's a very different kind of island a bit farther away to the south. It is Cozumel, which is much larger than Isla Mujeres, much more lush, and much more expensive.

One of Mexico's biggest islands, Cozumel lies in the Caribbean about 19 km. (12 miles) off the coast of the Yucatán peninsula and about 80 km. (50 miles) south of Cancún. The island is 45 km. (28 miles) long and 17.5 km. (11 miles) wide at its widest point, and, from a visitor's standpoint, is best known for the diving opportunities afforded by the nearby *Palancar Reef.*

Historically, Cozumel was probably a Mayan pilgrimage site, attracting worshipers of Ix-chel, the goddess of both fertility and the moon. The first Spaniard to set foot in what would one day become Mexico was Juan de Grijalva, who made a landfall on Cozumel in 1518 as he and his men sailed from Cuba into the Gulf. (This was a year before Cortés rescued Jerónimo de Aguilar, a shipwrecked sailor who had been marooned and enslaved by Indians three years earlier, from the island.)

From the 17th to the 19th centuries, Cozumel and other islands in the vicinity served as a refuge for pirates such as Henry Morgan and Jean Lafitte. During World War II, the United States established a base on the island for the Army Air Corps; the airfield it built was later to become the international airport that today is the first stop for the hordes of vacationers from around the world who come to this tropical setting in search of sun and fun. Few, however, are prepared for what they find. For lushness of vegetation, perhaps only Jamaica (also in the Caribbean) is more "tropical," and in this respect Cozumel is more naturally beautiful than either Isla Mujeres or Cancún (for that matter, it's more beautiful than most of the Yucatán peninsula).

The capital city of Cozumel is *San Miguel,* a town of about 25,000. Its main plaza is situated across from the ferry terminal, which is served from *Puerto Morelos* and *Playa del Carmen.* Playa del Carmen is also the customary port of call for cruise ships, whose passengers usually have a choice of visiting either Cancún or Cozumel.

Once on the island, a favorite pastime of visitors is browsing in the shops lining the pedestrian malls near San Miguel's plaza, where Cozumel's leading specialty, black coral jewelry, is found in abundance.

For more adventurous visitors, mopeds and cars can be rented to explore the island, which is encircled by a 65.5-km. (41-mile) drive. Among Cozumel's best-loved destinations is the *Laguna Chancanab* nature park. The lagoon, though small, is a veritable natural aquarium of exotic fish. Also on the grounds are a tropical botanic garden and a reconstructed Mayan farm. (Even if you choose not to rent a car or moped, the lagoon can be reached by public transportation.)

The beach at San Miguel is a popular spot for sunbathing, swimming, diving, and snorkeling along the coral reefs. There is also a shallow, sandy beach 8 km. (5 miles) away called *Playa San Francisco.* Restaurants at both beaches specialize in fresh seafood.

Of the 30 or so Mayan ruins on Cozumel, only *San Gervasio* has been restored and is relatively easy to reach. (It's about 6.5 km.—4 miles—off the main road that more or less bisects the island.) Although the miniature temples, which date from the Post-Classic period, aren't particularly impressive from an architectural standpoint, the walk through the dense tropical growth to reach them can be pleasant (except after a rain, when bugs come out in force; be sure to come equipped with insect repellent just in case).

Once you've returned to the mainland from Cozumel—either at Puerto Morelos, which is served by the car ferry, or Playa del Carmen, which offers passenger ferry service—your trip south along the coast of the peninsula will be highlighted by a series of idyllic beaches fronting palm-fringed, crystal-clear lagoons, with bungalows or tents for rent and Mayan ruins hidden in the bush. The archaeological high point of this stretch, however, is *Tulum,* impressive not so much for its architecture—which is Post-Classic like Cozumel's ruins—as for its dramatic setting high on a coral cliff. (Excursion boats can be hired to take you directly to Tulum from Cozumel.)

Let's assume, however, you've decided to drive along as much of the coastline as possible before exploring Tulum. Leaving Cancún on Highway 307, you'll come to an access road to Puerto Morelos, which leads to the ferry dock. At *Punta Bete,* 60 km. (37 miles) south of Cancún, a number of sandy paths lead to the beach. Here you'll find bungalow accommodations at *Capitain Lafitte* and

El Marlin Azul, among others, as well as a rather expensive tent colony, the *Camptel Kau Luum.*

Your next chance to stop is **Playa del Carmen,** 9 km. (5 miles) south of Cancún and the dock for the passenger ferry to Cozumel. The town has two comfortable hotels, as well as more modest, reasonably priced lodgings. The *palapa*-style (thatchroofed) restaurants and bars such as Mascaras and El Jardín near the beach, attract a young crowd.

*Akumal, about 104 km. (65 miles) south of Cancún, lies in a gently curving bay with a very long beach. Its bungalows tucked away among the palm groves were the first tourist accommodations developed on the eastern coast of the peninsula.

The beautiful lagoons and protected bays of ****Xel-ha,** slightly farther south, have attracted so many visitors of late that the area has developed into a lively tourist center. In particular, it's become popular with divers and snorkelers. The local ruins west of the highway consist mainly of the *Casa del Jaguar,* a small temple with an upside-down jaguar painted on its façade.

Finally, some 128 km. (80 miles) south of Cancún, you'll come to the village of ****Tulum** and then, 3.5 km. (2 miles) to the east, the site of the most important pre-Columbian ruins on the east coast of the Yucatán peninsula.

The ruins sit atop a 40-foot-high cliff overlooking the sea and are protected on their inland side by a thick wall, originally 13 feet high. Five gates with corbeled arches provide access to the grounds, and two temples resembling guard towers rise from the corners of the wall.

Developed late in the Mayan era, Tulum features temples and palaces that are smaller than most of those characteristic of the earlier Classic period. In addition, they were built on low foundations or platforms instead of the pyramid bases found at Uxmal and Chichén Itzá. Although the buildings here do not seem to have been constructed with the usual care associated with the Mayas, and the decorative work on the façades is considered less elegant than elsewhere, there are a number of well-preserved murals.

The *Templo de los Frescos* stands in the center of the zone, and like most of the other structures at Tulum has been rebuilt several times. The original building, with frescoes on both its exterior and interior walls, was later enlarged by the addition of a portico. This protected the Late-Classic wall paintings, which are similar to Mixtec codices in their subject matter. The roof ledge of the temple is richly ornamented, and one of its niches holds a stucco statue of the Mayan diving god. The two faces in the corners of the western façade, which probably represent the creator-god Itzamna, may seem bizarre, but they're more realistic than the Chac masks of the Classic Mayan temples.

As at other Mayan archaeological sites, the largest building is the *Castillo*. Situated at the edge of the cliff, it does, in fact, resemble a castle when seen from the sea. A wide stairway leads to a terrace and the entrance to the temple, which is supported by two serpent columns—probably a legacy of Toltec influence.

The *Templo del Dios Descendente* (Temple of the Diving-God) in the northeast corner of the zone is typical of most Mayan structures on the coast in that the walls taper slightly. In a niche above the entrance is a stucco mural of the diving-god, who seems to have been the most popular deity in Tulum.

Another variant of the stucco image can be seen in the entrance niche of the *House of the High Priest,* which is a bit to the northwest. The structure has a colonnade in front, as does the *House of Columns* to the south.

After visiting the ruins at Tulum, you may choose to take a swim in the small bay or get a snack or souvenir at one of the many shops (there seem to be more souvenir shops at Tulum than at any other archaeological site in Mexico) clustered around the entrance to the site.

Just south of the village of Tulum is a turnoff to the right that will take you to ***Cobá,** a one-way trip of about 40 km. (25 miles). In Mayan *cobá* means "water rippled by the wind," and the name is certainly appropriate, for Cobá lies in a region of small lakes, one of the few such regions on the Yucatán peninsula (and probably the only one at a Mayan site).

Although much excavation remains to be done, early indications are that Cobá was one of the largest, if not the largest, Mayan settlement on the peninsula, an achievement that can be attributed to the fact it had access to an abundant supply of fresh water. Judging by the many ruined structures still overgrown by jungle, Cobá must have had at least 40,000 inhabitants in its heyday between A.D. 600–900, and was probably both an important ceremonial center *and* trading center, for it lies at the junction of a far-flung network of roads. One of these roads, an earthen embankment with a flat, rolled surface of limestone mortar, was 99 km. (62 miles) long and reached all the way to Yaxuna in the west. (A stone roller has been found at the site.)

Few of the building complexes have been cleared, but the group between Lago Cobá and Lago Macanxoc (the two main lakes) has been partially excavated and is the easiest to reach. The *Castillo,* with its monumental staircase leading to a temple platform, is particularly impressive.

The temple atop another fortlike pyramid in the *Nohoch-Mul* group, about a mile to the northeast, is better preserved, however. In one of the three niches above its entrance is a statue of the diving god with remnants of paint on it. You might also consider a climb to the top: You'll be rewarded with a magnificent view of the dense jungle and the lakes embedded in it, the tops of overgrown pyramids barely visible above the canopy of green.

Among the finds at Cobá is a series of stelae, eight of which have been set up in the *Macanxoc* complex west of Lago Macanxoc. The area has also been designated as a nature reserve, thus preserving the jungle environment. One hotel, a branch of the Villas Arqueologicas, faces the lake and offers comfortable, if somewhat spartan, accommodations.

Continuing south toward Chetumal on Highway 307, you'll eventually reach **Felipe Carrillo Puerto,** the last bastion of the rebellious Mayas during the War of the Castes, which started in 1847. (The town and surrounding countryside were not reunited with the rest of Mexico until troops sent by Porfirio Díaz "liberated" it after the turn of the century.) From Felipe Carrillo Puerto, Highway 184 crosses the peninsula to *Muna,* near Uxmal, in the Puuc region of the state of Yucatán. The route, though scenic, is lightly traveled, and motorists should prepare accordingly.

If you keep travelling south on Highway 307, however, you'll come to the turquoise *Laguna de Bacalar* after 72 km. (45 miles), with the village of *Bacalar* dozing on its western shore. The ruins of the *fort of San Felipe,* which was built in 1733 by the Spanish as protection against English buccaneers, now houses a small museum.

The *Cenote Azul,* named for its deep blue waters, is south and west of Bacalar. Ranging in depth from 90 to 150 meters (200 to 500 feet), the cenote is truly the place for a memorable swim. The entrance can be found in the restaurant at its rim.

Not too far past the cenote, Highway 186 (toward Francisco Escárcega) heads off to the right, while the left fork, Highway 307, continues on toward **Chetumal.** Formerly the Mayan city of Chactemal, Chetumal, with a population of 90,000, is the capital of the state of Quintana Roo and is situated at the mouth of the Río Hondo, which forms Mexico's border with Belize.

A boat-building center in the days before the Spanish Conquest, the present city was founded in 1898. Today a free port, Chetumal is an important trading center for the east coast of the Yucatán peninsula and a way station for visitors making the grand tour of Mayan ruins (although the city itself lacks any major historic or cultural attractions).

About 56 km. (35 miles) west of town on the way to Francisco Escárgega is the former Mayan city of ***Kohunlich,** where the chief attraction is the *Pirámide de los Mascarones,* built on a high hill and decorated with huge, artfully executed stucco masks. Each mask bears the face of Itzamna, the Mayan creator-god, and six of the original eight are well preserved. They are now protected by palm roofs, however, which have greatly impaired their photogenic quality.

The modern settlements along

Mask relief, Kohunlich

this stretch of Highway 307 are poor, and contrast sharply with the Mayan ceremonial centers on Highway 186. The latter were all constructed in the Rio Bec style, which is named after its archaeological prototype, the temple at the jungle sanctuary of Rio Bec. The style is characterized by a covered one-story building complex flanked by two or three tower-like "false" pyramids (so-called because their stairs are indicated but cannot actually be climbed, in the same way that their temples cannot be entered). Rio Bec façades, however, are almost always richly decorated with stone mosaics in the shape of monster masks.

The next stop of interest along Highway 186 is ***Xpuhil,** where three pyramidal towers, remnants of an old Mayan ceremonial center, stand guard at the edge of town. A closer inspection reveals that they surround a main building that contained many rooms but is

now in ruins. All three are typical examples of the Rio Bec style. On the rear wall of the central pyramid—another false pyramid—is a well-preserved mask ornament that's usually well lighted by the afternoon sun.

From the village of Xpuhil, Maya enthusiasts can walk to a couple of remote archaeological sites that are accessible only on difficult paths through the surrounding jungle.

*Becan, with two towers similar to those in Xpuhil, is on the north side of the road about 6.5 km. (4 miles) away. Judging from the many temples and palaces grouped around its three large plazas, it must have been a more important ceremonial center than Xpuhil. The complex devoted to ritual worship was uncharacteristically laid out on a large limestone platform that is surrounded by an artificial ditch about 5 meters (15 feet) deep and, in some spots, up to 15.5 meters (52 feet) wide. One of the most interesting buildings at the site is a step pyramid with a number of rooms, which is located on the north side of the central plaza.

A kilometer and a half (1 mile) farther on, a road turns off to the left and after almost 1 km. (a half mile) ends in the midst of jungle at the entirely different site of ***Chicanna.** Take time here to walk around and admire the magnificent façades. The best one is the grandiose monster mask on the restored building known simply as *Structure II:* its open jaws form the entrance to the building, and it's particularly impressive in the late afternoon when the sun beats down on the western façade.

The stylistic connection with the Chenes region is much in evidence at Chicanna, and is repeated at the main temple of *Hormiguero,* a ruin in the jungle about 19 km. (12 miles) southwest of it.

The jungle scenery along this route becomes rather monotonous after a while and has little to recommend it apart from the archaeological sites mentioned above and the *Laguna Non.* Finally arriving at *Francisco Escárcega* (646 km.; 387 miles from Cancún), your circuitous tour of the Yucatán peninsula and its wonderful Mayan towns and ruins will have come full circle.

Practical Information

The following chapter is divided into two sections. The first, **General Trip Planning,** offers information you'll need for planning and researching your trip as well as tips on transportation to and around Mexico and other items of interest. (See listing in Contents for the full range of subjects covered.)

The second section, **Town-by-Town,** is organized alphabetically by town and provides information that will be helpful on site, such as local tourist offices, hotels, and transportation.

General Trip Planning

Choosing When To Go. Any time of year is the right time for a trip to Mexico, but regional climatic variations should be taken into consideration when preparing for your vacation. The coastal lowlands are very hot and humid in the rainy season, and prone to flooding (particularly on the Gulf coast). Thus, the best months for traveling to coastal resorts are late October and November, the early part of the dry season when everything is still green. (It's always best to avoid Christmas and Easter vacations due to the heavy domestic travel at those times of year.) High season prices are in effect from the middle of November to the end of May; the best travel bargains can be had during the summer months.

Pack light, comfortable clothing. For Mexico City and the highland areas you'll need a few woolen items—a warm sweater and pair of pants—for it can be cool, even cold, in the morning and evening. Some sort of rain protection should also be included, even during the dry season. Pack sturdy, flat-heeled shoes for visits to archaeological sites in case you decide to do some serious climbing. And remember: Beach attire or shorts are frowned upon in places like town markets and churches, especially in the southern part of the country.

Climate. Although much of Mexico lies in tropic and subtropic latitudes, the mountainous character of the country and its location between two large oceans results in four major climate zones. The torrid zone, or *tierra caliente,* with an annual average temperature above (25°C) 80°F and summertime highs well over (38°C) 100°F, is found between sea level and 760 meters (2,500 feet), and includes the coastal lowlands, the Yucatán, and the eastern slope and south of Baja. The temperate zone, or *tierra templada,* is found at elevations of 1,800 meters (6,000 feet), has an annual mean temperature range of (15–21°C) 60°–70°F, and includes much of the central plateau. The cool zone, or *tierra fría,* with a mean range of (13°–18°C) 55°–65°F, begins at elevations of 1,830 meters (6,000 feet) and extends up to timberline, which in Mexico lies between 4,000–4,600 meters (13,000–15,000 feet). Above that is the perpetual snow zone, or *tierra helada* (frozen zone).

Within each zone you can expect to find a substantial range between daytime highs and nighttime lows, especially at the higher altitudes. On a yearly average, day and night temperatures along the coasts will vary in the area of 10°F, while a difference of 20°F is common in the highlands. Don't be surprised, however, if you encounter frost at night between December and February in the *tierra fría,* while springlike temperatures return during the day.

Generally speaking, the coasts and Yucatán are hot and become more tropical the farther south you travel. The old Colonial cities of the central plateau are springlike year-round, a little warmer in summer and cooler in winter. In the north, the highlands gradually flatten, so that the effect of latitude is greater and seasonal temperature changes increase. Baja, with the exception of the Pacific-cooled northern coast, is mostly desert and always hot. You'll no doubt find it interesting, however, to travel through various zones and climates over relatively short distances—the trip from Pachuca to the Gulf coast, for instance.

Instead of four seasons, the year in Mexico is divided into a dry season from roughly November through April, with occasional dust storms and tornadoes in the highlands; and a rainy season from May to October, with afternoon thundershowers a common occurrence. Because of the Atlantic tradewinds, the eastern flank of the Gulf coast highlands are subject to precipitation throughout the year, and during the winter months the coast itself experiences unpredictable *nortes,* extensions of Canadian cold fronts, that can bring sudden temperature drops and heavy rain for days on end. The Yucatán and Gulf coast are visited by the occasional hurricane during the season from July to October, and the Pacific coast, too, will sometimes experience tropical storms blown north from the Gulf of Tehuantepec.

With the exception of the evergreen rain forests of the tropics and the mist forests of the mountains, Mexico is characterized by its vibrant greens during the rainy season and its dominant browns the rest of the year. September to December are the ideal months to visit in the opinion of most people—rain is scarce by then, but most plants, nourished by the moisture of the recently ended rainy season, are in full, glorious bloom.

Average Daily Temperatures

The temperature in Mexico is measured in degrees centigrade. Below is a listing of average daily temperatures by month in different areas of Mexico:

	Jan.		Feb.		March	
	F°	*C°*	*F°*	*C°*	*F°*	*C°*
Acapulco	78	26	78	26	78	26
Hermosillo	80	27	81	27	82	28
Manzanillo	74	23	76	24	74	23
Mérida	76	24	74	23	76	24
Mexicali	75	24	76	24	75	24
Mexico City	57	14	56	13	57	14
Monterrey	63	17	62	17	63	17
Oaxaca	66	19	67	19	67	19
Veracruz	72	22	73	23	72	22

	April		May		June	
	F°	*C°*	*F°*	*C°*	*F°*	*C°*
Acapulco	79	26	82	28	82	28
Hermosillo	89	32	89	32	87	31
Manzanillo	77	25	80	27	84	29
Mérida	81	27	83	28	83	28
Mexicali	83	28	84	29	84	29
Mexico City	64	18	66	19	66	19
Monterrey	73	23	78	26	81	27
Oaxaca	70	21	71	22	71	22
Veracruz	78	26	81	27	81	27

	July		Aug.		Sept.	
	F°	*C°*	*F°*	*C°*	*F°*	*C°*
Acapulco	82	28	82	28	82	28
Hermosillo	83	28	82	28	82	28
Manzanillo	85	29	85	29	83	28
Mérida	83	28	82	28	82	28
Mexicali	78	26	77	25	77	25
Mexico City	63	17	64	18	64	18
Monterrey	80	27	82	28	78	26
Oaxaca	69	21	68	20	68	20
Veracruz	81	27	81	27	80	27

	Oct.		Nov.		Dec.	
	F°	*C°*	*F°*	*C°*	*F°*	*C°*
Acapulco	81	27	81	27	78	26
Hermosillo	75	24	73	23	73	23
Manzanillo	84	29	79	26	78	26
Mérida	79	26	76	24	73	23
Mexicali	78	26	77	25	76	24
Mexico City	60	16	57	14	55	13
Monterrey	72	22	65	18	58	14
Oaxaca	65	18	64	18	65	18
Veracruz	79	26	75	24	73	23

Metric/U.S. Weight, Measure, Temperature Equivalents.
Mexico uses the metric system. Thus, throughout the text distances and
elevations have been followed in parentheses by their U.S. equivalents.
The following table is a quick reference for U.S. and metric equivalents.

Metric Unit	U.S. Equivalent	U.S. Unit	Metric Equivalent	
Length			**Length**	
1 kilometer	0.62 miles	1 mile	1.6	kilometers
1 meter	1.09 yards	1 yard	0.914	meters
1 decimeter	0.3 feet	1 foot	3.04	decimeters
1 centimeter	0.39 inches	1 inch	2.5	centimeters
Weight			**Weight**	
1 kilogram	2.2 pounds	1 pound	0.45	kilograms
1 gram	0.03 ounces	1 ounce	28.3	grams
Liquid Capacity			**Liquid Capacity**	
1 dekaliter	2.64 gallons	1 gallon	0.37	dekaliters
1 liter	1.05 quarts	1 quart	0.9	liters
1 liter	2.1 pints	1 pint	0.47	liters
Dry Measure			**Dry Measure**	
1 liter	0.9 quarts	1 quart	1.1	liters
1 liter	1.8 pints	1 pint	0.55	liters

To convert centigrade (C°) to Fahrenheit (F°):
$C° \times 9 \div 5 + 32 = F°$.
To convert Fahrenheit to centigrade:
$F° - 32 \times 5 \div 9 = C°$.

National Holidays. Listed below are the major national holidays in
Mexico. In addition, numerous fiestas and festivals are celebrated each
month; check with a travel agent for a complete schedule of calendar
dates.

January 1	New Year's Day
January 6	Twelfth Night, or Day of the Three Kings—traditional Christmas gift-giving day
February 5	Constitution Day—marks the signing of the Constitutions of 1857 and 1915

March 21	Birthday of Benito Juárez—remembered as the "Abraham Lincoln of Mexico"
May 1	Labor Day
May 5	Cinco de Mayo—commemorates the defeat of the French in 1862 in the Battle of Puebla
September 1	National Day—marks the president's State of the Union address and the official opening of Congress
September 16	Independence Day—commemorating Father Hidalgo's original cry for independence in 1810
October 12	Columbus Day, or the Día de la Raza, as it's called in Mexico
November 1–2	All Souls' Day and the Day of the Dead—highly important religious festivals in remembrance of the dead
November 20	Revolution Day—anniversary of the Revolution of 1910
December 1	Date of the presidential inauguration, which occurs every six years
December 12	Day of Our Lady of Guadalupe—in honor of Mexico's patroness saint
December 16	Christmas week, including *posadas* (reenactments of Mary and Joseph's trip to Bethlehem)
December 25	Christmas Day
Moveable festivals	Holy Week, which occurs prior to Easter, and Corpus Christi, which is celebrated at the end of December

Time Zones. Mexico is divided into three time zones: Central Standard Time, Mountain Pacific Time, and Pacific Standard Time. Most of the country lies in the Central Standard Time zone; if it's noon in New York, then it's 11:00 A.M. in Mexico City. If it's noon in London, it will be 6:00 A.M. in Mexico City. If it's noon in Melbourne, it will be 8:00 P.M. the previous day in Mexico City. Baja California Sur and the western states of Sonora, Sinaloa, and Nayarit are on Mountain Pacific Time, which is an hour earlier than Central Standard Time. Pacific Standard Time, which is two hours earlier than Central Standard Time, applies to Baja California Norte.

Passport and Visa Requirements. To enter Mexico, you must obtain a tourist card, which allows you to remain in Mexico for up to six months. The requirements for a tourist card are proof of citizenship (which may include a birth certificate, a voter's registration certification, or naturalization papers), a valid passport (not applicable to U.S. citizens, who may enter without one), and proof of financial solvency (i.e., traveller's checks). If you're not a U.S. or Canadian citizen, you must also receive approval from the Ministry of Government, Immigration Department, Dr. Jiménez 47, Col. Doctores, 06720, Mexico, D.F., tel. (915) 761–6286 or 761–5078. (Replacement cards may also be obtained at this address if you lose your tourist card.) U.S. citizens may visit border towns for up to 72 hours without a tourist card, but the card is required if you plan on making a longer trip into Mexico. Tourist cards can be procured from any government tourism office, Mexican consulates, the government border offices at any place of entry, your local travel agencies, and any airline associated with the International Air Transport Association (IATA). Children who are travelling alone, or with anyone other than their parents, are required to carry notarized permission.

Customs Entering Mexico. Visitors to Mexico may import the following duty-free: one carton of cigarettes; 50 cigars; 1.1 liters of alcohol/8.2 liters of beer; one still and one portable camera with 8 rolls of film each.

Customs Returning Home from Mexico. U.S. citizens returning from Mexico may declare $400 worth of purchases duty-free; for the next $1,000, there's a 10% duty tax. For goods exceeding $1,400, the duty rates vary. Specific arrangements can be made to combine individual allotments within a family of four to permit up to $1,600 in duty-free exports. You may also return with 200 cigarettes, 100 non-Cuban cigars, and one liter of alcohol. Another option is to mail packages under $50 duty-free, as long as they're not mailed to your own address. You can send only one package marked UNSOLICITED GIFT—VALUE UNDER $50 to each address during a 24-hour period. The U.S. has recently established the GSP, or Generalized System of Preferences, which allows a U.S. citizen to export particular items that exceed the $400 limit duty-free. A list can be obtained at a customs office. It is illegal to export any authentic archaeological artifacts from Mexico. There are many products that you may not bring back to the U.S. (e.g., plants, items made from tortoise shell, or certain animal skins, etc.). The U.S. Customs Service publishes a pamphlet called "Know Before You Go," that details prohibited products. To receive it, write to: U.S. Customs Service, Customs Information

Room 201, 6 World Trade Center, New York, N.Y. 10048; tel. (212) 466-5550.

Canadians may bring back duty-free purchases of $100, or $300 if they've been away for seven days or more. This includes 200 cigarettes, 50 cigars, 2 pounds of tobacco, and 40 oz. of liquor. Packages marked UNSOLICITED GIFT—VALUE UNDER $25 may be mailed to Canada duty-free.

British residents may return with $250 of duty-free purchases plus 200 cigarettes (or 50 cigars, or 250 grams of tobacco), 1 liter of alcohol over 38.8% proof (or 2 liters of alcohol not over 38.8% proof), 2 liters of table wine, and 50 grams of perfume.

Australian residents may return with $400 worth of duty-free purchases, 250 grams of tobacco, and one liter of alcohol.

Embassies and Consulates in Mexico. Help and information can be obtained at the following offices:

American Embassy
Paseo de la Reforma 305
06500, Mexico City, D.F.
tel. (915) 211–0042

Canadian Embassy
Schiller 529
11550, Mexico City, D.F.
tel. (915) 254–3288

British Embassy
Lerma 71
11550, Mexico City, D.F.
tel. (915) 511–4880

Australian Embassy
Plaza Polanco–Torre B–Piso 10
Jaime Balmes 11
Col. Los Morales
11510, Mexico City, D.F.
tel. (915) 395–9988

In addition to the above, there are consular offices throughout the country in the major cities and most of the touring areas.

Mexican Embassies and Consulates. Listed below are a few offices of the Mexican Embassy or Consulate.:

In the U.S.:	540 North LaSalle Street Chicago, IL 60611 tel. (312) 670–0240
	8 East 41st Street New York, N.Y. 10017 tel. (212) 689–0456
	125 Paseo de la Plaza Los Angeles, CA 90012 tel. (213) 624–3261
In Canada:	130 Albert Street, Suite 206 Ottawa, Ontario QAP SG Canada tel. (613) 233–8988
In Great Britain:	8 Halkin Street London, England SW 1 tel. (01) 235-6393
In Australia:	14 Perth Avenue Canberra, Australia ACT 2600 tel. (062) 73–3905

Ministry of Tourism. The offices listed below can provide you with detailed information on various tourist issues, from general problems such as renewing a lost tourist card to obtaining good road maps.

In Mexico:	Ministry of Tourism Avenida Presidente Masaryk 172 11550, Mexico City, D.F. open Monday–Friday, 8:00 A.M. to 7:00 P.M. tel. (915) 250–8555 or 250–4298 24-hour hotline for tourists: (915) 250–0123
In the U.S.:	2 Illinois Center 233 North Michigan Avenue, Suite 1413 Chicago, IL 60601 tel. (312) 565–2785
	405 Park Avenue, Suite 1002 New York, N.Y. 10022 tel. (212) 755–7261

10100 Santa Monica Blvd., Suite 224
Los Angeles, CA 90067
tel. (213) 203–8151

In Canada: 1 Place Ville Marie, Suite 2409
Montreal, Quebec
H3B 3M9 Canada
tel. (514) 871–1052

181 University Avenue, Suite 1112
Toronto, Ontario
M5H 3M7 Canada
tel. (416) 364–2455

700 West Georgia Street
Vancouver, B.C.
V7Y 1B6 Canada
tel. (604) 682–0551

In Great Britain: 7 Cork Street
London, England W 1
tel. (01) 734–1058 or 734–1059

There is no Mexican Tourist Office in Australia.

Getting to Mexico by Air. The major international carriers that service Mexico from the United States are Air Canada, Air France, American, Continental, Mexicana, Northwest, Pan Am, TWA, United, and Western. The carriers that fly from Canada include Air Canada and Japan Airlines. Iberia Airlines, KLM Airlines, and British Airways all fly to Mexico from Great Britain, with connections in the U.S. There are no direct flights to Mexico from Australia; most airlines, like Quantas or Australian Airlines, make stops in Los Angeles or London, and you must change airlines to complete your trip.

For more extensive information, write to Consumer Reports for their travel letter, which includes information on discount package tours, current air fares, rental cars, et cetera. The address is: Consumer Reports Travel Letter, Box 5248, Boulder, CO 80322. (A year's subscription is $37.)

There's a variety of ever-changing special fares and package deals that depend upon the season, the amount of time you plan to spend in Mexico, the number of places you wish to visit, et cetera. Keep an eye on the advertisements in your local newspaper's travel section and make your travel arrangements through a reliable travel agent or tour operator to get the best fares and packages available.

Getting to Mexico by Boat. There are a number of cruise lines that offer package deals to Mexico. Listed below are some of the more popular ones:

Admiral Cruises
1220 Biscayne Blvd.
Miami, FL 33101
tel. (800) 327–0271

Carnival Cruise Line
5225 N.W. 87 Avenue
Miami, FL 33166
tel. (800) 327–9501

Exploration Cruise Lines
1500 Metropolitan Park Bldg.
Seattle, WA 98101
tel. (800) 426–0600

Holland American Lines
300 Elliott Avenue West
Seattle, WA 98119
tel. (800) 426–0327

Norwegian Caribbean Lines
2 Alahambra Place
Coral Gables, FL 33134
tel. (800) 327–7030

Princess Cruises
2029 Century Park East
Los Angeles, CA 90067
tel. (800) 533–1770

Royal Viking Line
750 Battery Street
San Francisco, CA 94111
tel. (800) 422–8000

Sitmar Cruises
10100 Santa Monica Blvd.
Los Angeles, CA 90067
tel. (800) 421–0880

Special Expeditions
720 Fifth Avenue
New York, N.Y. 10019
tel. (800) 762–0003

Getting to Mexico by Rail. Railroad lines that run to Mexico include the Aztec Eagle, which departs from Nuevo Laredo (just across the Río Grande from Laredo, Texas) and goes to Mexico City, and Amtrak, which originates in Chicago and stops overnight in Nuevo Laredo before continuing into Mexico. For more information on rail connections, contact the National Railways of Mexico, 1500 Broadway, New York, N.Y. 10036.

Getting to Mexico by Car. If you plan to drive your own car in Mexico, you must have proof of ownership, a valid driver's license, and registration in order to obtain a tourist's car permit at the border. (Your car may not be resold while in Mexico.)

Only Mexican automobile insurance is valid in Mexico; therefore, it's highly advisable to purchase the most comprehensive insurance policy available. Any package should include liability and property damage coverage, physical liability, and theft insurance, and should be guaranteed by a reputable Mexican firm. (In the case of an accident, this will assure the police of your ability to cover the cost of any damages incurred.) The Mexican Insurance Commission sets policy rates.

Listed below are the major highways leading into Mexico from towns along the border. All are accessed by the U.S. interstate highway system. U.S. 89 ends in Arizona just across the border from Nogales, where it becomes Mexico Highway 15 and heads south to the coast and Mazatlán; Ciudad Juárez, across the border from El Paso, is the starting point for Highway 45 (also known as the Interamerican Highway), which drops south through Chihuahua, Torreón, Durango, and Zacatecas on its way to Mexico City; Highway 57 begins across the border from Eagle Pass, Texas, and continues to San Luís Potosí. Highway 180 runs along the Gulf coast from Matamoros to Veracruz; and from Laredo, Texas, take Highway 85 to Monterrey, then Highway 40 to Saltillo, where you can pick up Highway 57 to San Luís Potosí.

Hotels and Other Accommodations. Mexico offers lodging of all kinds in all price ranges, especially in the major cities and resorts. Accommodations run the gamut from luxury hotels, some featuring bold, modern architecture, to comfortable hotels in old *haciendas* or Colonial-style buildings, to boarding houses (*casas de huespedes*). The price of the room generally covers basic lodging only (no meals). Hotels in Mexico are categorized as Gran Turismo (Super Deluxe), Deluxe, First Class, Moderate, and Inexpensive. Each hotel is rated by the Ministry of Tourism, which also regulates prices on accommodations throughout the country.

Most hotels in major cities and resort areas accept credit cards; smaller hotels and guesthouses in the countryside may not, however. High-season prices are in effect from the middle of November to the end of May. At other times, prices are 10–30 percent less.

We have classified accommodations in the Town-by-Town section (see page 337) using the following categories:

🏨🏨🏨 Luxury (Gran Turismo and Deluxe)
🏨🏨🏨 First Class
🏨🏨 Moderate
🏨 Inexpensive

Colonial hotels/haciendas: The many private estates (*haciendas*) and monasteries from Mexico's Colonial period that have been converted into hotels are usually romantic and often expensive places to stay. *Haciendas* were once the spoils of the Spanish *conquistadors*, who received them as rewards for their services rendered a grateful crown. Most were destroyed by peasant armies during the Revolution, and newer accommodations have been built on their ruins. Often, these country hotels are popular weekend resorts for Mexican city-dwellers, so advance reservations are advisable.

Apartments and pensiones: In larger cities, you can usually find listings for short-term furnished apartments, which you may find convenient if you intend to spend a lot of time in one place. Reasonably priced *pensiones* (boarding houses) offering simple, clean accommodations also abound in Mexico, and frequently provide meals.

Currency Regulations and Credit Cards. The Mexican monetary unit is the peso, which is composed of 100 centavos. The government issues bank notes for 500, 1,000, 2,000, 5,000, 10,000, and 20,000 pesos, and coins in denominations of 20 and 50 centavos, and 1, 5, 10, 20, 50, 100, and 200 pesos. The peso rate fluctuates, with Mexico's recent economic problems contributing to its continued devaluation. Try to change only as much money as needed into Mexican currency, since it's difficult to convert large sums back into dollars. Non-U.S. residents should carry traveller's checks in U.S. dollars to facilitate their transactions. You'll usually find the best rates of exchange in banks, but money exchanges (*cambios de moneda*) frequently offer competitive rates.

Hotels, car-rental agencies, and many large stores and boutiques accept major credit cards. Personal checks are quite another matter; it's practically impossible to cash them.

Business Hours and Closings. Banks are generally open Monday through Friday from 9:00 A.M. to 1:30 P.M., and occasionally on Saturday mornings. All banks are closed on national holidays. Most business offices are open Monday through Friday, 9:00 A.M. to 2:00 P.M., then close for a two-hour *siesta* period, and re-open from 4:00 to 7:00 P.M. Stores are usually open from 10:00 A.M. to 7:00 P.M. Museums, monasteries, and archaeological sites are generally open Tuesday to Saturday, 9:00 A.M. to 5:00 P.M. (or 10:00 A.M. to 6:00 P.M.), and Sundays 10:00 A.M. to 4:00 P.M.

Postage. Post offices in large cities are open from 8:00 A.M. to 6:00 P.M., Monday through Friday. Postcards and airmail up to 20 grams (0.7 ounces) going to the U.S. and Canada cost 100 pesos. Mail to all other destinations outside the country costs 140 pesos. Mail in Mexico is infamous for being slow, particularly outside urban areas; to improve the likelihood that your mail will arrive at its intended destination, post your letters in major cities or airports.

Telephone. You can dial long distance directly from your hotel in Mexico; however, there'll a 39-percent tax, plus an additional 15-percent IVA (Value Added) tax figured into your bill. It is possible to make cheaper calls at a long-distance concessionary (*caseta de larga distancía*). You can only make local phone calls (1 peso) from pay phones, however.

Listed below are numbers for basic information:

Long distance operator (within Mexico):	02
International operator (English-speaking):	09
Local information:	04
Time:	03
Ambulance:	557–5758/59
Police:	06
Fire department	768–3700
Telegrams (international):	519–5929
Tourism hotline (Mexico City):	250–0123

Travelling in Mexico. *Taxis:* Despite a recent law requiring meters in taxis, few have them. For your own protection, negotiate the fare *before* you enter a cab. In metered cabs, the average fare starts at 180 pesos, with an additional 90 pesos for each kilometer (0.6 miles) travelled. Service at night costs approximately 10 percent more. *Colectivos,* or vans, are another way to get around town; they operate along set routes (usually from airports into cities), and cost less than taxis. It's customary not to tip a cab driver unless he performs a special service for you.

Buses: Travelling around by bus is relatively inexpensive, and falls into three categories: first class, second class, and local. You should always try to travel on air-conditioned first-class buses, especially for long-distance trips—you'll be glad you did. Some also have restroom facilities. You should also be aware that in some towns there are different stations for each bus company and category, so double check to avoid confusion. Buses generally run on time, due in part to very speedy drivers who do not seem daunted by even the most twisting mountain road. If you have bad nerves or difficulties with your stomach, you should seriously consider taking the train.

Try to purchase tickets on the day of your departure, or have them delivered to your hotel by phoning Central de Autobuses, tel. (915) 533–2047/49. In Mexico City, most of the larger bus lines are located at one of the newly built super-terminals: the Northern Terminal (Terminal Central del Norte), Av. de los 100 Metros 4907; the Southern Terminal (Terminal Central del Sur), Tasquena 1320; the Eastern Terminal (Terminal Central del Oriente), Calzada Ignacio Zaragoza 200; or the Western Terminal (Terminal Central del Poniete), Av. Sur 122.

Greyhound Bus lines are also located in Mexico City at Paseo de la Reforma 27, tel. (915) 535–4200/2618.

Trains. Train travel through Mexico will expose you to some of the world's most heartbreakingly beautiful vistas. The only drawbacks are that the trains are not always punctual, and they usually won't get you to where you want to go any faster than buses.

Nevertheless, you can obtain a schedule before your trip by writing to the Mexican Railway System, 1500 Broadway, Suite 810, New York, N.Y. 10036, or to the National Railways of Mexico, Av. Central 140, 06356, Mexico, D.F.

Once in Mexico City you can obtain a schedule at the main railroad station (*Estación Buenavista*) located on Av. Insurgentes Norte. Reservations can be made in Mexico City at Aviamex, Paseo de la Reforma, and in Chihuahua at Expresso Cañon del Cobre, V. Carranza 505. Below is a list of the four major railroads in Mexico:

Ferrocarriles Nacionales de Mexico
Estación Buenavista Departamento de
Trafico de Pasajeros
06358, Mexico, D.F.
tel. (915) 547–1084/1097

Ferrocarriles del Pacifico
Av. Central 140–Piso 6 ALA "C"
06358, Mexico, D.F.
tel. (915) 547–8545/6939

Ferrocarriles Sonora–Baja California
Av. Central 140–Piso 6 ALA "C"
06358, Mexico, D.F.
tel. (915) 547–8545/6939

Ferrocarriles Chihuahua-Pacifico
Av. Central 140–Piso 6 ALA "C"
06358, Mexico, D.F.
tel. (915) 547–8545/6939

One of the most breathtaking railroad routes anywhere goes through Copper Canyon. The train leaves from Ojinaga in northern Chihuahua, climbs the mountain peaks of the Sierra Madre Occidental, crosses the Continental Divide three times (stopping at the *divisadero* to give passengers an unforgettable view of a canyon whose span is four times greater than that of the Grand Canyon), and descends into the state of Sinaloa on its way to the coastal city of Los Mochis.

Other scenic train routes include Mexico City to Veracruz, which crosses the Sierra Madre Oriental and descends into lush countryside and tropical jungles, and Mexico City to Mérida, which passes by many of Mexico's most majestic architectural ruins.

Ferry Service. Ferry service for passengers and vehicles is provided between Mazatlán–La Paz; Puerto Vallarta–Cabo San Lucas; Guaymas –Santa Rosalía; Topolobampo–La Paz; and Puerto Morales–Cozumel. Schedules and rates can be obtained from the Servicio de Transbordadores, Juan de la Barrera 63, 06410, Mexico City, D.F.

Car Rental. While it is probably less expensive to bring your own car into Mexico, renting one may save yours from the rather poorly maintained condition of most Mexican roads. Car-rental agencies at the major airports include Avis, Budget, Hertz, National, and Quick Rent-a-Car. Remember: It's extremely important to purchase a comprehensive insurance policy that includes protection against robbery or other potential damage. Occasionally, airport car-rental agencies will not have enough cars in stock; be sure to reserve ahead rather than waiting until you arrive—even with a reservation, there are no guarantees.

Driving in Mexico. Driving through Mexico can be a highly pleasurable experience, but the key is to practice defensive driving. Because of the potential difficulties you can encounter during a road trip, you should plan ahead carefully and acquaint yourself with Spanish road signs.

Whether driving your own car or a rental, it's mandatory to have a comprehensive insurance policy protecting you and your car. In an accident, you will more than likely be jailed if you cannot prove your ability to cover damages. It's also good advice to wait until official assistance comes rather than settle matters yourself in the event of an accident. (In Mexico, you can be held responsible if you try to help an accident victim and the person dies.)

Mexican roads are infamous for their gaping potholes and unfinished sections. Pack a repair kit that includes everything from a tire pump and water for the radiator to extra fan belts and spark plugs.

Be sure to check road conditions before you proceed on a trip. In the rainy season, mud and torrential rains can make roads impassable, even the major highways. Always build in extra time for unexpected obstacles—including roads blocked by farm animals—that may slow you down. Avoid night driving as a rule, especially on dark country roads where animals who've wandered onto the road are a constant threat. Bear in mind, too, that some areas are unsafe at night; assaults and muggings are not unknown.

Gasoline is controlled and regulated by the Mexican government; Pemex, the government-owned oil company, franchises all gas stations. Unleaded 92 octane gas, called Extra, is frequently, though not always, available. Leaded 81 octane gas, called Nova, is always available. Gas stations accept pesos *only* (no credit cards or U.S. dollars). And it's customary to tip gas station attendants (see page 332).

You can get a good road map of Mexico from the Mexican Ministry of Tourism, or you can write away for the *Atlas de Carreteras,* a road atlas, from Guía Rojí, SA de CV, Calle Republica de Colombia 23, 06020, Mexico, D.F.

If your car breaks down on one of the major roadways, you can signal the emergency service trucks (called "Green Angels") by raising your hood. The fleet patrols the highways daily from 7:00 A.M. to 8:00 P.M. You can also call Mexico's automobile clubs, the AMA (*Asociacion Mexicana Automovilistica*) and the ANA (*Asociacion Nacional Automovilistica*), both of which are affiliated with the American Automobile Association. The AMA's main offices are at Orizaba 7, 06700, Mexico, D.F., tel. (905) 528–5815 or 588–7055.

There are four road types in Mexico: *autopistas* (superhighways), which connect the larger towns and cities; *rutas federales* (federal highways); *rutas estatales* (state highways maintained by individual states); and secondary roads, which are unpaved. Speed limits are 110 km. (68 mph) or 100 km. (62 mph) on highways, 80 km. (50 mph) on federal highways, and 40 km. (25 mph) on secondary roads.

Watch out for *topes*, or speed bumps, meant to encourage you to slow down. You'll encounter them here and there, but particularly as you approach towns.

The following is a list of common road signs and their meanings:

Road Sign	Meaning
Aduana	Customs
Alto	Stop
Aparcamiento	Parking lot
Arena suelta	Loose gravel
Atencion (or *Cuidado*)	Caution
Autopista	Superhighway
Avenida	Avenue, wide road
Bifurcacion	Junction, or fork in road
Calzada	Road
Camino angosto	Narrow road
Canada	Track for livestock
Carretera	Highway
Carretera de Cuota	Turnpike
Caseta de cobra	Toll booth
Ceda el paso	Yield
Cerro	Hill
Curva peligroso	Dangerous Bend
Derrumbes	Landslide zone
Despacio	Slow down
Desviacion	Detour
Circulacion	One-way traffic
Estacionamento	Parking
Hombres trabajando	Men working
Llevar la derecha (or *la izquierdo*)	Keep right (or left)
No rebase	Do not pass
Paso prohibido	No entry
Peaje (*Cuota*)	Toll
Peatones	Pedestrians
Peligro	Danger
Playa	Beach
Preferencia	One-way street
Topes	Speed bumps
Transbordador	Ferry

Tipping. Tipping is standard practice here, even for services you wouldn't ordinarily cover at home. (Tipping helps to stretch a small Mexican salary a long way.) The following guidelines may help you determine who and what to tip: bellhops receive 300 pesos per bag, 500 pesos a day to the maid; 50–100 pesos to someone who offers to watch your car (this ensures it won't be vandalized on the street); 500–1,000 pesos a day for tour guides; 100–200 pesos to gas station attendants; and 200 pesos to theater ushers. Cab drivers receive tips only if they perform a special service for you.

Health. To avoid the intestinal bugs variously nicknamed "Montezuma's Revenge" or "the Aztec two-step," which occur as a result of the different bacteria in Mexican water, you're better off avoiding unbottled water (to the point of not even brushing your teeth with it). It's probably also wise not to eat raw, unpeeled fruits or vegetables, or prepared foods from open market stands. If you do succumb to Montezuma's Revenge (and most visitors who stay for any length of time will), effective over-the-counter anti-diarretics such as Kaomycin and Kaopectate are widely available. In more severe cases, a paregoric such as Lomotil or Vibramincin can be prescribed by a physician.

Sunburn is another health concern. Remember, the intensity of the sun and heat in Mexico easily rivals most tropical climates. With the recent health warnings concerning skin cancer, you should take along a good sunblock, sunglasses, and a hat. Also, be sure to drink plenty of liquids to avoid dehydration.

Restaurants. All types of service are available in Mexico, from elegant restaurants to simple street-side carts or beach-side booths under a palm roof. Although the temptations will be many, food served on the streets is not recommended for anyone with a sensitive stomach. If you nevertheless find yourself caught up in the spirit of Mexican *machismo,* a few simple rules will serve you well: Stay away from uncooked greens and vegetables, peel all fruit, avoid dairy products (unless you're sure they've been pasteurized), and don't drink the water (unless it's been purified). You can bet on most soups (which in Mexico are delicious) being safe, as are breads, candy, eggs, beans, meat, poultry, and fish.

Even in Mexico City there are small, reasonably priced restaurants offering complete fast-food (Mexican-style) menus for working people. You'll find the cheapest prices at the *fondas* in the covered markets, where the hygiene is often better than its reputation. When in doubt, however, a glance into the open tiled kitchen will give you an idea of what (or what not) to expect. One more word about prices: Even the simplest dishes in the resort areas of the coast will be far more expensive than their cousins in the highlands.

If you're staying in a hotel, you'll always be able to get the same old

Continental breakfast of coffee, juice, toast, butter, and jam. Or you can do as most Mexicans do and start the day with heartier fare. National favorites include *huevos revueltos,* scrambled eggs with pieces of tomatoes and chiles, *huevos rancheros,* eggs scrambled and then baked with a tomato sauce, or *huevos estrallados,* fried eggs on a tortilla with a spicy tomato sauce—any of them just the thing to get your motor started for a long day of sightseeing and shopping. If you want a treat, ask for *café de olla,* coffee that is freshly brewed in an earthenware pot and flavored with brown sugar, cinnamon, and cloves. Tea drinkers will be surprised to find that tea is rare, even in the best hotels. If you can't do without, try one of the many herb teas available, or bring a few bags of your favorite type along.

Breakfast is dawdled over by most Mexicans, since it must last until lunch, the *comida,* which is eaten between 2 and 4 P.M. and is the main meal of the day. Both meals, even in the least expensive restaurants, consist of several courses (the *comida corrida* is a five-course extravagaza widely available), but, of course, dishes can be ordered individually. Not surprisingly, dinner is also served relatively late in the European style, usually after eight, and is quite leisurely.

A final remark concerning public establishments in Mexico. Apart from hotel lounges or specially marked "ladies' bars," the typical Mexican *cantina* is still off-limits to women. If a visitor should go ahead and damn the torpedoes, she should not be surprised to find everything made for the male half of the species—including the public facilities.

Sports. Mexico is a hub for aquatic sports such as waterskiing, sailing, windsurfing, snorkeling, and deep-sea diving and fishing. The mountainous regions offer excellent hiking and climbing opportunities. Spectator sports include boxing, wrestling, soccer, and jai alai. The *charreada,* the Mexican equivalent of a rodeo, is a popular spectator event. Cockfighting also draws large crowds, but the most widely attended spectator sport is bullfighting, and bullfighting arenas (*Plaza de Toros*) can be found in every large town and city; bullfights, or *corridas,* are usually held on Sundays and public holidays.

Shopping. While in Mexico, expect to find some wonderful items for sale that reflect Mexicans' unique sensitivity to color, style, and design. Native crafts are usually less expensive in local markets—where bargaining with vendors is an honored tradition—than they are in city shops. Fortunately, Mexico abounds with outdoor markets offering a huge variety of handmade items. You'll find beautiful garments such as *huipils* (embroidered dresses), *huraches, rebozos* (special shawls woven of wool, silk, or cotton), and *serapes* in almost every good-sized town you visit. If you so choose, you can spend a bit more money for fine hand-worked jewelry made from gold, silver, semi-precious stones, and other gems. Mexico is also famous for its traditional pottery and lacquerware featuring bright, striking colors and complex geometric patterns.

Different areas of the country are renowned for producing different specialties. You can find wonderful *guayabaras* (a cotton sport shirt with a pleated front) for men in both Acapulco and the cities of the Gulf coast, where they serve as perfect antidotes to the hot weather. At Guadalajara's Mercado Libertad, that city's central outdoor market, you can find a variety of items, from ceramics to hand-blown glassware to *rebozos*. Jocotepec is known for the quality of its white wool *serapes*. Mazatlán specializes in American designer clothing. Mérida offers a wide selection of straw goods including hammocks and Panama hats, as well as gold and silver filigree. Mexico City boasts superb hand-blown glass. Monterrey is known for its full-leaded crystal, and Morelia offers fine folk art and lacquerware. Oaxaca's excellent crafts center has a variety of items ranging from exquisite pottery to intricate jewelry. The Indian market at Pátzcuaro offers lacquerwork and embroidery of superior quality, and Paracho is famous for its handmade guitars. Puebla's main craft is its pottery, which is accented with an enamel glaze that is manufactured according to a recipe that dates to the days of the Conquest. Puerto Vallarta sells excellent tequila, Querétaro offers fine gems, and Saltillo, like Jocotepec, makes beautiful *serapes*. San Miguel de Allende is renowned for all kinds of things, including weaving, sculpture, and handicrafts. Taxco's major offering is silver, and Tijuana sells quality liquor, expensive crystal, and hand-blown glass. Tlaxcala and Toluca both offer fine woven articles, and Uriapan specializes in lacquerware.

Mexican design ranges from the ethereal—exemplified by the predominance of angels in much of its artwork—to the funereal, which is personified by the *pan de muerto* and skeleton-shaped confections offered in the weeks preceding All Souls' Day. Patterns on embroidered clothing are often highly complicated, with symbolism varying according to the particular region in which the clothing is made.

Do not buy anything that's touted as a genuine archaeological relic; more often than not it will be fake, and if it is authentic, it's illegal to take it out of the country. Be wary of designer items, as well, for they may be imitations. Any pottery you buy should not be used for cooking, due to the high lead content of the materials sometimes used in the manufacture of these goods. Silver should be marked clearly with a stamp—STERLING or .925, which indicates the amount of grams of silver per every 1,000 grams of weight.

Clothing sizes correspond to those used in the U.S., but tend to run a bit smaller. A conversion chart follows:

		U.S.	U.K.	Europe
Chest	*Small*	34	34	87
	Medium	36	36	91
		38	38	97
	Large	40	40	102
		42	42	107
	Extra Large	44	44	112
		46	46	117
Collar		14	14	36
		$14^1/_2$	$14^1/_2$	37
		15	15	38
		$15^1/_2$	$15^1/_2$	39
		16	16	41
		$16^1/_2$	$16^1/_2$	42
		17	17	43
Waist		24	24	61
		26	26	66
		28	28	71
		30	30	76
		32	32	80
		34	34	87
		36	36	91
		38	38	97
Men's suits		34	34	44
		35	35	46
		36	36	48
		37	37	$49^1/_2$
		38	38	51
		39	39	$52^1/_2$
		40	40	54
		41	41	$55^1/_2$
		42	42	57
Men's shoes		7	6	$39^1/_2$
		8	7	41
		9	8	42
		10	9	43
		11	10	$44^1/_2$
		12	11	46
		13	12	47
Men's hats		$6^3/_4$	$6^5/_8$	54
		$6^7/_8$	$6^3/_4$	55
		7	$6^7/_8$	56
		$7^1/_8$	7	57
		$7^1/_4$	$7^1/_8$	58
		$7^1/_2$	$7^3/_8$	60

	U.S.	U.K.	Europe
Women's dresses	6	8	36
	8	10	38
	10	12	40
	12	14	42
	14	16	44
	16	18	46
	18	20	48
Women's blouses and sweaters	8	10	38
	10	12	40
	12	14	42
	14	16	44
	16	18	46
	18	20	48
Women's shoes	4½	3	35½
	5	3½	36
	5½	4	36½
	6	4½	37
	6½	5	37½
	7	5½	38
	7½	6	38½
	8	6½	39
	8½	7	39½
	9	7½	40
Children's clothing *(One size larger for knitwear)*	2	16	92
	3	18	98
	4	20	104
	5	22	110
	6	24	116
	6X	26	122
Children's shoes	8	7	24
	9	8	25
	10	9	27
	11	10	28
	12	11	29
	13	12	30
	1	13	32
	2	1	33
	3	2	34
	4½	3	36
	5½	4	37
	6½	5½	38½

Town-by-Town

This section is organized alphabetically by town. To help you locate each town in this large country, we've also identified the state in which it is situated. Each listing provides information on tourist offices, air and ground transportation, including connections to other cities, and accommodations. Hotels are classified according to our own rating system which is based on the one used by Mexico's Ministry of Tourism (see page 323 for a full explanation).

Acapulco (Guerrero)

Information: Costera Miguel Alemán 187 (opposite Hotel El Cid). **Transportation:** *Air:* The one-way price of a taxi from the airport to the city costs as much as a roundtrip fare. Airport bus. Mexico City, USA, Canada. *Bus:* 1st-class bus station Estrella de Oro, Av. Cuauhtémoc 1490; 2nd-class bus station Flecha Roja, Av. Cuauhtémoc 97. Mexico City, Taxco, Pto. Escondido and Pié de la Cuesta. **Accommodations:** 🏨🏨🏨 (*Luxury*) Acapulco Plaza, Costera Miguel Alemán; Acapulco Princess and Pierre Marqués, Playa Revolcadero; Las Brisas, Carretera Escénica 5255. 🏨🏨🏨 The international hotel chain of *Costera Miguel Alemán* (*CMA*); Acapulco Malibú, CMA 20; El Presidente, CMA; La Palapa, Fragata Yucatán 210; El Cano, CMA. 🏨🏨 Caleta, Playa Caleta (traditional small hotel is an inlet); De Gante, CMA 265; El Mirador, Quebrada 74; Los Pericos, CMA 255. 🏨 Gran Motel Acapulco, CMA 127; Lindavista, Playa Caleta; San Francisco, CMA 219; Villa Sofía, CMA 53.

Aguascalientes (Aguascalientes)

Information: In Hotel Francia. **Transportation:** *Train:* Mexico City, Cd. Juárez. *Bus:* Central bus station, Av. Circunvalación Sur. 12 bus lines go to Mexico's major cities. **Accommodations:** 🏨🏨🏨 Francia, Av. Madero/Plaza Principal; Motel Castel las Trojes, Ctra. Panamericana Norte (outside Club Campestre). 🏨🏨 Río Grande, José María Chavéz 101 (by the plaza); Motel Medrano, José María Chávez 904. 🏨 Señorial, Colón 104; San José, Hidalgo 104. **Spas:** Thermal baths. Ojo Caliente.

Ajijic (Jalisco)
See Lake Chapala.

Barra de Navidad/Melaque (Jalisco)

Information: In Hotel Tropical. **Transportation:** *Bus:* Manzanillo, Puerto Vallarta, Guadalajara. **Accommodations:** 🏨🏨🏨 Cabo Blanco, Armada/Puerto Navidad. 🏨🏨 Tropical, López de Legazpi 96; Melaque, Paseo de la Primavera, Melaque. 🏨 Barra de Navidad, López de Legazpi; Delfin, Morelos 23. Other inns (mostly family hotels) are in Melaque.

Barranca del Cobre

Transportation: *Train:* Los Mochis–Chihuahua. For accommodations, *see Cerocahui, Creel, Cuauhtémoc, Divisadero Barrancas and El Fuerte.*

Cabo San Lucas (Baja California Sur)

Transportation: *Bus:* La Paz, Tijuana. *Boat:* Puerto Vallarta. **Accommodations:** 🏨🏨🏨 (*Luxury*) Cabo San Lucas; Hacienda del Cabo. 🏨🏨🏨 Finisterra; Solmar; Twin Dolphin, toward San José. 🏨🏨 Mar de Cortéz. 🏨 Marina, Malecón; Mi Ranchito, Guerrero y Marina. *See also San José del Cabo.*

Campeche (Campeche)

Information: By the Palacio de Gobierno, on the beach promenade. **Transportation:** *Train:* Palenque, Mexico City. *Bus:* Mérida, Uxmal, Villahermosa. **Accommodations:** 🏨🏨🏨 El Presidente, Av. Ruíz Cortines 51; Baluartes, Av. Ruíz Cortines. 🏨🏨 América, C. 10 No. 252. 🏨 Castellmar, C. 61 No. 2; López, C. 12 No. 189.

Cancún (Quintana Roo)

Information: Centro Comercial Cancún, Av. Tulúm. **Transportation:** *Air:* Mérida, Monterrey, Mexico City, USA. *Bus:* Archaeological zones around Chetumal, Mérida, Mexico City. *Boat:* Cozumel, Isla Mujeres (hydrofoil, glassbottom boat). **Accommodations:** 🏨🏨🏨 (*Luxury*) Camino Real, Punta Cancún; Cancún Sheraton, Paseo Kukulkán (lote 18); Krystal, Paseo Kukulkán (lotes 9/9a); Misión Miramar, Paseo Kukulkán. 🏨🏨🏨 El Presidente, Blvd. Cancún 7; Fiesta Americana, Playa Caracoles; Hyatt Cancún Caribe. 🏨🏨 Calinda Cancún, Paseo Kukulkán; Bojórquez, Paseo Kukulkán; Suites Dos Playas, Paseo Kukulkán. 🏨 Carrillos, Claveles 2 y 4, supermanzana 22 (in the city center); Komvaser, Av. Yaxchilán 15 (inner city; pool).

Catemaco (Veracruz)

Transportation: *Bus:* Veracruz (transfer in San Andres Tuxtla). **Accommodations:** 🏨🏨 Finca, as you enter the city coming from Villahermosa; Posada Konipan and Hotel del Lago, both on the shore promenade Malecón. 🏨 Cristal, C. Madero; Fonseca, C. Madero.

Cerocahui

Transportation: *Train:* Train station Bahuichivo (12.5 km., 8 miles, away), Los Mochis, Chihuahua. *Bus:* Bus to train station from Hotel Misión. **Accommodations:** 🏨🏨 Misión, Reserv. Hotel Sta. Anita, Los Mochis.

Lake Chapala Area (Jalisco)

Transportation: *Bus:* Guadalajara. **Accommodations:** 🏨🏨🏨 Hotel Real de Chapala, Paseo del Prado 20, Ajijic (pool); Brisas de Chapala, between Chapala and Ajijic (tennis, golf, pool). 🏨🏨 Nido, Madero 202, Chapala (pool); Nuevo Hotel Chapala, Madero 200, Chapala; Hotel Posada Ajijic, 16 de Sept. 2, Ajijic (pool); Motel San Juan Cosalá, about 5 km. (3 miles) west of Ajijic going toward Jocotepec. 🏨 Chapala Haciendas Hotel, off the highway between Guadalajara–Chapala (pool); Motel la Carreta, Colón 7, Ajijic.

Chetumal (Quintana Roo)

Transportation: *Air:* Intra-Mexican flight connections. *Bus:* Cancún, Mérida, Villahermosa; Belize City (Belize). **Accommodations:** 🏨🏨🏨 El Presidente, Av. Héroes 138 (central). 🏨🏨 Continental, Av. Héroes 171. 🏨 María Dolores, Av. A. Obregón 183; Laguna, Blvd. Costera 143, Laguna de Bacalar (seaside hotel, no telephone).

Chichén Itzá (Yucatán)

Transportation: *Bus:* Mérida, Puerto Juárez. **Accommodations:** 🏨🏨🏨 Hacienda Chichén, Zona arqueológica (former hacienda); Hotel Misión; Mayaland, Zona arqueológica. 🏨🏨 Villa Arqueológica, Zona arqueológica. 🏨 Dolores Alba (outside town); Posada Novelo.

Chihuahua (Chihuahua)

Information: Av. Universidad 505. **Transportation:** *Air:* Airport 20 km. (12 miles) outside town, mini-bus; major cities in Mexico, USA. *Train:* Los Mochis. Reservations, Expresso Cañón del Cobre, V. Carranza 505. *Bus:* Bus station about 20 km. (12 miles) outside town (buses in city center). Ciudad Juárez, Zacatecas, Mexico City, Cd. Cuauhtémoc. **Accommodations:** 🏨🏨🏨 Castel Sicomoro, Blvd. Ortíz Mena 411; El Presidente, Libertad 9; Exelaris Hyatt, Av. Independencia 500. 🏨🏨 Nueva Avenida, Av. Juárez/V. Carranza; Victoria, Av. Juárez/Colón. 🏨 Casa Blanca, Av. Vicente Guerrero 1205; Reforma, Victoria 809. For hotel reservations, contact *Cabaña Divisadero,* Barranca del Corbre: Aldama 407-C, tel. 23362.

Cholula (Puebla)

Transportation: *Bus:* Puebla. **Accommodations:** 🏨🏨 Villas Arqueológicas, 2 Poniente 601 (by the pyramid); Calli Quetzalcoatl, Portal Guerrero 11. 🏨 Las Américas, 14 Oriente 102.

Ciudad Juárez (Chihuahua)

Information: Av. Lerdo. **Transportation:** *Train:* Mexico City. *Bus:* Chihuahua, Mexico City. **Accommodations:** 🏨🏨🏨 Camino Real, Centro

Commercial PRONAF; Rodeway Inn, Lincoln/Coyoacán. 🏠 San Antonio, 16 de Septiembre 634 Ote.

Ciudad Lázaro Cárdenas (Michoacán)
Information: Guillermo Prieto 42, tel. 20576. **Transportation:** *Bus:* Bus station, Av. Lázaro Cárdenas. **Accommodations:** 🏠🏠🏠 Costa Brava, Nicolás Bravo 475; Hacienda Jacarandas, Ctra. L. Cárdenas–La Orilla; María Margarita, Corregidora/8 de Mayo. 🏠🏠 Internacional, Matamoros 508; Las Truchas, J. Mina 50; Plaza, Morelos/Nicolás Bravo. 🏠 Atzimba, Allende 219; Delfin, Av. L. Cárdenas/J. Mina; De la Curva, Vicente Guerrero.

Ciudad Obregón (Sonora)
Transportation: *Air:* Guadalajara, Mexico City and other Mexican cities, Los Angeles (USA). *Bus:* Guaymas, Hermosillo, Los Mochis, Guadalajara. **Accommodations:** 🏠🏠🏠 Valle Grande, Miguel Alemán/Tetabiate; Motel Costa de Oro, Miguel Alemán 201 N. 🏠🏠 San Jorge, Miguel Alemán 929 N. 🏠 Kuraica, 5 de Febrero 211 S; Jardín, Galeana 411 Oriente.

Ciudad Valles (San Luís Potosí)
Transportation: *Bus:* Ciudad Victoria, Tampico, San Luís Potosí, Mexico City. **Accommodations:** 🏠🏠 Valles, Blvd. 36 Norte (Carretera México); San Fernando, Ctra. México-Laredo. 🏠 Piña, Av. Juárez 210.

Colima (Colima)
Information: Hidalgo 75, tel. 24360. **Transportation:** *Train:* Guadalajara, Ciudad Guzmán. *Bus:* Ciudad Guzmán, Guadalajara, Manzanillo. **Accommodations:** 🏠🏠🏠 María Isabel, Blvd. Camino Real (pool). 🏠🏠 Villa del Rey, Blvd. Camino Real (pool); Los Candiles, Blvd. Camino Real (pool). 🏠 Gran Hotel, Av. Rey Colimán 18; Ceballos, Portal Medellín 16; Casino, Portal Morelos 11.

Cozumel (Quintana Roo)
Information: Near the pier. **Transportation:** *Air:* Mexico City, Mérida, Guadalajara, Monterrey; USA. *Boat:* Ferry to Playa del Carmen; car ferry to Pto. Morelos. **Accommodations:** 🏠🏠🏠 Cabañas del Caribe, Playa Santa Pilar 9; El Presidente, central Chankanaab; Mayan Plaza, Playa Santa Pilar; Cozumel Caribe, Playa San Juan; Sol Caribe, central Chankanaab. 🏠🏠 Playa Azul, Playa San Juan. 🏠 El Cozumeleño, Playa Punta Norte; Mesón San Miguel, Av. Juárez 2.

Creel (Chihuahua)

Transportation: *Train:* Los Mochis, Chihuahua. **Accommodations:** ♙ Cabañas del Cobre, 25 km. (15 miles) south in the mountains (Res. Hotel Sta. Anita, Los Mochis); Parador de la Montaña, Res. Chihuahua, tel. 22062. ♙ Hotel Nuevo; Korachi; Creel, all of them near the train station.

Cuauhtémoc (Chihuahua)

Transportation: *Train:* Los Mochis, Chihuahua. *Bus:* Chihuahua. **Accommodations:** ♙ Motel Tarahumara Inn, Av. Allende 5a; Rancho la Estancia (hunting trips, sports equipment), Res. Chihuahua, tel. 22282.

Cuautla (Morelos)

Transportation: *Bus:* Bus station, 5 de Mayo/Zavala; Mexico City, Cuernavaca, Atotonilco. **Accommodations:** ♙♙♙ (*Luxury*) Hacienda Cocoyoc, 10 km. (6 miles) outside Ctra. Cuautla–Cuernavaca. ♙♙♙ Hotel Cuautla, Batalla 19 de Febrero 104. ♙♙ Jardínes de Cuautla, 2 de Mayo 94. ♙ Mesón del Rey, Av. Progreso 505; El Paraiso, Av. Reforma 104. **Spas:** Balneario El Almeal; Agua Hedionda (thermal and sulphur baths); Agua Linda (sulphur); Los Limones.

Cuernavaca (Morelos)

Information: Av. Morelos 802, tel. 143920; C. Comonfort 2 (by the cathedral). **Transportation:** *Bus:* There are three bus stations in town, Estrella de Oro, Av. Morelos Sur 900; Estrella Roja, Leyva 10; Flecha Roja, Av. Morelos 255; connections in the surrounding area and to Taxco, Mexico City, Acapulco, and others. **Accommodations:** Most hotels have a park or garden. ♙♙♙ (*Luxury*) El Presidente, Naico 58 (Rancho Cortés, about 10 km., 6 miles, outside). ♙♙♙ Casino de la Selva, Leandro Valle 1001; Las Mañanitas, Ricardo Linares 107 (1st class garden restaurant); Posada Jacarandas, Av. Cuauhtémoc 805; Villa del Conquistador, Paseo del Conquistador (view of the city). *On Lake Tequesquitengo:* Hacienda Vista Hermosa. ♙♙ Posada Xochiquetzal, Francisco Leyva 200; Posada San Angelo, Cerrada de la Selva 100. ♙ Papagayo, Motolinia 13; Roma, Matamoros 405; España Colón, Morelos 105-c (lodging in the Alberguistas).

Culiacán (Sinaloa)

Transportation: *Air:* Mexico City, Los Angeles (USA). *Bus:* Los Mochis, Mazatlán, Mexico City. **Accommodations:** ♙♙♙ Camino Real Tres Ríos, C. Internacional K. 1423. Del Valle, Blvd. Leyva Solano y Andrade. ♙♙ Gran Hotel, Madero 376 Oriente; Francis, M. Escobedo 135 Poniente. ♙ Heredía, Madero 369 Poniente.

Divisadero Barrancas (Chihuahua)
Transportation: *Train:* Los Mochis, Chihuahua. **Accommodations:**
🏨 Cabañas Divisadero (with view of the canyon), Res. in Chihuahua,
tel. 23362.

Durango (Durango)
Information: Hidalgo 408 Sur, tel. 12139. **Transportation:** *Air:* Airport 5 km. (3 miles) outside town; Mexican cities. *Train:* Torreón. *Bus:* Chihuahua, Monterrey, Mazatlán, Mexico City, and others. **Accommodations:** 🏨 El Presidente, 20 de Noviembre 257 Oriente. 🏨 Casablanca, 20 de Noviembre 811 Poniente; Durango, 5 de Febrero 103 Oriente. 🏨 Posada San Jorge, Constitución 102 Sur; Huicot, Bruno Martínez Norte 165.

El Fuerte (Sinaloa)
Transportation: *Train:* Los Mochis, Chihuahua. **Accommodations:**
🏨 Posada, Res. Hotel Sta. Anita, Los Mochis.

Ensenada (Baja California Norte)
Transportation: *Bus:* Tijuana, Tecate, Mexicali, Mexico City. **Accommodations:** 🏨 El Cid Hotel; Estero Beach Hotel, about 10 km. (6 miles) from town on the beach; San Nicolás Hotel, Av. Adolfo López Mateos (pool). 🏨 La Pinta, Paseo Bucaneros (Floresta); Motel Puesta del Sol; Motel Quintas Papagayo. 🏨 Motel America; Ensenada Fiesta Inn; Misión Santa Isabel.

Guadalajara (Jalisco)
Information: Morelos 102 (Pl. Tapatía); Calle Juárez 638 (in former Convento del Carmen), also information for all Jalisco. **Transportation:** *Air:* Airport 20 km. (12 miles) outside town; taxis and Colectivos. *Train:* Mexico City, Manzanillo, Mazatlán. *Bus:* Bus station C. Estadio, near Parque Agua Azul. Buses and taxis in city center. Tijuana, Zacatecas, Cd. Juárez, Morelia, Lake Chapala, Mexico City. **Accommodations:** 🏨 (*Luxury*) Fiesta Americana, Aurelio Aceves 225 (ultramodern); Camino Real, Av. Vallarta 5005 (outside town); El Tapatío, Blvd. Aeropuerto 4275 (between the city and airport, bungalows); 🏨 Aranzazu, Av. Revolución 110 (central); Fenix, Av. Corona 160 (central); Holiday Inn, Av. López Mateos 2500; De Mendoza, V. Carranza 16 (central); Sheraton, Av. Niños Héroes/16 de Septiembre. 🏨 Colón, Av. Revolución Poniente 12; Fontana, Hidalgo 2301; Del Parque, Juárez 845. 🏨 Astoria, Calz. Independencia Sur 482 (former private house); Asturias, Morelos 381 (central, 19th-century patio); Guadalajara, Av. Colón/Colonial, near the bus station.

Guanajuato (Guanajuato)

Information: Av. Juárez 129. **Transportation:** *Bus:* Bus station (Central de Autobuses): Av. Juárez 131; Querétaro, San Miguel de Allende, Dolores Hidalgo, Guadalajara, Irapuato. **Accommodations:** 🏠 Castillo de Santa Cecilia, on the same street as the church, La Valenciana; Real de Minas, Nejayote 17; El Presidente, Ctra. Marfíl (2 km., 1 mile, from town). 🏠 Hacienda de Cobos, Padre Hidalgo Tercera/Av. Juárez 153 (near Alhóndiga); Hostería del Fraile, Sopeña 3; Posada Santa Fé, Jardín Unión; San Diego, Jardín Unión. 🏠 Murillo, Insurgentes 9; Posada del Convento, Calz. Guadalupe 17; Casa de Huéspedes Cloister, Alonso 32.

Guaymas (Sonora)

Information: On the harbor. **Transportation:** *Train:* Nogales, Los Mochis (from Empalme). *Bus:* Hermosillo, Mexicali, Tijuana. *Boat:* Santa Rosaliá and La Paz (Baja California). **Accommodations:** 🏠 Miramar; Playa de Cortés, both Bahía de Bacochibampo; La Posada de San Carlos, Bahía de San Carlos. 🏠 Motel Armida, Calz. García López; Motel Flamingos, C. Internacional, Col. Loma Linda. 🏠 Loma Linda, C. Internacional K. 1983; Rubi, Paseo Obregón/Calle 29.

Guerrero Negro (Baja California)

Accomodations: La Pinta, 5 km. (3 miles) outside town going north on Highway 1. 🏠 Dunas, Emiliano Zapata; Baja Sur, F. Legal/Emiliano Zapata.

Hermosillo (Sonora)

Transportation: *Air:* Mazatlán. *Train:* Mazatlán. *Bus:* Nogales, Tijuana, Los Mochis, Guadalajara. **Accommodations:** 🏠 Internacional, C. Rosales/C. Morelia; San Alberto, C. Rosales/C. Serdán. 🏠 Motel Gandara, Blvd. Eusebio Kino; Motel El Encanto, C. Rodríguez N. 🏠 Kino, C. Pino Suárez 151; Fermar, C. Morelia/C. González.

Huasca (Hidalgo)

Accommodations: 🏠 Hacienda San Miguel Regla.

Isla Mujéres (Quintana Roo)

Transportation: *Boat:* Punta Sam, Pto. Juárez. *Air:* Mérida. **Accommodations:** 🏠 El Presidente Caribe. 🏠 Posada del Mar, Calle 20 No. 85. 🏠 Zazil-Ha Bojórquez, Playa los Cocos (on the island's northern point). 🏠 Rocas del Caribe, Av. Francisco I. Madero 2; Rocamar, Av. Nicolás Bravo; Hostal Poc Na, similar to a youth hostel, near the Playa los Cocos.

Ixtapa/Zihuatanejo (Guerrero)

Information: Pedro Asencios 5. **Transportation:** *Air:* Mexico City, USA. *Bus:* Acapulco, Lázaro Cárdenas, Mexico City. **Accommodations:** *Ixtapa:* 🏨🏨🏨 (*Luxury*) Camino Real, Playa Vista Hermosa; Dorado Pacífico, Paseo de Ixtapa (PI); Ixtapa Sheraton, PI; Krystal, PI. 🏨🏨🏨 El Presidente, PI; Holiday Inn, PI; Riviera del Sol, PI. 🏨🏨 Castel Palmar, Av. del Palmar. *Zihuatanejo:* 🏨🏨🏨 Villa del Sol, Playa la Ropa (PR). 🏨🏨 Irma, Playa de la Madera; Sotavento, PR. 🏨 Calpulli, PR; Catalina, PR; Tres Marías, Noria 4.

Ixtapan de la Sal (Estado de México)

Transportation: *Bus:* Toluca, Taxco. **Accommodations:** 🏨🏨 Vistahermosa, Av. Jacarandas; Bungalows Lolita, Av. Jacarandas 33. 🏨 Casablanca, Av. Juárez 615; Casa Guille, Av. J. M. Morelos 212; Salvador, Independencia 77; Ideal, Av. Jacarandas 809.

Jalapa (Veracruz)

Information: Corner of Zaragoza/Carrillo Puerto. **Transportation:** *Air:* Airport 15 km. (9 miles) southeast on the road to Veracruz; Mexican cities. *Train:* Train station in northern part of town (bus); Veracruz, Mexico City. *Bus:* 1st class bus station (ADO), Av. Pte. M. Avila Camacho (corner of B. Juárez, 1 km., half a mile, northwest of Parque Juárez); 2nd class bus station (Autobuses Unidos): near Parque Juárez; Veracruz, Poza Rica. **Accommodations:** 🏨🏨🏨 María Victoria, Zaragoza 6. 🏨🏨 Del Prado, Revolución 40; Salmones, Zaragoza 24. Countless simple inns in the area.

La Paz (Baja California Sur)

Information: 5 de Mayo (opposite the cathedral). **Transportation:** *Air:* Airport 10 km. (6 miles) outside town; taxis; Los Mochis, Tijuana, Mexico City and other Mexican cities; *Bus:* Bus station, Jalisco/Josefa Ortíz de Domínguez; Tijuana, Los Cabos. *Boat:* Guaymas, Los Mochis, Mazatlán, Puerto Vallarta. **Accommodations:** 🏨🏨🏨 Gran Baja, Rangel; El Presidente, 5 km. (3 miles) from town; Castel Palmira, 2.5 km. (1.5 miles) from town; Los Arcos, Alvaro Obregón 498. 🏨🏨 Acuario's, Ramírez/Degollado; Gardenias, Aquiles Serdán 521 Norte; Perla, Av. Obregón 150. 🏨 La Posada, Reforma/Playa Sur; La Purísima, 16 de Septiembre 48.

León (Guanajuato)

Transportation: *Air:* Airport about 13 km. (8 miles) from town, toward Irapuato. *Bus:* Guadalajara, Guanajuato, Chihuahua, Mexico City. **Accommodations:** 🏨🏨🏨 Real de Mínas, López Mateos 🏨🏨 Condesa, Portal Bravo 14.

Loreto (Baja California Sur)
   Transportation: *Air:* Tijuana, La Paz. *Bus:* Tijuana, La Paz. **Accommodations:** 🏨🏨🏨 Presidente Nopolo, Blvd. Misión de Loreto, Nopolo Beach; Presidente La Pinta, Fco. I. Madero. 🏨🏨 Misión de Loreto, Blvd. López Mateos 1; Oasis, López Mateos/Baja California. 🏨 Salvatierra, Av. Salvatierra 223.

Los Mochis (Sinaloa)
   Transportation: *Air:* Airport 15 km. (9 miles) from town; taxis; Mexico City, Tijuana, La Paz, USA. *Boat:* La Paz. *Bus:* Tijuana, Mazatlán, Mexico City. *Train:* Chihuahua. **Accommodations:** 🏨🏨🏨 Holiday Inn, Ctra. Internacional. 🏨🏨 El Dorado, Gabriel Leyva/ Valdez; Santa Anita, Gabriel Leyva/Hidalgo (with reservations for a few hotels along the train line to Chihuahua; bus to train station). 🏨 Beltrán, Hidalgo/Zaragoza; Lorena, Alvaro Obregón 186 Poniente.

Manzanillo (Colima)
   Information: Juárez 111. **Transportation:** *Air:* Airport 45 km. (27 miles) north toward Barra de Navidad; taxis; Guadalajara. *Train:* Guadalajara, Colima. *Bus:* Guadalajara, Mexico City, Tijuana. **Accommodations:** 🏨🏨🏨 (*Luxury*) Las Hadas, Calle los Riscos y Vista Hermosa. 🏨🏨🏨 Club Santiago Acosa, Playa de Miramar; Club Maeva, between Manzanillo–Barra de Navidad. 🏨🏨 La Posada, Playa las Brisas km. 2; Casablanca Alamar, Av. Olas Altas 34. 🏨 Las Brisas, Playa las Brisas; Motel Star, Playa las Brisas.

Matamoros (Tamaulipas)
   Transportation: *Air:* Mexico City. *Train:* Monterrey, Mexico City. *Bus:* Ciudad Victoria, Monterrey, Mexico City. **Accommodations:** 🏨🏨🏨 El Presidente, Alvaro Obregón 249. 🏨🏨 México, Abasolo 123; Ritz, Matamoros/Siete.

Matehuala (San Luís Potosí)
   Transportation: Saltillo, San Luís Potosí. **Accommodations:** 🏨🏨 Las Palmas, northern section of the city.

Mazatlán (Sinaloa)
   Information: Av. del Mar 1000. **Transportation:** *Air:* Airport 26 km. (16 miles) from town; taxis; other cities in Mexico; USA. *Bus:* Bus station, Centro Colonia; Los Mochis, Guaymas, Durango, Guadalajara. *Boat:* La Paz. **Accommodations:** 🏨🏨🏨 (*Luxury*) El Cid, Av. Camarón Sábalo. 🏨🏨🏨 Camino Real, Punta del Sábalo; Hacienda Mazatlán, Av. del Mar/Flamingos; Holiday Inn, Av. Camarón Sábalo 696. 🏨🏨 Aqua Marina, Av. del Mar 110; Las Brisas, Av. del Mar 900; Motel Bungalow's

Dummy, Av. del Mar 1200. 🛏 Joncol's, Belisario Domínguez/Simón Bolívar; Motel del Sol, Av. del Mar.

Melaque (Jalisco)
See Barra de Navidad.

Mérida (Yucatán)
Information: Itzáes 590, corner of C. 59. **Transportatiòn:** *Air:* Airport 7 km. (4 miles) from city center; shuttle bus; Mexican cities, Europe, USA. *Train:* Mexico City (via Villahermosa, Córdoba), Tizimín. *Bus:* 1st and 2nd class bus station (ADO): corner of C. 69/68; 2nd class, C. 50; all directions and tickets to surrounding archaeological zones. Taxis and sitios in main plaza (agree on fare beforehand). **Accommodations:** The airport and ADO bus station have offices for hotel reservations. 🛏🛏🛏 Casa del Balam, C. 60 No. 488; Holiday Inn, Av. Colón 498/ C. 60; Mérida Misión, C. 60 No. 461; Montejo Palace, Paseo de Montejo 483; 🛏🛏 Caribe, C. 59 No. 500; Cayre, C. 70 No. 543; Colonial, C. 62 No. 476. 🛏 Del Parque, C. 60 No. 495; Montejo, C. 57 No. 507; Mucuy, C. 57 No. 481; Nacional, C. 61 No. 474.

Mexicali (Baja California Norte)
Information: Calle de Comercio (between Av. Reforma and Alvaro Obregón). **Transportation:** *Air:* Mexico City, USA. *Train:* Guadalajara, Mexico City. *Bus:* Tijuana, San Felipe, Hermosillo, Mexico City, San Diego (USA). **Accommodations:** 🛏🛏🛏 Holiday Inn, Benito Juárez; Castel Calafia, Calz. Justo Sierra 1495, Fracc. Los Pinos. 🛏🛏 Lucerna, Benito Juárez 2151. 🛏 Motel Cosmos, Justo Sierra 1493; Motel La Siesta, Justo Sierra 899.

Mexico City (D.F.)
Information: Secretaría de Turismo, Presidente Mazaryk 172 (corner of C. Hegel), Colonia Polanco, tel. 2110099 (also complaint office). Oficina de Turismo, Av. Juárez 92. Departamento de Información e Auxilio Turismo, telephone for help on the road, 2500123. Cámara Nacional de Comercio (Chamber of Commerce), Paseo de la Reforma 42 (maps and legal advice). **Transportation:** *Air:* Aeropuerto Internacional Benito Juárez, 13 km. (8 miles) outside town. Taxi service to the city can be arranged in the airport lobby. *Train:* Gran Estación Central de Buenavista. Connections to all major cities and to the USA. For information, call 5478971/72. Reservations are recommended. Train stations for overland travel with connections in all directions: *T.A.N. (Terminal del Norte;* Av. de los 100 Metros 4907, Metro stop), Teotihuacán, Tula, northern Mexico, USA. *Terminal Indios Verdes* (Metro stop), Teotihuacán and northern suburbs. *T.A.P.O. (Terminal del Oriente;* Calz. Ignacio

Zaragoza 200, Metro stop San Lázaro), Puebla, Oaxaca, Mérida. *T.A.S.* (*Terminal del Sur;* Av. Taxqueña 1230, Metro stop Taxqueña), Cuernavaca, Taxco, Acapulco. *T.A.P.* (*Terminal del Poniente,* Av. Sur 122 in Tacubaya, Metro stop Observatorio), Toluca, Morelia. For long trips, you can reserve a seat through *Central de Autobuses,* Reforma 52 (Mexicorama), tel. 5921199, or at the train station from which you will be departing. *Bus:* About 60 bus lines serve the city. The most important route (Ruta 100) goes along Reforma and Insurgentes. There are 15-day passes available for all intracity transportation (bus, trolley, subway) that are very inexpensive; otherwise, public transportation costs about 20 pesos (exact change). *Metro:* The subway system or "Metro" (see map on page 40), is the best and cheapest form of public transportation in the city. It runs from 6:00 A.M. to midnight on weekdays, until 1:00 A.M. on Saturday, and from 7:00 A.M. to midnight on Sunday. It's best to avoid the subway mornings before 11:00 A.M. and in the evenings between 5:00– 8:00 when it's at its most crowded. *Taxis:* There are a few different options for taxis. Be sure to negotiate the fare *before* you get in the cab; also, of you don't know the exact address to which you are going, the least you should do is to tell the driver to which quarter you wish to be taken. Limosines with English-speaking drivers are comfortable but very expensive. "Peseros" circulate on 20 routes throughout the city. VW taxis have meters (which don't keep pace with inflation so the registered fare is never what you pay) and are generally inexpensive. "Sitio" cabs, identified by their white with red stripe design, can be requested from call boxes in various locations around town. **Accommodations:** The hotel reservation office at the airport is open from 9:00 A.M.–11:30 P.M. The following hotels are in popular tourist areas of the city. 🏨🏨🏨 (*Luxury*) Camino Real, Mariano Escobedo 700 (near the National Museum of Anthropology; Westin); El Presidente Chapultepec, Jorge Eliot 16; Ma. Isabel Sheraton Hotel, Reforma 325 (Sheraton). 🏨🏨🏨 Aristos, Reforma 276; Calinda Geneve, Londres 130; De Cortés, Av. Hidalgo 85 (building from the 18th century; Best Western); El Presidente, Hamburgo 135 (Zona Rosa); Crowne Plaza, Reforma 80; Galería Plaza, Hamburgo 195 (Zona Rosa); Holiday Inn, at the airport; Krystal, Liverpool 155 (Zona Rosa). 🏨🏨 Ambassador, Humboldt 38; Avenida, Lázaro Cárdenas 38; Majestic, Madero 73 (Colonial style building on the Zócalo; Best Western); Palace Hotel, Ignacio Ramirez 7 (between Reforma and the monument to the Revolution); Regente, Calle Paris 9 (near the intersection of Reforma/Insurgentes); Ritz, Madero 30 (Best Western); Romano Diana, Río Lerma 237; Suites Havre, Havre 74 (Zona Rosa; for longer stays.) 🏨 Bonampak, Mérida 81; Centro Diana, Av. Universidad 1861; Fleming, Revilla-gigedo 35; Roosevelt, Insurgentes Sur 287. More simple hotels are located north of the Plaza de la República and in old quarter around the Zócalo.

Monterrey (Nuevo León)
Information: Av. Emilio Carranza 730 Sur, tel. 401080. **Transportation:** *Air:* International airport 24 km. (14 miles) from town; cities throughout Mexico, USA, Paris, Madrid. *Train:* Train station, Calz. Victoria y Nieto (northern part of the city); Tampico, Mexico City. *Bus:* Bus station, Avenida Colón at the Arco de la Independencia; Nuevo Laredo, Mexico City. **Accommodations:** 🏨 Ambassador, Hidalgo/E. Carranza; Gran Hotel Ancira, Hidalgo/Escobedo; Holiday Inn Monterrey, Av. Universidad 101; Monterrey Plaza, Constitución 300. 🏨 Río, Padre Mier 194 Poniente; Quinta Avenida, Madero 246 Oriente (relatively central). 🏨 Amado Nervo, Amado Nervo 1110 Norte (relatively central); Del Norte, Democracia 260 Poniente; Los Reyes, Hidalgo 543 Poniente. *Outside Monterrey:* 🏨 Chipinque, Meseta de Chipinque. 🏨 Cola de Caballo, by the waterfall of the same name (30 km., 18 miles, southeast of town).

Morelia (Michoacán)
Information: Palacio Clavijero, Calle Nigromante 79, tel. 32654; information kiosk in the bus station. **Transportation:** *Train:* Mexico city; 1st class only from Uruapan. *Bus:* Pátzcuaro, Uruapan, Irapuato, Mexico City, Acapulco, Zihuatanejo. **Accommodations:** 🏨 Hotel de la Soledad, C. Zaragoza/C. Ocampo (central location; charming, quiet guest house); Mansión de la Calle Real, Av. Madero Oriente 766; Villa Montaña, Calle Patzimba (above the city, pool); Virrey de Mendoza, Portal Matamoros 16 (on the Zócalo). 🏨 Mansión Acueducto, Av. Acueducto 25 (garden, pool); Casino, Portal Hidalgo 229 (on the Zócalo); Catedral, Zaragoza 37 (central). 🏨 Hotel Central, Zaragoza 37; Posada del Cortijo, Eduardo Ruiz 673; San Miguel, Av. Madero Poniente 1069.

Mulegé (Baja California Sur)
Accommodations: 🏨 Hotel Serenidad, 3 km. (1.5 miles) outside town going south. 🏨 Las Casitas, Madero 50.

Nuevo Laredo (Nuevo Laredo)
Transportation: *Air:* Flight connections to major cities in Mexico. *Train:* Mexico City. *Bus:* Monterrey, Guadalajara, Mexico City; Greyhound Bus to USA. **Accommodations:** 🏨 El Río Motor-Hotel, C. Reforma/C. Toluca; Motel Santa Mónica, Reforma/Candela; Motel Villa del Monte, Guerrero/Perú. 🏨 Confort, Guerrero/Canales; Alameda, González 2715; Motel del Centro, Héroes/Nacataz 3108. 🏨 Motel El Toro, Guerrero 2309; Motel del Mar, Reforma 3760.

Oaxaca (Oaxaca)

Information: Corner of 5 de Mayo/Morelos and Matamoros/García Vigil. **Transportation:** *Air:* Airport 8 km. (5 miles) south of town; taxis; Mexico City. *Train:* Rail station, Calz. Fco. I. Madero (1 km., half a mile, west of Zócalo); Mexico City, Puebla. *Bus:* 1st class bus station, Calz. Niños Héroes (1.5 km., 1 mile, from Zócalo), interregional connections; 2nd class bus station, Calz. Valerio Trujano/Periférico West (1 km., half a mile from Zócalo), regional service. **Accommodations:** 🏨🏨🏨 El Presidente, Calle 5 de Mayo 300 (former cloister of Sta. Catalina); Misión de los Angeles, Porfirio Díaz 102; Victoria, Ctra. Panamericana (situated on a hill below the Observatorio). 🏨🏨 Margarita, Madero 1254; Monte Albán, Alameda de León 1; Señorial, Portal de las Flores 6. 🏨 Central, 20 de Noviembre 104; Mesón del Rey, Trujano 212; Principal, 5 de Mayo 208. Other simple patio hotels are located along the Av. 20 de Noviembre.

Orizaba (Veracruz)

Transportation: *Bus:* Puebla, Tehuacán, Oaxaca, Veracruz. **Accommodations:** 🏨🏨 Aries, Oriente 6 No. 265; Trueba, Poniente 6 Sur No. 11. 🏨 Gran Hotel France, Oriente 6 No. 186.

Pachuca (Hidalgo)

Transportation: *Bus:* Mexico City, Tampico, Poza Rica. **Accommodations:** 🏨🏨 Emily, Pl. Independencia; Sahara, Blvd. Felipe Angeles. 🏨 Noriega, Matamoros 305.

Palenque (Chiapas)

Transportation: *Train:* Francisco Escarcega. *Bus:* Villahermosa, Mérida, San Cristóbal de las Casas, Mexico City. **Accommodations:** 🏨🏨🏨 Misión Palenque, Zona arqueologica; De las Ruinas, Zona arqueologica; 🏨🏨 Centro Turístico y Cultural Chan-Kah; Hotel Vaca Vieja, Av. 5 de Mayo 42. 🏨 Palenque, Av. 5 de Mayo 15; Tulipanes, Cañada 6.

Papantla (Veracruz)

Transportation: *Bus:* Jalapa, Veracruz. **Accommodations:** 🏨🏨 Papantla, Zócalo; El Tajín, José J. Nuñez 104.

Pátzcuaro (Michoacán)

Information: Portál Hidalgo 9, tel. 21214. **Transportation:** *Train:* Morelia (Mexico City), Uruapan. *Bus:* Bus station ADO: C. Lloreda y Titere 1-A; Tres Estrellas de Oro and Flecha Amarilla: C. Ahumada 63. Morelia, Guadalajara. **Accommodations:** 🏨🏨🏨 Posada Don Vasco, Av. de las Américas 450 (pool). 🏨🏨 Mansión Iturbe, Portal Morelos 59; Mesón del Gallo, Dr. Coss 20; Posada de la Basílica, Arciga 6. 🏨 Motel Pátzcuaro, Av. Lázaro Cárdenas 506.

Playa Azul (Michoacán)
Accommodations: 🏨 La Loma, V. Carranza; María Teresa, Independencia; Playa Azul, V. Carranza. 🏨 Bungalows Delfin, Plaza Principal; Delfin, V. Carranza.

Playa del Carmen (Quintana Roo)
Transportation: *Air:* Cozumel. *Boat:* Cozumel. *Bus:* Mérida, Puerto Juárez, Chetumal. **Accommodations:** 🏨 Molcas; Playacar. 🏨 Posada Lili.

Puebla (Puebla)
Information: Av. 5 de Oriente 3 (near the cathedral), tel. 461285.
Transportation: *Air:* New airport near Huejotzingo. *Train:* Rail station, 80 Poniente y 9 Norte; Mexico City. *Bus:* Bus stations: ADO, M.A. Camacho 604 (departures every 20 minutes for Mexico City); Estrella Roja, 5 Sur 105; Autobuses Surianos, 14 Poniente 114. **Accommodations:** 🏨 Mesón del Angel, Hermanos Serdán 807 (on highway west of town); Misión de Puebla, 5 Poniente 2522. 🏨 Hotel del Portal, M. A. Camacho 205 (on the Zócalo); Lastra, Calz. de los Fuertes 2633; Palacio San Leonardo, 2 Oriente 211; Posada San Pedro, 2 Oriente 202. 🏨 Imperial, 4 Oriente 212; Hostal de Halconeros, Av. Reforma 141.

Puerto Angel (Oaxaca)
Transportation: *Bus:* Oaxaca (via Pochutla), Puerto Escondido.
Accommodations: 🏨 Angel del Mar. There are a number of other small hotels and guesthouses.

Puerto Escondido (Oaxaca)
Transportation: *Air:* Mexico City, Oaxaca. *Bus:* Acapulco, Oaxaca, Puerto Angel, Salina Cruz. **Accommodations:** 🏨 Castell Bugambilias, Blvd. Juárez; Paraíso Escondido, Unión 10. 🏨 Las Palmas, Av. Alfonso Pérez Gazga. 🏨 Loren, Av. A.P. Gazga; Nayar, Av. A.P. Gazga 407; Rincón del Pacífico, Av. A.P. Gazga.

Puerto Vallarta (Jalisco)
Information: Palacio Municipal, corner of Juárez/Independencia.
Transportation: *Air:* Airport 7 km. (4 miles) from town, taxis; major cities in Mexico, Los Cabos (Baja Calif.), USA. *Bus:* Mazatlán, Tepic, Guadalajara, Manzanillo. *Boat:* Cabo San Lucas, La Paz. **Accommodations:** 🏨 (*Luxury*) Bugambilias Sheraton, Ctra. aeropuerto; Camino Real, Playa las Estacas; Fiesta Americana, Ctra. aeropuerto; Posada Vallarta, Av. de las Garzas. 🏨 Calinda Plaza las Glorias, Ctra. aeropuerto; Holiday Inn, Ctra. aeropuerto; Los Pelícanos, Ctra. aeropuerto. 🏨 Eloisa, Lázaro Cárdenas 179; Playa los Arcos, Olas Altas

270; Posada Río Cuale, Aquiles Serdán 242. 🏠 La Misión, Lázaro Cárdenas 205; Marsol, Francisca Rodríguez 103; Océano, Paseo Díaz Ordaz y Galeana.

Querétaro (Querétaro)

Information: Palacio Municipal, Pl. Independencia. **Transportation:** *Bus:* Bus station, Ctra. Panamericana (in Alameda-Park); Mexico City, Guadalajara, Guanajuato, San Miguel de Allende. **Accommodations:** 🏨 Hacienda Jurica, 9 km., (5 miles) from town; Holiday Inn, Av. Constituyentes 13 Sur; Mirabel, Corregidora/Av. Constituyentes; Real de Minas, Av. Constituyentes 124 Poniente. 🏨 Plata, Juárez Norte 23; Señorial, Guerrero e Hidalgo. 🏠 Corregidora, Av. Corregidora Sur 138; Del Marquez, Av. Juárez Norte 22; Gran Hotel, Madero Oriente 6 (on Zócalo).

Saltillo (Coahuila)

Information: Av. Fco. Coss/M. Acuña. **Transportation:** *Bus:* Monterrey, Nuevo Laredo, San Luís Potosí. **Accommodations:** 🏨 Camino Real, Ctra. 865. 🏨 Arizpe Sainz, Victoria 418; San Jorge, Manuel Acuña 240 Norte.

San Cristóbal de las Casas (Chiapas)

Information: In the town hall, Plaza 31 de Marzo. **Transportation:** *Air:* Charter flights to Bonampak and Yaxchilán. *Bus:* 1st class bus station (Cristóbal Colón), Av. Insurgentes Sur (on the Panamericana); 2nd class bus station, on the Panamericana between Fco. Sarabia and I. Allende. Tuxtla Gutiérrez, Palenque over Ococingo, the Guatemala border area, and other villages. **Accommodations:** 🏨 Ciudad Real, Plaza 31 de Marzo 10; Posada Diego Mazáriegos, María Adelina Flores 2; Santa Clara, Av. Insurgentes 1. 🏠 Capri, Av. Insurgentes 54; Español, 1° de Marzo 16; Casa de Huéspedes Diana, C. Real de Guadalupe 124. Other guest houses are located near the bus station.

San Ignacio (Baja California Sur)

Transportation: Tijuana, La Paz. **Accommodations:** 🏨 La Pinta, near Ortsrand. 🏠 Motel La Posada, V. Carranza.

San José del Cabo (Baja California Sur)

Transportation: *Air:* Mexico City, USA. *Bus:* La Paz, Tijuana. **Accommodations:** 🏨 (*Luxury*) Punta Palmilla. 🏨 Presidente San José; Castel Cabo. 🏨 Costa Aquamarina. 🏠 Nuevo Sol. *See also Cabo San Lucas.*

San Luís Potosí (San Luís Potosí)

Information: Jardín Hidalgo 20 (Plaza de Armas), tel. 23143. **Transportation:** *Train:* Laredo, Tampico, Aguascalientes, Mexico City. *Bus:* Bus station about 1.5 km. (1 mile) from city center; inner city buses; Querétaro, Nuevo Laredo, Mexico City. **Accommodations:** 🏨 Panorama, Av. V. Carranza. 🏨 Filher, Zaragoza/Av. Universidad (375); María Cristina, J. Sarabia 110 (pool); Napoles, J. Sarabia 120. 🏚 Plaza, Jardín Hidalgo 22; Progreso, Aldama 415.

San Miguel de Allende (Guanajuato)

Information: Plaza Principal. **Transportation:** *Bus:* Querétaro, Dolores Hidalgo, Guanajuato. **Accommodations:** 🏨 Hacienda Taboada, 8 km. (5 miles) outside town on the road to Dolores Hidalgo; Posada de la Aldea, Calle Ancha de San Antonio 11; Posada la Ermita, Pedro Vargas 64. 🏨 Posada de las Monjas, Canal 37; Posada San Francisco, Plaza Principal 2. 🏚 Casa Sautto, Dr. Hernández Mácias 59; Posada Carmina, Cuna de Allende 2; Quinta Loreto (hotel with garden).

Santa Rosalía (Baja California Sur)

Information: At the harbor. **Transportation:** *Boat:* Guaymas. **Accommodations:** 🏨 Francés, 11 de Julio 30; El Morro, 1.5 km. (1 mile) on the road south. 🏚 Blanco y Negro, Av. Sarabia 1; Palencia, Calle No. 1.

Tampico (Tamaulipas)

Information: Palacio Municipal, Plaza de Armas. **Transportation:** *Train:* Monterrey (via Cd. Victoria), San Luís Potosí. *Bus:* Monterrey (via Cd. Victoria), San Luís Potosí. **Accommodations:** 🏨 Camino Real, Hidalgo 2000; Holiday Inn, on the road between Tampico–Cd. Mante. 🏨 Impala, S. Díaz Mirón 220 Poniente; Imperial, López de Lara/Carranza. 🏚 Tampico, Carranza 513 Oriente; Sevilla, Rivera 300 Oriente.

Tapachula (Chiapas)

Transportation: *Bus:* Tehuantepec, Oaxaca. **Accommodations:** 🏨 Camino Real, C. Costera. 🏨 San Francisco, Central Sur 94. Fenix, 4. Av. Norte 19; 🏚 Internacional, Av. Central 119.

Taxco (Guerrero)

Information: Casa Borda, Plazuela Bernal. **Transportation:** *Bus:* 1st class bus station (Estrella de Oro): Av. J. F. Kennedy south (at the junction of C. Pilita); 2nd class bus station (Flecha Roja): Av. J. F. Kennedy (between C. M. Hidalgo and C. Veracruz); Guadalajara, Mexico City, Acapulco, Cacahuamilpa. *Cable car:* Teleférico Monte Taxco. **Accommodations:** 🏨🏨🏨 (*Luxury*) Monte Taxco, Fracc. Lomas de Taxco (located on a mountain outside the city; cable car). 🏨🏨🏨 De la Borda, Cerro de Pedregal 2; Hacienda del Chorrillo, near Los Arcos. 🏨🏨 Posada de la Misión, Av. J. F. Kennedy 32; Rancho Taxco-Victoria, C. J. Nibbi 14; Villa del Conquistador, Paseo Conquistador 134; Agua Escondida, Guillermo Spratling 4 (on the Zócalo, pool); Los Arcos, J. R. de Alarcón 12; Santa Prisca, Cena Obscuras 1 (lovely garden). 🏨 Posada de los Castillo, J. R. de Alarcón 3; Posada del Jardín, Celso Muños 4 (near Sta. Prisca).

Tehuacán (Puebla)

Transportation: *Bus:* Puebla, Oaxaca. **Accommodations:** 🏨🏨🏨 Aldea del Bazar, Calz. A. López Mateos 3351 (on the road from Puebla). 🏨🏨 Spa Peñafiel, near the thermal springs. 🏨 El Riego, Unidad Industrial El Riego, near the thermal springs (pool).

Tepic (Nayarit)

Transportation: *Bus:* Mazatlán, Guadalajara, Pto. Vallarta. **Accommodations:** 🏨🏨 Motel La Loma, Paseo de la Loma 301; Sierra de Alicia, México 180 Norte. 🏨 Motel Cora, Av. Insurgentes 100 Poniente.

Tijuana (Baja California Norte)

Information: Via Oriente 1. **Transportation:** *Air:* Mexico City, USA. *Bus:* Baja California Sur, Mexico City, USA. **Accommodations:** 🏨🏨🏨 (*Luxury*) Fiesta Americana, Blvd. Agua Caliente 4500. 🏨🏨🏨 Calinda, Blvd. Agua Caliente 1; El Conquistador, Blvd. Agua Caliente 1777. 🏨🏨 Motel León, Calle Séptima 1937; Padre Kino, Blvd. Agua Caliente 3. 🏨 Nelson, Av. Revolución 100; Sosa, Av. C. 565.

Tlaxcala (Tlaxcala)

Information: Plaza de la Constitución 21 (on the Zócalo), tel. 20027. **Transportation:** *Bus:* ADO and Flecha Azul to Puebla, Mexico City, and others. **Accommodations:** 🏨🏨🏨 Misión, Ctra. Tlaxcala-Apizaco (Colonial-style hotel near waterfall). 🏨🏨 Mansión Xicotencatl, Juárez 15. 🏨 Jeroc's, Blvd. Revolución 4; Hostal del Cid, Blvd. Revolución 6; Don Quijote, Constitución 23.

Toluca (Estado de México)

Information: Palacio de Gobierno, Lerdo Poniente 300. **Transportation:** *Bus:* Mexico City, Calixtlahuaca and other villages in the region.

Accommodations: 🛏️ Mansión de Milled, Hidalgo Poniente 310; Nuevo San Carlos, Portal Francisco I. Madero 210. 🛏️ Colonial, Av. Hidalgo Oriente 103.

Torreón (Coahuila)
Transportation: *Air:* Chihuahua, Cd. Juárez. *Bus:* Chihuahua, Cd. Juárez. **Accommodations:** 🛏️🛏️🛏️ El Presidente, Paseo de la Rosita; El Paraíso del Desierto, Blvd. Independencia; Palacio Real, Av. Morelos 1280. 🛏️🛏️ Diana, Reforma/Av. Hidalgo; Savoy, Acuña 257 Sur. 🛏️ Galicia, Cepeda 273 Sur; Plaza, Rodríguez 153 Sur.

Tuxtla Gutiérrez (Chiapas)
Information: Blvd. Belisario Domínguez 950, tel. 33028. **Transportation:** *Air:* New airport far from the city is often closed due to unfavorable weather conditions. Mexico City. *Bus:* 1st class bus station (Cristóbal Colón), 2 Av. Norte Poniente; 1st and 2nd class bus station (Transportes Tuxtla), 2 Av. Sur Oriente 712; Villahermosa, San Cristóbal, Oaxaca, Mexico City. **Accommodations:** 🛏️🛏️🛏️ Castell Flamboyan, Blvd. Belisario Domínguez 1081; Real de Tuxtla, Ctra. Panamericana 1088. 🛏️🛏️ Bonampak, Blvd. Belisario Domínguez 180; Gran Humberto, Av. Central Poniente 180. 🛏️ Balun-Canan, Av. Central Oriente 944; La Misión, Primera Poniente Norte 221.

Uruapan (Michoacán)
Information: Hotel Progreso, 5 de Febrero 17, tel. 20633. **Transportation:** *Air:* Mexico City. *Train:* Mexico City. *Bus:* Bus station in the northeast part of the city; buses and taxis to city center. Morelia, Pátzcuaro, Guadalajara, Zihuatanejo, Mexico City. **Accommodations:** 🛏️🛏️🛏️ Mansión del Cupatitzio, Parque Nacional; Plaza Uruapan, Ocampo 64; Real de Uruapan, Nicolás Bravo 110. 🛏️🛏️ Concordia, Portal Carrillo 8; Nuevo Alameda, 5 de Febrero 11; Paraíso Uruapan, 2 km. (1 mile) from town on the road to Pátzcuaro; Villa de Flores, Emilio Carranza 15. 🛏️ Hernández, Portal Matamoros 19.

Uxmal (Yucatán)
Transportation: *Bus:* Mérida. **Accommodations:** 🛏️🛏️🛏️ Hacienda Uxmal, Ctra. Mérida–Campeche. 🛏️🛏️ Villas Arqueológicas, Zona arqueológica.

Valladolid (Aguascalientes)
Accommodations: 🛏️🛏️ Hacienda Vinícula.

Valladolid (Yucatán)

Transportation: *Bus:* Chichén Itzá, Mérida, Pto. Juárez, Cobá, Tulum, Playa del Carmen, Chetumal. **Accommodations:** 🏨🏨 El Mesón del Marqués, Pl. Principal (former hacienda); Don Luis, Calle 39 No. 38 (pool).

Valle de Bravo (Estado de México)

Accommodations: 🏨🏨🏨 Los Arcos, Bocanegra 310 (central, pool); Posada Rincón del Bosque, Fracc. Avándaro (suburb). 🏨🏨 Motel Avándaro, Fracc. Avándaro (suburb). 🏨 Bravo, Bocanegra 102. Posadas familiares (private accommodations) A. Vendrel, Benito Juárez 101; S. Mondragón, Priv. del Vergel.

Veracruz (Veracruz)

Information: On the Zócalo and at the airport. **Transportation:** *Air:* Mexico City, Guadalajara, Monterrey, Tijuana. *Train:* Mexico City. *Bus:* Bus station, Av. Salvador Díaz Mirón (corner of Xalapa) south of city center; Mexico City, Jalapa, Orizaba, Puebla, Oaxaca, Villahermosa. **Accommodations:** 🏨🏨🏨 Hostal de Cortés, Blvd. Avila Camacho/B. de las Casas. 🏨🏨 Colonial, Zócalo (pool); Emporio, Av. Insurgentes Veracruzanos; Real del Mar, Blvd. Avila Camacho 2707. 🏨 Concha Dorada, Zócalo; Santillana, Landero/Coss No. 209 (central, by the fish market).

Villahermosa (Tabasco)

Information: Corner of Malecón/I. Zaragoza. **Transportation:** *Air:* Airport 15 km. (9 miles) from town; VW bus, taxis; Mexico City, Tuxtla Gutiérrez, Mérida, Palenque; charter flights to Bonampak and Yaxchilán. *Bus:* 1st class bus station (ADO), C. Constitución (with baggage room); 2nd class bus station, C. Constitución (2 and a half blocks from 1st class station); Chetumal, Mérida, Palenque, Oaxaca, Veracruz, Mexico City. **Accommodations:** 🏨🏨🏨 (*Luxury*) Tabasco Plaza, Paseo Tabasco 1407. 🏨🏨🏨 Argos, Paseo Tabasco 1502; Maya Tabasco, Av. Grijalva 907; Villahermosa Viva, Paseo Tabasco 1201. 🏨🏨 Manzur, Av. Madero 422; Ritz, Madero 1113. 🏨 Los Arcos, Madero 207; Palma de Mallorca, Madero 516.

Xalapa (Veracruz)

See Jalapa.

Zacatecas (Zacatecas)
Information: Palacio de Gobierno and Blvd. López Mateos 923a.
Transportation: *Train:* Mexico City, Chihuahua. *Bus:* Mexico City,
Chihuahua. **Accommodations:** 🏨 Calinda, Av. López Mateos;
Aristos, Lomas de la Soledad. 🏨 Motel del Bosque, Paseo Díaz Ordaz
(panoramic view; funicular); Posada de los Condes, Av. Juárez 18-A. 🏨
Posada de la Moneda, Av. Hidalgo 413 (central); Condesa, Av. Juárez 5.

Zihuatanejo (Guerrero)
See Ixtapa.

Index

(If more than one page number appears next to the name of a site, the number in boldface indicates the page where the detailed description appears in the text.)